Liberators and Patriots of Latin America

Liberators and Patriots of Latin America
Biographies of 23 Leaders from Doña Marina (1505–1530) to Bishop Romero (1917–1980)

by
Jerome R. Adams

McFarland & Company, Inc., Publishers
Jefferson, North Carolina, and London

The illustrations are by Alix C. Hitchcock.

British Library Cataloguing-in-Publication data are available

Library of Congress Cataloguing-in-Publication Data

Adams, Jerome R., 1938–
  Liberators and patriots of Latin America : biographies of 23
leaders from Doña Marina (1505–1530) to Bishop Romero (1917–1980) /
by Jerome R. Adams.
      p.   cm.
  Includes bibliographical references (p.   ) and index.
  ISBN 0-89950-602-X (lib. bdg. : 50# alk. paper) ⊚
  1. Latin America — Biography.   2. Heads of state — Latin America —
Biography.   3. Revolutionaries — Latin America — Biography.
4. Heroes — Latin America — Biography.   I. Title.
F1407.A33   1991
980′.00992 — dc20
  [B]   91-52511
                                                           CIP

Manufactured in the United States of America

McFarland & Company, Inc., Publishers
  Box 611, Jefferson, North Carolina 28640

for Jan,
Beth, Matthew,
Daniel and Rebecca

Contents

Introduction

The purpose for compiling these biographies is to bring Latin American heroes out of the shadow cast over them outside their own region. Their life stories, so well-known to generations of followers, have been obscure to Europeans and North Americans. Although their lives are rich with actions and associations that reveal the history of Latin America, their stories are neither taught in schools nor exposed in popular culture outside their own lands.

These figures were agents of change, and as such were both damned and venerated. Except for Pedro I, who was brought to the New World as a child, they were born in the hemisphere they did so much to change. They were nation builders.

At the beginning of the nineteenth century, leadership generally meant driving out Europeans after three centuries of colonization. Here the emphasis was on freedom and equality. European monarchs had imposed economic strictures that thwarted development. Not until the Treaty of Utrecht in 1713, for example, was France able to trade with the Spanish colonies of Peru and Chile; students of Indian or mixed blood were never, until after independence, allowed to matriculate at the University of San Marcos in Lima.

After independence, leadership, perforce, meant dealing with less easily defined political issues. When leaders took up arms, it was usually against their own countrymen.

The first period, winning independence, opened countless possibilities. Independence opened countless wounds, many of which are still unhealed.

Octavio Paz, the Mexican philosopher whose father followed Zapata, has described the racial, philosophical, and political mixture that has shaped Latin America, where, he says,

> thought begins as a justification of Independence, but it is transformed almost immediately into a quest: America is not so much a tradition that continues as a future to be realized. Quest and utopia are inseparable . . . from the end of the 18th Century to today. The quest includes, indeed requires, Iberian and mestizo, former slave and former clerk. Only by embracing all does it have meaning: the future must be imagined by us all to be built by us all, no more with imperial design, stamped in Europe, than imperialist design, price-tagged in the United States.

A future imagined by all has proved elusive. The inability of neighbors to cooperate destroyed the hopes of Bolívar and made his death especially bitter, although that has not stopped others—Pedro II, Martí, Bishop Romero—from articulating the dream.

There are, in fact, other patterns that run through these stories. There is the recurring reminder of the Indian heritage in Latin America, a heritage that not only extols the ways of the past but suggests solutions for the future. The Indian identity is an important aspect in the stories of Malinche and Juárez, Sandino and Zapata.

One also sees a compulsion to rebel, an interpretation of reality that drives Manuela Sáenz and "Ché" Guevara and others to fight on when compatriots have abandoned hope.

There is also, sadly, a continuing refrain of betrayal, tales written in treachery, blood, and disillusionment like those of Toussaint L'Ouverture and Sandino.

A much overlooked pattern has been the place of women in defining revolutionary values: Gutiérrez and her contemporaries and Eva Perón are voices that have been dramatized—*soldaderas* and *Evita*—but have not been listened to with sufficient respect.

Intertwined with many of these patterns is the role of the United States, which was developing its own foreign policy during the period 1800 (Toussaint's slave rebellion) to the present (Bishop Romero's plea to President Jimmy Carter). Over this period, U.S. troops failed to catch rebels like Sandino and Villa, and U.S. presidents were equally unsuccessful in understanding Latin American leaders.

These patterns suggest the history of the region and also define the humanity of twenty-three individuals. Like all truly useful heroes, these have endured by the examples they set — not so much of elevated virtue, but rather fallibility, even pain. They are persistent. Their images hover just beyond the limit of Latin American progress, beckoning. It is possible, they say, so keep trying. Their very weaknesses confirm, in Erich Fromm's term, their "relatedness." They have tried; so must others. They have won followings, some of them in enormous numbers, so it behooves others, at the very least, to learn of their goals, their methods, their lives.

A final word about learning is in order. In Cali, Colombia, in 1964, that most ignorant of pupils, a callow Peace Corps volunteer—blinded by the lustre of his North American methods and instruments—met two teachers, Luís Espinoza and Raúl Adames. Neither was by trade a teacher; Luís worked for a European tire manufacturer, Raúl sold contraband. Their initial lesson was in their friendship, for Luís was a Conservative, Raúl a Liberal, and Colombia a battleground in which members of those two parties had been killing each other by the thousands for fifteen years.

We were neighbors. Although neither of them had finished elementary school, they knew a great deal. They knew about their own country, which they cheerfully shared; they had opinions about the United States' relations with its Latin American neighbors, which they modestly asserted; and they knew a very great deal indeed about the history of the United States — more, by conservative estimate, than would the vast majority of that country's high school graduates.

There is an embarrassing difference between how much Latin Americans know about the United States and how little curiosity flows in the other direction. The purpose of this book is to strengthen that flow.

Doña Marina (La Malinche)
c. 1505–1530
(Mexico)

Mother of Conquest

Doña Marina was an Indian woman whose life was deeply interwoven with Spanish conquest and settlement of the New World, a contradiction that has, for Mexicans, taken on historic proportions. Although she was flesh and blood, some view her as mythical. Although she was a slave, she rose to a position of leadership that is unique in the history of the New World. Without an army, she employed her wit to begin the conquest of a continent by leading Cortés to his destiny. In the words of Haniel Long, "she represents more than any one moment of history can hold."

Yucatan juts like a clenched fist from the Mexican isthmus to form the southern coast of the Gulf of Mexico. It is harsh country. Inland, broad plains of limestone over coral soak up rainfall so fast that vegetation is sparse; along the marshy lowlands of the coast jungles of mahogany and rosewood grow. It was here, using the offshore islands and safe harbors, that Spanish explorers stepped ashore on a mainland the extent and fierceness of which they could only imagine.

Accepting the theory that the New World was populated by way of the Aleutian archipelago, it is thought that nomadic people made their way diagonally across the great expanse of North America to reach Yucatan at least ten thousand years before Christ was born. Those arrivals became the Mayas, who built what historian Alfred Percival Maudslay calls "the highest culture ever attained by natives on the continent of North America."

Art and architecture, and the educational structure supporting both, were highly developed. The Mayan fascination with time led to calendric measurement more precise than that devised by their European counterparts of the Middle Ages.

In fact, notes archeologist Elizabeth P. Benson, the Mayas enjoyed their Classic Period, from A.D. 300 to 900, during Europe's Dark Ages.

> They used a mathematical notation system more sophisticated than their contemporaries. They counted time past in hundreds of thousands of years, noted the movements of the planet Venus, and predicted eclipses of the sun and moon. Yet they never invented the wheel, that most basic of mankind's accomplishments, and they worked with only primitive stone tools and manpower. Technologically they were a Stone Age people. This combination of intellectual and esthetic sophistication with technical primitivism is the hallmark of the Mayan character.

Perhaps because they were peace-loving and unprepared to fight, perhaps because they were simply overwhelmed by the more populous Nahua tribes from the north, the Mayas began to die out after A.D. 900, leaving their temples to crumble with time and be overgrown by vegetation. Their less gifted descendants, the Maya Quiché, migrated southward toward the mountains of Nicaragua and Honduras. In the mythology of the tribes, the demise of the Mayan civilization is associated with the triumph of the warlike Huitzilopoctli over the civilized Quetzalcoatl.

The peninsula was next populated, still before the cultivation of grain or the smelting of iron, by the Toltecs, a Nahua tribe of considerable attainment, but a people destined to generations of subservience. Their masters were the fierce Aztec peoples farther north, whose government centered on the island city of Tenochtitlán. That city, in the great lake that then existed in Central Mexico, was the nucleus of today's Mexico City. The Aztecs, Maudslay tells us, "became the head of a military and predatory empire, dependent for their food, as well as their wealth, on tribute drawn from subject tribes and races. They were not a civilizing power."

Non-Aztec communities, long dominated and humiliated, hated their Aztec oppressors, a hatred that Doña Marina was instrumental in fanning and directing against the Aztecs. Absent such a strategy, the small band led by Hernán Cortés could never have conquered. Thus, responsibility for that conquest must be ascribed in large measure to the young woman who was originally known as Malinal.

Malinal (or, some suggest, "Malinulli") was the daughter of a *cacique*, a Cuban term for an aboriginal nobleman. She was born around 1505 in the village of Painalla in the province of Coatzacualco, at the north end of the base of the Yucatan peninsula. Historian William Prescott is convinced her father was "rich and powerful," and Marina herself was described by

Bernal Díaz del Castillo, a foot soldier with Cortés, as "a *cacica* with towns and vassals."

When Malinal was young, however, her father died. Her mother remarried, bore a son, and was determined that her son be heir to her first husband's estate. To clear the way, she sold her daughter into slavery — at night, to prevent discovery. Malinal's mother took the body of a slave's child who had died and buried it, telling the townspeople it was her own child. Malinal was carried off to the town of Xicalongo. "Her early years," notes Jon Manchip White, "were singular and melancholy."

Malinal ended up in the possession of a cacique of Tabasco, and it is clear that through her earliest years she developed two important characteristics. Apparently because of her noble birth, she demonstrated a bearing and an education that commanded respect. She was chattel, perhaps, but high-born chattel. "She had a rare liveliness of spirit," suggests Antonio de Solis, "and natural gifts that accorded with the quality of her birth." A Spanish poet called her "a most beautiful Amazon."

Second, because she was well educated being moved around allowed her to develop her facility with language. She would learn Spanish, by all accounts, in a matter of weeks, and her principal value to Cortés was that she had learned Nahuatl, the tongue used throughout the northern, Aztec, reaches of the country.

Those characteristics made her more than a translator. As she was alternately cajoled, harangued, and threatened, she represented the new might of Europe in league with exotic, unpredictable allies and against awesome, innumerable enemies. "Cortés is discovering a new country," Haniel Long has her say in his fanciful portrayal of her life, "but I am discovering myself."

The man who would benefit from her self-discovery was, of course, Hernán Cortés, the archetype of the conquistador, the most *macho* of men. Like many great figures, Cortés was sickly as a child. Sent to university in Spain, he was undistinguished as a scholar and early aspired to a military life. After missing several opportunities to join expeditions, he arrived in the New World in 1504 at the age of nineteen.

He acquitted himself well against hostile Indians — whose crude weapons were inadequate against Spanish guns and crossbows — and was awarded an *encomienda*, a royal grant of land, and the Indians who were to work the land in feudal subservience. Cortés, although he prospered, was better suited for a more active life. His checkered record shows he was twice elected mayor of Santiago and once thrown into jail. When the governor, Diego Velásquez, ordered Cortés to take an expedition to the mainland in February 1519, Cortés' enemies tried to get the order rescinded. Cortés was forced to embark hastily. For the entire time Cortés led his small army through harsh territory and battle after battle, he was constantly attacked from the rear by Velásquez, who resented his arrogant independence and tried, in vain, to recall him.

On the mainland Cortés, in fact, declared himself captain-general and began communicating directly with King Carlos V. When his men mutinied, he had his ships burned so there could be no turning back. When Velásquez sent a troop to arrest him, Cortés captured its leader and bribed its men to follow him, obtaining gold for the bribery by short-changing his own men. If it can be said Malinal was discovering herself, Cortés was sculpting the role of conquistador with his bare hands.

It was after the Spanish won their first significant victory, at Tabasco, that, Malinal, among twenty women to be used as cooks, was given to Cortés by Tabascan caciques. Solis, an Argentine historian, imagines her lowly state, with her "humble clothing disguising her nobility." Díaz, however, who had been on two Mexican expeditions before joining Cortés, was there. He describes an extraordinary person: "One Indian lady who was given to us here," he writes, "was christened Doña Marina, and she was truly a great *cacica* and the mistress of vassals, and this her appearance clearly showed." The Tabascans were defeated in a brutal battle, losing at least eight hundred of their warriors, who at first thought Spanish horsemen and their horses were one and the same. They brought many gifts, cloth, gold, ornamented masks. "These gifts, however, were worth nothing in comparison with the twenty women given us," Díaz says, "among them one very excellent woman called Doña Marina, for so she was named when she became a Christian."

Although Díaz fails to explain, Indian women were commonly christened, a sacrament the Spaniards felt ameliorated their taking the women as mistresses, or, as in the case of married men like Cortés, their adultery. There were at least two priests among Cortés' troop, occasionally offering their advice on how to treat the Indians, sometimes "baptizing" tens of thousands of them in one fell swoop.

Thus Malinal became known as Doña Marina. The term *doña* (for a man, *don*) is placed before a person's Christian name as a mark of respect. Invariably, Spanish references to her are as Doña Marina. She is listed in the Codex Florentino and the Lienzo de Tlaxcala as "standing beside Cortés and translating his words or issuing her own instruction." The Spanish have taken her to themselves as if she had never been Malinal. After all, the bargain that the Spanish struck with their own conscience was that they would baptize and civilize and "protect" the Indians in exchange for the Indians' back-breaking labor in the mines or under the oppressive *encomienda* system. For the Spanish, Doña Marina was a crucial possession.

There is another view that is less benign. Originally, Indians referred to her as Malintzin, a term of respect associated with her position at the side of Cortés. The Spanish transliterated the Indian word to "Malinche." That is, Cortés was *El Malinche* and she was *La Malinche.* But among Mexican xenophobes, the term has came to be synonymous with betrayer. *Malinchismo* denotes the opening of Mexico to outsiders, those who have rendered Indian stock "impure" and have sullied Indian culture. Although she "showed an invariable sympathy" with "the conquered races," Prescott points out, Marina "always remained faithful to the countrymen of her adoption." Without her, he continues, it would have been Cortés who was conquered, for "her knowledge of the language and customs of the Mexicans, and often of their designs, enabled her to extricate the Spaniards, more than once, from the most embarrassing and perilous situations."

When the twenty women were brought into the Spanish camp, Cortés distributed them among his officers. Cortés gave Marina, described as "good looking and intelligent and without embarrassment," to his close friend, Alonzo Hernández Puertocarrero. Then, either because he recognized his mistake in giving her away — "women had always a great affection for him," notes translator J. Bayard Morris — or because he needed a trusted messenger for his audacious direct communication with the king of Spain, Cortés designated Hernández as bearer of his first missive to Carlos V. After Puertocarrero left camp, Cortés took Marina for himself.

There had been, and were, other interpreters, and their position was critical. The Spaniards — 508 soldiers embarked with Cortés, plus about a hundred sailors and ships' masters — were lost on an uncharted plane of hostility, with hundreds of thousands of warriors surrounding them. "Communication" meant many things. First, the invaders, with a mule train and artillery, had to find the best route through inhospitable territory in their search for Moctezuma. Second, Indian communities had to be intimidated if possible, defeated if necessary, and, ideally, persuaded to march with Cortés against Moctezuma.

As soon as he had landed, Cortés was fortunate to encounter Jerónimo de Aguilar, a priest who had been captured by Indians, escaped, and had taken refuge with a friendly cacique of another tribe. He learned a language spoken in the south and was so assimilated into his Indian life that when spotted by Cortés' men, he was not recognized as a European. A European companion, in fact, whose situation was similar, chose to remain with his Indian wife and their sons rather than follow Cortés. Aguilar formed an important link with Marina. Before she learned Spanish he took Cortés' words and translated them into a language Marina understood, and she retranslated the words into the needed language, especially as they moved northward, where Nahuatl, the language of the Aztecs, was spoken.* Marina and Aguilar, writes Díaz, admiringly, "always went with us on every expedition, even when it took place at night."

Nahuatl is still spoken by more than a million Mexicans.

Any interruption, any distortion, in Cortés' line of communication could be fatal. Before the Battle of Tabasco, an Indian interpreter had run off, joined the Tabascans, convinced them they could hold out, and helped direct the defense against Cortés. (After the battle, which took eight hundred Indian lives, the defeated Tabascans repaid him for bad advice, sacrificing him to their gods.) Communication meant psychological warfare as each Indian community tried to decide whether it benefited more by challenging Cortés' advance or by aiding that advance in the hope of throwing off the hated yoke of the Aztecs. Under these circumstances, Marina rose above the role of interpreter, to that of confidante and fellow strategist. Jon Manchip White describes her as "continuously at Cortés' elbow. In the eyes of the Indians they formed an inseparable pair.... Cortés consulted her on matters of general policy and on all matters relating to Indian psychology." According to Prescott, "she is said to have possessed uncommon personal attractions, and her open, expressive features indicated her generous temper."

Always surrounded, always outnumbered, Cortés had to communicate a variety of messages, sometimes simultaneously. He had to negotiate with the particular community that lay in his path while at the same time entertaining emissaries from Moctezuma. Even Moctezuma himself was of two minds, undecided whether this Cortés and his men were demigods sent by Quetzalcoatl, or mere flesh and blood, to be crushed like any other enemy. Moctezuma's ambassadors were often accompanied by Aztec artists, whose charge it would be to paint likenesses of the Spaniards. There had been other expeditions, Moctezuma knew, but this one was different, piercing like a lance ever deeper into his kingdom.

Cortés, shrewdly and with Marina's help, created a system of intelligence that embodied the advice of a contemporary, Niccolo Machiavelli, who warned in *The Prince* that "the lion cannot protect himself from traps, and the fox cannot defend himself from wolves. One must be a fox to recognize traps, and a lion to frighten wolves." This duality suggests why the Indians came to see Cortés and Marina as one.

Cortés was convinced, at least at first, that Indians believed his men — godlike shooters of lightning and eaters of human hearts — could not be killed. So he had his dead buried rather than let them be seen by Indians. In sight of a legation of caciques, Cortés made a show of "talking" to a horse to convey that horses were independent, rational beings. He had a cannon fired with a full load of powder to terrify his visitors with its noise and smoke. Deception and strength. Bluster and power. Advance and negotiation. All the time, Moctezuma was uncertain how to respond, and it might have been, historian R. C. Padden suggests, that Marina found out about and informed Cortés of Moctezuma's ambivalence. It was another weakness to be exploited, another stratagem to be employed.

Terror, intimidation, and bribery were augmented by continual, crafty negotiations conducted by Marina. She must have had a part in their strategic conception. Confrontations could not be prepared for, but occurred unpredictably along the trail. Delay could be deadly; allies had to be reassured and adversaried confused. These labrynthine considerations converged at Cholula, as Cortés confronted the fierce and brave Tlaxcalans.

They were his enemies, and he needed them as allies. Cortés described Cholula, holy to both Tlaxcalans and Aztecs, to Carlos V. It was, he said, "more extensive than Granada, and better fortified. Everywhere good order and good manners prevail. The people are full of intelligence and understanding. Their way of life is superior to anything to be found among the Moors."

Pondering his relations with the Tlaxcalans, Cortés was befuddled by their relations with Moctezuma. Díaz tells of watching five of Moctezuma's tax gatherers arrive unexpectedly. The officials studiously ignored Cortés and his men, walking past them — the officials were sniffing bunches of roses — to discuss the Spanish not with Cortés, but with the Tlaxcalans. Díaz was aghast at their "utmost assurance and arrogance." Moctezuma's men chastised the Tlaxcalans for providing the Spaniards with a place to stay. Cortés was insulted, but also somewhat abashed, and not at all sure what to do. "Doña Marina, who understood full well what had happened," Díaz writes, "told him what was going on."

Cortés made an instant, bold judgment, instructing that Moctezuma's men be captured. He then informed the captives that he, personally, was chagrined that they were captured, allowing two to escape, to take word back to Moctezuma. The Tlaxcalans, presumably, were impressed with Cortés' temerity, and Moctezuma was both impressed and confused.

Cortés could trust no perception of his own and had to rely on Marina to see the truth. Were these people harboring so much hatred for their Aztec oppressors that they would ally themselves with Cortés, or was treachery afoot? Ambiguous attitudes were the most menacing. "The suspicions of Cortés increased," writes Cantu, "and he called the Indian woman Malinche to explain his apprehensions to her. She was ordered to mingle with the people to see what she could uncover."

Cortés himself, in one of the infrequent references he made to Marina in his letters to Carlos V, told of her part at Cholula. "And being somewhat perplexed by this [the Cholulans' indifference and the Aztecs' arrogance]," Cortés wrote, "I learnt through the agency of my interpreter, a native Indian girl who came with me from Putunchan (a great river of which I informed your majesty in my first letter), that a girl of the city had told her that a large force of Moctezuma's men had assembled nearby, and that the citizens themselves, having removed their wives, children and clothes, intended to attack us suddenly and leave not one of us alive."

Díaz, as always, is more colorful. His account is of an elderly woman from the village who approached Marina, remarking that Marina was "young and good-looking and rich." Rather than be slaughtered in the imminent attack, the old woman suggested, Marina should gather possessions and seek refuge at the old woman's house, where, later, she could marry the woman's son. Marina pretended to accept the offer, as Díaz tells the story, but put the old woman off until night, warning her that Cortés' troops were on guard and would hear them. Marina then pumped the woman for more information, asking the ironic question, "If this affair is such a secret, how is it that you came to know about it?" The woman's husband, it turned out, was a Tlaxcalan captain who had, along with others, received gifts from the wily Moctezuma to help ambush Cortés.

Barrancas outside of the town were alive with Moctezuma's warriors. Planned was a monumental ambush. So confident of success were the Tlaxcalans, Díaz observes, that they were "laughing and contented as though they had already caught us in their traps and nets." Forewarned by Marina, however, Cortés took a townsman captive, interrogated him secretly to learn more of the plot, and then launched a preemptive attack. His troops killed three thousand Tlaxcalans while Moctezuma's warriors fled. Cortés fought his way out of the city "on horseback [with] Doña Marina near him."

Díaz offers this brief panegyric, the remarks of a soldier who recognized that his life was saved by the action of another: "Let us leave this and say how Doña Marina who, although a native woman, possessed such manly valor that, although she had heard every day how the Indians were going to kill us and eat our flesh with chili, and had seen us surrounded in the late battles, and knew that all of us were wounded and sick, yet never allowed us to see any sign of fear in her, only a courage passing that of a woman."

Fear was rational. The Indians' *macanas* — heavy, flat wooden blades with flint or obsidian chips embedded in their edges — could sever the head of a horse. Javelins flew by the hundreds, many of them thrown a considerable distance by the use of *atlatls,* the cupped throwing sticks that extended an arm's length. The worst fate, however, was capture.

Capture meant sacrifice. The Spaniards, for all of their own ferocity, were appalled at the Indian priests, whose hair and animal-skin robes were matted with dried blood from sacrifices and who sliced their own ears in a form of worship, allowing the blood to coagulate in foul-smelling clots. Most shocking to the Spaniards, though, was the practice the priests had of cutting open captives' chests, sawing with an obsidian knife through the breastbone, to rip out still-beating hearts. The Spaniards and their allies knew — and would see confirmed before their expedition was ended — that such execution was the fate that awaited them if captured.

Cortés, whose troops were killing thousands in the name of the Christian god, was determined to end the Indian practice of sacrifice by destroying the temples in which it was conducted — tall, pyramidal structures that reeked like abattoirs. He ordered destruction of the temples, although for Marina this left the delicate task of convincing allies that such profane destruction was a good idea. Already fearful of Moctezuma's wrath, now they had their gods, too, to fear. Convincing the Tlaxcalans, Díaz notes, involved a complex process of threats from Cortés, reminders of what Moctezuma would do to them if they failed to conquer, encouragement, and flattery. Marina, Díaz writes, "knew well how to make them understand."

In addition to threats and negotiations, there were sermons. Cortés and his chaplains did not neglect their Christian duty to seek converts — who would, presumably, make more steadfast allies. Díaz was amused by the proselytizing, explaining that both Marina and Jerónimo de Aguilar had become expert at portraying the story of Christ in a variety of tongues and "were so expert at it that they explained it very clearly."

So, with a diminishing band of soldiers and with Indian allies who were seeing their faith shaken and their culture demolished, Cortés pressed on toward the most formidable fortress in the New World, the Aztec capital of Tenochtitlán. Each village along the way was offered a choice of battle or alliance. At Cempula, when a great cacique, Xicotenga, considered a sneak attack, Indian friends of Cortés who heard of it considered the idea a joke, and failed to tell him. Marina made no such error, informing him in time for soldiers to capture seventeen of Xicotenga's spies. Cortés sent them back to their own camp, some without their hands, some without thumbs. Xicotenga threw his support behind Cortés, even arranging for one of his daughters to marry one of Cortés' officers.

In early September 1519, the expedition reached Tenochtitlán, a city that seemed mystical, with condensation rising from the great inland lake to give reality a quality no European had ever experienced. "Gazing on such wonderful sights," wrote Díaz years after the event, when he was blind and old, "we did not know what to say, or whether what appeared before us was real."

Tenochtitlán had emerged as dominant over the complex of settlements, including two other cities, built around an unusual geographical phenomenon. Four hundred and forty-two square miles were covered by trapped water, actually two shallow lakes, at 7,244 feet above sea level. In the distance were snow-capped mountains reaching more than 17,000 feet. The great expanse was formed by the heavy rainfall that, for the most part, was taken away only by seepage and evaporation. Where water was able to escape in streams, it stayed fresh, but another part of this inland sea was saline because salt accumulates in stagnant water over time. The Aztecs had constructed a system of dikes separating the clear and salt waters; causeways provided access to cities. Tenochtitlán itself had a population of 300,000 in 60,000 dwellings, mainly two-story houses of dull-red volcanic stone and lime-covered adobe. Scattered about were reed structures on stilts, islands, and floating gardens. The latter were formed by mats, heaped with mud and cultivated until roots intertwined into tangled, floating bases. Eminently fecund, these dreamlike gardens of flowers astonished the members of the expedition — as did the entire sight.

The expedition crossed Lake Texcoco on a "broad causeway running straight and level," Díaz writes. The soldiers passed "edifices of lime and stone that seemed to rise out of the water. . . never yet did man see, hear, or dream of anything equal to the spectacle that appeared to our eyes on this day."

As Cortés approached the city, before he could decide how to deal with Moctezuma, he had to cover his rear. The still-angry governor, Diego Velásquez, had sent an eighteen-ship expedition to bring Cortés back to Cuba in shackles.

Therefore, Cortés had to halt his progress upon nearing Tenochtitlán in order to lead men back to the coast, fall upon the newcomers, capture their commander, and bribe the men into returning with him to Tenochtitlán as reinforcements. To effect the bribe it was necessary to use bounty already claimed by soldiers who had been with him all along, but Cortés was a determined man. "The shadow of a fern does not interest him," Haniel Long has his fictional Marina say, "nor does he pick up a blue pebble to look at it more closely, nor pass his fingers over the bark of a tree. Only what can be of use to him will he stay for. Me he loves because I can be of use to him."

Marina's use at Tenochtitlán was to help perpetrate the final treachery, the theft of an empire. While the Aztec federation that Cortés confronted was not as sophisticated as the long-departed Mayan culture, it was a functioning system that had extended its reach to the Gulf of Mexico and to the Pacific Ocean. The Aztec language was complex, their gods fierce, their buildings ornate.

The Spanish, especially the men who followed Cortés, were brigands, professional soldiers, some of whom fought with the brutal Gonsalvo de Córdoba in Italy and all of whom were interested in rape and plunder. "When our compatriots reach that remote world," wrote a contemporary of Cortés, "they become ravenous wolves." It would take another quarter of a century for the Spanish to begin to bring into subjegation this far-flung empire, and conquering Tenochtitlán was the key.

Ostensibly in Tenochtitlán as the honored guest of Moctezuma, with his Tlaxcalan allies camped on shore, Cortés and his men were isolated. The Tlaxcalans numbered about 2,000, while the Spanish, their number quadrupled by the reinforcements of Cortés brought back, were about 1,300 strong. Although Cortés knew Moctezuma was subject to conflicting advice, it was presumed that he was stalling until reinforcements could reach the city to crush the Spaniards once and for all. Moctezuma, a wily man, had served eighteen years as Aztec leader; he was in the ninth in succession of a line of powerful caciques. The principal burden of dealing with him was settled on the thin shoulders of Marina.

Cortés decided to invite Moctezuma to his quarters and there capture him, making him a prisoner in his own city. Marina first talked him into captivity and then tried to persuade him to surrender all his forces, yielding his riches and his kingdom to the Spaniards.

The longer Moctezuma delayed, however, and the longer he remained a captive, the less influence he had with his own people. He offered Marina bribes if she would desert the hated Spanish, perhaps saving herself in the process, but every day he was closer to his own destruction. Ancient Spanish paintings show Marina at Moctezuma's side when he was brought onto a roof to calm his people, who were restive, for Moctezuma had become a target of contempt. When the crowd below finally revolted, rocks were thrown and one struck Moctezuma in the head. He died three days later. Cortés was without his bargaining chip.

The resulting Aztec onslaught drove Cortés and his men out of the city with great loss of life as soldiers, weighted down with all the gold they could carry, were pitched from bridges and sank from sight. Cortés managed to save himself a sizable fortune by sending on ahead Tlaxcalans and horses loaded with gold ingots. Along the causeway of escape, Indians attacked from the sides from dugout canoes, and in the confusion Cortés was almost captured. It is known in Spanish lore as *la noche triste* (the Night of Sadness). Those soldiers who reached shore established a perimeter and listened through the night to shouted epithets and throbbing of drums, punctuated by the screams of sacrificed companions.

"But I have forgotten to write down," interjects Díaz in his chronicle of that terrifying night, "how happy to see Doña Marina still alive." She and several others had been guarded by a contingent of troops and their final escape was made possible, Díaz notes, with the help of Tlaxcalan warriors.

The departing Spanish were pursued, and the continuing fight was fierce. At the Battle of Otumba, 860 members of the expedition were killed or captured and sacrificed, and, at Tustepec, seventy-two more were lost.

As a result of this retreat, Spanish romantics have portrayed yet another side of their Doña Marina. The woman of *la noche triste*, the nurse to defeated soldiers, the comforter of Cortés, drying the tears that stained his lined face, has proved irresistible to Spanish chroniclers of the conquest.

The Spanish imagination has raised Doña Marina to levels approaching those of Dante's Beatrice, Milton's Eve, Jason's Medea. She remains, asserts Haniel Long, "the simplest and clearest expression in history or mythology of the union and the disunion of man and woman." Marina and Cortés were one and opposed, united and at eternal odds. Analysts, depending on their points of view, have compared Cortés with Christ or with the Devil. Marina — La Malinche — had been considered, if not the Virgin of the story, the Eternal Weeping Comforter. Mexicans still see *La Llorana*, an important part of their mythology. *La Llorana*, according to Cecilio Robelo, is "a white ghost who utters prolonged and tearful laments on dark nights, who is the soul of Malinche, who walks in pain for having been a traitor to her country, helping the Spanish conquerers."

Marina's own fate was more prosaic, but, apparently, satisfying. Cortés returned to Tenochtitlán, this time with thirteen assault boats so his attack would not be limited to the causeways. He prevailed and became, in Spanish eyes, a hero, living to lead several expeditions to explore the isthmus of Mexico and Central America.

Marina bore Cortés a son, named Martín, for his grandfather. Díaz describes her accompanying Cortés on an expedition to Honduras that took her to her old hometown, where she met, and forgave, her mother and half-brother, whose greed had been the cause of all her adventures.

Eventually, Marina married Juan Jaramillo at the small town of Ostotipec, in the province of Nogales, and the couple is said to have had a daughter. Cortés attended the wedding and as a present gave Marina an estate at Jilotepec, fifty miles north of Mexico City. He later gave her a plot adjacent to her house at Chapultepec in Mexico City. Still later, Cortés gave Marina another plot, this one, in a small, ultimate irony, having belonged to Moctezuma. The Aztec heritage had already been reduced to choice plots of real estate.

Diego de Ordáz, a Spanish adventurer, reported seeing Marina, her husband, and young Martin in 1529. The line of Marina's progeny, according to Gustavo A. Rodríguez, extended at least until the death of a nine-year-old boy, Fernando Gómez de Orosco y Figueroa, who was born in Tlzapan on July 23, 1930.

Pierre François Dominique Toussaint L'Ouverture
1743–1803
(Haiti)

Commander of a Slave Army

One afternoon in 1799, Pierre François Dominique Toussaint returned to his villa after meeting with emissaries of Britain's King George III and U.S. President John Adams. The villa, at Gonaives, in the Haitian hills overlooking the Caribbean, was Toussaint's favorite, and the afternoon glare off the sea must have been like the attention being paid to a former slave by powerful nations — intense, a bit blinding, quick to fade. Not only had Toussaint been meeting with British and American messengers, his plans were also of great interest to the First Consul of France, Napoleon Bonaparte. Because Toussaint's tiny half-island was the focus of so much international concern, his task that afternoon was to decide how best to keep Europeans and Americans at bay while he tried to found the New World's second republic, the only one ever created by slaves. In battle, things were more simple. Toussaint earned his sobriquet at the head of cavalry when an admiring French adversary dubbed him "L' Ouverture" for his ability to break openings in enemy lines where least expected.*

*A less romantic suggestion is that in northern Haiti many slaves were named "L'Ouverture" for the gaps in their front teeth.

Dealing with diplomats, Toussaint had learned that armed enemies were the least dangerous.

Toussaint L'Ouverture is thought to have been born on May 20, 1743. His father, Gaou-Guinou, was the second son of a chief of the Arradas tribe, taken in a raid by a neighboring tribe and sold at the port market at Ouidah, Dahomey, built by the French in the mid–1700s especially for the slave trade. It was a major exchange point on Africa's Slave Coast, part of a commercial system that would, in all, ship some 10 million Africans to the New World, counting those who died in transit and were thrown overboard.

Two months after his sale, Gaou-Guinou was unloaded at Cap François on the northern coast of the French colony of Saint Domingue, which slaves would later name Haiti. It is likely that in the slave society Gaou-Guinou was known by other slaves to be descended from Arradas royalty and treated with respect. Although slave languages were many and communication among them was kept difficult as a method of control, such was Gaou-Guinou's bearing that the Comte de Noé, his owner, mandated *liberté de savane*, which gave him both freedom and protection. He was also given land and five slaves and later baptized a Catholic. His wedding occasioned a plantation holiday.

Gaou-Guinou's freedom, under the careful French system of colonial law, did not extend to his children. Although the position of mulattoes would become ambivalent, there was no uncertainty regarding *noirs.* Children of freed slaves were slaves.

Toussaint was the oldest of several brothers and at least one sister, but was a sickly, moping boy, who was dubbed *fatras bâton* ("fragile stick"). Because of his weakness, he was relieved of herding, the job of young slaves, and was in and out of the plantation infirmary so often that he ended up working there under the tutelage of his godfather, an old slave named Pierre Baptiste. Baptiste had been taught to read and write by Jesuits and he taught Toussaint. The head of the infirmary, struck by Toussaint's ability to learn, put him to work in the slaves' dining hall.

Toussaint's education continued to be part European, part African. In the home, old ways were retained. The family spoke an African dialect, and his father taught him the uses of herbs (as an adult, Toussaint was a vegetarian). Toussaint began tending animals on the plantation. He was assumed by some slaves to have "magical" powers of the kind that still form, as "voodoo," an important part of Haitian culture.

Nature had left Toussaint weak, relatively short, rather ugly, and thin. He was surviving in a world that valued brute strength, and he compensated by being "diplomatic" with everyone.

It is possible that when Toussaint was about fourteen he witnessed—

such occurrences were, after all, carefully prepared lessons — the burning of a fugitive slave, François Macandal. As a fugitive, Macandal had conducted his own, one-man guerrilla warfare, hiding in the bush, conjuring potions, and inducing other slaves to sneak them into their masters' food. Whole families had been killed.

Slavery was efficient only insofar as discipline was rigidly enforced, and revolts erupted right from the beginning. In 1522, just twelve years after King Ferdinand of Spain authorized African slaves as replacement workers in the mines of the New World, there was an outbreak on Hispaniola, an island about the size of Ireland that Haiti shares with the Dominican Republic. Before 1550 there were at least three more outbreaks of sufficient magnitude to be recorded. In the next two hundred years, until Macandal was burned at the stake, there were continual outbreaks under a series of renegade leaders who wreaked havoc on both Spanish and French plantations. Thousands of people, black and white, were killed, and any atrocity that could be conceived — exploding gunpowder in a slave's rectum, rolling men and women down mountainsides in spike-lined barrels — was perpetrated. In this way slavery maintained the rich commerce of the Americas, which, in turn, supported European societies that were defining what is now called the Enlightenment.

Yet within the slave system, Toussaint was well on his way, as it were, to working his way up. He married a slave, Suzanne Simone Baptiste, and adopted her son, Placide, whose father was a mulatto. Suzanne bore Toussaint two sons, Isaac and Saint Jean. M. Bayou de Libertad, Toussaint's overseer, had placed Toussaint in charge of livestock, and although the choice led to Toussaint's being used as an example of proper subservience, a model not universally popular among his peers, it was for Toussaint a step up. He then became personal coachman to Libertad and, eventually, steward of the plantation. When he was thirty-four years old, Toussaint was freed. The year was 1777.

By 1791, two years after the Bastille had become a symbol of freedom in France, slave unrest on Hispaniola was at the point of explosion. On the Saint Domingue end of the island rebellion was more difficult to quash because the rough terrain afforded so many hiding places. It is said that when Napoleon asked a lieutenant to describe the topography of Saint Domingue, the lieutenant took a sheet of paper and crumpled it into a ball. It is beautiful countryside, but so mountainous, with peaks rising to nearly 8,800 feet, as to leave only 13 percent of its land arable. Yet on that small portion of rich land, France had grown fat.

Before slave uprisings began to diminish productivity, the colony was instrumental in paying France's huge war debts, a point not lost on the newly installed republicans, who had their own expenses. About 1800, Haitian exports were valued at 27 million U.S. dollars annually, greater than what was produced by all thirteen American states combined. Napoleon was prepared to hold the Mississippi Valley in order to grow and ship the food needed to keep Haitian slaves alive — as long as the system remained efficient. Slave revolts, however, upset the bookkeeping. In 1799, Saint Domingue's plantation production was valued at 176 million francs; by 1801 it was one-third that figure because the work was not being done.

The first cracks in the facade of Haiti's strange society appeared along the line carefully constructed between white men and their mulatto sons. It was Louis XIV, the Sun King, who had done a bit of human accounting in 1674 and decreed that all children of slaves, regardless of whether either or both parents had been freed, were slaves. In economic terms, this assured that capital stock was not depleted. Colonial customs emerged, however, that mixed parental feelings of obligation with amorous drives and civil codes. What evolved were traditions that insured social conflict. At age twenty-four mulattoes would be freed, although at age thirty, they had to serve three years in the militia. In effect, the French plantation owners were providing military training for their offspring *cum* future enemies.

Mulattoes paid a special tax to maintain roads, but were supposed to humbly dismount upon entering a city's gates. Many were educated in Europe, where, posing no threat, they were widely accepted. They came home to oversee plantations and own their own slaves. Yet they were excluded from the professions and from public office. Laws prohibited a mulatto from praying in his father's pew, eating at his father's table, finding rest in the family crypt, and, especially, inheriting the family estate.

By the beginning of the nineteenth century, these contradictions had caused deep cuts, the scars of which remain today.* There was a pyramid of 700,000 to 820,000 black slaves; about 100,000 mulattoes; some 10,000 whites of different nations, extracting what they could of the colony's riches or shunted aside because of their low social status; perhaps 1,500 aboriginal Indians who had, by necessity, clustered in a few isolated areas; and, in charge, about 500 Frenchmen.

Mulattoes led the charge against the old régime. After the French revolution, Haitian mulattoes pledged six million francs and one-fifth of their property to help pay the national debt, a gesture for which they expected recompense. Thus on March 8, 1790, in the first flush of the Republic, the

---

*Few countries have divided people by color with such attention to detail as Haiti. An homme de couleur was free, while the generic mulatre was not. After the revolt began, however, who was to say which was what? Marron or chestnut, means in Haiti a domestic animal run wild, hence a slave — a noir — who had fled to the hills. There were inland marronage colonies. The law of Saint Domingue decreed that Negro blood "decreased" for six generations, after which it vanished. Today, however, an authentique is one whose lineage is untainted by "white blood."

National Assembly resolved that mulattoes were entitled to seats in their colonial assemblies. So, in October, Vincent Oge, a Haitian mulatto, strode into the assembly at Cap François to demand that the pledge be fulfilled. The landowners refused. He pressed his case with two hundred armed mulattoes. The eventual outcome, in February 1791, was that he was broken on the wheel, screaming for mercy, along with seven other leaders of the insurrection. Nineteen others were sentenced to the galleys for life, and twenty-two were hanged.

At first, the slaves stayed out of the mulattoes' fight. But as the revolt spread, Toussaint, then forty-seven years old and steward of his plantation, became in effect the protector of his benefactor, Libertad, the man who had freed him. By autumn of 1791, when the fires of renegade slaves could be seen in the hills at night, Toussaint informed Libertad that protection was no longer possible. Toussaint helped the family embark for North America and turned to find his place in the revolt.

That summer, a Jamaican slave named Boukman had been calling self-selected leaders like Toussaint to clandestine meetings, moving through the northern hills where Macandal had operated thirty years before. Boukman inspired several strikes by factory workers, but found that such disruptions were easily put down. So, as fall approached, he held meetings to shape a new strategy. What followed was violence without bound.

Slaves wielding machetes, pruning hooks, stolen fowling rifles, pitchforks, and anything at hand that might be lethal "surrounded the houses, slaughtered the men, drank the rum, raped the women and fired the estates and cornfields," according to an account cited by historians Robert and Nancy Heinl. Particularly hated men were chopped to pieces or nailed up, alive, while their wives were raped. One counter-attack by whites was "overwhelmed by furious slaves whose standard was the body of a white baby impaled on a spike."

The slaves' massive numbers sustained the revolt, for they fought largely with simple implements, often did not know how to fire captured cannon, and sometimes charged hostile fire convinced that African gods protected them. By the time Toussaint joined the revolt, the plain around the port city of Cap François was littered with bodies. Broad assaults led to hundreds being cut down at once, while the gallows and the wheel took care of those who were captured. A white man captured while fighting at the side of slaves was roasted by his white adversaries over a charcoal fire. Boukman was finally captured, burned to death, and beheaded.

While slaves besieged Cap François on the northern coast, mulattoes, some using arms hidden earlier by Oge, fought in the west and south. At the same time, there was a standoff between white Jacobins and royalists as the same forces that divided France fought in Haiti. Then, throwing fuel on the fire, the national assembly, some members of which were dismayed by Oge's martyrdom, decreed in the spring of 1791 that mulattoes be admitted to colonial governments.

In part, the enfranchisement of mulattoes fulfilled the Rights of Man. More pragmatically, however, the deputies knew mulattoes were the only trained republican troops able to withstand Haiti's climate. Because of the decree, however, colonial representatives walked out of the national assembly in Paris, and their brethren in Haiti continued to deny political rights to mulattoes. The situation was further confused by royalists, including priests, who recruited gullible blacks with empty promises of a black, royalist colony. As several permutations of alliance formed, the national assembly, faced with both rebellious slaves and irridentist royalists, threw up its hands and rescinded the decree. The color line for mulattoes, briefly erased, was redrawn, casting mulattoes against whites and blacks against both. Into this chaos came Toussaint.

"The rebel horde was made up of an assortment of tribes from all parts of the African continent," writes Stephen Alexis, "Congos, Senegalese, Dahomeans, Lybians, Abyssinians, Bambaras, Peuhls, Ibos, Yoloffs, Guineans, Aradas, Touregs, Moroccans. It was a mixture of humanity, of violent, unstable tribesmen who were as uncertain of themselves as they were of what they wanted. . . . And it was out of this heterogeneous mass that Toussaint was to forge a striking force, crush the enemy, and build up a nation."

Toussaint accomplished the task, it must be added, along with other leaders, mulattoes like Alexandre Sabes Petión — who would later provision Bolívar against the Spanish — and the redoubtable mulatto known as "Candy." He did it with the help of his own lieutenants, the formidable Jacques Dessalines and Henri Christophe, who would later struggle with governing the social snakepit left to them. Together, they freed Haiti, Napoleon's prized possession, by making it so expensive to hold onto that even the man who would rule Europe could not bear the expense.

Toussaint's most important contribution may have been his personal dignity. He stepped into leadership alongside men like Biassou, who favored an orange costume of his own design that included a black, silk scarf, and Jean-François, who wore crimson velvet, gold braid, and a tri-cornered hat and declared himself "Grand Admiral of France." Toussaint continued to wear plantation garb: a white silk jacket, blue cotton pants, and a felt hat with the brim turned up.

The national assembly's idea of colonial government was to send an almost endless series of commissions to reestablish order, to redraw color lines, to punish rebels. Biassou and Jean-François, in exchange for freedom for themselves and a few hundred favorites, offered to betray the rest of their followers, whom they described as ignorant warriors uprooted from their African homeland. The Heinls point to this arrangement, which was accepted by the commissioners, as "a readiness to betray followers that students of Haitian politics would come to recognize." In the assembly at Cap François, however, landowners refused to recognize the deal, so slaves redoubled their violence.

The French response — signed by Louis XVI on April 4, 1792, within a year of losing his head — was yet another decree giving full political rights to mulattoes and free blacks. For enforcement, another commission was dispatched, accompanied by six hundred soldiers. In command was Etienne-Maynard Laveaux, who would become Toussaint's principal adversary.

A member of the commission was Léger-Félicité Sonthonax, whose antislavery sentiments and democratic beliefs made him profoundly distrusted by other governments with interests in the Caribbean. Because republican France had declared war on all monarchies, the English in Jamaica and the Spanish at the eastern end of Hispaniola were not eager to tolerate this penetration of their territory by such a democratic radical. On August 29, 1793, Sonthonax lived up to his enemies' worst expectations. Without authority from Paris, he declared all slaves free.

The British and Spanish immediately joined in an effort to destroy this threat to their own slave systems — at the same time seizing what they could of French territory. By early 1793, Biassou and Jean-François had thrown in with the Spanish. Biassou was named "Generalissimo of the Conquered Territories," while Jean-François was awarded the title "General and Admiral of the Reunited Troops." Both got new uniforms.

Toussaint, whose literacy and knowledge of medicine made him valuable, became secretary to Biassou. He was also given command of six hundred men, mostly mounted. Before long, Toussaint's command had swelled to four thousand and, making himself a colonel, he began to take orders directly from the Spanish at his headquarters at Marmelade.

By the autumn of 1793, the slave revolt had turned into a confused, extremely violent extension of the European wars. *Noirs* under Jean-François, Biassou, and Toussaint controlled the north; mulattoes established a lasting base in the south; the English took several port towns.

Toussaint began to build his reputation. "I am Toussaint L'Ouverture," he would announce to a conquered town. "My name has perhaps become known to you. I am bent on vengeance. I desire the establishment of Liberty and Equality in St. Domingue." Even as Toussaint's men confronted Laveaux's troops, however, Toussaint himself was in contact with the French commander. He had decided that the future of Haiti was better shaped against a background of the French Republic than the Spanish monarchy. In the spring of 1794, with Laveaux at the point of defeat, running out of ammunition and provisions, Toussaint switched sides. The Heinls write:

> Toussaint repaired to Marmelade. There, at the side of the Spanish commandant, he heard early mass. These devotions concluded, he mounted his horse, drew sword, unfurled the Tricolor and, at the head of his regiment and like-minded *noirs*, cut the throats of the Spanish garrison.

In one stroke, Toussaint had won the appreciation of the French, arrayed his forces against, rather than beside, one of the harshest slave systems of the New World, the Spanish; and, not incidentally, moved from beneath the command of Jean-François and Biassou to become his own man.

Through the spring of 1794, the Spanish were immobilized. Toussaint's army held the north, and his new allies, under an ambitious mulatto named Rigaud, held the south. Toussaint used the time to recruit and train; Rigaud plotted. In the meantime, the English were succumbing to an enemy that took no prisoners, yellow fever.

In July, the French and Spanish, each trying to stake out what was sure, agreed to split the ownership of the island, although Spanish troops were to remain and administer the eastern end in France's name. Biassou, idled, wandered off to Spanish southern Florida, where he died in a brawl. Jean-François retired, like a landowner, to Cádiz. Toussaint remained to fight.

Now his adversary was Rigaud. The mulatto commander had Laveaux, the French commander, wrestled from his office in Cap François and thrown in jail. As soon as Toussaint heard, he informed Laveaux's abductors that if the governor-general were not immediately released, everyone in the town would die. Laveaux was returned to his office. Immediately, he named Toussaint lieutenant-general, assuring the jealousy of every mulatto officer.

Toussaint was approaching a pinnacle as the most powerful man on the island. Laveaux himself had dubbed him "the black Spartacus" who, according to the prediction of Abbe Raynal in the sixteenth century, would one day avenge his people. On the horizon, however, there appeared more French commissioners. They included the fiery Sonthonax, who had been recalled to France, tried, and acquitted.

Real power was divided, uneasily, between Toussaint and Rigaud, and when the commissioners exiled several of Rigaud's lieutenants Toussaint's power was enhanced. In Toussaint's view, which tended toward the Olympian, that was not enough. It would be better, he thought, if the commission turned around and went back to Paris, leaving him to deal with Riguad. Indeed, eventually — and perhaps at Toussaint's instigation — both Laveaux and Sonthonax were elected to the national assembly in Paris. Laveaux sailed immediately, choosing France's violent political environment over Haiti's. But Sonthonax lingered, a white man, for all his republican intentions, administering a black society.

For a time Toussaint was preoccupied with trying to contain the British in their coastal strongholds, or put down mutinies of *noirs,* who were now called "cultivators" but were still prone to discontent when encouraged by royalist bribes. After a year, Toussaint ran out of patience and bundled Sonthonax aboard a ship bound for France. With the last French official finally gone, it is said that Toussaint was seen in Cap François, laughing. The scene was memorable, for Toussaint rarely laughed.

Now he was paramount. French authorities had named him *général de division,* and he was given Laveaux's old title, *général-en-chef des armées de Saint Domingue.* His two young sons had been sent to France to school. He commanded approximately 20,000 soldiers, as many as George Washington ever led.

With the Spanish at bay and French civil authority practically eliminated, it was still necessary to loosen the grip of the English on their coastal redoubts. The English, already devastated by yellow fever, found the nine hundred troops they had committed to Haiti fell far short of what was necessary. With the help of Rigaud — who commanded some 12,000 men — Toussaint forced the English to withdraw. The withdrawal, however, was allowed with honor. Toussaint remarked that republican France had never treated him with as much respect as had imperial England. The English, indeed, promised their support if he should crown himself "king of Haiti," but Toussaint declined.

Now Toussaint could concentrate on consolidating his power — after receiving yet one more commission from France. The spring of 1798 found the economy of the island, not surprisingly, in shambles. Toussaint was trying to revive agriculture by inviting *colons* to return to participate in a kind of feudalism, called *fermage,* conceived by his lieutenant, Henri Christophe. One reform under the plan was that only the slaves truly strong enough to work were to be sent back to the fields. In general, however, it was difficult for former slaves to understand and accept differences between feudalism and slavery.

The commissioners' benighted decision was to foment division in order to weaken the colony against the day that France might recoup its loss. Therefore, Rigaud was raised to equal rank with Toussaint.

So it was that Toussaint found himself at his villa at Gonaives, ardently courted by the English and Americans. The French had left the island with difficult problems, but Toussaint knew that Anglo-American intentions were hardly to solve those problems, simply to capitalize on them. As far as the great nations were concerned, all discussions, like those at Gonaives, turned on what benefit Toussaint and his slave army could be in the international struggle. Toussaint was no longer a slave in their eyes, but they still saw him as a pawn.

Toussaint is criticized for being indecisive. He did not, for example, simply declare Haiti independent and dare everyone to fight. He was encouraged to do so by the British envoy, Thomas Maitland. Toussaint, however, knew he was dependent on British and American manufactured goods — especially arms and ammunition — for a protracted war against France. Furthermore, what he did not need was to rush into the embrace of either Britain, which did not abolish slavery in its colonies until 1833, or the United States, which gave up slavery only reluctantly two generations later.

What Toussaint did was try to reach agreement with the mulattoes to strengthen Haiti internally. First, he made overtures to Rigaud. Then Toussaint called together mulattoes at the principal cathedral of Port-au-Prince, a mulatto stronghold. Combining accommodation with arrogance, Toussaint said that even though he understood their goal was to reenslave *noires*, he would forgive them. If they would accept as their goal the rebuilding of the island's economy, all would be well.

Rigaud, however, was quick to make his intentions clear. Unwilling to accept alliance, Rigaud led an army northward in June 1799, crossing the bridge at Miragoane — along the traditional dividing line between southern and northern Haiti — and launching civil war.

Hispaniola is shaped like a giant fish, its mouth wide open, swimming westward. Rigaud was driving out of the lower jaw toward Port-au-Prince, which is flanked by the two jaws. Rigaud's march, once it became known, inspired uprisings among mulattoes in several central and northern towns. Toussaint's army outnumbered Rigaud's, but the south was well fortified after years of fighting, and mulattoes, now that the French were gone, saw themselves as destined for domination. They would resist interference by *noires*. The result was some of the bloodiest conflict in Haiti's history.

Toussaint himself took charge of the mounted forces that struck at the uprisings; he sent Dessalines to subdue Rigaud's main force. So terrible was the feeling that the two sides adopted a particularly horrible method of punishment for captured leaders; they were stuffed down cannon barrels on top of grapeshot and literally blown to bits. Haitians had learned the technique from the British.

Toussaint's forces prevailed — with the help of the United States and after a brief interruption by France. Toussaint needed American shipping to maintain a line of supply, but he also asked U.S. naval forces to blockade and bombard southern ports controlled by Rigaud. The U.S. State Department, trying out its wings, complied, beginning what would become a long, troubled relationship between the two republics. As a result of the bombardments, Rigaud was squeezed into a corner by the spring of 1800. Dessalines was poised to deliver the final blow when Toussaint, in deference to the French, ordered him to hold back. Arriving was one more — the last — commission.

This commission had been personally dispatched by Napoleon, but that was of no importance to Haitians. Ostensibly, every commission from Paris had the goal of reestablishing Haitian productivity, but to Haitians that implied reimposing slavery. The three commissioners landed at the Spanish end of the island and traveled overland to the frontier. At the border, Toussaint had them arrested and let them sit and cool their heels. He then ordered their release, saying it had all been an unfortunate mistake. One commissioner got the message, turned around, and went back to France. Another, a mulatto lawyer and landowner, also opted out of the proceedings, busying himself instead with seeing to his properties. The third, a European engineer, offered his services to Toussaint to help build the country. The commission was thus disbanded, a turnabout of the type that is said to have caused Napoleon to grumble that never again would he put epaulets on the shoulders of a *noir*.

Then Toussaint unleashed Dessalines, who drove Rigaud's forces into the sea. Rigaud — after a final battle in which his horse was shot from beneath him and bullets pierced his jacket and hat — sailed into exile to await the chance to return that Napoleon would eventually provide. In triumph, Toussaint entered Les Cayes and went on to Port-au-Prince. Having acquired a European flair, Toussaint instituted a practice of entering the local cathedral while the choir sang a *Te Deum*. Then he would deliver a sermon, sometimes on the theme of forgiveness. Sometimes, however, Toussaint was capable of ordering enemy fighters bayoneted and shot; the total grew to more than a thousand. Dessalines, made governor of the south, is estimated to have ordered some ten thousand more to be executed.

Toussaint returned to his headquarters at Cap François intent upon conquering the other end of the island, which was still being administered by the Spanish on behalf of the French. In Toussaint's way stood a French civil commissioner, who yielded, and a Spanish general, who did not. The general made it clear he would not give up without a fight. Toussaint's response, dispatched in January 1801, had two parts: one was a column of 3,000 men under a *noir* general, descending from the north; the other was a column of 4,500 men marching across the south and commanded by Toussaint's brother, Paul. Toussaint rode with his brother, and three weeks later, after weak resistance, Toussaint accepted the keys to Santo Domingo.

His pronouncement has the ring of being directed not so much at Haitians as at the world. "The measures of prudence and humanity which I have taken," the *London Times* quoted him as saying, "prevented the effusion of blood; and with very little loss I have put myself in possession of the whole island." The Olympian tenor of the proclamation was typical of Toussaint, and, in truth, he had put himself, not France, in possession of the island. The message did not escape Napoleon.

Toussaint stood where important forces were converging. The time was February 1801. Many nations had reason to dread Toussaint's slave army, with its record of retribution. Abolitionists, in fact, cheered Toussaint on as a "Negro Spartacus" and "the Napoleon of the Antilles"; he was the subject of poems, dramas, and news stories; William Wordsworth sang his praises.

No one was more acutely aware of what Toussaint represented than Thomas Jefferson, just elected and to be inaugurated the next month. Jefferson was ambivalent — as was his wont in matters related to slavery. On the one hand, the father of his own mulattoes feared a revolution in which, as Jefferson wrote to an abolitionist friend, "we shall be the murderers of our own children." On the other hand, Jefferson was a realist in affairs of state, and Toussaint's successes benefited the United States by distorting relations among nations. Jefferson knew that the threat of revolt by the slaves of other nations — Britain, Spain, Portugal — tied down their troops in Latin America, preventing mischief along still-contested North American frontiers. If Toussaint was a bad example for slaves in the United States, he was also a constant problem to France and other slave-owning nations, and Jefferson could not discount the possibility that Napoleon planned a thrust northward from New Orleans to reclaim the Mississippi Valley from Spanish interlopers.

Toussaint did not dally over his newly acquired power. He returned to Cap François, where, according to a fascinated *Times* correspondent, he "declared most positively that he is determined not to suffer any strong naval force belonging to the [French] Republic to enter his harbor. Several engineers are now employed by him in fortifying the different ports at the east end of the island; and at Port Plata they have thrown up a long range of battery and mounted all the guns of the English frigate 'Tartar,' wrecked there in 1795."

Thus barricaded, Toussaint sent a brief message to Napoleon. It was a simple report on civic affairs, but the tone of the message made it clear that the sender considered himself, in all ways, equal. Napoleon did not respond.

In late May, a *Times* correspondent reflected:

> It does not appear that *Toussaint L'Ouverture*, the Negro-Chief of Hispaniola, has deigned to make any communication to the French Government of the important incorporation he has made of the Spanish part of the Island. The Black *Chief-Consul* is not inclined to acknowledge the White superiority, even in *Bonaparte*, and is certainly a rival and independent Prince.
>
> The state of all the West-India Islands will doubtless experience a very considerable change from the establishment of a Negro Empire in that Archipelago. St. Domingo must either prove a neutral, independent power

at the Peace, or be left at that period to be reclaimed by the Metropolitan Government in France. In either predicament the state of the slaves in all the Plantations, and West-India Commerce in general, will perceive the effects of it. The moralist will observe the experiment with anxious curiosity; but the statesman cannot contemplate it without serious apprehension.

The same spring Toussaint convened a "central assembly" to draft — or to approve his draft of — a constitution that named him *gouverneur-général-à-vie.* His government, however, was in reality an empty shell, its insides lost over a decade of warfare. It is estimated that more than three hundred thousand people had been killed; the white planter class had been reduced by at least two-thirds, mulattoes by one-fourth, blacks by one-third. Haiti had to try to make productive a bottomless pit of hatred, ignorance, and uncertainty. Toussaint's military administrators simply could not cope.

Rumors continued that slavery, in order for the island to survive, would be restored. When troops threatened to rebel at Cap François, Toussaint assembled them in front of townspeople and ordered suspects to step forward. Then he told them to shoot themselves. Understanding the alternatives, they complied, raising pistols to their heads. At the same time, Napoleon was concluding the Treaty of Amiens, meaning that England would no longer interfere with his plans for the Indies. Now Napoleon and Toussaint faced only one another.

Toussaint professed his loyalty to Napoleon, whatever might be the impression left by his arrogance, but Napoleon was not convinced. Trusting only French generals, Napoleon assembled at several European ports an armada of sixty-seven ships with 21,175 French and mercenary troops commanded by some of France's best officers. Overall command was given to Victor-Emmanuel Leclerc, husband of Napoleon's sister, Pauline. Leclerc was named captain-general of the colony, and Pauline accompanied the force. Overlooking no detail, Napoleon also sent two of Toussaint's sons, taking them from their studies in order to convince their father that it was time to lay down his arms.

It is said that Toussaint, knowing of the approaching armada, rode to a hill to watch its approach, remarking, "We are lost. All France has come to Saint Domingue." His own army included 17,000 regular troops and an undetermined number of militiamen.

As the armada rode at anchor, a proclamation from Napoleon was sent ashore, telling all inhabitants of the island that "whatever your origin, or your color, you are all French, you are all free, and all equal before God, and before the Republic." While the island was "a prey to factions," Napoleon noted, he asked the people to "embrace the French and rejoice to see again your friends, and your brothers of Europe." So strong was his feeling of brotherhood, Napoleon declared, that he had sent Leclerc, his own brother-in-law, as captain-general.

Leclerc had specific orders and a timetable. With deadlines for each of three steps, Napoleon instructed Leclerc to talk his way ashore, secure major towns, and clear the interior of resistance. Promises could be made, but the point was to get men to lay down their arms and return to the fields. The tactics partially worked, isolating several of Toussaint's *noir* commanders, some of whom, confused, capitulated. Others, however, were not going to allow the French to take the island without a fight. Some put their stores to the torch and retreated inland, and many prepared to burn or blow up everything they could not defend.

Toussaint also, when the French secured the coastal towns, retreated into the rough interior of the island. He was declared an outlaw; people were warned to neither follow nor help him. Leclerc, however, was surviving on bluster. He would later write that at this point if Toussaint had been able to contact his scattered commanders "there can be no doubt that he would have been victorious."

Toussaint's sons were sent to him, but he was not swayed; he was convinced that the French were determined to resubjugate all *noirs.* He told his sons he could not lay down his arms, so Isaac, saying he was a French subject, returned to Leclerc, while Placide, the older, whom Toussaint had adopted upon marrying Placide's mother, remained with his father.

The French advanced, some units led by mulatto officers, including Rigaud. Napoleon had instructed Leclerc to use the mulattoes if necessary, but, if not, to put them all on a ship and send them to Madagascar. Pockets of resistance were led by Dessalines, Christophe, and Toussaint. Dessalines, surrounded and with ammunition almost gone, earned the admiration of even his enemies by slipping his men through their lines in the night, leaving behind only the dead and wounded. Later, when Christophe and Toussaint were finally forced to open negotiations toward surrender, Dessalines, the fiercest *noir* of them all, refused to join them, fighting on.

After Christophe had given up, Toussaint went with four hundred mounted men to meet Leclerc at Haut-du-Cap. Leclerc waited, flanked by several *noir* officers who had surrendered. As Toussaint walked forward, his brother Paul, who had been at Leclerc's side, stepped forward to embrace him. Toussaint turned away. Leclerc asked Toussaint to betray Dessalines; he refused. After an uneasy dinner with Leclerc, Toussaint retired to his plantation at Ennery, near the villa at Gonaives.

As were other *noir* commanders, Toussaint was given nominal authority over a region, but within days he was summoned to another meeting with the French. Showing a lack of caution that suggests he had given up, Toussaint rode to the meeting accompanied only by two officers and an aide. He was captured, trussed like a subdued slave, and taken by carriage at night to Gonaives. At Cap François he was placed on board a ship with his family and valet. The ship was bound for France. Almost immediately, Napoleon signed decrees restoring slavery.

Toussaint arrived in Paris, where he was separated from his wife and family. Suzanne, given a pension after the Bourbon restoration, died in Paris in 1816. Toussaint was taken to an isolated fort in the Jura Mountains on the frontier between France and Switzerland. He was locked in a room twenty-five to thirty feet long and twelve feet wide. Its stone floor was almost always damp in the summer; in winter, a small stove was brought in to augment the fireplace.

It is said that Toussaint's harsh treatment might have been to make him disclose where he had buried 15 million francs, later killing the slaves who dug the hole. The story is as hollow as Napoleon's conscience. John Bigelow, an associate of William Cullen Bryant at the New York *Evening Post*, visited the fort and was struck by the structure's grimness. Seven centuries old, Bigelow wrote, the fort stood "upon the very summit of a solid rock about five hundred feet high." Bigelow concluded that the cruelty of Toussaint's treatment was caused by his having addressed a letter to Napoleon "from the First of the Blacks to the First of the Whites."

The two physicians who were brought in to certify Toussaint's death attributed it to apoplexy and pleuropneumonia, but it is likely that he was poisoned, perhaps by Napoleon's order. His body was found on April 6, 1803, lying on the stone floor.

Biographer Alexis allows himself a poignant smile in imagining the scene after the superstitious French jailer hurried out of the cell to inform others. He hesitated, Alexis writes, because "you can never tell, he thought, with these black princes.... To make quite sure, he went back and carefully locked the door."

Simón Bolívar
1783–1830
(Venezuela)

Liberator of the North

Spain, wrote Simón Bolívar, had kept its colonies "in a sort of permanent infancy." He described a vast colonial system that had bred three centuries' worth of Creoles who were given no part in the governance of their own land and of slaves whose only purpose was to extract wealth in the name of a distant monarchy. Peru, Bolívar wrote, was built on "two factors that clash with every just and liberal principle: gold and slaves. The former corrupts everything; the latter are themselves corrupt. The soul of a serf can seldom really appreciate free-

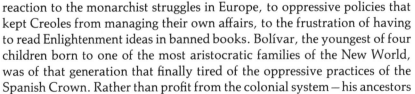

dom. Either he loses his head in uprising or his self-respect in chains." Bolívar's vision was of an "America fashioned into the greatest nation in the world, greatest not so much by virtue of her area and wealth as by her freedom and glory." To that end, Bolívar helped drive out the Europeans, but the Creoles he helped free rejected his vision and drove him to despair. Nevertheless, Bolívar's vision has inspired every Latin American generation for a century and a half.

Simón Antonio de la Santisima Trinidad Bolívar y Palacios was born July 24, 1783, just four years before the first abortive rebellion in Caracas. The revolt was in reaction to the monarchist struggles in Europe, to oppressive policies that kept Creoles from managing their own affairs, to the frustration of having to read Enlightenment ideas in banned books. Bolívar, the youngest of four children born to one of the most aristocratic families of the New World, was of that generation that finally tired of the oppressive practices of the Spanish Crown. Rather than profit from the colonial system — his ancestors through two centuries had been richly rewarded for service and loyalty in administering the orders of the monarch, helping build the port of La Guaira, laying roads, digging mines, and creating plantations — Bolívar followed a more torturous path.

He was orphaned early in life. Although biographers' dates vary, it seems certain his father died when Bolívar was very young and his mother before he had reached his middle teens. Nevertheless, Bolívar led what one biographer called a "spoiled and precocious boyhood" as a result of his family's wealth and the devoted attentions of slave women. Equally attentive were his tutors, including Andrés Bello, who would become a noted scientist, and Simón Rodríguez, a young dévoté of Jean-Jacques Rousseau.

Rodríguez began his lessons about the time Bolívar's mother died, and Bolívar later acknowledged the power of the Enlightenment ideas Rodríguez conveyed: "You have molded my heart for liberty, justice, greatness and beauty. I have followed the path you traced for me." Their relationship had its fullest effect for five years, and after Rodríguez returned to Europe Bolívar sought him out. Thus Bolívar was both protected by great wealth and schooled, from childhood, in revolutionary notions.

Bolívar's training also included athletics, and about 1797, when he was fourteen, he was given military training for two years; he rose to the rank of lieutenant. When he was sixteen he was sent to Madrid to live with relatives and get further schooling. As a wealthy Creole he was introduced to people in the most privileged positions of the system he would later help destroy. In 1800, at the age of seventeen, Bolívar met María Teresa Rodríguez del Toro, a few years his elder, the niece of a Caracas merchant. Of their meeting, no biographer fails to note Bolívar's immediate and profound infatuation.

Impatiently, he waited two years before he could marry her and take her home, but within ten months of their arrival back in Caracas, in the tropical climate to which she was not accustomed, she was dead of yellow fever. Her death was crushing; six months after she died, Bolívar, restless and disconsolate, was back in Europe. He later wrote, explaining his singlemindedness, "The death of my wife pushed me very early into politics." He would never remarry.

On this trip, Bolívar traveled to Paris, where, in the spring of 1804, he found Napoleon, whom he had admired, undermining republicanism by crowning himself. That Bonaparte would aspire to be "a Caesar" disappointed Bolívar, although he recognized the need for structure that was represented by Napoleonic law. The pomp of Napoleon's Paris also impressed Bolívar; he never lost his sense of wonder at the way cheering crowds sounded and would reconstruct the sensation again and again. In Paris, Bolívar was directed to the eminent German naturalist, Alexander von Humboldt. Humboldt, it is said, told Bolívar that a recent trip to Mexico had convinced him that the natural wealth of Latin America promised its peoples a great future — if a man dared lead them. In 1805 Bolívar went to Vienna to visit his old tutor, Rodríguez, with whom he set out on a walking trip to Rome. Admirers — and Bolívar, through his writing, did much to create his own myth — accept the dramatic story that while in Rome Bolívar took Rodríguez to the top of Mount Aventino. There Bolívar swore to God he would never rest until his homeland was independent.

After continuing on to Naples and spending more time with Humboldt, Bolívar, in 1806, went on to the United States. He traveled from Boston to New York, Philadelphia, the District of Columbia, and Charleston, observing the nation with its brand-new constitution. All this time, tremors of independence were being felt from Mexico to Argentina, and Bolívar saw the United States as the model for a united Latin America.

In 1810, after Bolívar had returned, Caracas cast its die. On April 19, the town council declared allegiance to the deposed Ferdinand VII of Spain rather than the dissolute Charles IV, placed on the throne by Napoleon and represented in Caracas by a Spanish captain-general. Ferdinand's restoration to the throne, of course, was but a convenient cause. It came too late if it was to be followed by restoration of the colonial system in America. Political freedom — and the commercial advantages it held — was not like some dried flower, to be saved between the pages of a book. For the group of independentistas to whose leadership Bolívar, then twenty-six, had risen, any monarchy represented oppression. In the summer of 1811 Venezuela declared its independence.

"Venezuela has placed herself in the number of free nations," it was announced. "'Virtue and moderation' have been our motto. 'Fraternity, union and generosity' should be yours, so that these great principles combined may accomplish the great work of raising America to the political dignity which so rightly belongs to her." The differences between the ideals of fraternity, union, and generosity, on the one hand, and reality, on the other, would become increasingly apparent. Even upon his return, according to historian J. B. Trend, Bolívar had to adjust. "The contrast between his ideals, acquired in Europe and from European books, [and] the actual conditions in South America which he found on his return came with something of a shock. Humboldt's glib and superficial view...proved to have no foundation in fact."

The revolutionary junta sent Bolívar to Great Britain to solicit aid, and he was instrumental in bringing back to Venezuela the elderly Francisco de Miranda, a colorful character who had long advocated freedom from the Crown. Under Miranda's erratic leadership Creole armies were at first successful. Then human frailty and natural disaster combined to cloud the picture. First, Miranda came to consider himself a virtual dictator, rendering himself as unpopular in some circles of the New World as he was with the Crown. Second, earthquakes struck.

There were two severe tremors. The first was on March 26, 1812, a Maundy Thursday when churches were full. Entire towns were leveled; corps of troops were buried. Ten thousand people were said to have been killed in Caracas alone. Royalists shouted that it was the dissident towns that most suffered God's wrath for their opposition to the divine right of Ferdinand. They pointed to a Caracas church that bore the royal coat-of-arms on one of its pillars and was completely leveled—except for that pillar. Surely a sign, the royalists averred, angrily roaming the streets. Then, on April 4, another quake struck. Bolívar, too, took to the streets, arguing against the doomsayers and helping to dig out corpses. Rebel determination, however, was shaken.

Military setbacks followed with the result that rebel ranks were broken. In June, the rebel army was devastated in battle, and Miranda tried to flee. He was caught and turned over to the Spanish by Bolívar and other officers and gentlemen, whom the Spanish, in return for the favor, allowed to go into exile. The treachery was excused by Bolívar and his brother officers as justified in light of Miranda's excesses. Miranda would eventually die in a Spanish dungeon, but if honor was sullied, the rebellion's leadership was preserved. Bolívar fled first to safety on the island of Curacao.

From there he returned to the northern coast of Colombia, where his declaration from Cartagena suggests that his principal task was convincing Creoles that they, after three centuries of being told of their colonial inferiority, were capable of successful rebellion. They were, he declared, the equals of "those wretched Spaniards who are superior to us only in wickedness, while they do not excel us in valor, because our indulgence is what gives them their strength. If they appear great to us, it is because we are on our knees. Let us avenge three centuries of shame. War alone can save us through the path of honor." With such words Bolívar was able to gather about two hundred men, whom he led overland back into Venezuela. At Caracas, the Creole residents declared him "Liberator" and "Dictator." Then the Spanish once again drove him out.

During this brief campaign, in 1813, Bolívar helped codify another unfortunate practice of rebellion, one that ranks alongside treachery: retaliatory violence. Bolívar's decree, "War to the Death," warned royalists that they could "be sure of death even if you are indifferent. Americans: Be sure of life even if you are guilty." The declaration contributed to an atmosphere of rabid violence like that which had obtained in Haiti, and Bolívar is blamed for having condoned extreme violence. For decades, however, virtually every Spanish officer, surrounded by hostile Creoles, had demonstrated a taste for terrorism in order to keep adversaries, who were countless and usually invisible, at bay. Survival for Europeans had meant the enslavement of Indians and Africans, so it was but a small step to terrorizing rebellious Creoles. One of the practices the Spanish had perfected by Bolívar's time, for example, was the suffocation of captives. Bolívar responded with equal ferocity. Yet he made plain to the civilians who acknowledged his military leadership that his role was military alone. Once the war was won, he wrote, "I shall not retain any part of authority, even if the people themselves should entrust it to me."

In exile again, this time on Jamaica, Bolívar was protected, but not assisted, by the British, who were hewing a narrow line between protection of their own crowned head and development of new markets. Recognizing this, Bolívar argued that their long-term interests lay with eschewing support for old, European monarchies and supporting New World rebellion. "Europe itself, by reason of wholesome policies," Bolívar wrote in 1815, "should have prepared and carried out the plan of American independence not only because it is so required for the balance of the world, but because this is a legitimate and safe means of obtaining commercial posts."

Trying once more to return to the mainland, Bolívar was again chased out by royalist troops, this time to Haiti. There, he was more warmly welcomed than he had been by the British and he was able to get assistance from the government of former slaves. This new Haitian government, so feared in Europe and the United States for the example it set, formed an immediate ligature with Bolívar, and Bolivarian constitutions would all have a provision prohibiting slavery.

Bolívar, again, gathered an officer corps. His ability to continually recruit patriot armies suggests the attractiveness of his personality and the degree of his commitment. "Bolívar," writes J. B. Trend, "who had made himself into an army commander through sheer force of character and strength of will, never forgot his own men, and, for that, they adored him." With his nascent army, he landed again in the spring of 1816, on the coast of Venezuela. As he had promised, his first "official" act was to abolish slavery. The people hailed him. Again, they declared him Liberator, but they did not join his army. Royalists chased him back to Haiti.

Finally, in 1817, Bolívar was successful in making his return trip stick because he allied himself with an early practitioner of guerrilla warfare, Jose Antonio Páez. Unable to beat disciplined royalist troops in open battle, Bolívar needed time to build an army. By joining forces with Páez — whose rough, illiterate frontiersmen fought as effectively as had the farmers of New England forty years earlier — he got that time and much more besides. Páez, in fact, is directly responsible for the successful beginning of the wars of independence. Páez recruited peasants — many of whom had at first fought on the royalist side as mercenaries — and turned them into a feared division of the patriot army.

Bolstered by Páez' men and instructed by his tactics, Bolívar stopped trying to march on cities and instead lived off the bounty of the countryside, keeping his own troops provisioned while denying supplies to the enemy. Tactics ceased being attack-and-retreat and were stretched into an effort at outlasting the royalists. Its legitimacy growing with every day and able to stay in the field, the army further benefited from thousands of mercenaries who began arriving from Britain and Germany. Under Bolívar's command, this reinvigorated army secured part of Venezuela, but avoided the strong Spanish force there and turned toward Nueva Granada, which was not as stoutly defended.

Bolívar's political philosophy was articulated at this point, early in 1819, in an essay written for the congress gathered at Angostura, Venezuela. Like pronouncements from Jamaica, these remarks expressed the ideals, set the standards, for the whole independence movement. "The continuation of authority in one individual has frequently been the undoing of democratic governments," he said, foreshadowing precisely the problem that would dog his later years. "Repeated elections are essential. . . . The most perfect system of government is the one that produces the greatest possible happiness, the greatest degree of social safety, and the greatest political stability." His goals for government would ring like bells over the continent, until, sadly, their pealing was drowned out by raucous shouting in the streets.

In the spring of 1819, however, those were ideas that ignited men's souls, and Bolívar led a patriot army of more than 2,000 men — roughly, 1,300 infantry and 700 cavalry — through the Orinoco jungles during the rainy season and up into the frozen passages of the Andes, which lay across his path to Nueva Granada. A portion of this army was recent European immigrants, some of whom had seen action in the Napoleonic wars. There was a full battalion of British troops. At thirty-six, Bolívar was the oldest commander; Francisco de Paula Santander, leading the forward contingent, was only twenty-eight.

At Paya, in late June, the patriots defeated a strong Spanish position and began their ascent. When they passed 10,000 feet the tree line was below them and they passed over narrow, treacherous, slippery trails, often in fog, beneath peaks that reached 14,000 feet. Men of the lowlands, they had never experienced such bitter cold. The feat came after San Martín's Andean crossing, but was through passes approximately a thousand feet higher. "Other crossings of mountains may have been more adroit and of a more exemplary strategy," remarks the Uruguayan José Enrique Rodó, "but none was so audacious, so heroic and legendary." Trend describes the crossing this way: "Bolívar, wrapped in a great scarlet cloak, was indomitable; but even the devoted aide-de-camp, O'Leary, almost gave up. Many died of exposure, including 56 of the English, and when the rest reached Socha (6th July, 1819) they had practically nothing on but their weapons. All the pack and saddle animals had died on the way."

With this army, Bolívar won three engagements in the middle of July against well-trained troops holding good positions. Then, with the Spanish rocked back on their heels, Bolívar pursued his advantage to a final victory at the Battle of Boyacá. The viceroy fled from Bogotá, and Bolívar rode, almost completely unattended, into the city. His entry, according to the official dispatch, was possible "after having overcome difficulties and obstacles much greater than could be foreseen . . . and destroyed an army three times superior in number to the invaders." Victory was complete.

"After Boyacá," writes historian Guillermo A. Sherwell, "the campaigns of Bolívar were very swift, very successful and on a very different footing from his past campaigns. His enemies henceforth had to give up calling him the chieftan of rebels and bandits, and to treat him as an equal." Control of New Granada was assured; Bolívar was proclaimed Liberator — and before the year was out had to hurry back to Venezuela because officers and civilian politicians were plotting against him. It was a scene that would be repeated again and again. The Spanish could be defeated, but the Creoles could not conquer their wrangling for power or control their predilection for divisiveness.

The plans of both Bolívar and San Martín were enhanced by events in Spain. In Cádiz, the great army being prepared for embarkation by Ferdinand VII revolted on New Year's Day 1820. The Spanish were politically divided between supporters of the monarchy and adherents of the idea, embodied in the Constitution of 1812, of a constitutional system. The army, influenced by constitutionalists, declared itself more interested in staying home than mounting an expediton to reconquer the colonies. Although Bolívar still faced at least 15,000 royalist troops in Nueva Granada and royal garrisons in major cities, his task was considerably eased. The commander of royalist forces in Nueva Granada, Gen. Pablo Morillo, was ordered to negotiate; reluctantly he agreed and during 1820 the war in the north dwindled into discussion between equals. Late in the year, after Bolívar and Morillo met, Morillo described "one of the most pleasant days of my life in the company of Bolívar and various members of his staff. . . . Bolívar was wildly excited; we embraced again and again, and determined to put up a monument to the perpetual memory of our meeting."

Thoughts of a monument faded, however, when relations between the two sides, after Morillo had been recalled to Spain, deteriorated. The armistice was ended, and after two inconclusive engagements in the spring of 1821, the situation in the north moved toward its final resolution during the summer. It was the second great battle fought on the plain of Carabobo, south of Caracas, where Bolívar had won one of his early victories seven years before.

This time, Bolívar confronted approximately 5,000 skilled enemy troops in a strong position. From a hill, they covered with cannon and rifle the trails that were cut through rough, tall grass; a frontal assault was out of the question. Bolívar had 6,500 infantrymen, 1,500 mounted *llaneros* commanded by José Antonio Páez, and his faithful battalion of British, still with him, still willing to follow him anywhere. He first sent his cavalry around the enemy's flank over an obscure trail in a move that was supposed to be a surprise. The horsemen emerged from their two-and-a-half hour encirclement in plain view, however, and the royalists were able to wheel their artillery around to deliver withering fire as the cavalry found itself attacking over unexpectedly rough terrain. The day would have been lost for the patriots were it not for the British.

The battalion's determined attack cost it two-thirds of its nine hundred men, but it drew fire until the *llaneros* could reform, climb the final hill, and attack again toward the royalist rear. Then, with Bolívar leading a frontal attack, the three segments closed in, causing huge royalist losses in dead, wounded, and captured. The Spanish commander was chased with his few remaining troops to refuge in Puerto Cabello; within days, the Caracas garrison surrendered. The war in the north was essentially over.

The time, July 1821, had come for Bolívar and San Martín, who had just conquered Lima, to meet. The two had corresponded as their armies approached each other; San Martín had sent troops to help bring order to Ecuador's periodic madness, and now Bolívar was in Guayaquil trying to calm the excitable citizens of that city. Logically, the meeting should have paved the way for joint action, but that is not what happened. These were not logical times.

San Martín, unexpectedly, requested the meeting and sailed northward from Callao. He wanted to decide the proper government for Guayaquil — being pulled apart by forces favoring Peru, Colombia, or its own independent government — and to get reinforcements for his army. San Martín was also willing to discuss the idea of some form of constitutional monarchy for new Latin American countries, perhaps importing European princes for the purpose. He had been, after all, thoroughly chastened by his experiences in Chile and Peru; he was unable to point to any example of stable government and was uncertain whether any was possible under a republican form.

Bolívar, on the other hand, approached the meeting transfixed by his own grand idea, to create *Gran Colombia* out of New Granada (modern Colombia) Venezuela, and Ecuador and to weld a union of Latin American states that would be a model of strength against aggression from outside and of cooperation inside. He had reluctantly accepted the presidency of *Gran Colombia* from a congress assembled at Cúcuta — "I am not the kind of ruler the Republic wants"—and left Santander in charge of civic affairs while he journeyed southward to try to complete the war.

He wanted no part of winning a war against Europeans only to import European problems.

Like other Latin American thinkers, he saw Europe as fundamentally flawed. "The lessons of experience should not be lost on us," he had written. "The spectacle presented to us by Europe, steeped in blood in an endeavor to establish a balance that is forever changing, should correct our policy in order to save it from those bloody dangers."

Rather than the constant cross-border conflict that characterized Europe, he envisioned cooperation, the creation of an all-encompassing republic in order that "a single government may use its great resources [to] lift us to the summit of power and prosperity."

In his favor at this particular juncture, Bolívar had appearances. He was at the height of his apparent power, and as long as military, not political, solutions were sufficient, Bolívar was supreme. His triumphal entry into Quito—the one that had won him the affections of Manuela Sáenz—made it look as if he had gloriously completed his vision of creating *Gran Colombia.*

Despite sniping by local politicians and nationalist fervor that would soon break his union into pieces, Bolívar in mid-1821 stood head and shoulders above any alternative in Latin America. As if to press home this point when San Martín stepped ashore at Guayaquil, Bolívar welcomed him to "Colombian soil."

The two had never met, although they had exchanged cordial, general messages as they and their armies approached each other. San Martín, in fact, was reading messages from the fluent Bolívar right up to the time his schooner sailed into the Guayas River. At a banquet, Bolívar, never self-effacing, toasted "the two greatest men in South America, General San Martín and me." There is a bit of irony in that Bolívar missed the chance to extend his characterization beyond continental boundaries: Napoleon had died three months earlier, so perhaps they were the greatest in the world.

The two men conferred in private, without even aides accompanying them, out of earshot and sometimes strolling out of sight of their solicitous lieutenants. History, as a result, does not record precisely what was said. Because, predictably, so much of what was written immediately after the meeting was written by Bolívar or his aides, there is the school of thought that Bolívar was somehow "superior." It is only certain, however, that San Martín was more humble. He looked at reality, while Bolívar tended to be constantly glancing in a mirror.

Probably the most crucial information exchanged in Guayaquil was that which arrived from Bolívar's minister to Lima. It was word of an uprising — of which San Martín was unaware — that had erupted as soon as the Protector left the city. The news must have confirmed everything San Martín had come to believe about the impossibility of stable government. Three days after his arrival, San Martín, disgusted with failure and apparently embarrassed by the gaudiness of the celebration, quickly and quietly left Guayaquil, sailed to Peru, resigned as Protector, went to Chile and traveled overland to Buenos Aires, and then sailed to Europe. He left, as it turned out, the remaining heartache to Bolívar.

The problem of clearing Peru of royalist troops remained. Bolívar sent a Colombian force for that purpose, but it was sent back, either because of Peruvian ingratitude or Colombian arrogance. It was difficult to tell with Peruvians, who tended to cover royalist sentiments with the thinnest of republican veneers. Whatever the reason, in early 1823, Bolívar sent the troops again, this time with Sucre at their head. Then Bolívar himself, at the insistence of Peruvians, went south, still looking for the last, great battle and determined not to slip into the bog of civil administration. "My repugnance to work in governmental affairs," he warned, "is beyond all exaggeration. . . . The Congress of Peru may count, nevertheless, on all the strength of Colombian arms."

The Battle of Junín on August 7, 1823, was a fitting last battle for the Liberator. It has been called the "Battle of the Centaurs" because it was fought entirely by cavalry with swords and lances. Before the battle, on a plain 14,000 feet above sea level in the Andes, Bolívar told 7,700 troops, "Men, the enemy you are going to destroy boasts that he has been winning for fourteen years. Thus, he is worthy of measuring his arms against yours, which have also shone brilliantly in a great number of engagements." The patriot victory was complete. The royalists retreated south where, after Bolívar had returned to Lima, Sucre destroyed them on December 9, 1824, in the Battle of Ayacucho. When the news of Ayacucho reached Bolívar, he ripped off his uniform jacket and threw it to the ground, saying, "Thank God. Never again shall I have to command."

For eight months in 1825, Bolívar traveled through Upper Peru, which would form the country named for him, Bolivia. His last government effort was to write the constitution for the new nation, and, like his pronouncements from Jamaica and his Angostura remarks, the constitution is a testament to Bolívar's concern for a stable, republican government. Notably, the only thing the new republic rejected was Bolívar's provision for freedom of religion. "Should the state be the conscience of its subjects?" Bolívar asked, and the Bolivians gave their answer by requiring that the state be Roman Catholic.

More serious differences of opinion awaited him back in Colombia in 1826, where internal disputes and bankruptcy threatened, but the story was the same in every new republic. "His presence," writes historian Trend, "seemed necessary everywhere to inspire that loyalty and common sense without which his schemes would not work." Guayaquil and Quito left the union and, in January 1827, Bolívar returned to a Venezuela disenchanted with him and unable to live up to his requirements.

Bolívar rode into Caracas accompanied by Páez, but Páez was a dissident too. Bolívar spent six months trying to reorganize the government, working on agriculture and education and worrying over the budget; his thanks for his effort was a resolution asking that he never return to his native country.

He returned to Bogotá and Manuela Sáenz, the mistress who had been among his few devoted followers. Santander, privately, accused him of ruling "not constitutionally, but capriciously," and, indeed, Bolívar's mind was addled. His orders were often contradictory. Tuberculosis wracked his body, ingratitude was destroying his mind. His behavior only contributed to the widespread confusion. At the same time opponents were trying to hound him into exile, several town councils were declaring him dictator for life. If Bolívar was without direction, so was everyone else.

The attempt on his life in 1828 was a final ignominy. Saved by Manuela Sáenz, Bolívar hid beneath a bridge through most of the night, damaging his health and honor. As he spent the night beneath the bridge with the pastry cook, with whom he had escaped from the presidential palace, Bolívar listened to hoofbeats on the cobblestones and shouts of "*Viva el Libertador*," but he was never sure whether supporters or assassins were trying to draw him out of hiding. The coup attempt was never actively, overtly supported by more than a battalion of troops and a few officers, but it was clear that many more hung back, hoping for the attempt to succeed. Santander was at the root of it, and was at first condemned to death, although Bolívar commuted the sentence to exile. Still, he found himself condemning to firing squads men, including Gen. José María Córdoba, who had been brave soldiers throughout the wars of independence. He despaired. "I shall go away to the country for several months," he wrote late that year, "to a place where there are nothing but Indians. . . . I can no longer abide such ingratitude. I am not a saint. I have no wish to be a martyr. Only the luck of having a few good friends enables me to withstand this torture."

The torture continued. In the south of Colombia, Popayán, an old royalist stronghold, revolted against the central government; Peru invaded Colombia; Venezuela and Quito left the union. Finally, the charge of being a monarchist was leveled at Bolívar. After sacrificing his physical and mental health for the cause of democracy, Bolívar was now subject to the same accusation that had been aimed at San Martín, that was thrown up to anyone who lost faith in Creoles' capacity for order.

The strain showed on Bolívar. In January 1830, returning to Bogotá from a trip, Bolívar was described as "ghastly pale." His voice was "almost inaudible." Addressing the congress, he pled: "The national treasury must claim your attention. . . . The public debt, Colombia's cancerous sore, demands that its sacred obligations be honored. The army, which has innumerable claims to the nation's gratitude, is in need of thorough reorganization. Justice demands codes capable of protecting the rights and the honor of free men. All this is for you to create.

"Fellow citizens, I am ashamed to say it, but independence is the sole benefit we have gained, at the sacrifice of all others."

In the spring, even as New Granada and Ecuador pulled apart, Bolívar, his tuberculosis having ravaged his health, tried to find peaceful exile. He rode off, accompanied by his long-time servant, José Palacios, and only a few others, seeking refuge on the northern coast of Colombia, on the sere, northern edge of what he had envisioned as a great political union.

Although Gen. Rafael Urdaneta — encouraged and aided by Manuela Sáenz — was successful in briefly leading pro-Bolívar forces back to power, Bolívar himself refused to return. He knew it would lead to bloody civil war. "In every civil war the winning side has been the more ferocious and energetic," he wrote, having learned the lesson that still eluded his countrymen. "From the beginning, no recourse remains to you except flight from the country or bringing despair to your enemies, because the response of your enemies would be terrifying. In order not to place myself between those cruel alternatives I have not dared take part in this rebellion, since I am convinced that our authority and our lives would not be saved without the cost of the blood of our adversaries, achieving through this sacrifice neither peace nor happiness, much less honor."

Bolívar stayed to die. "To the sepulchre, that's what my fellow citizens have meted out [for me]," he told the French doctor attending him, "but I forgive them. . . . I only wish I could take with me the consolation of their having stayed together."

He received, when he was not too weak to see them, a scattering of visitors, including one sent by Manuela Sáenz because he had not allowed her to accompany him. "Prepare yourself," she was informed in the winter of 1830, "to receive the final and fatal news."

The Liberator moved in and out of coherence. "They may take my kit aboard," he told aides who were not there in preparation for a voyage that would never be. In December, before he died, Bolívar had his last confession, and uttered plaintively, "Oh, how shall I get out of this labyrinth?"

Manuela Sáenz
1797–1859
(Ecuador)

Spirit of the Liberation

Manuela Sáenz created her own image; she was feisty, intelligent, indomitable, outrageous. Her beauty was legendary, her intelligence freely and piquantly expressed, her spies feared. Her sexual fidelity to the Liberator was certainly stronger than his faithfulness to her. She never lost hope in the Liberation and never abandoned her will to fight, even when Bolívar, who was given to periods of depression, lapsed into despair. "Her passion for Bolívar is so explosive," writes a biographer, "that its sparks appear like lu- minaries in Bolívar's life." She was his "gentle, crazy woman." For eight years, Manuela Sáenz was at Bolí- var's side, and when he went off to die she fought on without him.

Manuela Sáenz was born on De- cember 27, 1797, to Simón Sáenz y Vergara and María de Ais- puru, both of whom were rea- sonably affluent, but who were not man and wife. Simón Sáenz had come to Quito by way of Popayán, Co- lombia, arriving on horseback in the late 1700s. He was without money and with little to recommend him except his Spanish birth, which would open doors for him that were closed to Creoles. María de Aispuru, although a Creole, had no cause to make excuses for her background; her grandfather was Spanish (Vizcayan), an ancestry that biographer Alfonso Rumazo González says explained Manuela's "aggressiveness, compulsiveness, invincibility."

Although illegitimate, Manuela Sáenz grew up well provided for and could even count on a modest inheritance, something bastards had not always been allowed under royal law. Her illegitimacy, however, was a thorn she could not ignore; biographer Mercedes Ballesteros writes that to call her a bastard "lit in her angry character a desire for revenge that would never be extinguished."

Simón Sáenz prospered in commerce and was appointed to political office. He did not neglect his daughter, who frequently visited the home he shared with his aristocratic wife and their four children, Pedro, José María, Ignacio, and Eulalia. Manuela's relationship with her half-brothers and half-sister was mixed; they might have considered her beneath them. Later in life, the tragic realities of civil war that affected Ignacio and José María would rub off on Manuela.

As a youth, Manuela closely observed a black servant who was a few years older. From Jonatás Manuela learned the art of survival, the trick of pleasing everyone, most of all herself. "If she was sent to play in the street," Rumazo writes of Jonatás, "she returned full of news; if she was taken to mass, she prayed more than anyone, if with glazed eyes. She appeared to be shameless, laughing loudly. She detested work; she loved the sensational. For little Manuela, she was an intimate friend, almost indispensable." Manuela learned to ride and to handle sword and pistol, preferring to ride astride a horse and to dress like a man.

Manuela's father was a staunch, unyielding royalist who was named a life member of the *cabildo*, the city council, after he had attained some prosperity in commerce. Sáenz was able to transform himself into a relatively big fish in Quito's small pond. A city of some 60,000 people at the time, Quito had a stagnant economy that was hindered by the city's being 9,350 feet above sea level and far from the sea. Politics were predictable; the city was royalist by default. In general, Ecuador did not have enough political will to protect its borders, which were periodically nibbled away by aggressive neighbors. Bolívar thought of Ecuador as part of his grand schemes because its borders conformed to the ancient Incan kingdom of Quitu, but within those borders there was little revolutionary ferment.

Nevertheless, after 1810 Ecuadorans were aware of revolutionary movements in other places, and they duplicated the unrest on a small, sometimes violent, scale. Manuela, when she was but twelve years old, watched from a balcony of her mother's house when soldiers brought into town shackled prisoners, rebels who were arrested after a short-lived "declaration of emancipation." The city government was even briefly overturned and her father jailed along with other royalists. Because of a brief flare-up in August 1810 — disembodied heads sent through the mail was one manifestation — Manuela's mother took her to a country home for safety.

At the age of seventeen, Manuela was sent by her mother to the

Convent of Santa Catalina, where young ladies were taught, among other things, the preparation of desserts. The convent, founded two centuries earlier, took in a few non-novitiates like Manuela. It had a scandalous history. The nuns enjoyed such worldly privileges as private maids, and were rumored to be under the influence of their Dominican mentors, who were described as "masters of sensuality." Manuela was untouched by such considerations, however, indulging in little more between prayers than surreptitious lessons in dancing and smoking. She was allowed out only once a month, on Sunday, after mass.

That, however, was enough time to meet a young army officer, Fausto d'Elhuyar, and soon Manuela was in love. Little is known about the affair; Manuela got permission to leave the convent one Sunday morning, met her young man, and simply did not come back. Manuela never spoke of what happened or where the young lovers were able to go. She was found and taken home, and before long a solution was found. She would be courted by Dr. James Thorne, a forty-year-old English physician and merchant.

In 1817, after Manuela and Thorne had been meeting at her mother's house once a month, never without a chaperone, they were married. She was not enthusiastic, calling the whole affair "supremely ridiculous," but the marriage stopped the gossip. Manuela was expected to be like other wives — chatting, sewing, praying, living an empty life in full skirts — but the opportunity for something more exciting emerged when Thorne decided in 1818 to take her to Lima, seat of the vice-royalty. There she met Rosa Campuzano, a society flirt from Guayaquil with a predilection for soldiers. Among those passing through Lima in 1819, in fact, was Manuela's half-brother José María. By then he was a royalist captain whose sympathies lay with the revolutionaries, and by December of the next year he would join San Martín, rising eventually to the rank of general.

Lima, of course, was the last prize of the wars of independence, caught in a vice. In August 1819 Bolívar entered Bogotá and drove southward. A year later San Martín embarked from Valparaiso. Guayaquil declared independence on October 9, 1820, stealing the Crown's arsenal on the Pacific in the process. On July 10, 1821, San Martín quietly entered the city.

At the obligatory grand ball, Rosa Campuzano, who had set her cap for San Martín, was determined to shine, but Manuela was asked by Thorne not to attend. She obeyed, and stayed home until three weeks later, when she went to observe the parade commemorating the formal declaration of independence. With her dark eyes and long, straight, black hair, Manuela appeared in a blue silk, sleeveless dress. The dress, in Rumazo's enthusiastic description, "exhibited her amber bosom from which boastfully emerged incredibly graceful breasts that beckoned toward pleasure." She wore no jewelry.

Rosa Campuzano's play for San Martín was of fleeting success. Lima's society, always royalist to the core, settled back into the unwelcome business of defining itself under patriot administration.

In 1821, Bolívar completed the conquest of Venezuela and in 1822, Gen. Antonio José de Sucre — who would become a firm friend of Manuela — helped free Ecuador. With San Martín's success in Peru, these victories set the scene for the Conference of Cúcuta, at which Bolívar's totally unrealistic dream, *Gran Colombia*, was accepted. What are today Venezuela, Colombia, Ecuador, Peru, and Bolivia were shaped into one unruly entity, and Bolívar was named president.

Meanwhile, in early 1822, Simón Sáenz played his role in destiny by arriving in Lima on business. Manuela decided, with Thorne's approval, to accompany her father back to Quito for a visit. She arrived about the time of the May 24 Battle of Pichinchá, after which Quito declared itself independent and a part of *Gran Colombia*. Manuela was introduced to Sucre and took part in the elaborate preparation for the triumphal entry of Bolívar.

June 16, 1822, has been lovingly documented — and embellished — by romantic biographers. The parade route was crowded with happy people; the sun was bright; aristocratic women rode to the parade route in sedan chairs borne by bare-footed slaves in bright colors and powdered hair. True patriots showed their enthusiasm for independence — no matter how recently acquired — by wearing simple muslin.

Bolívar — five feet, five inches tall — was splendid in uniform astride a white horse, at least from a distance. Up close, it was clear that although he was only forty years old, his face — described as "long, dark and ugly" with a prominent nose and lower lip — already showed signs of the strain of tuberculosis. He was, however, at the height of his strength in the popular imagination, in the eyes of a public that knew or cared nothing of his detractors, opponents, and critics. Masses were offered, banners were unfurled, line after line of troops marched by with bands playing. Manuela Sáenz, then twenty-six years old, was enthralled.

She watched from a balcony with the governor, wearing a crimson sash with the Order of the Sun, the highest decoration conferred by the new Peruvian government. The story is thus: She threw a laurel wreath. Bolívar looked up to see who threw it, and their eyes met.

Her white dress exposed her arms and shoulders and, of course, all the other endowments on which biographers have commented. It was the beginning of one of the most ardent love affairs of history. "Of the many women in Bolívar's life," writes historian Hubert Herring, "none held his loyalty and affection longer than she." After she saved Bolívar's life, he would refer to her, only half in jest, as "the Liberator of the Liberator." Even when she grew old, Giuseppe Garibaldi, the Italian adventurer, would describe her as "gracious and gentle" — and, still, "eccentric." Gen. Daniel

Florencio O'Leary, Bolívar's aide de camp, would write, quite simply, that Manuela Sáenz "looked like a queen."

At the ball that night, Juan Larrea, a friend, introduced them. The ball lasted until dawn; no one knew at what time they left, together.

For the next eight years, she would follow him, often arduously because he was a man at the head of an army, chasing a grand idea. She was often dependent upon him for support; her mother's death left her some estate, but not much, and she was constantly at the mercy of Bolívar's largesse or loans from friends and acquaintances.

After their meeting, they spent twelve days together in Quito before Bolívar left for his fateful meeting in Guayaquil with San Martín; she did not accompany him, and he did not write. By early 1823, Manuela had begun her life of either being with Bolívar or corresponding with him. She became close friends with Sucre — they were two of the few people Bolívar could trust completely — and is thought to have had some influence with other generals as well, if only because no one could ever be sure how much influence she had with Bolívar. She was not shy about expressing opinions. It appears that her influence was limited to winning mercy for out-of-favor royalists who had been her friends, but she also operated a spy network. Her friends and her servants provided her with information, and with war a constant reality and distrust common, information was an important asset. Manuela never wavered in her candor, and Bolívar learned to appreciate that.

Her presence was not always appreciated. After she followed him to Callao, the Peruvian seaport, traveling behind in a stagecoach, patriot officers objected. "My general," one said to Bolívar, "we're about to go swordfight with the Goths and you're carrying on with women."

Manuela left for a while, returning to Quito, where her father was fatally wounded in one of the string of royalist uprisings that plagued Sucre's administration of Ecuador. Bolívar faced similar problems in Lima, so Manuela joined him there. Familiar with Lima's society, Manuela, with the help of her servant, Jonatás, collected information. Jonatás, a big woman in a brightly colored turban, worked the street for news. So helpful was Manuela's service, in fact, that O'Leary suggested she be named a colonel. When Bolívar complied, Manuela delightedly manifested her rank by wearing a blue military tunic with a red collar.

Manuela also acquired more direct military experience. By the middle of 1824, Bolívar had moved his army over a difficult trail to Cerro de Pasco, northwest of Lima, determined to finally stamp out royalist resistance. The 950-mile trek cost him 700 men to death and desertion while crossing the mountains. Manuela made the entire trip with the army and stayed at Bolívar's side to within ten kilometers of the enemy. At that point, Bolívar sent her back to be with the infantry.

The battle was a victory for the patriots, and when the royalists turned tail for Cuzco, seeking reinforcements among the friendly populace, Manuela joined in the pursuit. Maneuvering continued through August and into the beginning of the rainy season, both sides recognizing that the next battle would be important, perhaps definitive. The next battle, in fact, was the Battle of Ayacucho, which Bolívar missed, but Manuela did not. Bolívar had to leave the field because he needed to raise money to keep his army provisioned and because he was being implored to do something about the problems tearing apart patriot governments from Caracas to Bogotá.

Manuela stayed in the field with Sucre. Much has been made of the intimacy of their relationship — Sucre was twenty-nine at the time, Manuela almost twenty-seven — but all that is known for sure is that Manuela would be known after December 9, 1824, as having been "on the field at Ayacucho," a claim not even Bolívar could make.

The armies faced each other on a high Andean plain. The night before the battle men from both sides crossed to embrace brothers and friends. The royalists counted on at least 3,000 more men — more than 9,000 royalists against fewer than 6,000 patriots — and ten times the artillery, but when the battle was over, the royalists had suffered a humiliating defeat. At least 1,800 royalists had been killed, 500 officers captured, and 2,000 enlisted men taken prisoner. The rest deserted. The viceroy and several important generals were taken by the patriots.

Manuela rode alongside the reserve force, the commander of which was wounded. "Ayacucho marked the virtual end of the wars for Spanish American independence," notes Herring. As a bizarre remembrance, Manuela cut from a dead enemy soldier his mustache, making for herself a false mustache that she wore with a military outfit to costume balls. This, as might be imagined, was not universally appreciated.

Indeed, her place beside Bolívar was becoming the subject of censure, and some people suspected the Liberator would crown her. Over the next months, however, as Bolívar traveled back and forth across a disintegrating *Gran Colombia*, Manuela would have been the first to scoff at such speculation. She saw herself as having to fight for his attention in letters, or, when he was in Lima, to share him with admirers and sycophants — and other women.

Manuela dealt as well as she could with Bolívar's reputation as a Lothario. Upon finding a diamond earring in his bed in Lima, she gave him a tongue lashing that she knew would have but temporary effect; the cards were stacked against her. Bolívar was continually being seduced, as it were, by custom. Every time he entered a new town, for example, local leaders chose the prettiest girl for the honor of delivering a crown of flowers. If she delivered more, well, he was the Liberator. In Huaylas, for example, the damsel was Manolita Madroño, eighteen years old. When Manuela found out, she counter-attacked in a letter that, preserved through the years, still carries its original pout: "The disgrace is mine," she wrote. "Everything comes to an end. The general does not think of me. He has written only two letters in nineteen days."

Manuela was by turns furious or philosophical about Bolívar's amorous activities. His *quinta* outside Lima was legendary. Rumazo writes of Bolívar's being "solaced by Lima women who line up at the country house like a procession of love." Bolívar's private secretary blushed: "We are in a Babylon wherein all the beautiful women have been conjured in order to make us lose our heads." A visitor asked, "How many women loved him here? No one can be sure."

In the winter of 1825 Manuela despaired. A long separation could only exhaust his love, not hers. For his part, he tried to convince her that he loved her more for her spirit than her "delicious attractions." At such times their relationship was a study in the ambiguity that results from two strong personalities. Bolívar, for all his conquests, knew of the gossip and the need to preserve some modicum of propriety. He was, he wrote to Manuela, "determined to live up to my obligation to tell you of the cruel destiny that separates us from ourselves. Yes, from ourselves, since the soul that gives us existence, that affords us pleasure in living, flees. In the future, you will be alone, though at the side of your husband; I will be alone in the midst of the crowd."

When left behind, Manuela was forced to stay with Thorne — of whose jealousy and drunkenness she complained in letters — and then would rush to Bolívar whenever possible. She was convinced, with some justice, that her love was among the few things Bolívar, increasingly despised for his ambition, could trust. The accuracy of that belief would soon be proven.

In the autumn of 1826, Bolívar left Lima for Bogotá. Although in June the Panama Conference had given lip service to unity, everyone knew dissent was tearing *Gran Colombia* apart. Few trustworthy friends remained. On the road, Bolívar wrote back to Manuela, "You asked me to tell you that I love no one else. Oh, no! I love no one; I will love no one. The pedestal you occupy will not be profaned by another idol nor another image beyond that of God Himself." In November, he arrived in Bogotá; he had been away five long years and much had changed. A trip to his native Caracas would be his last, so intense had the hostility become.

At the same time — January 1827 — Manuela was demonstrating just how far she was prepared to go in her commitment to Bolívar. In Lima, a Colombian division garrison there declared that it was terminating its allegiance to the Bolivarian constitution. Twenty-four hundred soldiers were in revolt. Manuela, determined to intervene, tried to reach the commanding general in person, but was turned back. Then she sent a message, which was intercepted. Frustrated, she took matters into her own hands. She rode at full tilt into the courtyard of the divisional barracks of the dissidents. She wore a man's clothing. Clutching the reins in one hand, she brandished a pistol in the other. She called upon the soldiers to remain loyal to Bolívar, and, as an inducement, she offered money.

For this dramatic gesture she ended up in jail, held for several days incommunicado at a convent and ordered to leave the country within twenty-four hours. So determined was she, however, that she was able, while still in the convent, to contact supporters, who distributed bribe money on her behalf. The nuns, driven to distraction by her disruptive behavior, were forced to station a sentry, a nun whose orders were never to let Manuela out of her sight.

The governor who had ordered her jailed, according to the official bulletin, said that she and an accomplice had "not ceased trying to seduce, promise and spread bribes," the latter in considerable quantities. "With evidence implicating Armero and that woman, whose scandalous conduct has so insulted the public honor and morality, I called on her at four in the afternoon to say: You must embark within twenty-four hours." The alternative was prison.

Manuela left Ecuador by way of Guayaquil, embarking on the same ship with Gen. José María Córdoba, a Colombian general who was one of Bolívar's principal critics. Manuela and the general crossed verbal swords. Her dislike of Córdoba would prove prescient.

By mid–1827, Bolívar was on his way back to Bogotá, periodically receiving gloomy messages that one or another capital had renounced membership in *Gran Colombia*. A revolt in Quito was put down with much bloodshed; not long after he left Caracas, dissidents had to be suppressed there. Depressed by the task of presiding over an embattled, shrinking government, he wrote to Manuela: "The ice of my years [he was forty-four] is melted by your warmth and grace. Your love renews a life that is expiring. I can't be without you; I can't voluntarily deny myself my Manuela . . . . I see you even though far from you. Come, come, come."

Manuela was, as always, ready. She moved into a borrowed house a few yards down the street from Palacio San Carlos, the presidential palace. It was a fortuitous choice.

The atmosphere in the city, then with only about 22,000 inhabitants, was tense. Bolívar and his vice president, Francisco de Paula Santander, could not even speak to each other; rumors of plots surfaced constantly. This was the kind of environment, however, in which Manuela was at her best. Sexually, she would always have rivals, but in gall, audacity, and loyalty, she was without peer.

Juan Bautista Boussingault, a French contemporary, describes Manuela as "always visible." "In the morning, she wore a housecoat that was not without its attractions. Her arms were bare; she didn't bother to cover them; she embroidered, showing the most beautiful fingers in the world; she spoke little; she smoked gracefully. She imparted and received news. During the day, she went out in proper clothes. At night, she was transformed, wearing a bit of rouge, her hair artfully brushed. She was very animated and unafraid of making, from time to time, risqué remarks. Her self-possession, her generosity, were limitless." Manuela enjoyed her reputation for having "fought on the fields of Ayacucho."

Biographer Rumazo takes pains to suggest that Manuela was "a lady of State, who entered into politics, offered her opinion, made political suggestions, made decisions, unmasked enemies, made energetic determinations." The reality is less clear. Certainly, Manuela was only one of many voices, but she was not afraid to use that voice. She herself acknowledged, in pleading the case for some acquaintance, that if Bolívar decided to the contrary "I know well how much I can do for a friend and that certainly does not extend to compromising the man I idolize." It was in laughing off suggestions of her power that Bolívar, perhaps defensively, called her "that kind, crazy woman." That anyone even suggested she might have influence, of course, affirms some measure of influence.

Manuela often presided at Bolívar's Colombian country estate, "La Quinta." Although the atmosphere of La Quinta was less carefree than that of La Magdalena, for Bolívar was less adored, Manuela still managed to be outrageous. Among the frequent callers when Bolívar was away were men rumored to be her clandestine lovers. She kept at the house a small bear, which delighted her and terrified unprepared visitors.

In one instance, however, she went too far in the eyes of many. At a particularly boisterous La Quinta party a crude effigy was made and dressed to look like Santander, the vice president and Bolívar's adversary. The figure was set on a bench, facing a wall, its back to the boisterous, drunken crowd. A priest administered "last rites" and a firing squad was assembled. A young ensign, appalled at what was going on, refused to give the order to fire and was promptly arrested. Someone else gave the order, and the firing squad's bullets ripped into the back of the dummy.

Córdoba, the general who liked neither Bolívar nor Manuela, wrote to Bolívar to protest. Thanking him for his friendship and loyalty — thanks that would prove misplaced — Bolívar replied, "I know my friends and their craziness. But only the commander of the Grenadiers is to blame. The others have committed no legal wrong." Bolívar conceded, however, that the affair was "eminently shabby and stupid."

Of Sáenz he wrote: "As for the crazy one, what do you want me to do? You've known her for some time; after this event I'm thinking about making her go back to her own country or wherever. Moreover, I'll say that she has never meddled with the exception of asking favors, but she has never been accommodated except in the matter of C. Alvarado." Unrepentant, Manuela would always believe that the mock execution was clairvoyance.

After writing to Córdoba, Bolívar ignored the affair when he wrote to Manuela. He referred, rather, to having received her three most recent letters: "One...pierces me with its tenderness, the other amuses me with your good humor, and the third convinces that you have suffered past, undeserved injuries." This was hardly a reprimand.

In August 1828, Colombians—some of whom had insisted that Bolívar assume total power—scheduled a great celebration of the Battle of Boyacá. Manuela was afraid. Alerted by her spies and conscious of the animosity surrounding Bolívar, she told him she did not think he should go to the masquerade ball. The ball, however, was dedicated to him, and she ran out of arguments to keep him away. One Marcelo Tenorio describes what happened:

Descending from an upstairs corridor toward the main ballroom about eleven o'clock, Tenorio found his way blocked by someone dressed as an old man in traditional Spanish garb. When Tenorio bristled at being detained, the man leaned close, lifted his mask, and said, "Don't you recognize me? In half an hour, at midnight, the tyrant will die." To drive home his assertion, the man pulled back his jacket to expose the hilt of a dagger. "There are twelve of us," he whispered. "Silence."

Looking down into the ballroom, Tenorio could see Bolívar chatting with generals. Then, suddenly, Bolívar's attention was drawn to a clamor at the door. It was Manuela, described as "disheveled and dirty, but laughing uproariously," She was being denied entry, apparently because of her manly costume, a hussar's uniform. "I am Manuela Sáenz," she said loudly. It did not matter if she were Saint Manuela, she was told, she was not going to get into the ball without proper attire.

Bolívar, apparently embarrassed and hauling Gen. Córdoba along with him, strode to the door, took Manuela by the arm, and departed. Tenorio heard someone gasp, "The tyrant has escaped." Later it was determined that a plot had been planned, the suspected mastermind being Santander, who innocently arrived at the party later. It was never known for sure, but widely suspected, that Manuela's timely disruption was also planned, to provide Bolívar with an exit.

Another plot was hatched almost immediately, for September. Again, to Manuela's dismay, Bolívar did nothing to prepare. Even when one group of conspirators gave itself away by bickering over who should be in command, Bolívar, hearing reports, brushed the story aside.

Then news of an assassination attempt was brought directly to the presidential palace by a lone woman who insisted on anonymity. After a servant had heard the woman's story, Bolívar sent his aide, Col. James

Fergusson, to hear the woman out. She accused Santander, who was said to be condoning the plot without sticking his neck out, and also implicated Gen. Córdoba. Bolívar did not believe her story, saying it was an unsubstantiated slur on a faithful officer, Córdoba, who had fought valiantly at Ayacucho. Fergusson, however, was beginning to believe the woman, and Manuela, always cautious, was thoroughly convinced. To their dismay, however, Bolívar did nothing, neither assigning extra guards nor even telling the sergeant of the guards of the warning.

Then, on September 25, a drunk artillery captain was overheard blurting something about a Masonic conspiracy to kill "that old man Bolívar, who is a tyrant." The captain was arrested, and other conspirators, apparently fearful that further delay would undo them, resolved to act that night.

At seven o'clock in the evening, the conspirators met at the home of Bolívar opponent Vargas Tejada. They knew the chief of staff of the Bogotá garrison, while not joining them, had agreed to absent himself by spending time at the house of a friend, effectively washing his hands of the affair— and waiting to see how it turned out. By ten o'clock, more than one hundred officers and civilians were on their way to arm themselves, although the vast majority got cold feet.

In the meantime—Manuela disclosed in a letter to old friend O'Leary in 1850—Bolívar had sent for her early in the evening, and she had responded that she was ill. He sent a second summons, however, suggesting that she was less ill than he and that she should reconsider. As always, she went to him, pulling on a pair of boots over her slippers because the streets were wet.

When she arrived at his apartment, he was in the bath. He told her a revolt was planned, then tried to reassure her as she admonished him for being so casual. She calmed down enough to read to him while he was in the bath, and they went to bed without the guards being increased. As always, Bolívar kept a sword and pistols by the bed. He slept soundly.

About midnight, two groups entered the palace. One was made up of ten to twelve civilians led by a man named Augustín Horment; in the other group sixteen to twenty-five soldiers followed Pedro Carujo. One of the conspirators, Florentino González, wrote in his memoirs that successful overthrow of the government depended on the terror that "would result from the death of Bolívar, and in that moment that end was supreme."

Horment's civilians killed three sentinels. Then the soldiers acted as lookouts while the civilians penetrated farther, breaking down two doors and disarming and wounding Lt. André Ibarra, officer of the guards. The band shouted, "Long live liberty." Behind the third door was Bolívar's apartment.

Manuela had heard dogs barking, then other noises as the conspirators made their way through the palace. Awakened by her, Bolívar sprang to his feet, seized a pistol and the sword, and started out the door. Manuela held him back and told him to get dressed. Then the two were unsure what to do next.

Should they barricade themselves? Deciding against that course, according to Manuela's account, Bolívar again thought to open the door, and again she had to stop him. Manuela reminded Bolívar that earlier he had remarked to a friend that the bedroom window was perfect for escape should it ever be needed. That was now the course they decided on.

Suddenly they realized that Bolívar's boots had been taken out for cleaning. Quickly, he pulled onto his small feet the boots she had worn. He started out the window, and once again she held him back momentarily while people in the street passed by. Then he dropped nine feet to the ground. Moments later, the bedroom door flew open.

Manuela confronted the assassins in the light of a lantern one of them carried.

"Where is Bolívar?" they demanded.

"In the council room," Manuela replied, a response that caused some consternation. Perhaps he and others were preparing resistance. Their concern was heightened by the fact that the one among them who knew the layout of the palace had lost his nerve along the way and deserted them. "Some believed me and some did not," Manuela wrote. "They saw the open window and the rumpled bed."

"Why is the window open?" they asked. She had opened it to hear the shouting outside.

Why was the bed warm? She had been waiting for the Liberator, to wash his back.

Where was the council room? She did not know exactly, she had only heard them speak of it. She, after all, lived down the street. They insisted she lead them to the council room, but on the way they encountered the wounded Ibarra, and she delayed further by tending to his wound with her handkerchief. Have they killed the Liberator? Ibarra asked. No, she whispered, he lives. She insisted that Ibarra, wounded honorably, be lifted onto Bolívar's bed.

Outside, Col. Fergusson, the aide, clearly visible in the moonlight, shouted up to the window. He too, had been ill—so many at the palace were ill that Manuela referred to it as "a hospital"—and had heard noises. He was coming in. There was nothing he could do but endanger himself, she called back; stay there. He would rather face his duty honorably, he replied, and came ahead. He was dropped by a bullet in the chest. Carujo finished him with a sabre slash across the forehead.

In frustration after so much killing with still no sign of Bolívar, the assassins threatened Manuela, but one of their leaders intervened. Finally, however, the assassins were beyond restraint. According to historian Salvador de Madariaga, "The conspirators then vented their frustration and fury on Manuela, who was so severely beaten with the flat of a sword that twelve days later, on October 7th, she was still confined to bed." She was punched and kicked, all the while taunting, "Go ahead, cowards, kill me. Kill a woman."

Outside the window, the first person Bolívar met was his pastry cook, who had just left the kitchen on his way home. Together, the two hurried away, past a hostile sentry who thought, when he recognized the pastry cook, that the two were simply servants on their way home for the night. The cook hid Bolívar beneath a bridge, listening to the confused clatter of hooves above them, hearing shots fired and shouts of "*Viva el Libertador*," which Bolívar was afraid might be a trap to draw him out of hiding.

Men from both sides were looking for him, but Bolívar, in his hiding place, could not tell who was who. When he finally dared go out, he was given a horse and escorted to the main plaza, where he was welcomed by a crowd, among which was Santander. Even then, Bolívar had to know — Manuela had repeatedly warned him — that he was surrounded not only by friends, but by others who had hung back, waiting to see whether the attempt would succeed.

Once he was safe, Bolívar undertook to rewrite history, erasing Manuela's role in saving him, exaggerating his own. He saw to it that the official *Gazeta* reported that he had tried to confront his attackers, but they outnumbered him. So, "being singlehanded against so many, he tried to barricade himself in his bedroom and, as it became impossible to resist any longer, he flew to the street." He reached the barracks of loyal troops, "where he was received with indescribable joy."

Historian Madariaga, for one, is appalled at the *Gazeta's* "omitting, of course, all mention of Manuela Sáenz." In addition, Madariaga adds, "the omission of his three hours of hiding is pathetic." Manuela later told O'Leary that when Bolívar finally got back to bed that night he was so overwrought that he alternated between asking about what had happened while he was in hiding and telling her to keep quiet so he could get some sleep.

Bolívar was uncertain what to do with the captured conspirators. At first, he agreed the time had come to pardon his opponents, try to calm the situation, and retire because of his widespread unpopularity. Then he changed his mind and ordered that the assassins be summarily shot. Troubled by his decision, Bolívar was counseled by Manuela not to lose faith in his mission, which required making an example of the assassins: "May God ordain that all your enemies die . . . it would be a great day for Colombia . . . these and others are sacrificing you with their enmity in order to make you the victim day after day. The most humane idea is this: that ten die to save millions."

Some confessed and others denied their complicity. The governing council decided that all who actually entered the palace were to be executed, and it was suggested that Manuela identify them. Bolívar, however, intervened. "This woman," he declared, "will never be the instrument of death nor the accuser of such shameful ones."

Manuela did testify, nevertheless, and although it was Horment, one of the leaders, who apparently said, "We're not here to kill women," perhaps saving Manuela's life, Manuela attributed the remark to Florentino González. González, presumably, had that turn of fate in mind while writing in his memoirs, "When he broke down the door of the bedroom, a beautiful woman stepped before us with a sword in her hand and an admirable presence of spirit to very courteously ask what it was we wanted."

If Manuela had saved Bolívar's life, however, she could not save his idea. Weakened by consumption—which was exacerbated by the night under the bridge—Bolívar vainly fought to prolong his dream. He commuted Santander's death sentence to exile—which infuriated Manuela—without winning Santander's adherents to his side. He condemned Córdoba to death, but he could not, as Manuela wished, execute all his enemies. Unrest cropped up like so many malevolent mushrooms; Popayán rebelled; Peru invaded.

At this point Manuela received a letter from Thorne, asking yet again that she return to his hearth. Her reply has often been cited as an eloquent expression of her spirit, her assertion to the entire world that she did not "live by the social preoccupations invented for mutual torment."

Give it up, she wrote, so I don't have to say no again and again. "Do you believe," she asked rhetorically, "after being the mistress of this general for seven years, with the security of possessing his heart, I could prefer to be the mistress of the Father, the Son and the Holy Ghost, or the Holy Trinity?

"If I feel anything it is that you haven't accepted any better your having been deserted. I know very well that nothing can unite me with him under the auspices that you call honor. [But] do you believe me less honorable for his being my lover and not my husband? Ah! I don't live under the social preoccupations invented for mutual torment.

"Leave me, my dear Englishman. Let's make a deal: in heaven we'll marry again, but on earth, no."

Manuela concluded with a devastating comment on the difference between the rainy nature of the English and the fiery soul of a Latin: "Monotony is reserved to your nation," she wrote, "in love, for sure, but also in the rest; who else does so well in commerce and sailing?

"Love affords you no pleasure, conversation no wit, movement no sprightliness; you greet without feeling, rising and sitting with care, joking without laughter, these are divine formalities, but I am such a miserable

mortal that I have to laugh at myself, at you and at all your English seriousness.

"Enough of jokes. Formally, and without laughing, in total seriousness, truth and purity of an Englishwoman, I tell you that I will never be
yours again."

The historical evidence is that the letter was closely edited, as friends
apparently chuckled with Manuela over this final blow to her tortured ex-
husband's ego. Furthermore, she sent a copy to Bolívar. He replied, in part,
"The tone of the letter makes me love you for your admirable spirit — what
you tell me of your husband is at the same time both painful and humorous."

After both had fought to suppress dissent in the south, Bolívar and
Sucre met for the last time in Quito in March 1829. Bolívar then fell ill and
eventually made his way back toward Bogotá, where Manuela awaited him
at La Quinta early in 1830. He was a beaten man, his health destroyed, his
will weakened. In the spring, Ecuador formed itself as an independent state,
electing as its first president Juan José Flores, an illiterate. Bolívar's dream
of *Gran Colombia* had gone up in smoke. Preparing himself for exile, he
gave La Quinta to a friend in January, but stayed on until early March.
Then he moved into a house lent to him by one of his generals, and
Manuela moved into a rented house nearby.

On May 29, 1830, he rode by her house to say goodbye for what
Manuela thought would be a brief interruption in their life together, an interruption like so many others. She thought it was just a matter of time
before she would join him. His companions, including his long-time servant, José Palacios, waited outside while Bolívar talked to Manuela in the
front hall. She did not know it was the last time she would see him. As the
small group rode off, Palacios was weeping.

Hardly had Bolívar begun his trip north, however, when he got news
of Manuela, who had become a rallying point for his supporters. If the fight
was gone from Bolívar, it was not from Manuela, and that distressed him.
"My love," he wrote, "I love you very much, but I will love you more if
now, more than ever, you exercise judgment. Be careful in what you do,
or, if not, the loss might be for us both, losing you." The danger was real;
Venezuela declared that Bolívar was never to return to his native country;
and, in the south, Sucre was ambushed and assassinated.

Manuela, quite simply, fought on. She found out that the new government was allowing, as part of a celebration in Bogotá, a fireworks display
that included two effigies, one like Bolívar labeled "Despotism," the other
a likeness of herself labeled "Tyranny." Military guards were assigned to
protect the display before the celebration.

Manuela, predictably, was incensed. She dressed Jonatás and another
female servant, Nathán, in military uniforms and sallied forth with them

on horseback. Once again, her behavior sufficiently shocked the public consciousness that it made the official news. Sworn testimony portrayed the servants trying to disarm the guards. One witness said the attack was so fierce he ran to get a rifle to help defend the display. The three women were arrested, but not before they knocked down both the effigies and the elaborate fireworks. Jail merely added spice to their victory.

La Aurora, a newspaper supporting the government, described Manuela as a woman who "every day wears clothing that does not correspond to her sex and, similarly, allows her slave to insult decorum, and brags about her contempt for both law and morality." She had, *Aurora* gasped, "fired a pistol she carried, shouting against the government, against liberty and against the people." Manuela defended herself in a public statement, saying that while her detractors might revile her, they could "not make me take back one line of my respect for, friendship with, and gratitude to General Bolívar."

The conflict continued, even though Bolívar refused to be drawn back into it. Rumors that Europe's "Holy Alliance" would try to help Spain reconquer its colonies heightened tension as Gen. Rafael Urdaneta, a Bolivarian, sought to overthrow the new government. Neither Manuela nor the general was successful in luring the Liberator back from exile to lead their effort, and Manuela kept getting into hot water. "Manuela Sáenz is disturbing public tranquility with repeated scandalous acts," wrote the minister of state to the mayor of Bogotá in a bill of particulars, "that her servants have fixed posters in the streets; that she had tried to seduce with gifts the soldiers of the palace guard; and that she has committed other attempts, too, threatening public order."

A sentence to internal exile did not quell her, for she continued to turn up, spurring on dissidents. "Manuela was without doubt the soul of the revolution," writes historian Luis Augusto Cuervo — even when the revolution was over.

From afar, she agonized through Bolívar's final weeks in the autumn of 1830, informed by messages of personal emissaries, but unable to join him herself. He did not name her in his will, and, after his last confession, was not even allowed to utter her name because he was prohibited by church dictates from any mention of sin. When he died, she went to a small town and, like Cleopatra, caused a poisonous snake to bite her in a suicide attempt. Boussingault visited her, finding her with her right arm limp and swollen to the shoulder.

The virtual state of war between Urdaneta and Santander finally drove Manuela out of Colombia. In January 1834 she was told to leave, although she resisted so vehemently that it took a small squad of cadets and soldiers to force her out of her house. Because Guayaquil and Quito were at war — her brother José María was killed in the fighting — she was exiled to

Jamaica. From there, however, a steady stream of letters to Ecuador failed to win a visa to her native country because the government considered her too dangerous. Her reputation was too well known.

She wrote to Juan José Flores, the president of Ecuador, that he could not "ignore that a poor woman like me cannot do anything; but Santander does not think that way; he ascribes to me an imaginary valor." Flores did not think there was anything imaginary about Manuela's valor. When, after a year in Jamaica, she insisted on embarking for Quito she got as far as Guayaquil and the trail into the mountains; she was stopped by an official party. Her brother had been on the wrong side in the war, and the government was not going to allow Manuela back "in order to pursue her dauntless vengeance."

Without money, with only Jonatás and Nathán, she ended up just across the border in a miserable little Peruvian port called Paitá. She opened a small store — "Tobacco. English Spoken. Manuela Sáenz" — and after two years Flores informed her that Ecuador's legislature had approved her return. "How kind you are," wrote Manuela in reply. "The worst is that the damage is done; I will not return to my native soil since you know, my friend, that it is easier to destroy something than to make it new . . . a safe-conduct is not enough to revive my fond affections for my country and my friends."

Thorne sent her money, which she is said to have refused. When she was named in his will — he apparently was murdered — she refused any part of the estate. She grew fat from inactivity and was partly crippled by rheumatism; she was tired, outliving her beloved servants and eventually tiring of telling of her experiences with the Liberator. She was not, however, forgotten.

Ricardo Palma, the Peruvian writer, visited and told of her "strictly ceremonial" conversation. "In her tone," writes Palma, "was something of the high-born lady, accustomed to command, and to have done her will."

A ship's doctor who stopped in Paitá when Manuela was more than seventy years old remembered her having said that if Bolívar had been French "he would have been greater than Napoleon." More to the point was the physician's own evaluation: "If that woman had been French and the lover of one of the Kings, she would also have figured in the forefront of events."

She outlived Bolívar by twenty-nine years. In December 1859, her rheumatic pains sharp and exacerbated by a pain in her throat, her temperature high, and her breathing labored, she could fight no longer. She was buried in Paitá, and her clothes and belongings were burned to prevent the spread of diphtheria. Also destroyed was a box she had kept containing letters.

José de San Martín
1778–1850
(Argentina)

Liberator of the South

"It has been said," writes Bartolomé Mitre, "that San Martín was not a man, but a mission." He was also an enigma, a victor who walked away from history. San Martín was "the other Liberator," who was overshadowed by Bolívar. Liberation of southern South America and capture of the viceroyal seat at Lima were not enough to save San Martín from lonely, impoverished exile, a widower adrift in Europe with his daughter, an outcast from the lands he freed from the European yoke.

José Francisco de San Martín was born in an isolated outpost because his father, a Castillian army officer who had worked his way up through the ranks before emigrating, was assigned there. It was a remote Indian settlement called *Tupambac*, "God's Estate," an experiment that exemplifies the creativity and intelligence of the Jesuits. The priests organized some thirty *reducciones* (settlements of Indians) — in this case Guaraní, converted to Catholicism — into a self-sufficient, productive community. Under the tutelage of the Jesuits, the Indians raised palms, figs, and oranges, and they were educated. When San Martín's father was appointed administrator at *Tupambac*, the building into which he moved had a fully stocked library.

It was the very success of the Jesuits in such projects, of course, that made them the object of hatred for royal administrators, who were usually incompetent and always jealous of their prerogatives. At the urging of such men Charles III expelled the Jesuits in 1767, and in 1770 Capt. Juan de San Martín y Gómez was sent to *Tupambac* to take over.

So hastily was he dispatched that he had to leave his betrothed, Gregoria Mattoras, behind in Buenos Aires. His fellow officers raised enough money to send her along later, after the couple was married by proxy. Juan de San Martín eventually became lieutenant governor of the department of Yupeyú. "Much to the surprise of those accustomed to official rapacity," writes biographer J. C. J. Metford, "he did not abuse his position for personal gain, remaining a poor man for the duration of his tenure of office."

José Francisco was born on February 25, 1778 (although conflicting reports place the date over a range from early 1777 to as late as 1781). He was the youngest of three sons and had a sister, María Elena, who was probably younger. Money was short; in 1779 San Martín's mother traveled to Buenos Aires to try to obtain what was owed by her husband, and by about 1781 the San Martín family had been moved back to Buenos Aires. Finally, between 1783 and 1785, Capt. San Martín took his family back to Spain.

Western Europe was at that time constantly at war, and until his death in 1796 the elder San Martín supported his family at Málaga in military service. As an officer, he enjoyed certain prerogatives — as long as he could document that there were no Moors, Jews, or heretics in his family tree — and young José was accepted into Seminario de los Nobles, an aristocratic training ground for service to the Crown. All three San Martín boys became cadets at age twelve.

José de San Martín's military career was circumscribed by Charles IV's rather bizarre monarchy and France's expansionism. In 1793, at age fifteen, San Martín joined the Murcia Regiment. At that time, Spain still held, barely, the fort at the North African port of Orán. The fort had been under siege by warriors of the Bey of Máscara for two years, and the Murcia Regiment was sent in relief. After thirty days of fighting — through an earthquake — the Spanish surrendered; along with other prisoners, San Martín was allowed to return to Spain.

Shortly afterward, Charles made a feeble offer to help the deposed Louis XVI regain his throne, an offer that caused the Directorate to declare war. For the next two decades, San Martín would fight from one end of the Iberian peninsula to the other, from the foot of the Pyrenees to Lisbon and, finally, Cádiz.

At first, Spanish troops scored successes over the poorly trained soldiers hustled into combat by the Directorate. In time, however, Spanish commanders, warring among themselves, were outmaneuvered. In early 1794, San Martín, among the forces being driven southward, was again captured. He was only sixteen.

Upon release, San Martín demonstrated abilities that were recognized in promotions up the line to second lieutenant in 1795. He had grown into a tall man, broad-shouldered and erect, with a pale complexion and "a remarkably sharp and penetrating eye." His hair was dark, his sideburns long. "His address was quick and lively," wrote an admirer, "his manners affable and polite." He was not given to the depression that would plague Bolívar — the younger Bolívar, a wealthy Creole student, took his sojourn through Europe about this time — but he would develop physical problems, including bloody coughing that would weaken him during strenuous campaigns.

When the short-lived Peace of Basel was signed in 1795, France pulled its troops out of Spain (but acquired the entire island of Santo Domingo), and hostilities abated. Then, in 1801, as Napoleon's Continental System sought to exclude English ships from friendly harbors, 30,000 French troops were sent to help the Spanish invade Portugal. Again San Martín was at war, this time storming the fort at Olivares.

After the action, San Martín finally found relative quiet — he was once stabbed and robbed, another time assigned to cholera-ridden Cádiz — with garrison duty. To improve his chances for promotion he changed regiments and rose to the rank of second captain.

After a second invasion of Portugal, San Martín was stationed back at Cádiz, which was in turmoil as the Spanish fought over whether they would be a monarchy — and, if so, French or Spanish — or a republic. At Cádiz, San Martín witnessed the chaos that characterized the Old World and felt the force of fresh ideas blowing in from the New. French ships were trapped in the port, chased and held there by the British after the Battle of Trafalgar. San Martín was called upon to help defend the Spanish administrator as he was threatened by angry mobs. Ordered not to let his men fire into the crowd, San Martín was virtually helpless as the king's deputy was dragged from hiding and, on his way to the scaffold, stabbed to death. San Martín had to escape to Seville. Biographer Metford suggests that "the affair made a deep and lasting impression on his mind and influenced his political outlook."

With the Crown debilitated, the junta of Seville took over civil administration of Spain and the Indies. The junta had the allegiance of the army, which tried to turn back French advances. In a cavalry charge near Andújar, San Martín so distinguished himself that he was promoted to the rank of captain. "This valiant officer," said the *Ministerial Gazette*, "attentive only to his superior's orders, engaged the enemy with such courage that he completely routed them." In July 1808 San Martín earned a gold medal and promotion to lieutenant-colonel at the Battle of Bailén, a Spanish victory.

San Martín, in service for more than twenty years and a veteran of countless battles, seemed to have reached the zenith of his career in an army conditioned to defeat. After an illness in late 1809 and early 1810, San Martín was appointed adjutant to his commander, and in 1811 he continued to serve through the frustrating effort the Spanish know as the "war of independence." After the French were driven northward, San Martín was present at the Spanish defeat at Tudela. The Spanish again retreated southward, this time driven past Seville to the coast.

With their army essentially cornered at Cádiz, Spaniards fought among themselves. Partisans of the Bourbons preferred any monarchy to chaos; supporters of Ferdinand VII wanted a Spanish succession; republicans insisted on a constitutional monarchy. For his part, San Martín wanted more. He had met both English officers and Creoles, including Bernardo O'Higgins, the Chilean patriot. These men spoke of ideas, freedoms, causes, not tired European traditions. At this time, apparently, San Martín discussed the ideas of Locke and Montesquieu, and his dedication was raised a level, from obeisance to an unseen king to commitment to a political philosophy. He joined a clandestine cell, with O'Higgins. This fraternity would later, in America, be the Lautaro Lodge, a Mason-like organization with signs and passwords, named for the Araucanian Indian hero of a popular novel. It would be the vehicle of democratic ideas.

San Martín served in his last two battles, at Badajoz and Albuera, rising after the latter to become commander of a regiment of dragoons. The Spanish finally held Cádiz with the help of the English. San Martín, however, had turned his intentions toward America. It was the summer of 1811. Now thirty-three years old, San Martín requested retirement without pension and permission to travel to South America under the pretense that he had family matters to settle in Lima. This apparently reflects a conspiracy of military officers with democratic notions to enter the Spanish colonies. San Martín set sail, first for England, then Buenos Aires, where he arrived in early 1812.

Although discovered by Juan Díaz de Solis in 1516 — before Cortés landed at Yucatan — Buenos Aires was the least of the Spanish Crown's concerns. Direct trade between Rio de la Plata and Spanish ports was forbidden; all influence, all communication, all commerce, trickled down from the west, from Lima through Upper Peru. Not until 1620 was Buenos Aires made a provincial capital, and then mostly to try to stop smuggling as traders developed the obvious, direct link with European ports. The city was made a vice-royal capital in 1776 and trade restraints were lifted, so industry prospered; but its independent nature was fully formed.

Early in 1812, San Martín disembarked in a city nearly two years into independence. Within six months he had married María de los Remedios Escalada y de la Quintana — at fifteen, she was twenty years his junior — the daughter of a prosperous, and independence-minded, merchant.

The revolutionary government commissioned San Martín to form a corps of mounted grenadiers. He instituted a strict code of conduct, well aware that patriot troops had sometimes carried the day with raw enthusiasm, but convinced that iron discipline would be necessary in the long run. "Soldiers are made in the barracks and on the parade ground" was the axiom he cited; the troop was drilled daily in the bull ring.

In October, word reached Buenos Aires that the patriot general Manuel Belgrano had been defeated in the north. Then, amidst the anxiety caused by the defeat, a feud broke out between partisans of the administrative triumvirate and the legislative assembly. The city garrison, including San Martín's grenadiers, was called out to maintain order. Generally, the dispute was over which of several government alternatives should prevail. San Martín was among those wanting a clean, strong break with Spain, but factions continued to scuffle without resolution.

San Martín's first battle in the New World occurred a year after his arrival. Spanish troops had been disrupting river trade with the interior by sailing up the Paraná from their stronghold at Montevideo. San Martín took a contingent in pursuit and, when it appeared he would be outdistanced, he chose 120 grenadiers and left the others to follow. Near San Lorenzo, the Spanish put 250 men and some artillery ashore, giving San Martín his chance. He divided his small force and fell on the Spanish, losing 25 men, but forcing the surprised Spanish force to yield.

In the battle, San Martín's horse fell and rolled over on him and he would likely have been killed or captured had not a quick-witted soldier saved his life. The main Spanish force eventually had to turn back toward its base at Montevideo, and San Martín's small victory gave patriots something to cheer. "San Lorenzo," writes Metford, "was little more than a skirmish, but it had the effect of a great military victory. *Criollos* had proved themselves superior to Spaniards, even when outnumbered, and capable of tactical manoeuvres in the best European tradition." No fewer than nineteen of San Martín's men who saw their first combat that day would later serve him as generals. After the battle, the patriot government deleted references to the king in official documents and took the royal image off coins.

In the bigger picture, however, change was more difficult. Towns and provinces of the interior both declared their independence from Spain and their freedom from control by Buenos Aires. Belgrano fought on although essentially defeated and disgraced; loyalists held out in the hope that Ferdinand VII would regain the throne with the help of his foreign allies. San Martín, meanwhile, was "rewarded" for his victory by being ordered home to command the Buenos Aires garrison by jealous leaders who wanted no more dramatic victories to overshadow their efforts.

San Martín's patron and apparent friend in the Buenos Aires government was Carlos María de Alvear, a member of the Lautaro Lodge and a witness at San Martín's wedding, but a formidable politician with his own agenda. In late 1813, Alvear helped obtain for San Martín 100 artillery pieces and 250 mounted grenadiers to relieve Belgrano. It appeared to be a hopeless task. As San Martín departed, one observer predicted, "The man is finished."

Arriving at the patriot camp, San Martín took command reluctantly, not wanting to embarrass Belgrano. His dual responsibility was to hold the Spanish, 5,000 strong, at bay while he rebuilt the army, beginning with the 600 men he got from Belgrano. "I have found here no more than the sad remnants of a routed army," he wrote.

More important, however, San Martín recognized that he was not where he needed to be. He founded a school for math and military science; he tried to rein in the fiercely competitive, independent chiefs who made up Belgrano's force; and then he requested to be relieved of the command. San Martín knew that Upper Peru — the "direct" route to Lima — was a dead end for the patriot army, which could not sustain a supply line over jungle trails. A 1,500-man expedition would later prove his point. He also knew, however, that the Spanish had the same problem in reverse. Their supply trains could not withstand harassing raids by guerrillas. San Martín's vision was toward the mountains, traversing 1,200-foot-high passes used by Incan invaders.

The goal was the same, Lima, but the method was to emerge on the central plain of Chile, take Santiago and Valparaiso, then sail with an invading force to Callao, Lima's port.

In September 1814, after an illness, San Martín was granted his request to be appointed governor of the province of Cuyo. Alvear, figuring he had San Martín in a weak positon and wanting to destroy a rival, tried to replace San Martín with his own appointee. A popular outcry in Mendoza not only saved San Martín's job but cost Alvear his. Nevertheless, San Martín's position was widely seen as respectable retirement. Almost no one knew it was San Martín's carefully planned first step.

Slowly, he raised an army, imposed taxes, recruited seamstresses to make uniforms, and even found a monk, Luis Beltrán, who knew enough chemistry to direct the manufacture of explosives. María made the long journey to join her husband and gave birth to their only child, Mercedes, on August 4, 1816. For even his small family, because he was working at half-salary to help finance the expedition, San Martín had to borrow from the director of the revolutionary government, Juan Martín Pueyrredón. Pueyrredón, virtually the only leader in Buenos Aires who believed an attack over the Andes was possible, would remain a faithful friend and financier. "If I go bankrupt," he wrote to San Martín, "I will cancel my debts with everyone and come to you myself so you can give me some of the beef jerky I am sending."

In May 1816 the Congress of Tucumán "organized" the United Provinces of La Plata, although united was the last thing they were. Nevertheless, on July 9, shunting aside Ferdinand VII's apparent offer of a compromise, the congress proclaimed independence. Now the Spanish might invade any day, and San Martín, meeting Pueyrredón at Córdoba, got final support for his plan.

The threat of a Spanish invasion from Chile actually helped San Martín recruit, adding urgency to his words. Beginning with about 25 men from the Cuyo militia, he took in 1,200 regular enlistments, ordered slaves to enlist, fining their owners if they did not, and conscripted every Creole man between the ages of fourteen and forty-five. In addition, several companies of artillery and mounted grenadiers were sent from Buenos Aires.

Crucial to the invasion was military intelligence, and San Martín was something of a master of spies, who operated along the frontier, in Chile and up the coast to Callao and Lima. John Miers, an Englishman, observes, "The General was, from an early period, a great adept in cunning and intrigue." When spies from across the mountains fell into San Martín's hands, he made sure to send them back with greatly inflated estimates of his force, hoping to hold the Spanish off until he was ready. San Martín also met with the fierce Tehuelche Indians south of Cuyo, who agreed to provide safe passage. San Martín told them that his plan was to move his main army through the pass at Planchón, but that they were to tell the Spanish the route would be through the valley of Aconcagua. He assumed, correctly, the Indians would betray him upon receipt of bribes from the Spanish, and reinforced the game of mirrors by allowing interception of "orders" designating Planchón. All the time, of course, he intended to take a third route.

Meanwhile, in Chile, an army under Bernardo O'Higgins briefly established patriot supremacy, only to be beaten by the Spanish and royalists in October 1814. As a result, San Martín found his efforts hampered by the necessity of taking in refugees fleeing the battle at Rancagua. San Martín welcomed O'Higgins, his fellow Lautaro Lodgeman, and placed him in command of one of his divisions.

San Martín's Army of the Andes was ready by late 1816. He had prepared the way with misinformation, suggesting to the Spanish he was coming by each of six possible routes. The route he chose was the most direct, but he had spent months sending signals to his adversary, Marshal Marcó del Pont, that kept reconnaissance patrols constantly on the move and the defending army spread along a 1,300-mile frontier. He sent ahead a formal declaration of independence, making sure the officer who carried it gathered information about the pass at Uspallata during the trip.

On the morning of January 5, 1817, after a day of praying and parading and a night of feasting and dancing, the army, carrying an embroidered version of the blue-and-white flag adopted at Tucumán, lumbered toward the mountains, from which came the echo of a final ceremonial cannonade. Over more than two years, demonstrating the patience and persistence for which he would become famous, San Martín had built an army of 3,778 men, including 742 mounted grenadiers. They were supported by 1,392 auxiliary forces, from sappers, or field engineers whose specialty was hand-held bombs, to baggage handlers. Eighteen artillery pieces were slung between mules for the passage along mountain trails, through gorges, San Martín knew, which were so narrow they could be blocked by a handful of men.

There were 1,600 horses and 9,281 mules; the number of animals is the mathematical measure of the difficulty of the passage. The army would arrive with but 500 horses and 4,300 mules remaining. An English officer who accompanied the army, John Miller, wrote, "The intense cold on the summits killed many men." Although San Martín ordered an extra supply of garlic and onions, the only known remedy for *puna,* or vertigo, the sickening dizziness caused by the thin air of high altitude, the sickness affected virtually everyone. The crossing has been compared with feats of Hannibal, Napoleon, and, of course, Bolívar, who two years later would make his Andean crossing through passes a thousand feet higher.

Although royalists occupied the capital, San Martín counted on a friendly reception in other towns because Chile had harbored its own independence movement from 1781 and had been the site of a tax revolt as early as 1776. Del Pont, San Martín's spies informed him, would command 5,000 men, mostly mestizos and only 930 of them well-trained.

San Martín rode with O'Higgins and Gen. Miguel Estanislao Soler, who commanded the main force. A secondary force, including the artillery, was commanded by Juan Gregorio de las Heras, and two other, smaller, forces rode flanking movements through separate passes. Deposits had been laid along the routes, and careful surveys had been made of the potential battle sites. All four forces were to be in place at their respective summits by February 1, 1817.

The main and Las Heras forces combined on February 8 and the march on Santiago proceeded at six points. Del Pont, already confused, now split into fractions. He had received reports of rebel advances at Los Patos, Uspallata, and Planchón, all of which had some truth to them. San Martín's main force, however, was marching up the valley of the Aconcagua River.

The army Del Pont sent to stop San Martín at Chacabuco had 1,500 men and five artillery pieces. In addition, he could count on those troops who were retreating in the face of San Martín's advance. Unsure of exactly what he faced and where he faced it, Del Pont held onto 1,600 men to defend Santiago. It would all be to no avail.

The defense at Chacabuco occupied the crest of a hill—a hill that

San Martín's engineers had surveyed. San Martín knew of a narrow, rocky trail cut into the mountain and leading around the Spanish left. In addition, San Martín captured a reconnaissance patrol, effectively blinding the Spanish commander. Appraising the situation, San Martín sent Soler around the left flank to create pressure on the defenders' rear. O'Higgins was sent, by moonlight, to spring a frontal assault at daybreak, before the enemy was dug in.

At dawn, O'Higgins' men turned the defenders and set them to flight. Spanish officers, however, because Soler did not get into position in time, were able to establish a second line of defense. San Martín ordered O'Higgins to pursue and Soler to hurry.

Soler was not fast enough. The second time the Spanish established themselves, with two cannons, across a stream rushing through a deep arroyo. It was a formidable position, and O'Higgins impetuously attacked without waiting for Soler. San Martín, watching from an elevated command post, saw O'Higgins prematurely order an attack and be beaten back from the watercourse. Again hastening Soler, San Martín mounted and rode to help O'Higgins.

A furious assault by saber and bayonet — ex-slaves fought bravely — finally carried the position, but only after Soler's flanking movement contributed to the royalists' disarray. Of the enemy, 500 were killed and 600 captured; the patriots' losses were 130 killed and about the same number wounded. The Spanish succeeded in getting 500 men away and, eventually, to Lima. Others retreated southward to royalist strongholds.

"I think we must now be more prudent and look to the future," San Martín wrote to his friend Tomás Godoy Cruz after the Battle of Chacabuco. "Let us not become conceited with our glories, but let us take advantage of the occasion to determine the destiny of our country calmly and on a sound basis." Such prudence would take its place in San Martín's personal history along with his reputation for careful organization, but it would often be seen as crippling timidity. Failure to pursue the royalists southward prolonged the war at least a year.

Del Pont was captured, along with his hated commander of slave labor in Santiago, as he tried to escape to Valparaiso to embark for Lima. After initial chaos as royalists' property was stolen and their shops pillaged, San Martín restored order. He turned aside the people's request that he proclaim himself leader, naming O'Higgins and extricating himself — almost — from the vicious internal politics that followed independence.

It proved impossible to dislodge royalists from a stronghold at Talcahuano in the south, on the Bay of Concepción, where they could be reinforced and provisioned by sea. Leaving the problem to O'Higgins, San Martín, ill and wanting to rebuild his army for the final push on Lima, left for Buenos Aires.

In May 1817, San Martín returned to Santiago in good health, but found the royalists still occupying Talcahuano while O'Higgins and Las Heras argued. San Martín agreed to a land and sea assault in November, but it was to no avail, encouraging royalists, who were waiting for rescue from Lima. Meanwhile, San Martín tried to build a new army. In effect, he had to shout his promises of cash and supplies over the racket of internecine fighting among Chileans. In addition, his association with the Lautaro Lodge led to the accusation that Argentines were trying to dominate Chilean affairs.

In the meantime, Viceroy Joaquin de Pezuela did not sit in Lima waiting for San Martín to arrive. He sent 3,300 troops by ship to the royalist stronghold at the Bay of Concepción. The viceroy intended a feint toward breaking the siege of Talcahuano, drawing patriot strength south. Then, with Santiago left undefended, the Spanish troops would suddenly reembark for a sweep up the coast to Valparaiso before the patriots could return. The plan had one flaw: San Martín's spies in Callao told him.

With Chileans formally declaring their independence in early 1818, San Martín saw his chance to solidify their situation by exercising both caution and cleverness. "The preservation of the state," he said, "depends on our not risking any action the outcome of which might be doubtful. For the moment our plan of campaign must be the concentration of our forces in order to deliver a final and decisive blow." The viceroy's move gave San Martín his chance. Leaving Valparaiso fortified, San Martín marched south, but not too far. O'Higgins, at the same time, lifted the siege of Talcahuano and moved northward to consolidate with San Martín. They waited at Cancha Rayada as the Spanish, intent upon confrontation, were drawn in from the Bay of Concepción to follow O'Higgins. Four thousand Spanish and royalists moved north against seven thousand patriots.

There was contact between the hostile forces on March 8, 1818, and San Martín immediately ordered a cavalry attack. It achieved little on the field, but convinced the Spanish that the numbers were not in their favor. The Spanish halted their advance, but by now San Martín's army was swallowing them like an amoeba, threatening on three sides.

The Spanish commander, in despair, halted his advance and, not knowing what to do, prayed into the night. The second in command, disgusted with his superior's timidity, mounted a surprise night attack before the patriots had firmly fixed their defenses. The daring Spanish charge took them suddenly into the midst of the patriot camp, and a shot wounded O'Higgins. The patriots broke and fled.

Witnesses to the rout reported all kinds of dire events: that O'Higgins was dead, that San Martín had committed suicide in disgrace on the battlefield.

Both leaders, in truth, returned to Santiago to reorganize. Las Heras had managed to save a flank of 3,500 troops, and — perhaps because they ran too fast to get shot — the patriots had lost no more than 120. Desertion, however, had thinned their ranks so that they, like the Spanish, were now about 5,000 strong.

On April 3, 1818, the Spanish army crossed the River Maipú and two days later assembled for a classic European-style battle on the plain outside Santiago. After an exchange of artillery fire, the patriots attacked the royalist right but were turned back. The Spanish, however, overestimating the advantage they had gained, pursued, only to be turned back themselves, then put to flight by San Martín's reserves. In the meantime, the patriot cavalry had broken the Spanish left. Victory was complete.

After the tension created by the Spanish night attack and the fear that Santiago might fall, the patriots were nearly delirious. An English observer wrote: "People embraced each other, laughed, wept and shrieked as if deprived of their senses. Some went literally mad, and one or two of them have never recovered their reason."

San Martín had taken the first, arduous step. "The victory of Maipú," writes Samuel Haigh, "left the cause of independence on so solid a footing as to deliver the mortal blow to Spanish power in South America." Neither San Martín nor the Spanish, however, yet knew that.

The next step required crossing not the mountains, but the sea. That was accomplished only with the help of English officers, those other veterans of the Napoleonic wars. Foremost among them was the almost mythical Scot, Thomas, Lord Cochran, Tenth Earl of Dundonald, who terrorized the Spanish navy all along the coast, conducting daring raids and allowing San Martín safe passage. "The importance of Cochran's contribution to San Martín's great design cannot be underestimated," notes Metford. "Although he failed twice to take Callao, he so terrified the royalists that they were unwilling to risk their frigates on the high seas. This gave San Martín the necessary freedom to move his men into Peru."

But nowhere was San Martín moving until he could refinance the provisioning of an army and overcome the political infighting in both Santiago and Buenos Aires. Chile got a British loan, but O'Higgins was slow to pass along funds. Buenos Aires, as usual, was torn by dissension so San Martín was deprived of any help from Belgrano's Army of the North, with which he had intended to coordinate his assault on Lima. Leaders in Buenos Aires, in any event, had lost interest in Lima, wanting San Martín back to guard against an invasion rumored to be coming their way. Indeed, such an expedition was being mounted at Cádiz, but was brought low by yellow fever. In January 1820, moreover, a revolt forced Ferdinand VII, recently restored to his throne, to reinstitute the liberal constitution of 1812. Metropolitan Spanish, preoccupied with their own problems, were lukewarm to foreign expeditions.

San Martín, frustrated by the lack of support from either government, withdrew a division to Mendoza, halfway between Buenos Aires and Santiago. Finally, an agreement for joint financing was signed in February 1819, but then the United Provinces government was deposed. At wit's end, San Martín resigned his command. He instructed Las Heras that the army's authority to exist had evaporated. He suggested the men elect a general to fight on. The men, predictably, decided to stick with the general they had, but two long years had passed since Maipú.

"[I]f the expedition to Peru is not undertaken," San Martín wrote to a friend, "everything will go to the devil." Finally, in August 1820, he procured the last of what he needed — only to find that the docks at Valparaiso did not have the cranes he needed to load it.

Lima, South America's oldest vice-royalty, was there, waiting, fat from the wealth of silver mines, royalist by tradition, and this last fact troubled San Martín. Although Pizarro had been of an independent turn of mind, once burning the royal standard, and Peru had been home to four Indian uprisings and two Creole revolts, Lima was consummately loyal to the king. The city was not infested with patriots as Santiago had been, so there would be no internal revolt. In addition, there was so little trade with southern South America that San Martín's spies were of little help.

The viceroy could count on 23,000 regular troops, 7,800 in Callao and Lima, 6,000 in Upper Peru, and 9,000 spread from Arequipa in the south to Guayaquil in the north. Lord Cochrane, contemptuous of Spanish fighting ability, counseled attack. San Martín was cautious; his army would never number more than 14,000. On August 20, 1820, they set sail from Valparaiso.

To Cochrane's dismay, San Martín ordered a landing at Pisco, one hundred miles south of Lima. Critics still argue that Cochrane was right. San Martín, however, was negotiating, and so far killing had been averted. The viceroy, in line with the new liberal constitution his king was following, was ordered to seek an accommodation. One solution to avoid war was simply to set up a monarch in America who would send deputies to the Spanish parliament. San Martín was not interested. Recognition for Chile? asked the viceroy, and a halt to hostilities? San Martín accepted on condition that the viceroy pull his forces from Upper Peru and allow Britain and the United States to guarantee peace. The viceroy rejected the idea.

While the talks proceeded for two months, San Martín sent a force of 1,300 into the interior to recruit Indians, spread revolutionary propaganda, enlist deserters, and, if necessary, engage the enemy. The tactic worked in a defeat for the Spanish at Pasco, but the patriots then rejoined San Martín, leaving enough Spanish to slaughter Indians in revenge.

In late October, San Martín sailed again. Cochrane implored San Martín to be allowed to take Callao and march directly on Lima, but

San Martín ordered the fleet to sail past Callao to the Bay of Ancón, just north of Lima. From there, he moved a bit farther north and set his camp at Huacho. There, he waited.

By early 1821, further expeditions into the interior had recruited more Indians and the blockade of Callao had begun to squeeze Lima's residents. San Martín still waited.

In May he sent an emissary to armistice talks, but only to gain time, to let the viceroy stew a little longer. The military commander of Lima, seeing the folly of trying to keep the city governed and supplied while defending it, decided not to wait, but to retreat. Leaving a garrison and supplies in Callao, he took the viceroy and moved his headquarters to the mountains. San Martín was invited to enter the city, but he declined.

Instead, he moved to Miraflores, halfway between Callao and Lima. He would later explain his enigmatic tactics in words as modern as today's: "I do not want military renown. I have no ambition to be the conqueror of Peru. I want solely to liberate the country from oppression. Of what use would Lima be to me if the inhabitants were hostile in political sentiment?... The country has now become sensible of its true interests and it is right the inhabitants should have the means of expressing what they think. Public opinion is an engine newly introduced into this country; the Spaniards, who are utterly incapable of directing it, have prohibited its use; but they shall now experience its strength and importance."

Lima residents, with San Martín refusing to enter, were afraid of a slave revolt inside the city; outside city walls, moreover, hostile Indians could be seen setting up camp. Terrified, they again asked San Martín in. Again, he refused, although he provided troops for police duty. San Martín simply said he would not enter the city until its residents, once and for all, declared their independence.

On July 9 they did so, and the army marched in. Yet there was no triumphal entry, with San Martín, astride a white horse receiving garlands. Not until July 12, after commerce had been restored and governance reestablished, did San Martín, accompanied by a single aide, ride quietly into the city in the early evening.

He occupied not the vice-regal palace, but the home of the hastily appointed governor whom the viceroy had abandoned. When the people found out where San Martín was, they flocked to him. Capt. Basil Hall, an English witness, wrote: "During this scene I was near enough to watch him closely; but I could not detect, either in his manner or in his expressions, the least affectation... nothing which seemed to refer to himself; I could not even discover the least trace of a self-approving smile. His satisfaction seemed to be caused solely by the pleasure reflected from others."

On July 28, after a full dress parade, San Martín unfurled the flag he had designed, but other considerations were more complex. In Buenos Aires and Santiago patriots were eager to establish democratic processes; Lima was a royalist package, and in the unwrapping neither San Martín nor anyone else knew what to expect. Generations of slavery, both of Africans and Indians, an ingrained class system, and the departure of brain power with the vice-royal entourage all left the city's future unpredictable.

San Martín, who must have recalled the chaos of Cádiz, said, "Every civilized people is entitled to be free; but the degree of freedom which any country can enjoy must bear an exact proportion to the measure of its civilization." At the people's request, he proclaimed himself Protector of Peru.

He chose three men as administrators, including the wretched Bernardo de Monteagudo. Blame for many of Monteagudo's misdeeds would fall on San Martín, and Monteagudo was so hated for his thievery and brutish behavior that he was exiled as soon as San Martín was out of the city. When he dared return, he was stabbed to death in the street. San Martín, indeed, was blamed for everyone's transgressions. Limeños followed the ignoble pattern of reviling the Protector they so ardently had sought.

In August, the Spanish, about 3,200 strong, came out of their mountain redoubt and assembled on the plain. San Martín was as the theater in early September when informed the Spanish were approaching the city. After standing in his box to call for the citizens' help, he took charge of the army—some 12,000 troops—and committed what would be seen as a woeful abdication of his power.

San Martín assembled his troops with a strong anchor in the hills on his left, but left a passage on his right, along the shore. The Spanish, trying to reach their companions holding the fort at Callao, had to pass through this gauntlet. As the Spanish moved along the shore, San Martín was asked, even begged, to attack. Cochrane rode up, furious at the thought of letting them escape. The troops were shouting that they wanted to fight. San Martín would not give the order. His lack of decisiveness in this and other instances might have been caused by the opium he used to treat his persistent illness.

After the Spanish passed, he said, "They are lost. Callao is ours. They do not have enough provisions for a fortnight and the reinforcements from the mountains will eat them all. Within a week they will be obliged to surrender or be skewered on our bayonets."

Although his evaluation was right, when the Spanish had to leave the fort San Martín again let them pass. By the time two pursuing forces were sent, one was badly beaten by the Spanish rearguard and the other exhausted its provisions and had to turn back. Callao finally surrendered, but San Martín had again, as after the Battle of Chacabuco, failed to press his advantage to destroy his enemy.

An American diplomat wrote to John Quincy Adams that "it occurs to me that San Martín...prefers to continue his influence by protracting the military conflict...rather than to put down the remnant of the royal troops and leave the country to the agonies of conflicting factions; or, in a few words, to make himself, as his own choice, King, Dictator, or Director." The judgment could not have been more wrong.

Cochrane took his fleet and sailed away (to appear later fighting for Brazil), and San Martín was left to govern Peruvians. His orders advanced education and founded the National Library. He abolished the various forms of Indian servitude and proclaimed the freedom of all children of slaves born after July 28, 1821. He abolished hanging, except for traitors, and the whipping of schoolchildren. He drew the enmity of the established church by recognizing freedom of worship.

For his efforts, San Martín was thanked with a coup attempt. His ministers were hated. Perhaps in desperation, he petitioned the British Crown for a likely relative to serve as a monarch, then convoked a congress to lay the idea of monarchy to rest.

How to govern unruly Peruvians would soon, however, be someone else's concern. Bolívar's army was descending from the north. Although San Martín had sent troops north to help Colombians under Bolívar's command, and Bolívar had ordered two Colombian battalions to Peru, misunderstandings had doomed both cooperative ventures. There would be no further attempts. The two generals were like oil and water.

The dispute ostensibly focused on Guayaquil, a malarial port in what is now Ecuador, the citizens of which could not decide whether to join Peru, become part of *Gran Colombia*, or be independent. Bolívar made the choice for them.

Bolívar and San Martín had planned to meet. San Martín wrote that "the stability of the destiny that America is rapidly approaching makes our interview necessary." Bolívar wrote that the two of them would march together like "brothers." Nevertheless, each surprised the other in July 1822, when Bolívar appeared unexpectedly in Guayaquil and San Martín sailed up the coast aboard a schooner. Their situations were hardly equal. Bolívar had a large army that was ready to march farther southward; he had just been elected president of Colombia. San Martín was having trouble administering the affairs of Peru, and his army was in disarray. He had, of course, lost his entire navy.

On July 25, San Martín sailed into Guayaquil's harbor. Bolívar preempted any discussion of Guayaquil's fate by welcoming San Martín to Colombia. The next day, when San Martín went ashore for formal discussions, there was an awkward moment when a laurel wreath was offered by a young girl. Bolívar required such pomp, but it embarrassed San Martín. He took it off; then, not wishing to appear ungrateful, he uttered a brief speech.

Immediately the two men went off by themselves for an hour and a half, out of hearing, sometimes out of sight, of their lieutenants. According to an observer, they "emerged, frowning gravely."

The next day, before they met again, San Martín ordered his luggage put back on board. They would sail as soon as he could get away from a ball scheduled for that night. Then the two men met alone again, this time for four hours. Afterward, they were again silent. Both went to the ball that night, but at one o'clock in the morning, after dourly observing the festivities, San Martín summoned his aide, grumbled, "I can't stand this tumult any longer," and left. Bolívar saw San Martín off at the dock.

What happened? Despite later letters from the two principals and the recorded impressions of witnesses, what exactly transpired is unknown. We know, of course, that Bolívar was ambitious; he had a great design for the continent; he was a lover, in every sense of the word, of the grand. San Martín, the evidence shows again and again, was meticulous, careful, self-effacing. "In conversation," wrote a contemporary, "he goes at once to the strong points of the topic... [there is] nothing showy or ingenious in his discourse." A biographer observes, "His retirement was the greatest victory that man can achieve, for it was a victory over himself. He also had in him something of a saint." Perhaps San Martín himself disclosed everything in his disappointment when he wrote to O'Higgins after the meeting at Guayaquil: "The Liberator is not what we thought."

Disgusted with Peru, San Martín called an assembly for September 20, resigned, and left. (Bolívar's army would finish off the Spanish at Junín and, without Bolívar, at Ayacucho.) San Martín left six sealed envelopes. "I have fulfilled my promises," he wrote. "The presence of a victorious soldier, no matter how detached, is fearsome to states in the process of formation." Of San Martín's departure, Juan Bautista Alberdi declared that "as a final addition to a chest covered with medals of honor... we must add a medal for modesty."

Chile was his respite. He lived outside Santiago with O'Higgins' mother and sister until, although ill, he had to flee when O'Higgins was forced out of office. San Martín then found relative contentment in Mendoza — he hung his portrait between those of Napoleon and Wellington — but he could not go to Buenos Aires because he had been declared a "traitor." He was reviled by English friends of Cochrane, who described him as limited in imagination, intellect, and daring.

In the winter of 1823 San Martín was informed that his wife was ill at her parents' home in Buenos Aires, but he could not go. She died in August. When he was allowed to make arrangements for her burial, he took their young daughter — "Child of Mendoza" was his affectionate name for her — and sailed into exile in Europe.

He settled first in Brussels. His Peruvian pension was slow in coming, but he eked out a living on income from property. Both politics and penury—for San Martín was both a famous democrat and poor—condemned him to a fitful wandering, carefully watched by chiefs of police. Between 1824 and 1830, San Martín's passport was stamped with forty-seven visas; between 1831 and 1849, there were another ten. Returning briefly in 1826, however, he found Argentina, rent by its usual problems, a poor refuge. Back in Europe, his brother Justo joined him, and he managed to keep Mercedes in private schools in Brussels and Paris. Her schoolmates treated the old general like "a beloved father." Mercedes married Mariano Balcarce, a man who briefly served Argentina until he, too, was forced back to Europe, reuniting the only family San Martín had. Eventually, an old friend provided San Martín with an income to keep him, at long last, comfortable.

When he expressed himself, even writing from Europe, his views attracted opposition as honey attracts foul-tempered bees. Writing to a friend, Tomás Guido, he despaired, "Liberty! Give a child of two years a box of razors to play with and see what will happen. Liberty! So that all honest men shall see themselves attacked by a licentious press, without laws to protect them, or, if there are laws, they become illusory. Liberty! So that if I devote myself to any kind of work, a revolution shall come and ruin for me the work of many years and the hope of leaving a mouthful of bread to my children.... I prefer the voluntary ostracism that I have imposed on myself to the joys of that kind of 'liberty.'"

San Martín praised the strength of Manuel Rosas, which won him gratitude from the despot (and forgiveness from Sarmiento), but calumny from Rosas' many enemies. His countrymen were more gratified when San Martín criticized the British and French blockade of Buenos Aires in the late 1840s.

But the tangle of European and Latin American politics dogged San Martín's path. When Louis Philippe fell in 1848, San Martín and his family had to escape from Paris to the countryside. On August 17, 1850, he died at his daughter's home.

Bernardo O'Higgins
1778–1842
(Chile)

Chile's Irish Liberator

The dramatic role of Bernardo O'Higgins in the drama of Latin American history is no more remarkable than that of his father, Ambrose O'Higgins, "the English viceroy." The elder, in fact, was a model for the younger, despite the fact that they were estranged by the younger's illegitimate birth, separated by the elder's overweening ambition, and made enemies by the radical difference in their political philosophies. That last aspect, of course, is crucial; while the father was a lifelong royalist, the son was a zealous democrat. Their sequential careers overlap the end of Spanish domination of southern South America, a reign that Ambrose O'Higgins did his best to perpetuate and Bernardo O'Higgins did so much to end.

Ambrose O'Higgins' family, not a wealthy one, sent him, probably with a cousin who was a priest, to Spain as a young boy to earn his livelihood. Such emigration was not as unusual as it might seem, the bond between the Irish and the Spanish being woven from the dual strands of their Roman Catholic religion and their common antipathy toward the English.

O'Higgins ended up a bank clerk in Cádiz in 1751 and embarked for the Americas, following a brother, five years later. His commercial ventures failed in the tightly controlled economy of the Spanish colonies, so he became a draftsman, designing forts along Chile's southern frontier, where the Crown held the fierce Araucanian Indians at bay.

In the winter of 1763 O'Higgins had an experience that almost led to the attention he coveted. He had returned to Spain to press for a better posting, but was disappointed. Returning to Chile, he was crossing the Andes when he nearly froze — one of his bearers died — along the frigid, windswept passes. He conceived of a string of shelters for travelers. The royal administration eventually accepted the idea. While O'Higgins saw it through to completion, his career was little improved.

In 1769, however, when there was an Indian uprising, O'Higgins, then in Santiago, jumped at the opportunity to volunteer. At the age of forty-nine, he was made a captain of dragoons, the beginning of his military career. He rose to commander-in-chief of frontier forces and, at sixty-six, was named governor of the southern province of Concepción.

During this time, O'Higgins met Isabel Riquelme, the daughter of wealthy Creole landowner who traced his family's background to the Moorish occupation of Spain. Such loving, and necessary, attention to heritage was what would later drive O'Higgins to claim the spurious title of "baron of Ballinary." Isabel was a teenager, perhaps as young as thirteen or fourteen, when they met. She had a lovely oval face, straight black hair, light skin, and blue eyes. O'Higgins was an officer of the Crown, some forty years older. The relationship, which lasted several years, led to the birth in Chillán of their son in 1778, on August 20, the day of the feast of St. Bernard.

There was no question of marriage. O'Higgins, attentive to his career as a representative of the Crown, could not marry a Creole. He moved on, and Isabel later married a wealthy neighbor. After Bernardo's half-sister, Rosita, was born, Isabel was widowed in 1782. Her later liaison with another neighbor, which led to the birth of another daughter, Nieves, who was raised by her father, apparently hastened O'Higgins in his search for a foster home for Bernardo. Bernardo, however, remained steadfast in his devotion to both parents.

Little Bernardo, with curly, chestnut hair, was growing up to be as stocky, round-faced, and plain as his father. His early schooling was with Araucanian children, but when he was four he was taken to the estate of his father's friend, Juan Albano. Not until 1788, when Bernardo was ten years old, did he next see his father, briefly, when Ambrose had been named governor-general of Chile. About seven years later, when the father was named viceroy, Bernardo was shipped off to school in London.

This period of O'Higgins' life biographer Jay Kinsbruner describes as "exasperatingly void of familial love." His financial agents cheated him, and his guardian, Nicolás de la Cruz, a son-in-law of Albano who lived in Cádiz, had little interest in his charge. O'Higgins got no instruction in life from his distant father. The long distance relationship between father and son — Bernardo was known by the surname "Riquelme" — was a poignant one. The son, unstinting in his respect, wrote his father long, adulatory letters. His father ignored him.

"My dearest father and benefactor," he wrote in January 1799, "I pray Your Excellency will excuse my using this term so freely, for I do not rightly know whether I may address you thus or not; but if I must choose between the two expressions, I will follow the inclinations of nature (having no other guide), for had I different instructions I would obey them. Although I have written to Your Excellency on several occasions, fortune has never favoured me with any reply." Bernardo was then twenty-one, without a clue as to what his prospects for a career might be. His father had provided "no other guide" than a disdainful silence, leaving the son unsure even how to address him.

One man to whom Bernardo could turn in England was the enigmatic Francisco Miranda. The fiery Venezuelan was unsuccessful in his own attempts to lead democratic insurrections in South America — he would die in a royal dungeon for his revolutionary efforts — but his rhetoric was impressive to countless emigrés like O'Higgins. "Always bear in mind the difference that exists between the character of the Spaniards and that of the Americans," Miranda counseled his young admirer as O'Higgins left to return to the New World. "The ignorance, pride, and fanaticism of the Spaniards are invincible. . . . Do not forget the Inquisition, nor its spies, its dungeons and its tortures."

Indeed, O'Higgins' imminent return to America was watched by spies. Along with others of Miranda's circle, he had been identified as an insurrectionist, an enemy of the king and, therefore, an enemy of his father.

In the spring of 1799, O'Higgins returned to his guardian's house in Cádiz, where he was not welcome, in order to sail for home — only to have his ship captured by an English squadron blocking the port. Back he went to his guardian's house. In despair, he was giving up on seeking any help from his silent father. "I will not trouble you further," he wrote. "May God prolong your precious life for many years." It was too late. Ambrose O'Higgins, always despised by jealous Spaniards, had been deposed as viceroy. In forced retirement, he fell ill and died. On his deathbed, however, he finally acknowledged his only son.

Bernardo O'Higgins landed in Valparaiso in September 1802. He had not inherited a great deal. His father, a reformer, had simply not enriched himself and had distributed what little he had to nephews and protégés. Bernardo was still the illegitimate son, and he was unable to change that as far as the royal records were concerned. He was welcomed home by cousins and old friends, but he had to be satisfied at probate with an estate, Las Canteras, and 3,000 head of cattle. At Las Canteras he installed Rosita and his mother and ever after kept them close.

His mother would take charge of two Araucanian orphan girls O'Higgins adopted and, later, his own illegitimate son, born to a mistress after the Battle of Maipú. O'Higgins, like his father, never married but rather kept a series of mistresses. Also, like his father, he never paid much attention to his son.

Biographer Stephen Clissold asserts that the denial of his father's honors and titles — and the resulting bitterness O'Higgins felt — was a godsend for Chilean independence. "Would a marquis," Clissold asks, "have fought so passionately to establish a Republic?" O'Higgins himself would write: "If it had been my lot to be born in Great Britain or Ireland, I would have lived and died on my estates. But father wished that I should first see the light of day in Chile, and I cannot forget what I owe to my country."

O'Higgins worked his Chilean estate for six years and made it prosperous. Then, in February 1808, a cleavage opened in Chile's colonial politics, and in March Charles IV was forced to abdicate, raising the stakes. The question of independence had to be discussed in the context of support either for Charles' son Ferdinand, or Joseph, insinuated onto the throne by Napoleon. In Spain, there was civil war; in Chile, there was ferment. O'Higgins was among those who wanted to break with all royalty but figured their best strategy lay in supporting Ferdinand for the time being.

On September 18, 1810, a *cabildo abierto* replaced the colonial leader with an independence-minded junta, and economic independence, especially trade with Britain and the United States, followed. The rock slide toward democracy gathered the weight of an avalanche. Elected a representative from Los Angeles, O'Higgins wrote to Juan Mackenna, a fellow Irishman and friend of his father who had married into the prominent Larrain family, "I have enlisted under the colors of my country...never shall I repent."

Throughout this period, O'Higgins, still unsure of his place in life, played a secondary role. The dominant force in Chile was José Miguel Carrera, descended from conquistadors and everything O'Higgins was not. Carrera was dashing in appearance, favoring the colors of the Galician Hussars, with whom he had proved himself in the European wars. Carrera was followed slavishly by his brothers, Juan José and Luis. The Carreras were ruthless in their desire to lead, and the story of Chile's independence is written in the conflict between an honorable Bernardo O'Higgins and the dastardly José Miguel Carrera.

Seeking a clear direction, O'Higgins wrote to the independence-minded Mackenna. "If you study the life of your father," Mackenna replied, "you will find in it military lessons which are the most useful and relevant to your present situation, and if you always keep his brilliant example before your eyes, you will never stray from the path of honour." Ambrose O'Higgins had learned late in life to be a soldier and leader; now it was his son's turn.

José Miguel Carrera had his own ideas about leadership. In late 1811, only six weeks after returning from Spain, his troops surrounded a meeting of the new congress, which Carrera disbanded and replaced with a junta. Six weeks later, to consolidate his power, Carrera threw out that junta and named a new three-man group that included Mackenna and himself. Then, when the third member was out of the capital, Carrera prevailed upon O'Higgins to fill in. O'Higgins, whose most notable public service up until then had been a proposal to ban burials beneath church floors (because they were unsanitary), was reluctant, but agreed. Subsequently, having placed O'Higgins in an awkward position, Carrera ordered Mackenna arrested. O'Higgins saw he had been duped, but all he could bring himself to do was resign, leaving Carrera's power uncontested.

Sensing O'Higgins' uncertainty, Carrera convinced him his course was honorable and even persuaded him to intercede with the third junta member, who was, in effect, in exile in the southern city of Concepción. O'Higgins agreed. He made the trip, became a mediator, and sent back to Carrera a proposal for power sharing. Carrera's response, in March 1812, was to reject the overture, claim all power for himself, and march south at the head of an army.

At long last, O'Higgins recognized Carrera's all-consuming ambition. He offered to lead an army against Carrera, but held his fire while efforts were made to avoid civil war. Carrera and his opponents talked and talked, into the rainy autumn, the indecision effectively cementing Carrera's power. Finally, O'Higgins, disenchanted, retired from public life and returned to Las Canteras. The stalemate was only broken in March 1813, when the royalists returned in force to reconquer the colony.

The challenge reunited patriots. O'Higgins offered to serve Carrera, and they were soon joined by Mackenna, who came from the prison into which Carrera had him thrown. This was the real beginning of O'Higgins' rise to prominence; his star rose because of his bravery even as Carrera's plummeted because of his incompetence.

The Spanish moved north from their southern strongholds. As allies, ironically, they could count both on the Araucanians and the strong garrisons along the frontier, perhaps a thousand men in all, who were there to contain the Indians. The Valdivia garrison, 1,500 strong, had declared itself at the side of patriots, but switched sides and became the core of the royalist army. Three more towns quickly fell, and the royalists, now with 3,000 troops, grew stronger.

O'Higgins, quixotically, gathered one hundred sharecroppers and set out toward Concepción to do battle. His men were armed, for the most part, only with lances and swords. When he got word that his band was not only tiny but too late, he sent them home and rode with a handful of companions for the Maule River to join the main body of patriots.

At the Maule, about one-third of the way between Concepción and Santiago, the patriots would make their stand. José Miguel Carrera showed up, arrogating to himself the title of commander-in-chief.

"Command," however, would prove an elusive function among patriot forces. Carrera procrastinated, and O'Higgins and others feared that the patriot troops, without a sense of leadership, would go over to the royalists. So O'Higgins seized command of a squadron of horsemen and launched a sudden attack on the royalists' advanced detachment, stopping it long enough to recruit among local townsfolk.

Then, his band slightly enlarged, O'Higgins led them under cover of darkness to Linares, where royalists were encamped. As dawn broke, the patriots rode into the town's main plaza, making as much noise as possible to give the appearance of a major attack. They were rewarded with a slew of captives, who were taken to the patriots' camp at Talca, where they, too, were recruited. Although there had yet to be a major engagement, O'Higgins leadership was providing successes that heartened the patriots and forged the beginning of his reputation.

O'Higgins fell ill just as confusion, as it so often did, took the field. Carrera arrayed his forces along the Maule, and a patriot advance guard — command of which passed from O'Higgins, in his illness, to another — was sent to engage the enemy's advance units. Another surprise attack was supposed to emulate O'Higgins' success. This time, however, six hundred patriots, advancing at night, crept quietly and ineptly into the middle of the royalists' main encampment.

At first, the mistake had great effect. Flustered royalists fired at each other in the dark.

When a troop of royalist cavalry realized what was afoot, however, it charged, turning the tide, which washed back over the entire patriot army. The cavalry drove toward patriot lines, and from there cowardly patriot officers were the first to flee. Mackenna stepped forward, arguing that there was still a chance to rally, but Carrera, intent on flight, overruled him and ordered a general retreat.

Confusion had not completed its work yet, however. When the royalist commander ordered a drive toward Santiago in pursuit of the retreating patriots, it stalled. The core of the royalist army, recruited from the southern island of Chiloé, was still unsettled by the patriots' night attack and refused to advance beyond the Maule. Every step northward, they said, was farther from home. They simply quit. The dismayed royalist commander was forced to halt pursuit and, finally, to turn back south toward Chillán to winter his troops.

Carrera, however, proved so witless as to cause one more disaster. With his troops reinforced, he swung back with a final attack on the royalists' rearguard, the result of which was nought but more casualties on both sides. Out of this dreary, bloody exercise in war only O'Higgins seemed to be able to prevail. As Carrera organized a siege of the town, O'Higgins, recovered from his illness, once again demonstrated such daring that he inspired a wider belief — albeit false — that the patriots' cause might succeed.

O'Higgins, recovered, was sent to recruit his own workers at Las Canteras. O'Higgins raised thirty horsemen and surprised the nearby Los Angeles outpost, crashing in on the troops at their leisure. The post commander was caught in the middle of a game of cards with the local priest. Local residents, impressed with this act of daring, joined the impetuous O'Higgins, who found himself in command of 1,400 men.

No other use could be found for the new troops, however, than to join Carrera's rain-drenched siege of Chillán. O'Higgins and Mackenna argued for a frontal assault, and Carrera finally acceded, but the attack demonstrated little besides the folly of motivating fighting men with strong drink.

At night, O'Higgins stoked five hundred infantrymen with brandy and occupied a rise before the town, where they set up cannons. Mackenna and Carrera, meanwhile, plied four hundred foot soldiers with brandy and dramatically led them across the Nuble River on the right. On the other flank, a cavalry troop, presumably sober, advanced.

As the sun came up, royalists sallied out to quiet O'Higgins' battery, and the battle was joined. At first, the brandy seemed a good idea. Spirited patriots put the royalists to flight; O'Higgins was in the thick of fierce fighting as his troop not only defended its position but counter-attacked, invested the city, and pressed toward its center.

The royalists, however, regrouped on the other side of town and turned on the patriots — who were by this time more drunk than fierce and more interested in the spoils of war than war itself. The distracted patriots never quite occupied the center of town, and when a cannon shot exploded their gunpowder store they fled before a royalist counter-attack. Only nightfall ended the carnage, in which two hundred patriots were killed and as many wounded. Carrera called off the assault.

The patriots lost more than the battle. People in the countryside, earlier encouraged by O'Higgins' victories, were disheartened. Carrera, more bandit than statesman, allowed plunder and reprisals against royalist families, further sacrificing respect. O'Higgins was nearly captured in a guerrilla skirmish after the battle, and Las Canteras was pillaged, its crops destroyed root and vine, its cattle driven off. His mother and sister were taken hostage and had to be exchanged for a royalist officer's family. Patriot strength around Chillán was sapped.

In October, reinvigorated royalists launched a surprise attack that surged across the El Roble River and nearly captured Carrera, who spurred his horse away just in time. O'Higgins, wounded in the leg, bandaged it himself with rags and stayed to fight. He ordered that he be carried back to the front line, where, lying on the ground, he resumed command despite the pain. The contrast between the two leaders was not lost on their troops. After the patriots had fought off the attack, stories of O'Higgins' bravery circulated all the way back to the junta.

Nevertheless, junta members were unwilling to sack Carrera and risk being deposed in return. Furthermore, O'Higgins and several other officers informed the junta and Carrera that their support still lay with the commanding general as long as the royalist threat continued. Mackenna, however, was of another mind. He persuaded the junta to make the switch, and although Carrera resisted and the officer corps revolted, in the end O'Higgins, despite his own protestations, took command. On February 2, 1814, O'Higgins arrived at Concepción to find that desertions over the preceding four months had reduced the ranks to 1,800 men; provisions were low; ammunition was almost gone; uniforms were in tatters. "I dare not call it an army," O'Higgins wrote to Casimiro Albano, his boyhood friend, "as I can see nothing, absolutely nothing, in its equipment or morale that justifies that name."

The viceroy agreed. Encouraged by reports that the royalists, surrounded at Chillán but popular with local residents, were spoiling for an all-out fight, the viceroy sent reinforcements. The troops were to land at the Gulf of Arauco just south of Concepción to drive out the patriots once and for all.

The junta's defense plan called for O'Higgins to pull his troops back northward, where he could link with Mackenna's command. O'Higgins, however, vacillated, wanting to strike one more blow at royalists in the south before their reinforcements landed. When Carrera concurred with O'Higgins' misguided plan, the junta ordered Carrera off to Argentina on a diplomatic mission — on which he, along with a brother, was captured by royalists, suggesting a plot. Mackenna's troops, meanwhile, sank deeper into trouble.

The junta had been chased out of Talca, and Santiago was threatened. Mackenna could not rush to the defense of Santiago because that would leave O'Higgins isolated in the south. Mackenna began sending frantic messages asking why O'Higgins was delayed. "You, my dear friend," Mackenna wrote, "are responsible to your country for your present inactivity. . . . For God's sake, come, and all will be well." Finally, O'Higgins awoke himself and struck out northward, his troops ragged in appearance but so reduced in number as to be the patriots' hardest core of fighting men.

Even as he marched north, O'Higgins allowed himself to be delayed by royalist attacks on his rear. "These delays will be the ruin of us,"

Mackenna, who had been wounded, wrote to O'Higgins in frustration before the patriots finally consolidated their forces. Not until then, with a total of 1,500 infantrymen, 18 cannon, and several hundred mounted militia, did Mackenna feel confident — and O'Higgins finally understand — that they could defend Santiago.

Both armies then undertook a forced march to be first to reach the capital, and the result was a kind of tie. On April 3, 1815, both armies reached the Maule River and crossed it. The patriots set up a perimeter at a plantation called Quechereguas, which convinced the royalists they could neither turn their backs on the patriots to assault the city nor root the patriots out of their position. Neither could patriots advance, so a stalemate ensued and negotiations began.

At first, time was on the side of the patriots. The royalist army began to shrink as soldiers deserted. O'Higgins, on the other hand, was able to recruit and even to threaten the royalists' winter base at Talca. Eventually, however, negotiations led to the "Treaty of Lircay," a document neither side took seriously and both were ready to abjure at the earliest opportunity. Moderates greeted the treaty as an advance, but zealots on both sides continued to badger each other. Royalist troops, headed for embarcation, denounced the agreement and refused to board the ships. When their commander sent for orders from the viceroy, O'Higgins grew suspicious. He sent envoys to find out what was happening, and when they came back without an answer, O'Higgins lost patience and prepared to attack.

The royalists then unveiled a demonic plan. They still held the two Carrera brothers. Both sides knew that their release would serve to consolidate patriot opposition to the treaty, leading to such disruption that the royalists would gain an advantage. The patriots, however, including Mackenna, had to insist that as a point of honor the Carreras be set free. The royalists, happily, did so.

When the Carreras showed up at patriot headquarters, O'Higgins, as trusting as ever, welcomed them, although his officer corps was not so receptive. Sensing the chill, the brothers left for Santiago, where political leaders were outraged that these snakes in the grass had been allowed back among them. Sure enough, in late July the Carreras seized those political leaders, including Mackenna, and established another dictatorship.

O'Higgins, with his troops in Talca, 150 miles south of the capital, was outmaneuvered. His response was to demonstrate a naivete of monumental proportions. He thought Carrera might be induced to step down voluntarily rather than lead the country into yet another civil war. When O'Higgins suggested as much in a letter, Carrera put him off. In September, O'Higgins sought to force Carrera's hand by leading a troop of cavalry to the capital, but he took only 150 men, leaving the rest to contain the royalists. Carrera repelled this small force with little more than the back of his hand, and O'Higgins, charging into more than he had reckoned on, nearly got himself captured. O'Higgins then began to organize a full-scale assault on Carrera only to be informed by a messenger from the viceroy that the Treaty of Lircay was unacceptable. In addition, the patriots were expected to surrender forthwith.

This time the external threat healed Chilean divisions only after so much wrangling that the strengthened royalists were unstoppable. The diabolical release of the Carreras had paid off handsomely for the viceroy's strategy. Carrera threw the viceroy's messenger into jail and prepared to attack O'Higgins' position. O'Higgins sought accommodation, at least long enough to repel the threat. Carrera contemptuously rejected the overture. O'Higgins tried again. Carrera again rejected. O'Higgins then rode to Santiago to press his case in person.

Finally successful, O'Higgins tried to rally support to throw back the royalists, by now 5,000 strong, including well-trained troops. The patriots could muster no more than 4,000 men, counting ill-trained militia.

The final straw was that O'Higgins, in order to reach an agreement, had yielded command of those troops to the inept Carrera. Then Carrera refused, despite O'Higgins' repeated invitations, to take charge by going to the front. "I will be at your side," O'Higgins wrote, "serving as adjutant, or in command of some division or small detachment — or simply with gun in hand." Carrera, however, hung back, making no decisions.

On September 30, the royalists marched against a patriot line along the Cachapoal River south of Santiago. O'Higgins was on the left, toward the town of Rancagua, while on the center and right were divisions commanded by José Miguel Carrera's two brothers. The royalists broke through the patriot line and turned along the river toward Rancagua. O'Higgins moved his troops to meet the threat, expecting the Carrera brothers to join him. They did not. Juan José retreated with his division, taking refuge in Rancagua. Luís fell back.

O'Higgins' aides counseled him to fall back, too, joining Luís and leaving the other Carrera to destruction. O'Higgins would not take their advice. "It is because the Carreras are my greatest enemies that I cannot abandon them now," O'Higgins said. "Honor is more than life." When O'Higgins rode into Rancagua, Juan José embraced him and gratefully relinquished command. The patriots barricaded themselves in the central plaza, and on October 1 the battle was joined.

Had O'Higgins, at that point, been aware of an important bit of information, the patriots' tactics would almost certainly have been different, and probably more successful. The royalist troops were needed back in Peru. Their commander got orders to either strike a victorious blow or, failing that, negotiate a truce so he could remove his men to another front. The Spanish commander was convinced he had the strength for a quick victory and so launched his attack. O'Higgins fought back fiercely when he might have done better to string out the action, figuring that mere survival would have constituted the victory.

The royalists came on in a frontal attack, even though the narrow streets of Rancagua channeled them into the patriots' hellish field of fire. Some of the royalists' best troops were cut down in what Clissold describes as "an hour's fighting more intense than anything hitherto seen in Chile."

Thrown back, the Spanish commander reconsidered, but his lieutenants urged him on again. The royalists brought up artillery and blasted their way to the central plaza, but there the patriots fought back with bayonets, again repelling the attack.

O'Higgins knew, however, that his casualties were numerous, ammunition was low, and water — cut off by the enemy — was almost gone. A message was sent asking the main patriot force for help. A message came back promising help, but it did not come. O'Higgins was informed, however, that Carrera had a paid assassin in the camp, and should O'Higgins be successful in defending Rancagua he was to be murdered.

By the time the final assault came, the patriots had built barricades using their own dead. There was brief hope when a sentry espied, in the distance, a relief column. The royalists, surprised, swung around to meet the threat from the rear, and it looked as if the patriots were about to pull out a stirring victory. Then hope crashed into despair. The arriving troops, as suddenly as they had appeared, turned and retreated.

No longer was there room for hope. A spark ignited the patriots' powder store, and the invaders penetrated to the defenders' central trenches. The resourceful Juan José Carrera had kept himself a fresh horse and made good his own escape, but O'Higgins fought on alongside his men — the five hundred remaining. To try to break out, they drove pack mules ahead as moving cover.

As O'Higgins finally drove his spurs into his horse to climb the barricade and escape, his horse fell back, throwing him to the ground. Getting to his feet, he saw an aide killed beside him. A mounted royalist charged at O'Higgins, but was killed himself, allowing O'Higgins to swing into the saddle and rejoin his men. As the patriots fled, madness enveloped Rancagua. The attackers, crazed by the bitter resistance, killed prisoners and children and raped women, some in the cathedral where they had hidden. The house used as a patriot hospital caught fire and burned down.

With his troops now reduced to only two hundred soldiers, O'Higgins made for Santiago. He angrily asked why the relief column had turned back. Responses were several: the relief troops were inexperienced militia, untrustworthy in battle; O'Higgins had missed his chance to escape during the confusion; it appeared to be too late, that the patriots had surrendered.

It was October 1814. Following his mother and sister, O'Higgins went into exile in Argentina. A stream of refugees flowed over the Andes, using the shelters built there by Ambrosio Higgins years before. In Mendoza, San Martín welcomed O'Higgins, but knew the Carreras were not to be trusted. When it became apparent they intended to use what was left of their army to take control of Cuyo, San Martín ordered them arrested and banished to San Luís, where they were closely watched.

The Carreras' capacity for evil, however, was inexhaustible. Arriving in Buenos Aires, they encountered Mackenna, whom they had earlier tried unsuccessfully to goad into a duel. Now Luís succeeded, and Mackenna died from a bullet through the neck. The Carreras slithered into a conspiracy with Carlos María de Alvear, the bitter rival of San Martín.

O'Higgins settled into a modest life with his mother and sister in Buenos Aires, where he was initiated into the Lautaro Lodge, the secret cell of revolutionaries. Both O'Higgins and José Miguel Carrera presented to San Martín plans for the reconquest of Chile. When Carrera's was rejected, he petulantly left for the United States to try to garner support there. O'Higgins' plan, which called for a joint attack by land and sea, was also deemed impracticable, but he was extended an invitation to join the Army of the Andes. He was named a brigadier general in a force by that time grown to 1,500 trained men and 4,000 militiamen. His assignment was to complete by October 1816 a main training camp, which he accomplished, and at that camp the army grew to 4,000 trained troops by the beginning of 1817.

When the march began, O'Higgins was given command of the thousand men of the Second Division. As the army wended its way toward the Andes, a letter caught up with him from Juan Martín de Pueyrredón, the Argentine supreme director. The message had two parts: good wishes for O'Higgins' swift ascent to supreme director of an independent Chile; and a warning that Carrera was on his way to Chile on board a U.S. warship.

The royalists planned to stop the patriots near the village of Chacabuco, where a steep, rocky redoubt split the route to Santiago, one road passing through the village, the other rounding to the west. O'Higgins' responsibility was to lead his division — increased to 1,500 men — into the teeth of the royalist defense, up over the ridge toward the village. Miguel de Soler, meanwhile, would make a flanking movement to the right, along the longer route, so the two columns could coordinate a pincerlike attack.

O'Higgins' men faced not only a tough fight, but a difficult climb, during which they lost two cannon over a cliff. Near the top, O'Higgins took command of one column, assigning the other to Col. Ambrosio Cramer, a veteran of the European wars. They attacked just as San Martín galloped up to join them. Observing from the rear, San Martín had seen the difficulty into which O'Higgins was advancing and had sent a message to Soler to hurry, before O'Higgins' division was ground up.

O'Higgins' columns drove the royalists off the ridge, and as they retreated O'Higgins pressed to pursue them. San Martín consented, but only after stipulating that a general engagement not be risked until Soler was in position.

O'Higgins carried on, thinking the royalists had retreated all the way to the village. He led his men down a narrow trail, discovering too late that the enemy was not so far off as he'd thought and that his soldiers, vulnerable by being stretched out along the mountain path, were threatened. He had overextended himself and could advance only at great risk; retreat was worse.

In the heat of midday, O'Higgins had led his men to within three hundred yards of the enemy, which opened fire with artillery to devastating effect. Cramer's experience, however, told him that as problematical as their situation was, Soler's appearance, when it finally came, would so alter the balance that the royalists would be forced to retreat. He advised a bayonet attack, contrary to San Martín's orders not to engage the enemy without Soler's division in place.

O'Higgins hesitated, then followed Cramer's suggestion. In two columns, with cavalry arranged in the rear, the patriots charged. O'Higgins and Cramer led their infantry into the royalists' right wing, leaving the left to the cavalry. The royalists were forced back, but were nevertheless able to repel the cavalry attack because a protective gully channeled the horses back toward the center of the patriots' line. While the royalists regrouped, O'Higgins swiftly changed his plan, reversing the roles of cavalry and infantry, and charged again.

The attack was successful on both counts. No longer stopped by the gully, the cavalry kept up with the infantry charge. Together, they overran the royalist artillery, chasing the enemy toward the village. When Soler's division finally appeared, the royalists were being driven all the way to Colima.

The Battle of Chacabuco was won, although Soler was furious that O'Higgins, by pressing his attack, had deprived Soler of a share in the glory. O'Higgins cut off Soler's tantrum and looked in the confusion for San Martín. He asked for a thousand of Soler's men — who, after all, were spoiling for a fight — to cut the royalists off before they could reach the port at Valparaíso. San Martín, wary of royalist reserves, demurred. Instead, O'Higgins rode by San Martín's side at the head of the patriot army as it marched into Santiago.

In February 1817, O'Higgins accepted the supreme directorship when San Martín, graciously and astutely, declined. San Martín was thus able to turn to the task of rebuilding and refinancing his army in order to continue on to Lima. O'Higgins was left to try to manage an obstreperous new republic. He confiscated royal property, founded a newspaper, and asked "patriots" to declare themselves but ordered that "nonpatriots" not be harassed. Reprisals, nevertheless, cut to the heart of the new republic, and resentment, notes historian J. C. J. Metford, "eventually crystallized into a deep-seated enmity towards O'Higgins. It was one of the causes of the internal upheavals which for so long disturbed the peace and retarded the progress of the new Chilean state."

O'Higgins' association with the Lautaro Lodge was a problem, suggesting that the new nation would be managed by a cabal. The usual question of whether to continue Church privileges arose, deepening the conflict with a Church that had been divided on the question of independence in the first place. Many Chileans longed for the relative stability of the viceroyalty, a point that O'Higgins addressed in an 1821 letter to José Gaspar Marín:

"If Chile is to be a Republic," he wrote, "as is required by our oaths and suggested by its natural endowments; if our sacrifices have not been insignificant; if the creators of the revolution truly meant to make this land free and happy; then this can only be achieved under a Republican Government that is not just some variation of distant dynasty, but exists precisely because we shunned those cold schemers who crave a monarchy. How hard it is, my friend, to break old habits!"

Political problems, however, were no worse than military ones. San Martín's failure to follow and destroy the defeated royalists was an unmitigated mistake. By the time O'Higgins could assign Juan Gregorio de las Heras, the third of San Martín's division commanders, to pursue and wipe out the royalists they had fled to their traditional strongholds in the south near the Bay of Concepción. Las Heras failed, so O'Higgins chastised him and took command himself, but could do no better. The patriots found themselves once again bogged down in the unsympathetic south trying to root out royalists. Then it was learned from spies that the viceroy was sending three thousand reinforcements with the purpose of once again breaking out and marching north to reconquer the country. It was the same song, second verse.

Just as he had once moved an army northward to meet Mackenna, O'Higgins now hurried his 2,200 troops toward San Martín's main force of 4,400. Once again, the royalists followed. When the royalists got as far north as the Maule River, their commander, fearful of overextending, decided to dig in. His lieutenants, however, accused him of cowardice and insisted that the advance continue. So the royalists pushed on — until they saw the strength of the combined patriot armies and recognized their miscalculation. They tried to turn around toward better positions along the Maule.

San Martín saw the opening and sent his army racing to cut them off from the river. Outflanked, the royalists then turned toward Talca, and

San Martín countered with a cavalry charge to keep them from reaching the town. The rough terrain and the royalists' spirited response, however, were too much for the horsemen, despite superior numbers. San Martín, still anxious to deny the royalists the town, next sent O'Higgins into the breach.

O'Higgins ordered an artillery barrage and then followed with an infantry charge, but once again the royalists' fierce reply turned the patriots back. As night fell, both sides contemplated their next moves.

The royalists' plan was dictated by desperation, and it prevailed. All of their leadership now conceded they had come too far. They were too weak either to hold Talca or to retreat in safety. While the commander continued to wring his hands, however, his lieutenants organized a desperate charge in the night into O'Higgins' command.

O'Higgins was caught flatfooted, his artillery still limbered, his cavalry unready, his division completely flustered. Although the royalists, hurried into action, suffered from some confusion of their own, greater was the panic of the patriots. O'Higgins did gather his wits and enough men to defend his position for a time, but a bullet broke his right arm. Bleeding and in pain, he was carried to the Lircay River to San Martín's retreating headquarters.

Losses on both sides were about equal in terms of soldiers, but the patriots had lost stores, equipment, and animals. They were thoroughly demoralized. An inferior force had routed them, and some patriot officers had behaved abominably, running for their lives.

The patriot command, falling back to Quecheraguas, learned that Las Heras' division was unscathed; the patriot army was still four thousand strong. San Martín, predictably, counseled a slow, solid effort at rebuilding. The fiery O'Higgins argued for making a stand at Quecheraguas. The physician attending O'Higgins' badly damaged arm, made worse by the rigors of retreat, recalled later that he reminded O'Higgins that the patriots could again escape to Argentina. "One case of exile is enough," was O'Higgins' reply. "As long as I remain alive and have a single Chilean to follow me I shall go on fighting against the enemy in Chile."

In Santiago, few Chileans were enthusiastic about following. Rumors had San Martín dead of a battlefield suicide and O'Higgins hopelessly wounded. Some patriots packed and began trudging into exile. A public statement from San Martín was of some help in restoring order, but supporters of the Carrera brothers were rapidly making the situation impossible. Luis Carrera insinuated himself into a position of leadership, causing frightened O'Higgins partisans to send a frantic message requesting that he return to the capital. He did so, and displaying his bandaged arm for emphasis he told an assembly, "I am not asking for money. . . . I only ask you to be whole-heartedly with us."

While San Martín returned to the front, O'Higgins supervised the construction of fortifications and hastened troops from Argentina and Valparaíso into town. When it appeared the royalists might skirt San Martín's forces and take the city, O'Higgins was advised to find safety at San Martín's headquarters. "No, I'll stay," he said. "If the enemy attacks, I will die at my post."

O'Higgins' efforts were toward the definitive Battle of Maipú on April 5. By the time he himself rode out into the field with a thousand mounted militia, the battle was winding down. Fifteen hundred royalists and eight hundred patriots died in the battle. The patriots held more than 2,000 prisoners and had suffered a thousand wounded. Chile had won its independence.

Now O'Higgins had to secure independence from the depredations of the Carreras. Pueyrredón, in Buenos Aires, was initially swayed by the Carreras' unctuous words and wrote to O'Higgins suggesting that the Chilean government pay them a pension. O'Higgins replied that Pueyrredón had "been taken in by the cunning and double-dealing of men who ought to be branded as outlaws." Pueyrredón soon learned for himself. When the Carreras tried their old tricks with him, Pueyrredón chased them into exile in Montevideo.

There, Juan José and Luís plotted to return to Chile, abduct San Martín and O'Higgins, and impose yet another dictatorship with José Miguel at its head. The two were no more adept at conspiracy than they were at warfare. They were arrested, in disguise, before reaching the Chilean border. "They have always been the same," declared O'Higgins, "and only death will change them."

They were not put to death, however, but languished in prison. The imprisonment had decidedly different effects on the two siblings. Juan José was repentant and wanted only to be allowed to return home. Luis, contrarily, decided not only to escape from jail but to shoot the governor and organize a guerrilla band. News of these audacious plans leaked to citizens of Mendoza at a time when royalists appeared to be in the ascendent, just before the Battle of Maipú. Panicked, they were in a mood to deal severely with the brothers.

In Mendoza at precisely that time was one of the few men whose hatefulness was a match for the Carreras: San Martín's trusted administrator, Bernardo Monteagudo, who would later be exiled, then stabbed to death by outraged Peruvians. Monteagudo persuaded the town council of Mendoza to execute the Carrera brothers, a punishment much more severe than the normal exile. Just four hours before a messenger rode in from San Martín and O'Higgins, the victors at Maipú, ordering that the brothers be spared, they were executed by firing squad.

News of the executions surely deepened the historic divisions of

Chilean politics, but it was a drop in an already turbulent ocean of distrust. O'Higgins was adrift in that turmoil, blown from crisis to crisis.

O'Higgins was seen as having pardoned the Carreras only when he knew it was too late. An attempt was made on his life, getting as far as the courtyard of his mansion before its leaders were taken into custody. He was blamed for the murder of a Carrera supporter who was killed on his way into exile. Even the execution of José Miguel Carrera, captured, condemned as a common bandit, and shot in the same courtyard where his brothers died, did nothing to bring balance to Chilean politics.

O'Higgins was left surrounded by enemies. San Martín's labors to equip and build an army were crowned with the conquest of Lima; O'Higgins' reward was animosity. After Argentina reneged on its promises of support, it was O'Higgins who initiated the eminently successful naval fleet and who rebuilt the army to 7,500 troops; San Martín rode into Lima; O'Higgins was saddled with debt.

"Things have gotten to such a pitch that I even have the humiliation of having to find someone to lend me 500 pesos every month for my own needs," O'Higgins wrote to San Martín. A contemporary described O'Higgins' government as "hated by the entire population."

Improvements to the city required taxes. Church reform — although O'Higgins refused to try to confiscate church property — angered the faithful. Although he believed in the democracy envisioned by Miranda, O'Higgins manipulated politics as had the viceroys before him. Although he saw through the sycophants and scoundrels who surrounded San Martín, he was blind to those who closed in around him.

In his private affairs he was abstemious and plain. Another contemporary, describing his home outside Santiago, wrote that O'Higgins, "when here, sleeps on a little portable camp bed, and to judge by his room, is not very studious of personal accommodation."

In October 1822, two years after sailing off in high hopes of triumph, San Martín returned to Chile a broken man, deathly ill with typhoid and the target of harsh criticism. O'Higgins took in and protected his old friend and mentor, helping him recuperate before he departed for Mendoza and exile. Then O'Higgins was alone.

In early 1823, O'Higgins, in full uniform, strode into a rowdy congregation of dissident politicians clambering for his resignation. Civil war, again, loomed. Upon his resignation, the crowd outside shouted, "*Viva, O'Higgins. We hold nothing against you,*" but even after he had stepped down he was feared lest his supporters revolt. Only outside Chile would he and his family be safe, so he took them to Peru, settling into a modest house outside Lima.

He was granted a staff position in Bolívar's army and caught up with the army in July 1824, arriving, according to an old English friend, "the same honest, kind-hearted, straightforward, unsuspecting character we always found him to be." O'Higgins saw no combat, but joined Bolívar back in Lima, where he attended the grand fete celebrating the Battle of Ayacucho. "In contrast to the bemedalled Colombian, Argentine and Peruvian generals," Clissold writes, "O'Higgins appeared in plain civilian dress."

For nearly two more decades, until he died quietly on October 23, 1842, O'Higgins observed the tortured politics of both Peru and Chile, which included an abortive war between the two. Memories haunted him, and he once had to disavow any intention of returning home. Chilean biographer Miguel Luis Amunátegui Reyes concludes. "In spite of everything, the Government of the Supreme Director was one of neither tyranny nor oppression, but an epoch of fertile labor, in which patriots first tasted the blessed fruits of liberty."

Domingo Faustino Sarmiento
1811–1888
(Argentina)

Educator of a Continent

Faustino Valentín Sarmiento Albarracín was born on February 15, 1811, within a year of Argentina's declaration of independence from Spain. This correlation between his birth and that of his nation was the beginning of a long association, parallel paths over which Sarmiento would insist, again and again, that he be allowed to play a role in shaping Argentina. The young nation would prove a boisterous schoolyard on which to impose Sarmiento's standards of civility, but he never stopped trying.

That Sarmiento, while still a boy, took as his own saint, Domingo, was a bit the name of the family of independence typical of him bred into him by his surroundings. He was born in San Juan, capital of the western frontier province of the same name, where the Tulum Valley separates the rich pampas from the towering Andes along Argentina's border with Chile. The town of San Juan—then inhabited by 3,000 people, mostly in adobe houses—was founded in the mid- fifteenth century, a tiny outpost on the thinly populated periphery of a captaincy that was all but ignored by the Spanish Crown.

Sarmiento's biographers have stressed his mother's civilizing influence on him—so touchingly and thoroughly documented by Sarmiento himself—because his father was a rakehell. This is a bit unfair, because José Clemente Sarmiento had intriguing, if untamed, qualities. Although he was a financial failure—while his wife was a paragon of industry and organization—he was at his son's side at important times. Sarmiento himself, aware of the low opinion others held of his father, took pains to give him credit.

92

Sarmiento's life, in fact, is a mirror not just of those virtues his mother embodied, but also of the unpredictability that his father manifested.

Both of Sarmiento's parents were reared in families that were prominent in the settlement of Argentina and Chile, although both had been left penniless. Paula Albarracín's grandfather was mayor of San Juan and her father a landowner. Her father's death when she was twenty-three, however, and her brothers' inability to make the land productive, forced the sale of the family holdings. The wealth to which young Paula had been accustomed simply disappeared. Undaunted — the story goes — she and a slave laid the foundation for what would be her house. Then she set up her loom beneath a nearby fig tree and made fabric to sell to pay the builders. Only after her house was complete was she willing to marry José Clemente Sarmiento Funes, a man who had reacted to his impoverishment by ignoring it. "It was a family," notes biographer Allison Bunkley, "not of normal, average people, but of eccentricity." The couple had fifteen children, nine of whom died. Sarmiento's only brother died at the age of eleven. Growing into adulthood were Sarmiento and five sisters. As a toddler, because his mother supported the family with her weaving, little Faustino was literally tied to her apron strings lest he wander off.

Her weaving and dyeing provided what little income the family had. José Clemente, mostly working as a laborer on nearby farms, had no luck that could be measured in money. He did have, however, a certain flair, and Argentina's tumultuous times provided a wide stage. In 1812, when his son was still an infant, José Clemente made a modest name for himself by taking up a collection to relieve the plight of Gen. Manuel Belgrano, whose revolutionary army was bogged down at Tucumán. José Clemente braved the scorn of royalists to raise funds, and as a result he was entrusted five years later by José de San Martín with bringing Spanish prisoners back to San Juan after the Battle of Chacabuco. Sarmiento's guarded comment — "My father is a good man who has nothing more notable in his life than having given some service in a subordinate capacity in the wars of independence" — was condescending, but it revealed, at the very least, the son's recognition of his father's having lived up to a standard.

Sarmiento, meanwhile, was partly reared by uncles. In 1814, a forty-year-old uncle — a priest, later a bishop — took Sarmiento into his home, making him a kind of tiny acolyte and giving him his early education. This kind of education, seen at first as a bridge to formal schooling, would grow in importance when the formal schooling failed to materialize. Sarmiento's one stint in a regular school began two years later, when he entered, at about six years old, San Juan's first school, *Escuela de la Patria*.

Political struggles around Sarmiento would have more influence than education. In 1820 the province saw five governors take power. In 1821 Sarmiento's father took him to a more tranquil environment, the seminary at

Córdoba, 250 miles away. Enrollment, however, was prevented by what Sarmiento later described as "sicknesses," without hinting that perhaps the normal sickness for a ten-year-old was plain old homesickness. Sarmiento returned to San Juan.

For the next several years, Sarmiento's father tried every trick he could think of to win his son a scholarship, "in order that he may, if possible," José Clemente wrote to the government in Buenos Aires, "be of service to America, and since my resources are on the threshhold of beggary." It was to no avail.

The next step of Sarmiento's education was shaped by politics. Another of Sarmiento's uncles, José de Oro—a dynamic priest who served at the Battle of Chacabuco and held various political posts—was a vocal defender of the Church against anticlerical unitarists. In 1826, in the shifting sands of San Juan politics, Oro was exiled and took his nephew—fifteen years old and working for a civil engineer—with him.

Oro took up residence for a year in a cabin in San Luís province. An erudite man, he insisted that Sarmiento keep a journal recording their daily "dialogue between a citizen and a peasant." Sarmiento studied Latin and the Bible. Beginning the pattern of a lifetime, he founded a small "school," teaching fundamentals to rustic youths, including some older than himself. Again, however, his father reentered his life, appearing to inform Sarmiento that he had finally obtained placement at a school in Buenos Aires. Sarmiento resisted. He was growing into manhood and learning enough to teach. Why return? His father prevailed, but before they could get back to San Juan yet another revolt upset the political picture, erasing the school.

Sarmiento went to work in an aunt's store, continuing his self-education. He kept records, ordered inventory, and was entrusted with buying trips, at the same time finding time to read at the counter when there were no customers. He delved into *The Autobiography of Benjamin Franklin*, who had died about twenty years before Sarmiento was born. He read the classics and he was, almost, able to ignore the politics of San Juan.

A large region, including San Juan province, was then under the heel of Juan "Facundo" Quiroga, "the tiger of the llanos," whose name Sarmiento would make synonymous with Argentine barbarity. Sarmiento saw in Argentina's frontier crudeness an evil so profound as to affect every aspect of national life. It was a society, he believed, in which women were taught to provide the necessities while men were taught nothing except violence, handling horses, and throwing the three-pronged *bolo*. Children were little above animals. In the study titled *Facundo*, Sarmiento would write of Argentine boys: "When puberty approaches, they dedicate themselves to taming wild horses, and death is a minor punishment that awaits them if in one moment they lack strength or courage. In this youth first concerns are independence and idleness. Thus begins the public life of the *gaucho*, since his education is already over."

Given this disdain for the frontier, it was predictable that Sarmiento would have trouble with the frontier government. When the provincial militia impressed him into service, making him a sub-lieutenant in June 1828, Sarmiento sent a petition to the governor, explaining that he could not carry out his assignment because of responsibilities at his aunt's store. Therefore, he wrote, he was resigning his commission. He was promptly hauled, in uniform, before the governor.

Sarmiento later recalled the scene in romantic terms that not even his most enthusiastic biographers believe. The governor was seated on the patio and neither rose nor removed his hat. This offended Sarmiento, who at first refused to remove his own hat. The governor brought him up short with an angry admonition, however, and Sarmiento belatedly doffed his hat.

In the safety of his memoirs, Sarmiento described his and the governor's eyes meeting and flashing, as each tried to stare the other down. As Sarmiento remembered the scene, he won. The official resolution was that Sarmiento was clapped in jail. His family and friends told him he'd been foolish, but he figured he was being persecuted by Philistines. "This was my vision on the Road to Damascus," he wrote later, "of liberty, of civilization. All the ills of my country suddenly revealed themselves: barbarians!"

Unchastened, Sarmiento came to trial. The court was surprised to hear him swear that others, too, were critical of the government. This raised proceedings to a more dangerous level, but when he refused to give the names of other dissenters, he was dismissed by a court that obviously did not consider the impetuous sub-lieutenant a threat. Sarmiento remembered it this way: "At the age of sixteen [he was seventeen], I entered jail; I came out with political opinions. . . . It was not difficult to choose among the parties. . . . Nourished on the books I had read, pre-occupied by the fate of liberty which the history of Rome and Greece had taught me to live, without understanding how to realize this beautiful idea, I threw myself into the partisan struggle with enthusiasm and self-denial."

He became a unitarist in a family of federalists, a family that would more than once bail him out of political trouble. In 1828, Juan Manuel de Rosas — "the Caligula of the River Plate" — consolidated power for the federalists. Only Gen. José María Paz held out with a unitarist army in Córdoba, between San Juan and Buenos Aires. Although Rosas was unconcerned about Paz' stronghold, it constituted a threat to the *gaucho* leader Juan "Facundo" Quiroga. Quiroga held sway in the outlying provinces and wanted a clear road to Buenos Aires. So he led his *gaucho* army toward Córdoba, and riding as one of his officers was Sarmiento's father.

Sarmiento himself left his store counter to join Paz and was commissioned as a lieutenant. The bookworm had become a warrior, and in June 1829, at the Battle of Niquivil, Sarmiento distinguished himself in battle. He carried the commander's orders through enemy fire to an officer who then accomplished a maneuver that won the day. Meanwhile, Paz' main federalist force defeated Quiroga in a major battle. These battles left the unitarists, however briefly, in a commanding position, while Sarmiento's father returned toward San Juan, part of a defeated army.

Sarmiento was then sent with a squad to destroy a federalist depot. He returned to discover that in his absence his comrades had been put to flight. He had no choice but to take flight himself across the countryside — where he ran into his father on the trail. His father, demonstrating a paternal concern that is also a commentary on Argentine politics, switched sides in order to be with his son. Then the two men, along with a few soldiers from Sarmiento's squad, rode off across the barren land, warriors in search of a war.

If the scene seems to have been written by Cervantes, there is more. The hapless group soon encountered on the trail Francisco Laprida, a respected statesman who had presided over the Congress of Tucumán. As the small group picked up information about more garrison revolts, more sideswitching, Sarmiento was impressed, as he later wrote, that "even a distinguished leader such as [Laprida] felt disoriented and confused by the chaos into which national life had degenerated."

Finally alighting in Mendoza, Sarmiento was given a staff job with Gen. José Rudecindo Alvarado. His father accepted a unitarist commission, and the two comrades in arms awaited the siege that federalists were preparing. When the siege began, however, Sarmiento found it boring and endeavored to make his own action. He would sneak off to join skirmishers at the city's edge, and once was cut off on Mendoza's unfamiliar streets, requiring the help of his father to get back. A few days later, missing from his post again, Sarmiento was discovered by superiors and ordered to turn in his rifle. He was convinced his father had reported him in order to keep him out of trouble.

The siege ended with a rush, and Alvarado surrendered, but his troops would not, trying to fight their way out of the city. Sarmiento joined a detachment of San Juan soldiers, which, pausing at a waterhole, found themselves surrounded. There was an uneasy standoff until, as usual, confusion took over. The result was more brawl than battle because so many of the soldiers from both sides knew each other. "Over there were two Rosas brothers," Sarmiento would recall, "from the opposing parties, fighting over a horse; further on I joined Joaquín Villanueva, who was later lanced; I met his brother, José María, who had his throat cut three days later." One federalist who threatened Sarmiento before wheeling and fleeing had been a servant to friends of Sarmiento's family, a boy he'd once caned and who now saw his chance for revenge. Finally, Sarmiento was captured.

Other captured unitarists were being executed by firing squads, and Sarmiento awaited his turn. When the time came, however, a federalist officer spoke up for him, delaying the execution until Sarmiento's federalist relatives arrived and took him home with the simple agreement that he not return to the war. Meanwhile, his father, following the federalist army in search of his son, was also captured and condemned to a firing squad. The story in his instance was that his sangfroid so impressed the enemy commander — legend has it José Clemente ordered dinner and wine while awaiting the firing squad — that he, too, was sent home.

Between October 1829 and March 1830, Sarmiento was under a family-imposed house arrest. He studied French, translating twelve volumes of the *Memoirs of Josephine,* but it became clear that old animosities in war-embittered San Juan would not allow such a peaceful respite. Fearing reprisals, Sarmiento fled briefly to Chile, but returned to become a lieutenant in the militia after San Juan unitarists again took the province. Then given a command in the regular army, Sarmiento found the stricter discipline satisfying and rose rapidly to the rank of captain.

"Discipline," of course, Sarmiento wanted to define for himself. Considering certain duties boring or beneath him, Sarmiento would sometimes simply wander off. Thus it happened that one day, when he was one of two officers in charge, he was absent at the time sixty federalist prisoners attempted to escape from a San Juan guardhouse. Sarmiento was blamed for the bloody retaliation by the small squad that stopped the escapees. Sarmiento's defense was that when he heard of the revolt, he hid, unsure of how serious the threat was. He did not emerge from hiding, Sarmiento said, until his executive officer assured him the "revolt" had been quelled. Sarmiento argued his failure was one of being too casual. Others called the offense cowardice.

The war, meanwhile, took a turn for the worse. Preparing to help in the defense of San Juan, Sarmiento saw the provincial government fall from within. Off he went, barely twenty years old, into exile in Chile once again. Juan Facundo Quiroga entered San Juan at the head of his troops and summoned Sarmiento's mother to his desk. He told her that if her son were caught he would be shot.

To support himself and his father, he turned to teaching, which served him well on the frontier. Observing the lack of education in this backwoods, Sarmiento began to tie the need for better schooling to his notions about politics. He was appalled at the rigid, ineffective formality of the pedagogy of the day. Rather than using the boring letter-by-letter approach, Sarmiento began employing a method of teaching syllables developed by English educator Joseph Lancaster, of whom Sarmiento had read. Lancaster taught poor boys in the London borough of Southwark, and Sarmiento found himself in a similar position. Like Lancaster, Sarmiento came to be criticized by the elitist old guard for this heresy.

Sarmiento saw all of Latin America as stifled by cumbersome thinking. Change had to be encouraged in an atmosphere of discipline; new methods were necessary. He would suggest in *Facundo*, in fact, that the entire foundation of civil order is laid in primary school, a notion gleaned from his reading of Locke, Franklin, and Rousseau, all of whom devised educational strategies that were interwoven with their political philosophies. When Sarmiento was asked later in his life if he could distinguish among his many works which was most important, he answered without hesitation: his basic reader.

Still unable to return to Argentina, Sarmiento and his father pushed on to another rural town, where there was no school at all. Sarmiento set one up, and, using money sent by his family, also established an alehouse. At this point one of Sarmiento's periodic romances led, in July 1832, to the birth of his first child. A girl, named Emilia Faustina, was taken to San Juan to be reared by Sarmiento's mother.

Sarmiento, his alehouse a failure and his family urging him to stay out of trouble, wandered on. "His amorous adventures were becoming more complicated and increasingly serious in their results," notes biographer Bunkley. He ended up at the sea, in Valparaíso, where he found work as a clerk and spent half his salary for English lessons. Chile was then awash with Argentine refugees, and Sarmiento followed his army buddies to a silver mine recently bought by his commander at the Battle of Niquivil. Sarmiento took to the miner's life with a flourish, adopting the distinctive dress and behavior, gambling and drinking with sufficient gusto to keep his wallet thin. Invited into polite society, he would show up looking like a lowly miner, and then amaze unsuspecting guests with his erudition. For nearly three years he enjoyed his role, as he put it, as "the miner they always saw reading."

Over the years, Argentine politics, although still in turmoil, calmed a bit. Rosas remained in power, although Quiroga had been murdered, easing the danger for Sarmiento to some degree. Quiroga was succeeded in San Juan by Gen. Nazario Benavídez, who would become no less an adversary for Sarmiento but in 1835 yielded to Sarmiento's family in its request that their prodigal son, gravely ill with typhoid, be allowed to return. Benavidez, incorrectly as it turned out, saw no threat from a man, even a unitarist, at the point of death.

At home, however, Sarmiento's health and fortunes improved. Although penniless, he was well connected. Although a unitarist, his federalist family continued to protect him. For a while, he taught drawing and began practicing law, demonstrating real talent for neither. Finally, again with family help, he stepped onto safer vocational ground. In March 1839, Sarmiento founded a school for girls. He used capital invested by an uncle, Father Justo de Santa María de Oro, soon to be a bishop, and by the widow of the deceased bishop.

As headmaster, Sarmiento occupied a certain position in the town, and in the less oppressive atmosphere of the Benavídez government Sarmiento and his friends formed a salon. The governor saw no harm in literary discussions, occasionally appointed the headmaster to minor government posts, and even perceived no danger when Sarmiento, ever restless, proposed a weekly newspaper — completely apolitical, of course.

Sarmiento chose the name *El Zonda* and published the first issue in July 1839; his stated purpose was to publish for ten years. The paper lasted six weeks. Its comments on culture and morality were not the problem; its downfall was Sarmiento's biting satire. He wrote of the paper's having been attacked by "a little Cuzcan bitch [that] jumped out at it, seized it by the calf of the leg, shook it at will and sank its teeth into its flesh." The bitch was an unveiled reference to the wife of the governor, the man who had allowed Sarmiento to return from exile, who had supported his school, and who had allowed him to establish a newspaper.

Summoned to the governor's chambers, Sarmiento was told he owed a tax on his newspaper, and, when he refused to pay, saw the paper banned. He disconsolately completed his school's first year, during which he was for the second time refused when he proposed marriage to a pupil. To add to his problems, by late 1840 the civil war had begun to heat up again, and, after a successful unitarist uprising in a neighboring province, a nervous Governor Benavídez began rounding up unitarists. Other members of Sarmiento's salon took the hint and left San Juan province. Sarmiento refused to leave, was arrested, released, arrested again, and, finally, imprisoned. He was nearly lynched.

While Sarmiento was being held, federalist soldiers from a nearby encampment came into town one night on leave. As the liquor flowed, the soldiers thought a lynching might be amusing and gathered, along with a crowd, at the building where Sarmiento was held. They shouted for him to be brought out. When he refused to leave his room, the guard dragged out another prisoner, but the soldiers knew whom they wanted. Sarmiento was forcibly brought out to face an angry crowd, some of whom wore swords, some bayonets. Sarmiento was smacked with the flat sides of swords and prodded, and an officer ordered marksmen to report to the square to form a firing squad.

Sarmiento talked fast to buy time. Ducking under a porch, he scrambled to the other side to momentarily escape, but was recaptured. Eventually, his mother, informed of the ruckus, ran to the home of the governor and persuaded him to intervene. The next day, Sarmiento, accompanied by his father and a group of unitarists, was again on the road to exile.

Sarmiento would spend the next five years in Chile, essentially held at bay by Argentine federalists. During that five years, Sarmiento cemented his reputation as part of Argentina's "Generation of 1837," exiled unitarist intellectuals who attacked Rosas with their pens. Sarmiento's ardor would not subside, his style would not soften, and his predilection for trouble would never disappear. Argentine historian Antonio de la Torre describes Sarmiento as "a multiple personality...of diverse spiritual tendencies, at times in conflict with each other."

Sarmiento reached Chile in November 1840. Although his father was allowed to return home, Sarmiento settled in Santiago. He was now thirty years old, but age had not improved his looks. A friend described him as having "a high forehead, slightly bald, his cheeks fleshy, loose and shaven." His heavy body was beginning to bend a bit, giving him more of a bull-like appearance than ever.

His first major essay, on the Battle of Chacabuco, was published in *El Mercurio* in early 1841 and immediately established his ability. Sarmiento defended San Martín as deserving equal consideration with Bolívar as a giant of the wars of independence. He used the article as a framework for his battle with Rosas, whom he labeled "a despot sworn to exterminate all the soldiers of the War of Independence." The essay brought Sarmiento attention, although it is unlikely that it was, as he immodestly recalled later, "irreproachable in style, pure in language, brilliant in its imagery, nourished with sane ideas, embellished by the soft varnish of sentiment."

Doors opened in the young — Santiago's population was then sixty thousand — politically volatile republic. Sarmiento was welcomed by Chile's conservatives, who controlled the presidency during the nation's early years. Most important to Sarmiento was his association with Manuel Montt. The two shared an interest in education, and like schoolmasters with a nation full of unruly pupils, the two men delighted in planning classes for the future.

El Mercurio editorials became Sarmiento's main forum, although other newspapers served as platforms for his ideas and invective. He founded a newspaper for strictly Argentine news, but closed it in despair when Rosas delivered a crushing blow to unitarists in early 1843. Sarmiento later described his Chilean sojourn: "Five years of work in the daily press of Chile, five newspapers, six hundred editorial articles, various university papers and works for the instruction of the people, and several books, ephemeral but full of the true love of liberty and civilization, must have left...an awareness of the solidity of my convictions."

One of Sarmiento's pet causes was in the prickly area of Spanish grammar and usage. Sarmiento, despite his Romantic leaning, favored a modern,

American Spanish, unfettered by "classical" terms, open to invention. It was a manifestation of his distrust of most things European. Not all of Sarmiento's arguments were so lofty, however. In late 1842 a personal remark directed toward a notorious nun of the day got him into a legal suit, charges and countercharges in newspapers, and, ultimately, an atmosphere of rancor.

Such was Sarmiento's style that even compliments carried a poison tip. He set the tone for generations of Argentine thinkers by viewing the United States as a place with bulging pockets and no culture: "The people of North America have no literature," wrote Sarmiento in June 1842, two decades before being introduced to Emerson and Longfellow, "but in the absence of literature, they have liberty, wealth, the most complete civilization, inventions, steamships, factories, shipping and sixteen million men who know how to read and understand what they read."

Literacy was the key. Montt, as minister of education, called on Sarmiento to write the decree for creation of Chile's first normal school, the first in Latin America. Sarmiento also planned its curriculum and taught, with one assistant, its courses.

In May 1845, the first installment of his study, *El Facundo*, or "Civilization and Barbarity" appeared in the Chilean press. This was the book that would crystallize Sarmiento's thought, posing Argentina's notorious *gaucho* as the symbol of all that was wrong with a continent. A second newspaper picked up the serialization, and, in July, *Facundo* was published in book form.

The book was written in haste and contains numerous historical and factual errors, but it was received as a torch against the darkness that threatened all of Latin America's brand-new republics. The *gaucho*, the man on horseback, was the focus. Personalist politics, the "gauchocracy," Sarmiento declared, was the enslavement of sensibility. "The constant insecurity of life outside the towns, it seems to me, stamps upon the Argentine character a certain stoic resignation to death by violence," he wrote. The book expressed Sarmiento's strong, if simplistic, belief in a Manichean duality: good and evil, knowledge and ignorance, violence and justice, "the two different phases that struggle in the breast of [Argentine] society."

The book was anathema to many, especially Argentines, but a source of fascination for others who were hungry for information about this strange continent. The French critic Charles de Mazade would call it "new and full of attraction, instructive as history, interesting as a novel, brilliant with images and color."

Sarmiento's reputation grew, as did his propensity for trouble. After several inconclusive love affairs, he was keeping company with a twenty-two-year-old beauty, Benita Martínez Pastoriza de Castro. A native of San Juan, she was married to a very rich, very old, very sick man. In 1844, she became pregnant. A boy, Domingo Fidel, was born in April 1845 — just as *Facundo* appeared — and Montt concluded that it was time for Sarmiento go take a trip abroad.

Sarmiento was commissioned by the Chilean government to undertake a fact-finding tour. Embarking in October, he sailed first to Montevideo, then under siege by Rosas' troops. Bartólomé Mitre, a unitarist, had serialized *Facundo* in his Montevideo newspaper. Sarmiento sailed on to Le Havre, arriving in May 1846 and ready to give vent to all his prejudice. Europe, after all, was all that was wrong with everything: "Ah, Europe! Strange mixture of greatness and abjection, of knowledge and stupidity at the same time, sublime and filthy receptacle of all that elevates man and all that holds him degraded, kings and lackeys, monuments and pesthouses, opulance and savage life."

At first — before *Facundo* was published in Europe — Sarmiento was unknown. Thus in September, when he reached the heart of his discontent, Spain, he was widely ignored. "I came to Spain with the holy aim of verbally putting it on trial to give foundation to an accusation," he would write. By the time Sarmiento arrived in Barcelona, however, Mazade's review of *Facundo* guaranteed his reputation.

The next concern was his wallet. Sarmiento counted 600 pesos for the 700-peso trip back to Chile, but decided to head for England and the United States anyway. In England he met Americans who gave him a letter of introduction to Horace Mann, whom Sarmiento admired. Mann's ideas revolutionized public education in the United States, and Sarmiento began a life-long correspondence with Mann's second wife and collaborator, Mary Tyler Peabody Mann.

In the District of Columbia — where the Washington Monument was nearing completion — Sarmiento ran into a Chilean friend who agreed to help pay for the trip home. It was a fortuitous match, although it almost went awry; Sarmiento lost track of his new friend and had to chase him across Pennsylvania. "Great mental stess can be relieved only in one's own language," Sarmiento noted wryly, "and though English has a passable 'God damn,' for special cases I preferred Spanish, which is so round and sonorous for uttering rage."

Sarmiento returned to Chile in February 1848 after two years, four months abroad to find Benita a twenty-six-year-old widow. In May, they were married, and Sarmiento adopted little Dominguito. The family moved to Benita's estate at Yungay. For three years, Sarmiento remained at Yungay, writing and seeking ways to link himself with issues in his homeland.

Viajes en Europa, Africa y América was a catalogue of his fascination with practically everything, from signs in hotel lobbies to the future of religion. *Educación popular* was based on his official report. He then published the ill-fated *Arqirópolis*, dedicated to Gen. Justo José de Urquiza, the caudillo of the province of Entre Rios and the only man capable of driving Rosas from power. The book drew only contempt; even Urquiza ignored it. *Recuerdos de provincia* was less cloying, but no less self-serving: "In school I always distinguished myself with an exemplary veracity," Sarmiento wrote, "to the extent that the teachers acknowledged it by making me a model."

In 1851 a door was finally opened toward home. Urquiza led his own and two other provinces into revolt, allying himself with the *República Oriental*, which would become Uruguay, with Brazil, and with unitarist exiles in Montevideo. The end of Rosas' long, harsh reign was in sight. Urquiza's forces invaded Uruguay in July and broke the siege of Montevideo in September. Commanding 17,000 Argentines and 4,000 Brazilians and Uruguayans, Urquiza turned toward Buenos Aires.

Sarmiento's first thought was to lead an army of exiles over the Andes to attack the western provinces, a plan that elicited no support. So, in September, Sarmiento, Mitre, and other exiles boarded a frigate and sailed for forty days to reach Montevideo. Sarmiento appeared at Urquiza's headquarters in the uniform of a lieutenant-colonel, a rank Urquiza accepted in light of Sarmiento's military experience. Sarmiento wanted a command; instead, Urquiza made him official propagandist.

Sarmiento bought a printing press that Urquiza said was too expensive and a uniform at which the general laughed outright. The cost of the press, Sarmiento explained, was the result of haste. The uniform, he said, was a fashion statement, to elegantly separate him from the common *gauchos* riding for Rosas. The press rattled along behind the advancing army, printing leaflets.

On Christmas Eve the army crossed the Paraná River and marched toward Buenos Aires, but rising like the dust was the inevitable rivalry between Urquiza and Sarmiento.

On the one hand, Sarmiento was popular in some, although surely not all, quarters. Also, Urquiza recognized that exiles like Sarmiento had fought Rosas for years, well back to the time that he, Urquiza, was allied with the tyrant. "I just came to meet the writers from Montevideo and Chile," he remarked derisively. "They did it all." Sarmiento insisted that anti–Rosas propaganda had been and still was crucial, which brought from Urquiza the rejoinder: "[I]n regard to the feats that you say the press accomplishes in frightening the enemy, the presses have been shouting in Chile and other places for many years and until now Juan Manuel de Rosas has not been frightened. On the contrary, every day he grew stronger."

On February 3, 1852, at the Battle of Caseros, Sarmiento left his press and entered the fight, once again distinguishing himself. The Battle of

Caseros finished Rosas, who took flight with his British protectors on a gunboat to exile in England. In Argentine lore, the Battle of Caseros is symbolized by crossed pen and sword, but in early 1852 Sarmiento and Urquiza had the two instruments pointed at each other's hearts.

The split was not long in coming. Urquiza accused the unitarist Sarmiento of wanting "to make war on the governors." Sarmiento described Urquiza as just another caudillo; he refused to wear the red armband symbolic of the federalist cause. Sarmiento asked for and immediately got permission to return to Chile, losing no time in beginning to organize an opposition. Urquiza, for his part, set up a constitutional convention, persuaded governors to sign the cooperative Accord of San Nicolás, and set a date for a constitutional congress later in the year. That congress abolished internal tariffs, arranged for free congressional elections, and condemned local separatist movements. While Sarmiento sulked, Urquiza was trying to draw together an Argentine Republic.

Fourteen provinces ratified the agreement, but Buenos Aires, controlled by unitarists, refused and then seceded from a federation that had never been given a chance. Urquiza proceeded without the province. The result was the Constitution of 1853, shaped by the fertile mind of Juan Bautista Alberdi, which would stand as the charter of the nation until 1949. The constitution was drafted, improved, and ratified without Buenos Aires and without Sarmiento. While Mitre and other unitarists remained, Sarmiento fulminated from abroad, rejecting all offers of conciliation. Elected to a national convention, Sarmiento refused to attend. Mitre beckoned in vain, and Alberdi finally snorted that Sarmiento was a "caudillo of the pen."

In January 1854, when Sarmiento tried to return to San Juan, he was jailed, held incommunicado, tried for conspiracy and, finally, forced to flee back to Chile. A year later, he again returned. After a single-minded — if not monomaniacal — and fruitless attempt to persuade San Juan's Governor Benavídez to come over to his side, he trudged on to Buenos Aires, where he found a political home among unitarists.

Benita sold her estate in Chile and brought Dominguito to live in Buenos Aires, but the family's relationships deteriorated even as Sarmiento's political career emerged. Before 1855 was over, Sarmiento had been named editor of the newspaper El Nacional by Mitre and made director of public schools by the governor. He won elective posts as well, and established a successful experimental farm at Chivilcoy. After two and a half decades of contumacy and contumely, Sarmiento had arrived at his political destination despite an uncompromising nature.

Indeed, his acidic style of personal journalism was undiluted. Opposing editors — Urquiza supporters — countered, one challenging Sarmiento to a duel, a prospect Sarmiento ridiculed. He was accused of having poisoned Benita's late husband (although out of the country at the time) and won a slander suit. He got into a fistfight with another editor on a Buenos Aires street. When his old adversary, Governor Benavídez, was deposed, jailed, and shot in cold blood, Sarmiento published an article excusing the murder.

In 1858 Urquiza tired of waiting for Buenos Aires to find humility and sent an army to force it into the union. The provincial army, led by Mitre, was put to flight, and all that remained to Buenos Aires was to take advantage of a concession by Urquiza that the constitution might be amended and the national government restructured. Sarmiento was elected to the assembly drafting amendments.

Sarmiento's view of reforming the national constitution was to model it more along the lines of the constitution of the United States, expanding guarantees of civil liberties and freedom of the press, and, of course, strengthening central authority. He helped defeat a proposal to make Catholicism the official religion of the nation. The convention gave Sarmiento the chance to be seen as a responsible spokesman for provincial interests and he was soon elected to the provincial legislature. After Mitre was elected governor, he was appointed minister of state.

The barbarity that Sarmiento saw surrounding him, however, would not abate. In one of San Juan's periodic flareups, a boyhood friend was executed. Sarmiento, already depressed by other setbacks, rejected appointment as emissary to the United States and in January 1861 resigned as provincial minister of state. Yet another civil war threatened in mid–1861, but after a battle at Pavón, Urquiza forces withdrew, not because they were beaten but because it was clear no Argentine could benefit from the endless bloodshed. Out of this morass Argentina would have to build itself.

The following year Sarmiento got his wish to be named the national government's administrator of San Juan, but he returned to a province enervated by war. His parents were both dead, his mother having died the previous November at the age of ninety-one. To add to his misfortune, Sarmiento left his wife and son behind in Buenos Aires, and there were rumors there — widely discussed and evidently substantiated — that Benita was unfaithful. Sarmiento himself had not been a model husband, and the tension between the two adults poisoned Sarmiento's relationship with his son.

Finally in a position of real administrative power, however, Sarmiento embarked on ambitious plans. He organized a more rational school system, and for the first time each department of the province was required to maintain at least one primary school. His administration founded agricultural communities, mapped the province, reorganized the militia, established an agricultural school, and drew up a proposal for irrigation. Then the smoldering civil war was enflamed anew.

This time Sarmiento's nemesis was Angel Vicente "El Chacho" Peñalosa, who, when captured, was summarily executed. His head was mounted on the point of a lance for display. This act of barbarity was laid at the doorstep of Sarmiento, the supposed advocate of restraint and civility. The controversy brought Sarmiento low again. Coupled with marital strife, the infamy overshadowed any successes of the past months, and Sarmiento lapsed into the sort of despair that had engulfed him before. Mitre, knowing of his problems, appointed Sarmiento envoy extraordinary and minister plenipotentiary to the United States.

Sarmiento arrived in New York in the spring of 1865, at the end of the Civil War. He established his office in New York City and founded a newspaper, *Ambas Américas.* The next year personal tragedy struck as a result of the seemingly endless fighting in the River Plate Valley. Capt. Domingo Fidel Sarmiento was killed.

During this period, Sarmiento renewed his friendship with Mary Mann, who would translate *Facundo* into English. He met Emerson and discovered that Longfellow spoke "perfect Spanish." As in the past, neither political, pedagogical, nor publishing concerns kept Sarmiento, now estranged from his wife, from affairs of the heart. "Sarmiento," notes historian César Guerrero, "had women who loved him, who knew how to interpret his feelings, who understood little besides admiration for him, and who collaborated with him along the long road of this wandering civilizor — and who did not leave upon his troubled heart some sediment of tenderness?" Returning from a voyage to Paris, Sarmiento met Ida Wickersham, who offered to help him improve his English.

"The most womanly woman I have ever known," wrote Sarmiento to a friend. They spent time together in Philadelphia, studying. Ida Wickersham was married, to a physician, but assured Sarmiento that their correspondence, especially if he wrote to her in French, would not be a problem. Through 1867, their letters (only hers exist) were torrid, and she carried on her end of the writing for several years, providing Sarmiento with details of the Chicago Fire, continuing to write after Sarmiento had returned to Argentina. Her last letter, in 1882, pleaded for some response: "I keep all your letters and reread them in detail. I could write if I knew you felt some interest in me. . . . Please, write and tell me of your life." By that time she was divorced and living alone in New York City. Sarmiento was embroiled in the affairs of his country and did not reply.

In 1868, Sarmiento knew his name had been placed in nomination to succeed Mitre as president of Argentina. Mitre was riding out a six-year term, during which there were no fewer than 117 local coups. Sarmiento had told his daughter when he left for the United States that the trip might be a device to isolate him from presidential politics, but he was supported by several generals and by Mitre. All he could do from abroad was wait and hope. Asked for his platform, he replied, "My program is in the atmosphere, in twenty years of life, actions and writings." On his way home,

Sarmiento did not know until his boat entered the harbor at Bahía that he had won.

Along with Mitre, Sarmiento presided over a profound transition in Argentina that grew out of the country's natural strengths, a transformation that Sarmiento had helped to foster but that no one, once it was underway, could control. Awakening after decades of fitful, tormented wars, the country established a thriving sheep industry. Between 1830 and 1880 the number of sheep rose from 2.5 million to 61 million. The country also raised cattle and planted grain. While in the 1850s net immigration had averaged 5,000 people a year, by the 1880s the average was 50,000, peaking at 200,000 immigrants in 1889. Argentina's population grew from 1.1 million in 1857 to 3.3 million in 1890.

"Sarmiento initiated a period of bourgeois domination in Argentina," writes biographer Bunkley. "His presidency marks the advent of the middle and landowning classes as the pivot of power in the nation. The age of the gaucho had ended; the age of the merchant and the cattleman had begun. The aim of this group was stability, order, and material progress. . . . He had only to overcome the last vestiges of the old order to put his program into operation."

Alas, the last vestiges of the old order were not easily conquered. The caudillos, with Urquiza still in command of several alliances, persisted. A war with Paraguay raged on. In 1870, after Urquiza and his family were assassinated, the most virulent uprising of all, led by Ricardo López Jordán, raged. Even after Jordán's army was defeated and Jordán driven into hiding in Brazil, he returned in May 1873, overrunning Entre Rios and gathering followers.

Sarmiento blamed Jordán for an assassination attempt in August 1873 when two Italian seaman were hired to shoot Sarmiento as his coach carried him through the streets of Buenos Aires. An overloaded gun almost blew the hand off one of the inept assassins, and Sarmiento, by now quite deaf, did not even hear the blast.

In the end, the heavy-handedness that had characterized much of Sarmiento's writing did not serve him well as administrative technique. When a factional dispute split his own province of San Juan, Sarmiento issued a presidential decree that simply imposed his will, deciding the issue in favor of his supporters. In 1869, he imposed martial law in San Luis after a provincial leader was shot by a firing squad. Although presidents had issued arbitrary decrees before, Sarmiento's martial law was the first time this device had been employed, and even his old friend Mitre attacked the action as unconstitutional.

By the time the next presidential election came around, Sarmiento was glad to leave the wrangling to others; he had to call out the army to keep order. Tired, deaf, and thoroughly disenchanted, Sarmiento continued to be the center of criticism as if by national habit. Returning to the Senate, he was asked how, since he was deaf, he could debate. "I don't go to the Senate to hear them," he replied, "but for them to hear me."

In 1879 — after contemplating another run at the presidency — he made the mistake of resigning from the Senate to accept a presidential appointment as minister of the interior and head of the cabinet. His charge was to restore order to national debate. "The colt throws his ears back," he wrote confidently to a friend. "He will calm down, recognizing his old master. There will be government." Such confidence was unjustified, and he quit within weeks.

In 1883, Sarmiento wrote *Conflictos y armónias de las razas de América*, still trying to resolve the dilemma, as he saw it, of taking the best from various "races" while leaving old, European foibles behind. He continued to run for office and to lose to men of no reputation whatsoever. He founded *El Censor* to fight a censorship law and then, finally, gave up fighting anything at all. There was so much fighting all around that he was hardly being noticed, the worst possible fate for such a powerfully prideful man.

With Faustina, Sarmiento moved to a better climate in Paraguay, to a small house where his heart failed on September 11, 1888.

Brazil's Emperors
Pedro I (1798–1834)
and Pedro II (1825–1891)

Divine Right and Democracy

Prince Hal was Shakespeare's "rascaliest, sweet young prince," who eventually had to grow up, leaving behind Falstaff in order to become Henry V. Similarly, Pedro I of the House of Braganza, after a dissolute youth, was thrust into reigning over the largest country of Latin America. Pedro, however, was an anomaly — king of an independent nation, monarch of an emerging democracy. This unique scepter he passed on to his son, Pedro II, who proved better able to understand a country casting off the trappings of royalty. They were unusual men in a situation that has no historical parallel, and their roles were crucial. "History," writes Hubert Herring, "credits the empire with having held Brazil together; had it not been for the cohesive power of the crown, the nation might easily have split at its seams as did Gran Colombia, Peru and the provinces of La Plata."

On November 29, 1807, Portugal's insane Queen Maria I and the prince regent João VI fled their country, sailing down the Tagus and out to sea as Napoleon's army reached the hills outside Lisbon. Their choice had been to retain Portugal's long-standing ties to a selfish Britain, or succumb to Napoleon's jealous France. Five British men-of-war protected them and their entourage aboard 36 ships as they set a course for Brazil.

The trans–Atlantic maneuver had been planned and was not without precedent. Kingdoms were portable, and Portugal, in fact, a tiny nation with expansionist neighbors, had contemplated moving before. For three centuries the Portuguese had controlled Brazil, and the court was welcomed ashore at Bahía in January 1808.

Brazil is shaped like a mammoth, spinning top. Its shoulders bulge northwestward toward Colombia and the headwaters of the Amazon, 3,900 miles long, and northeast toward Africa, less than 2,000 miles away. The arid, impoverished northeast has historically sent its own rivers of poor people to work in the more prosperous states inland and southward, like Bahía and Minas Gerais. Forests and pampas have supported a rich agrarian economy and built great cities like Rio de Janeiro, where the royal family settled.

The arrival of the European court was a boon to Brazil; some reports say more than 15,000 Portuguese followed their government. The British, who had already built London into an international financial center on gold smuggled out of Brazil during the eighteenth century, now prospered from their relationship with this growing market. A few Irish and German settlers added their numbers.

Especially galling to the Brazilians, however, was the arrogance of the Portuguese, who made known their dissatisfaction with conditions, especially the lack of sanitation. This conflict between Creoles and Portuguese would continue through the reigns of both Pedros.

From the beginning, the relationship between gigantic Brazil and tiny Portugal was an odd one, like a huge organ grinder dancing on a monkey's chain. Portuguese navigators—from a nation of half a million people spread along the Iberian coast—were without peer. They had been to Labrador as early as 1474 and discovered Brazil before 1500. Soon after word of Columbus's feat, Pope Alexander VI was called upon to settle the argument between Spanish and Portuguese over who owned what. The pope drew the line of demarcation from pole to pole a hundred leagues (roughly, 350 miles) west of the Azore and Cape Verde Islands. The resulting slice of the New World did not satisfy the feisty Portuguese, who obtained, in the Treaty of Tordesillas in 1494, a line of demarcation set 370 leagues west of the Cape Verdes. Then they drove inland to take even more.

After 1500, when Pedro Álvares Cabral staked a formal claim to the territory, the Portuguese took advantage of Spain's fixation with the silver of Peru on the other side of the continent. The Portuguese pushed farther and farther inland, following gold prospectors and the ruthless, slave-seeking *bandeirantes*. Unlike North American colonists, the Portuguese did not trundle westward with all their possessions and their families. Without women accompanying these interlopers, historian João Pandiá Calogeras points out, "racial crossing began early and broke down all barriers." The demographic result has defied precise measurement.

The geographic result, of course, was a huge colony. Portugal is just a bit larger than the state of Maine, and Brazil is about the size of the rest of the United States, including Alaska and Hawaii. Brazil encompasses almost half the land mass of South America. Its name, originally Terra da Vera Cruz, is from the *Caesalpinia,* which was commonly known as the brazilwood tree because its interior turns red like a coal, or *braza,* when exposed to air.

Economically, the metropolis prospered. After 1550, reaping the harvest of Brazilian plantations, Lisbon became the sugar capital of Europe. Politically, however, even control of this huge kingdom—Portugal also had to concern itself with India—did not prevent Portugal from being a mere pawn to European ambitions. Crown Prince João was more than glad to have found escape in the New World. Brazilians liked him, and *fazandeiros,* plantation owners, joined his court and built houses in Rio. In December 1815, he signed an edict giving Brazil dominion status within the empire. Matters of state, however, were not so easily avoided.

Napoleon had fallen the year before and Ferdinand VII, as a condition of his return, had been forced to accept the liberal Spanish constitution of 1812. This had as much effect in Portuguese America as in Spanish America; republican ideas were contagious. At the same time, however, the crowned heads represented at the Congress of Vienna (1815), tidying up the world after Napoleon, accepted the Brazilian monarchy for the first time. Thus, when Queen Maria died in 1816 and her son was crowned King João VI of the "United Kingdom of Portugal, Brazil and the Algarve [the medieval Moorish kingdom at the southern tip of Portugal]," he was promptly caught between demands on both sides of the Atlantic.

By 1820, there were in Portugal sporadic uprisings against "monarchial absolutism"; many of João's Portuguese subjects wanted a constitutional monarch. They also wanted their king to return, reducing Brazil to its former colonial status. João, for his part, wanted to stay in Brazil, so he countered with a proposal for a "dual monarchy." It was rejected. On April 21, 1821, João tried another ploy: a separate constitution for Brazil. This idea was rejected when the Rio garrison stepped in to break up the drafting assembly.

João had run out of options; he knew that if he insisted on staying in Brazil, the House of Branganza would lose Portugal. So, on April 24, pressed by his Portuguese supporters, by the British, and by his oldest son, Pedro, João grudgingly sailed for Portugal. To the delight of Brazilians, he took with him his shrewish wife Carlota, Ferdinand's sister, who had made clear her contempt for Brazilians and had tried to carve her own realm out of Brazil's southern tip—a region Argentines had come to think of as Argentina. On his way out, João robbed Brazil's treasury of money and jewels. To his twenty-four-year-old son, Pedro Antonio José de Alcántara, whom he left as regent, he is said to have counseled: "If Brazil demands independence, grant it, but put the crown upon your own head."

The evidence suggests, in fact, that João foresaw Brazilian independence and, knowing the Portuguese would not allow a dual monarchy, thought his return would at least assure that both countries would be controlled by Braganzas. When he died, he reasoned, the two crowns might be united with his son. Such a tidy plan was not to be. In Portugal after João's death, the House of Braganza would fight with itself. In Brazil after João's departure, Brazilians would prove so independent as to reject Pedro's intention to serve as absolute monarch.

Biographers describe Pedro I in romantic terms. He was handsome, sentimental, impulsive, spoiled, and unschooled. Only irregularly was he seen in the presence of tutors. He was hated by his mother and ignored by his father, although he displayed a common sense and firmness that were likened to his mother's and an affability that he shared with his father. As a boy, he was allowed, even encouraged, to associate with lackeys at court and commoners—even in the street. Calogeras depicts Pedro I as "bold, inured to hardship, and adept in all sports, a marvelous horseman.... He could rise to heights of generosity and heroism, but was quite capable of falling into the opposite extremes.... As a consequence of his dissolute life and degraded companions he was ill-bred, coarse, and rude, addicted to low jests and practical jokes." Although he had avidly supported the cause of Brazilian independence from Portugal's yoke, he was so vain and shortsighted as to imagine he could exercise absolute control.

Pedro's principal saving grace was his first wife, the plain but exceptionally well-bred (Maria) Leopoldina. "His wife was an asset," writes biographer Mary Wilhemine Williams. Leopoldina's father was Emperor Francis I of Austria, who was served by that most famous of statesmen, Prince von Metternich. Her older sister was Napoleon's second wife. In matters of state concerning South America or Europe, Leopoldina was at her husband's side, advising. She read extensively—among her choices was Malthus' *Principles of Political Economy*—and she managed to assemble a library that has been described as "the best in Brazil at the time." Interested in botany and geology, she sent samples of New World discoveries to learned friends in Europe. At court, she raised the level of discourse above Pedro's ribaldry.

She, too, supported an independent Brazil. Quite apart from her bloodline, her intelligence, or her political views, Brazilians lionized Leopoldina because she endeavored to understand them, to meet them on their own terms. She was seen in counterpoint to her predecessor, the despised termagant Carlota. "In Brazil," notes Williams, "to whose independence she directly contributed, her memory is still held in gratitude and respect."

The marriage of Pedro and Leopoldina in 1817 was not, alas, particularly romantic. It began well enough; although they never met before the wedding they had corresponded. She, two years older than he, was unswerving in her dedication. Both were equestrians and took long rides through the Brazilian countryside. When Pedro reviewed troops, Leopoldina, wearing the blue uniform of the dragoons and heavy silver spurs, would ride beside him. The couple had four children.

Physically, however, Leopoldina, despite blond curls, fair skin, and blue eyes, was not particularly attractive. She had a figure that has been charitably described as "sturdy." Calogeras remarks, "The princess lacked many of those feminine traits which appealed to a man of the type of Dom Pedro." Felix Reichmann calls her "totally lacking in sex appeal." The faithless Pedro focused his attentions on other women, but especially on Domitila de Castro Canto e Mello, who in 1824 gave birth to his daughter and whom he named, with crude irony, lady of the empress' bedchamber. Later, he elevated her to a marchioness.

Leopoldina did not suffer these indignities quietly. She openly quarreled with her husband and let her father know of her predicament. Brazilians in the street were aware of the indignities their queen suffered, increasing their hostility toward a king they did not like in the first place.

In 1826, Leopoldina fell ill and died two weeks before Christmas, delirious and ranting, apparently suffering from an infection following a miscarriage. The story circulated among her many supporters that their empress had been killed by a blow from the boorish Pedro during a violent argument.

Pedro's management of an unruly country was no better than his handling of marital affairs. "As a monarch he was less than nothing," writes Calogeras. In the Portuguese *côrte*, where members yearned for the old metropolis-colony relationship, antipathy for Brazil increased. Delegates arriving from Brazil were ridiculed. Pedro responded in letters to his father criticizing the *côrte*. There were attempts to reduce the status of Brazil within the partnership, and the *côrte* excluded Brazilians from all high military and political offices in their own country. As a final insult, Pedro was summoned to Portugal to "complete his political education."

Pedro hesitated, and Leopoldina was among those who persuaded him not to return. The Masonic Order, into which he would be inducted, also fed the flame of defiance. Petitions arrived from the provinces asking him to stay, not totally for love of Pedro — several municipalities in Minas Gerais were perfectly willing to let him go — but because of his tactical usefulness in the strategic battle with Lisbon.

Central to Pedro's decision to stay in Brazil was the advice of José Bonifacio de Andrada e Silva, who has to come to be known as "the patriarch of Brazilian independence." Bonifacio, a member of one of São Paulo's most distinguished families, had studied and taught in Portugal before returning to Brazil in 1819, when he was fifty-four. During his thirty years in Europe, Bonifacio counted among his friends Alexander von Humboldt, the German naturalist, Allessandro Volta, the Italian physicist, and Joseph Priestly, the English clergyman and chemist. He served as secretary of the Scientific Academy of Lisbon and earned a reputation as a leading mineralogist. Back in his native country, Bonifacio went to work on some very rough ore indeed in an effort to shape Brazilian democracy.

While Bonifacio devoutly believed in the need for Brazil's independence, he had been shocked by what he observed of the French Revolution in 1789. He was convinced that the monarchy must remain strong within a constitutional framework. Balancing those elements against each other in the tropical climate of Brazilian politics would test Bonifacio's wisdom and skill. The Masons criticized his efforts, as did other of Pedro's advisors, and, in fact, did Pedro himself. Bonifacio proposed social and economic reforms, like land redistribution and a higher standard of living for workers, which placed him on a collision course with the landed aristocracy. Liberals, on the other hand, objected to his defense of the monarchy. Bonifacio's contentiousness got him fired and exiled by Pedro, but, fortunately for the future of Brazil, he returned to a position of influence.

By early January 1822, Pedro could hold out no longer; he had to indicate whether he would yield, returning to Lisbon as demanded by the côrte, or stay in Brazil. Pedro's formal rejection of Portuguese authority is known to Brazilians as the "Fico" — I will remain. "As it is for the good of all and the general felicity of the nation," Pedro declared, "tell the people that I will remain." Portugal's military garrisons angrily demanded compliance with the order to return, but popular uprisings in support of Pedro silenced the garrisons.

Later that same year, on September 7, while traveling in the provinces, Pedro received a dispatch from Portugal telling him that the battle was not yet done. The côrte was annulling all of his acts as regent and declaring his ministers guilty of treason. Standing by the bank of the Ypiranga River, Pedro delivered his second dramatic pronouncement, the "Grito do Ypiranga." Drawing his sword, he said, "The hour has come! Independence or death! We have separated from Portugal!" Leopoldina wrote him at the time, "The apple is ripe; pick it now or it will rot."

These two pronouncements ushered in the brief period — Brazil's modest "war" of independence — that would end on February 28, 1824, when the last Portuguese garrison set sail for home. In Pará, Pernambuco, and Bahía there was brief resistance, but no more. Bonifacio recruited the Scotsman Lord Cochran, who had performed a similar service for Chile, to sweep Brazilian seas clean of the Portuguese navy. "The war of independence in Spanish America had lasted fifteen years," writes Calogeras, "the independence of Brazil was won in as many months."

On December 1, 1822, he was crowned Pedro I, "Constitutional Emperor" of Brazil. When the Portuguese garrison at Rio, 1,600 strong, rebelled, outraged Brazilians chased them across the harbor, where they were captured under a virtual state of siege. Pedro ordered the artillery they left behind trained on their hiding place, and a third of the soldiers switched sides. The rest sailed for home. Reinforcements, which met them en route, were of no help; Brazilians simply would not allow the fresh troops to get off their ships, so they turned around and sailed back to Portugal.

Pedro's battles, however, were only half over. He would later write to his son, "The time when princes were respected simply because they were princes is past." It was a lesson reiterated every day by Brazilians who wanted to breathe life into this odd notion of a constitutional monarch. When a constituent assembly, fired by the idea of designing some brand-new form of government, opened in April 1823, Pedro's tolerance lasted only until November. The assembly went too far, so Pedro ordered it disbanded.

In its stead, Pedro appointed a commission to draw up a document that would serve as a legal foundation. The result Calogeras calls "a monument of political liberalism and well-balanced powers." Liberals of the day disagreed, wanting stronger republican institutions that made their own decisions. The country was left with ambivalence, a state in which the emperor's "moderating power" was no power at all if factions behaved immoderately. "The respect of a free people for their ruler," Bonifacio counseled, "should spring from the conviction that he is the leader capable of enabling them to attain that degree of well-being to which they aspire." Pedro I was not that leader.

An important political problem was that of the slave trade. Other new Latin American nations had immediately prohibited slavery, writing the prohibitions into their constitutions. In those instances, however, large slaveholders had often been peninsular Spanish, royalists who were defeated in the wars of independence. Thus slavery was toppled with other institutions of colonialism. In Brazil, slaveholders were supporters of independence and were helping to shape the new government. Slavery, therefore, was more imbedded.

Attempts to dislodge slavery were in vain. The British demanded in

1826 that by 1830 importation of slaves be ceased. The 1830 deadline was not met, and the issue divided Brazil as it did the United States, which had passed its own Missouri Compromise — assuring the continued admission of slave states into the Union — in 1820. Bonifacio was among those who argued for abolition. "He who lives on the earnings of his slaves lives in indolence," Bonifacio counseled, "and indolence brings vice in its wake."

The solution would not come for half a century, and, in the meantime, Pedro I's time was running out. It was always a source of resentment that Pedro's closest friends and advisors were Portuguese, not Creoles; Pedro isolated himself. His preferred venue was an army barracks. He submitted treaties to the legislature, but only after he had unilaterally ratified them himself. Expected to act as mediator of disputes among the far-flung provinces, Pedro argued with anyone in the room.

At his best, Pedro had risen to the drama of Brazilian independence. With cavalier gestures, he had been in the vanguard of independence. Nation building would require someone of more patience and wisdom.

On December 2, 1825, Pedro's youngest child was born, a son and heir. Pedro and Leopoldina had had two sons who died young — one in infancy, the other of pneumonia after the family was subjected to harsh conditions during their flight from a revolt in Rio. There were no more boys until — after three girls — the birth of Pedro de Alcántara, Pedro II, a child Brazil could rear in its own image.

Events quickly converged, as if on cue. João had finally recognized Brazil "to be in the category of an independent empire," but then, a few months later, in March 1826, João died. This left Pedro I to fight with his brother Miguel over who would take their father's throne. Brazilians wanted to keep Pedro in Rio, fearing that if he left they would become a second-class partner in the kingdom.

Initially, Pedro thought he could control the throne in Lisbon by shipping off his eldest daughter, Maria da Gloria, in July 1827 to claim it and by naming Miguel regent. The plan did not work. First, Portugal split into a civil war between partisans of democracy and reactionaries who intended that Miguel rule as an absolute monarch. Maria da Gloria never got a chance to take the throne, and within a year Miguel had seized it for himself.

Pedro's plans for Brazil were no more successful. Taxpayers were incensed over the debt Brazil had to assume as a condition for recognition as an independent monarchy, adding to the hostility directed at Pedro as a person. He was blamed for the long, expensive, bloody war that failed to hold onto the Cisplatine province, which in 1828 became Uruguay. With his predictable contempt for public opinion Pedro only incurred further wrath by continuing his relationship with Domitila despite his 1829 marriage to a Bavarian princess.

By 1831, relations had so deteriorated that mobs were in the streets, and soldiers were deserting to join them. Disgusted and frustrated, Pedro scribbled out a note abdicating his Brazilian throne and embarked for Portugal, where he would continue the effort to make his daughter the queen. He was at least successful in that effort, but died in 1834, only thirty-six years old. In the end, his greatest gift to Brazil was his departure, leaving behind as regent the five-year-old Pedro II and naming as Tutor the sage republican Bonifacio.

Pedro I demonstrated, according to biographer Williams, "a strong, deep affection" for his infant son. After the abdication, notes and letters were exchanged, a governess at first guiding the hand of "the crowned orphan," whose father would reply to "my beloved son and my Emperor." When his father died in 1834, Pedro II was nine years old. "They err," Bonifacio told him gently. "Dom Pedro did not die. Common men die, but not heroes."

Pedro II's sisters, Januaria and Francisca (Paula died in 1833), remained in Brazil with him, and among Pedro's closest friends was said to be one "Rafael," a black soldier who had been a favorite of his father. Rafael, whose rooms Pedro was allowed to visit, represented a kind of counterpoint to rigorous schooling, a thorough grounding in languages, the classics, and modern thought. There was an emphasis on reading.

He was taught, it is said, "to love labor as the foundation of the virtues, and to honor equally the men who toil and those who serve the state through political office." An elevated thought, yet early on Pedro was expected to don a uniform and review troops, and even as a child he received the credentials of arriving diplomats. His childhood papers, carefully preserved, demonstrate knowledge of the French revolution, of U.S. history, and of William Burke, the English conservative, all written in English. He translated Longfellow and Byron, and attained a working knowledge of fourteen languages, including Hebrew, which he mastered in order to study the Old Testament. To say, as biographer Reichmann does, that Pedro II was "totally different from his father" risks understatement. Reichmann adds primly, "His private conduct was impeccable."

His schooling, in fact, was characterized by strong religious influences, and a considerable moral example must have been set by his principal governess, Doña Marianna Carlota Verna de Magalhaes Continho, a widow who came to Brazil with her husband in 1808 to join the court of Dom João. Pedro's childhood name for her was "Dadama." Appointed head governess in 1831, Dadama was made a countess in 1844 and in 1855 opened her house to cholera victims, eventually dying of the disease after contracting it from her patients.

So important was Pedro's education that his relationship with Bonifacio became a political issue. Octavio Tarquinio de Sousa, a historian, dismisses objections about Bonifacio as "the hostility that invariably is felt toward superior men, above all when that superiority is felt as a result of the disdainful, even insolent, gesture." There was more to the hostile scrutiny of Bonifacio, however, than could be explained by his arrogance. There is the story of a European contemporary who made it his business to keep an eye on the comings and goings of the Brazilian court. Seeing a horse tied outside Bonifacio's residence, he asked if it belonged to Pedro. "Yes," came the reply, "it's the prince, José Bonifacio's assistant."

Bonifacio, clearly, had his hand on the hand that would be on the helm of Brazil's destiny, and the aging intellectual was determined to keep his grip firm. Bonifacio found in Pedro II "the fittest instrument," writes historian Manoel de Oliveira Lima, for his own republican goals. Bonifacio himself was "predestined" to shape the future of the continent's largest country. When Pedro I named Bonifacio to the task of educating his son, dissidents contested the nomination, saying the choice should rest with the legislature. Bonifacio — sixty-eight years old at the time — held a seat from Bahía, but he took his case to the people. He published a "Protest to the Brazilian Nation and to the Entire World." The council of regency took the side of the dissidents, but when the matter was put before the full legislature on June 30, 1831, Bonifacio was eventually deposed as tutor, but not until, more than two years after the appointment, his mark on the development of Pedro II and the future of Brazil was assured.

The reason for Bonifacio's downfall was his conviction that the monarchy must remain strong. Liberals condemned this view, but Bonifacio's thinking was shaped, while in Europe, by France's example of republican chaos, and, since returning home, by the cases of Peru, Chile, and Argentina. From the time of Pedro II's birth, Brazil had threatened to fly apart from the same sort of centrifugal forces that afflicted Mexico. Revolts in the northern provinces broke out in 1824, and mid–1825 brought the revolt of the Cisplatine province. Bonifacio argued that only a strong monarch could hold the nation together. Clinging to this opinion, Bonifacio saw his tutorial post terminated by the legislature in December 1833. He had to be removed forcibly from his office, after which he was imprisoned. Although acquitted in a criminal trial, Bonifacio was then driven to retire from politics.

Those who would get rid of the monarchy once and for all caused sporadic revolts, especially along the northern and southern borders, causing Pedro II's protectors to spirit him away from Rio seeking safety. Although democrats did not blame him personally, Pedro was the focus of their dissent just as he was the catalyst of monarchists' zeal. Brazil had grown to 4.5 million citizens in eighteen provinces — remote Amazonas and Paraná were formed during his reign — and it was by no means certain there would be a nation left to govern when he grew up. "While Dom Pedro's tutors were intent upon training him to be a good man and a good emperor," writes Williams, "the Brazilian regency was struggling to hold the country together—to preserve it for him to rule."

There were mutinies by soldiers who drove away civic officials and set up their own governments; there were republican rebellions, separatist movements, and conflicts between federalists and monarchists—with *moderados* in between. Civil war broke out in Rio Grande do Sul in 1835, in Maranhão in 1840, in São Paulo in 1841, in Minas Gerais in 1842, and in Pernambuco in 1847. From 1835, when he was only ten years old, there was pressure to bring Pedro II's minority to an end when he was fourteen in order to stabilize the nation. Another frantic proposal was to name his elder sister, Januaria, regent, although at the time she was only twenty-one and the minimum age for such an arrangement was twenty-five.

A national guard was formed to confront army mutineers, and in 1839 there was a move to grant the monarchy police powers. Conditions, however, did not improve. Creole unrest could only grow as long as the Portuguese controlled agriculture and commerce. In the spring of 1840, a legislative faction moved to end Pedro's minority and, after a parliamentary battle, succeeded in July. The coronation was held a year later.

At the time of his coronation Pedro was still very much an adolescent, a bit short and pudgy, with blond hair. He would grow to be six feet, three inches tall, and well proportioned; his hair and full beard would be brown. For all of his liberal education, it was noted of him that "an air of reserve discouraged familiarity." He was, as might be imagined, mature for his years. He immediately began opening and closing sessions of the legislature in full regalia, his costume including a scepter topped by a griffin, the symbol of the Braganzas.

"Yet in some ways," Williams writes, "the sovereign was but a child. His new dignity perhaps prompted him on December 2, 1840, to begin a diary which shows the naiveté of the average boy of fifteen. In his first entry he remarked that his birth was a historical event for Brazil. Then he solemnly proceeded to mention the coffee and eggs he had had for breakfast."

Almost immediately after the coronation, the regency began casting about for a wife. In Austria in April 1842, a betrothal contract was signed for Thereza, sister of Ferdinand II of the Sicilies. Metternich helped arrange the betrothal; Pedro gave his approval on the basis of a portrait. Thereza was apparently as close a relative as the House of Austria was willing to part with after the experience of Leopoldina. Thereza was related to so many of Pedro's relatives—including, of course, his irascible grandmother Carlota—that Pope Gregory XVI had to approve the marriage. On May 30, 1848, there was a proxy marriage and Thereza sailed; she was twenty-one, Pedro not yet eighteen.

Pedro went aboard her ship when it entered port. He had read the novels of Walter Scott and was thus familiar with scenes of romance such as to set a young man's heart throbbing. What he saw was a woman who was short, walked with a limp from a physical defect, and was "somewhat lacking in grace... unquestionably plain." Besides, despite sound schooling Thereza was a bit dull.

The portraitist had fudged the truth. Pedro is said to have turned away in momentary despair and remarked to his former governess, "They have deceived me, Dadama." Twenty years later, when his daughters were both to be married to grandsons of France's monarch in exile, Louis Philippe, Pedro made sure they met their prospective husbands before committing themselves.

Yet Thereza was devoted to her husband, and he, in turn, was faithful to a fault. She came to be known as "the Mother of Brazilians." They had two sons, both of whom died while young, and two daughters, Isabel and Leopoldina. This family served as the sort of model that its predecessor could not; it represented intelligence, compassion, and gentility, giving Brazilians, members of a large and boisterous society, an important focus. The reign of Pedro II was as effective as could be expected in a day when monarchies were ending, serving as an imprimatur on Brazil's republican birth. Pedro II and daughter Isabel were identified with the eventual, belated, end of slavery. When his time came, Pedro II was a paragon of graciousness as he sailed into exile.

Slavery was important to Brazil and suggests much of Pedro II's ambivalent role. Liberals won control of Pedro's education and brought him to power hoping he would lead their various causes, including abolition of slavery. Once he was monarch, however, Pedro had to deal with the realities of an unruly populace whose economy was inextricably entwined with slave labor.

After the mid–1830s, Brazilians gathered more power to democratic, if unpredictable, institutions, while stripping power from the monarchy. The power of the king's council was diminished, while elections were spun out to the provinces. In an atmosphere of untried institutions and uncertain allegiances, however, a clever monarch could hold sway. Pedro was not averse to ignoring the law, and there were many officers whom he would simply fire. As for the often raucous Chamber of Deputies — the law required voters to have some income but did not require them to have any education — its members were a rambunctious lot. Pedro suspended the Chamber of Deputies eleven times.

In addition, Pedro was constantly meddling in the affairs of ministers and of the aristocratic Senate, where members held life terms. His powers were weak, but his intellectual strength was great, suggesting that he could halt or delay undesired actions, but had a problem getting things to move.

Politicians from across a huge nation offered a variety of challenges, and Pedro's *poder moderador* was no power at all if not reinforced by popular will. Manoel de Oliveira Lima has called Pedro II's regime a "dictatorship of morality."

By 1845, Pedro ruled a population of 7 to 8 million subjects, virtually all along the coast: a few hundred mestizos; 1 million whites, Creoles, and Portuguese; 1.5 million full-blooded Indians; and 5 million slaves. Except for the Spanish colonies of Puerto Rico and Cuba, Brazil and the United States were the only important places in the western hemisphere clinging to slavery. To the dismay of Pedro II, Brazil would hold on even longer than the United States.

It is often asserted that the slave's lot in Brazil was generally better than it was in the United States. Gilberto Freyre has pointed out that the long and deep relationship between Africa and Portugal—from the Moorish penetration of tiny Portugal to miscegenation in Brazil—has created the special "influence of the African, either direct or vague and remote." The ambiguity of the relationship was evident through seventy-five years between the rejection of slavery by other Latin American republics and Brazil's grudging acceptance of emancipation.

Attempts to end the importation of Africans through 1845 were largely brushed aside. Internal disorder, massive geography, and a lack of will prevented enforcement. After that year, when the law imposed by the British expired, imports soared. In 1846, 19,453 slaves were imported; in 1847, the number was approximately 50,000 and rising.

When the British insisted on switching enforcement of slavery law to British admiralty courts, and, later, when British ships began entering Brazilian ports in pursuit of slavers, much more was done to enflame relations with white Brazil than to diminish the growth of black Brazil. Not until 1850 were Brazilian authorities able to begin to staunch the flow.

Relations between a proud Brazil and a haughty, powerful Britain continued a broken course throughout this period. Brazilians were quick to chaff, and otherwise minor incidents related to British sailors deteriorated into a six-day blockade of Rio by British ships in 1862–63. These violations of Brazilian sovereignty forced Pedro, a private opponent of slavery and anything but a firebrand, to affect a public posture of nationalism. When angry Brazilians rattled their untried sabers, the scholarly Pedro drew himself to his full, impressive height and offered to go to war to defend his country's honor. "I am the equal of any other Brazilian citizen," he soberly announced.

The fundamental problem, however, worsened. It is not surprising that the Brazilian legislature recognized the belligerency of the Confederate States of America. Slavery was a powerful bond. By 1862, fully one-fourth of the Brazilian population were slaves, some 1.7 million slaves in all. In

1870, one-fifth of Rio's 250,000 population was counted as slaves. Pedro and others, frustrated by their inability to curb slavery through legislative measures, began in 1871 a fund to buy slaves' freedom, and Pedro once went so far as to buy a slave's freedom in the street.

Adding to Brazil's general malaise and Pedro's inability to govern were military fanatics along the country's southern border. Pedro's father had suffered a loss of prestige from civil war in the south, but now the threats were tripled from across the border with three neighbors. Juan Manuel Rosas, the Argentine tyrant so vehemently opposed by Sarmiento, drew Brazil into the problem created by his capacity for malice; Uruguay was chronically unstable; and, worst of all, Paraguay's Francisco Solano López, along with his son, turned Paraguay into an armed camp, a nation of fanatics who would eventually, through virulent, mindless warfare, seriously deplete the population of men.

Pedro II, a friend of Argentine President Bartolomé Mitre, the man who did much to restore his country after Rosas, insisted on going to the front in 1865 as the three allies fought to bring López down. "I want to go," Pedro announced when his advisors sought to restrain him. "If not permitted to go as Emperor, I will abdicate and go as a private citizen. Though I may not be permitted to go as a general, the quality of a Brazilian cannot be taken from me; I will enlist with a musket as a volunteer for the fatherland."

In July 1865, he departed for the front, accompanied by one son-in-law, later joined by the other. He "attended" — a term that suggests gentility, certainly not fierceness — the siege of Uruguayana. He opposed, in his humanitarian way, bombardment of the town, and, indeed, the battle was won without bombardment. His visit is said to have "stimulatled allied solidarity" with Uruguay and Argentina, and he returned to Rio in November, unscathed.

This almost comical war record ought not disguise his determination, however.

When in 1867 a peace initiative was advanced by Paraguay, Pedro rejected it, with disastrous consequences. "For a time he stood almost alone in his demand that the war go on," writes Williams, "his was the responsibility for prolonging it." It dragged on in the face of insane determination on the part of the defeated, but unrelenting, Paraguayans. Paraguay's male population, almost literally, fought to the death.

The estimates of Brazilian losses range from 35,000 to 50,000 lives in five years of conflict. The war cost Brazil $30 million. Pedro's hair, light brown at the outset, was almost entirely white at the armistice. He was forty-four years old.

It was time for Pedro II to retire from the stage of history. In 1871–72 he made a trip, his first, to Portugal, then on to Europe and Egypt. He was nothing if not modest, carrying his own valise, his own umbrella. When Victor Hugo, weary of an endless stream of admirers, refused to accept an invitation to call on Pedro, Pedro called on Victor Hugo, who called him "the grandson of Marcus Aurelius" for the intelligence of his monarchy. If all monarchs were like Pedro, Hugo asked rhetorically, who could be a republican? In 1875 Pedro visited the United States, traveling from New York to California and back again.

The United States was rebuilding from the Civil War, and Europe was growing with the bulk of the Industrial Revolution. Brazil, Pedro knew, was entering its own difficult phase. "Very few nations are prepared for the system of government toward which we are headed," he wrote in a personal note in 1879, "and I certainly would be better off and happier as president of a republic than as constitutional emperor." Once again, however, despite the lofty philosophy he was disturbed by the political mediocrity he saw resulting from Brazilian elections.

He proposed progressive reforms, but his proposals were not joined by legislative force. Improved education was Pedro's principal concern — "if I were not an Emperor, I would like to be a teacher" — but he also wanted better irrigation in the northeast, a national school of agronomy, improved rail and telegraph lines, easier credit for investment. To rebuild the population after the war with Paraguay he wanted to encourage immigration.

Slavery was outlawed in 1888, while Pedro, very ill, was recovering in Milan. "Oh, what a great people. What a great people," he wired home, then broke into tears. He wrote a sonnet to commemorate emancipation.

When he returned to Brazil in August, however, he found resentment over emancipation was strong and weariness with the monarchy widespread. "The Emperor of Brazil is personally popular," wrote the U.S. representative to Secretary of State William Seward, "not so the Empire." Biographer Reichmann adds that "at the end of Pedro's regime nobody came to his aid, although almost everybody respected him." Pedro's response, typically, was gentle: "[I]f Brazilians do not want me for their emperor, I will go and be a professor."

The professor's massive class was almost over. He was criticized as "soft" on Freemasons, those enemies of the Church, and was overwhelmed by antimonarchists dominating both houses of the legislature. Only Pedro's personal popularity stayed the inevitable.

Enter the military, politicized by the slavery debate, disaffected by the long war against Paraguay, surly because of a reorganization plan, impatient with rioting. Gen. Manoel Deodoro da Fonseca, commandant and vice president of always troublesome Rio Grande do Sul, became the lightning rod for dissent. He was joined by a teacher at the military academy, Lt. Col. Benjamin Constant Coelho. The year 1889 was a long slide away from monarchy, and in November a republic was proclaimed.

Pedro's feelings were hurt when the revolutionaries held him in his palace, an insult for such a reasonable, gentle man. Although he said he wanted to stay in Brazil, he made it known he was ready for exile, and Deodoro informed him, "The country expects that you will know how to imitate, in submission to its desires, the example of the first Emperor." On the boat on November 24, Pedro's fourteen-year-old grandson suggested that a pigeon be sent back carrying a farewell message. Pedro wrote the note and attached it to the bird's leg, only to stand on deck and watch the pigeon beat its way against a strong headwind until finally, exhausted, it fell into the waves.

Soon after reaching Portugal, Pedro's beloved Thereza died, and he wrote in his diary, "I can only weep the happiness of forty-six years. . . . Nothing can express how much I have lost. . . . I wish that my daughter would come." His daughter came, but Pedro, visited by an endless stream of admirers, lived only two more years himself. He died at sixty-six in December 1891 in a Cannes hotel. A small placard outside his apartment said simply, "D. Pedro de Alcántara," but his countrymen remember him as Pedro the Magnanimous.

José Martí
1853–1895
(Cuba)

Revolutionary Poet

I cultivate white roses
In January as in July
For the honest friend who freely
Offers me his hand.

And for the brute who tears from me
The heart with which I live,
I nurture neither grubs nor thistles,
But cultivate white roses.

José Martí remains one of the most exalted figures of Latin America's wars of independence. He was a leader in the struggle to free Cuba, the last New World colony that Spain still clutched as the twentieth century approached. Yet he lived his life far from the fighting until that last, fatal moment when he thrust himself into the battle. Martí articulated revolution as a journalist, poet, and orator. Also, he was an ardent lover whose charms were known to many women, except, alas, his long-suffering wife. History cast Martí as an exile, condemning him to an odyssey throughout Europe and the Americas, circling, never settling on the island he sought to free. But his words, still heard, made him one of the region's most enduring heroes.

José Julian Martí y Pérez was born on January 28, 1853, into a Cuba as isolated and anomalous as the island is today. Half a century had passed since Haiti led the way, and between 1810 and 1824 the Spanish-American colonies had followed, making abolition of slavery a principle on which they formed themselves. Yet Cuba languished, along with Puerto Rico, as a royal colony with a slave economy.

There were independence movements in both Cuba and Spain, but dissent, even favoring modified autonomy as part of a commonwealth, was harshly put down by royal troops. Cuba lived in the preceding century because Mother Spain still dwelled there. The Martí family harbored no notions of independence and ignored politics in general. Everything was safer that way.

Don Mariano Martí y Navarro was a native of Valencia who served in the Royal Artillery Corps before emigrating to Cuba about 1850. He was a simple man, a policeman, sometimes a tailor of uniforms, sometimes out of work. He married Leonor Pérez, also of modest background, in 1852, when he was forty-seven and she was twenty-two.

José was born less than a year later. They had six other children, all girls. Life in the Martí home was one of constant economic strain, with Don Mariano periodically petitioning one government office or another to obtain a job. Martí was bright enough to have handled, while still a boy, the clerical tasks attached to his father's post as a policeman.

But if the home life of Martí was isolated from politics, school and the neighborhoods were not. The Havana school he attended — and where he won awards in arithmetic and sacred history — was directed by Rafael María de Mendive, whose tutelage included large doses of contemporary politics. Mendive's political activities made him a target of the authorities because the Spanish monarchy, threatened by republicanism at home and separatists on the island, clung to its final possessions with a blind tenacity. Royal interests were guarded by bands of armed roughnecks called "Volunteers." Much of the dissent emanated from small clubs, like Mendive's, who made public their literary aspirations, but kept secret their revolutionary publications. The mixture was one of art and politics, and the model was a strong one for the young Martí.

On October 10, 1868, when Martí was fifteen years old, there was an uprising in the small town of Yara. "The cry of Yara" would become a symbol of revolution. By the next year, the United States, which looked down on Cuba the way an anteater regards a particularly fat ant, threatened to recognize the insurgents as belligerents.

Mendive's school was a lightning rod in a charged atmosphere with revolutionary literature blowing through the streets. Much of it derived from the lack of accurate information. After every clash, Cubans' only source of news as to how each side acquitted itself had to be gleaned from propaganda sheets. One product of the tension was that combination of fire and arrogance for which defenders of the Spanish Crown have distinguished themselves. In January 1869, at a time the Crown was trying to mollify critics by recalling a particularly offensive captain general, a student was slain in Havana for not yielding the way to a Spanish officer in the street.

In response to indignation, someone, apparently the Volunteers, fired into a crowded Havana theater on opening night of a drama reputed to be unpatriotic. By exquisite coincidence, it was the next morning that Martí, days before his sixteenth birthday, broke into print. His dramatic poem told of Abdala, who sacrifices himself for the ultimate triumph of Nubia: "Oh, how sweet it is to die when one dies fighting boldly to defend one's country."

The poem was published in *La Patria Libre,* a democratic, cosmopolitan weekly conceived and edited — for one issue only — by a close friend and schoolmate of Martí, Fermín Valdés Domínguez. The publication was sponsored by Mendive, giving it the patina of advanced schoolwork, but Martí's parents were unimpressed. His father was, after all, an officer of the regime. Besides, when dealing with an enraged, dying monarchy, there is no such thing as a schoolboy's prank.

Mendive, who had been in a box seat at the theater, and whose mother-in-law was a part owner, was arrested, imprisoned for four months, and exiled to Spain. For the while, Martí was safe, but in the autumn, there was another disturbance. Some boys had the audacity to laugh during a Havana military parade honoring the birthday of the Spanish regent. One of the boys was the brother of Fermín Valdés. Officers searched the Valdés house and found the revolutionary literature of adolescents; Martí was implicated.

Most damaging, in the eyes of investigators, was a letter from Fermín and Martí to a third schoolmate who had joined the Spanish army as an officer. They accused him of "apostacy," a charge the authorities interpreted as mutiny. At their trial, both boys claimed authorship of the letter. But when the judge questioned them, it was Martí who delivered a speech proclaiming Cuba's right to independence. Fermín was sentenced to six months in prison. Martí got six years. He was sixteen years old.

From prison, he wrote to his mother and sent along a photograph showing him in a chain that stretched from his waist to his ankle. "I am sixteen years old," he wrote, "and already many old men have told me that I seem old. To a certain extent they are right, for if I have in its full strength the recklessness and effervescence of youth; I have, on the other hand, a heart as small as it is wounded. It is true that you suffer intensely, but it is also true that I suffer more."

His father, visiting him in prison, was shocked. He worked in a limestone quarry, where conditions were always harsh, and where men were sometimes blinded by the kilns. Using his position as a policeman — lowly, but one that put him in contact with notables — his father got Martí transferred to a cigar factory, where conditions were better and prisoners were only fastened to their work tables.

His mother was able to get his sentence changed to exile, and he was moved to the Isle of Pines. Until he was finally exiled to Spain in January 1871, Martí was confined for approximately a year. The harshness of his treatment was attested to by a recurring leg injury he carried for the rest of his life. It was a lesion caused by a blow from a chain, and, despite two operations, its pain returned periodically, sometimes debilitating him. By the end of his sixteenth year, Martí had been jerked from schoolboy revolutionary romanticism to the hard life of a nineteenth-century convict.

For some, the lesson learned would have been sufficient. Martí was not yet out of high school and could, eventually, have returned to Cuba. The alternative was one of the many émigré colonies that Spain's recalcitrance had sown around the world. The importance of his choice was made clear about the time Martí arrived in Spanish exile with publication of the *Book of Blood*, published by the exile community in New York. It listed the dates and places where 4,478 Cuban *independentistas* had been shot or garroted and suggested that more than 150,000 had been killed in the continuing civil war to free the last colony of the hemisphere.

A slight man, already in poor health because of his imprisonment, Martí took on a demeanor of pained sorrow. Upon hearing that eight Cuban students had been murdered by the Volunteers, he began wearing black. When his old friend Fermín Valdés saw him in Spain he described him, in the words of one Martí biographer, as "emaciated and melancholy."

Nevertheless, among émigrés he was introduced to more freedom of discussion than he had ever experienced. To continue his education, he enrolled in both secondary school and the university, in law, at the same time. He earned a living by tutoring and published in a Cádiz newspaper a fragment of what would be his first book, *The Military Prison of Cuba*. Although bothered, at times severely, by his leg, Martí spent some of his happiest years during this time. There were museums, the theater, art, the world of émigré salons — a wider world than he had ever known. There was also a love affair — his brooding disposition seemed a particular attraction to women throughout his life — with the wife of a host. This predilection for the wives of hosts would follow him.

Martí spent four years in Spain. But although he was there when the king abdicated in 1874 and during the short-lived republic the following year, he was apart from these events, writing poetry, completing his high school studies, and readying himself for university examinations. Martí's intellect and rhetorical power would allow him to assert himself as a leader of the rebellion against the claims of fighters. He could make no pretense of being a military man, despite his record of endurance in prison. Nor did his social status or age entitle him to respect within the émigré community. So he formed his prospects from intelligence and literary style and cast his future with the rebellion.

In the summer of 1874 he passed the preliminary requirements for a law degree, then took exams for a high school diploma in philosophy and letters. In late September and early October, he took, almost back-to-back, examinations in Greek language and literature and in critical studies of Greek authors, in metaphysics and historical geography, in Spanish history and the Hebrew language. On October 20, he asked that a date be set for this final examination, and it was set four days later. He drew three topics at random and chose "Roman political and forensic oratory: Cicero as its supreme expression; speeches analyzed according to his works on rhetoric." He was given three hours by himself to prepare, then summoned to develop his thesis before a committee, which asked questions for thirty minutes. He took a grade of *sobresaliente,* outstanding.

Because he could not pay either school the necessary fee, Martí was given only certificates, not the diplomas he needed to guarantee work as an accredited teacher. Still ahead of him was a life of wandering, without independent income, and the lack of accreditation would continually hinder him.

When he decided to leave Europe, Valdés insisted that they spend some time in the museums of France and England. In December 1874, in Paris, a fellow poet introduced Martí to Victor Hugo, who was, like most intellectuals of the time, a supporter of Cuban independence. At Valdés' expense, Martí sailed from Southampton first class.

His eventual destination was Mexico City, where Martí was to be reunited with his family, but he arrived just weeks after Ana, a sister with whom he had been particularly close, had died. His family, he discovered, had not prospered, but had been held together with the help of benefactors and what the women could earn by sewing.

In Mexico at that time the political and literary climates were perfect for Martí. President Sebastian Lerdo de Tejada carried on *La Reforma,* the liberalization set in motion by his predecessor, Benito Juárez, who had died two years before. Too briefly, nascent democracy offered Mexico promises that would never be fulfilled. But in that fragile environment, Martí found a home writing columns for *Revista Universal,* owned by a Lerdo liberal. Martí adopted the pen name "Orestes," the son of Agamemnon and Clytemnestra who avenged his father's murder by slaying his mother.

Martí's wit won him immediate acceptance in Mexican literary society, requiring, to his apparent delight, that he occasionally clear away the chiffon in order to clear his head. One prestigious salon was presided over by Rosario La Pena, whose beauty and perfidy had reputedly driven one poet to despair and suicide. Martí, as ever, brooding, seemed at the point of falling gladly into Doña Rosario's gossamer net. But the vehemence of his ardor scared her off. Martí was not a man of half-measures, and in this instance his exuberance apparently saved him.

In his writing, Martí was a willing conduit for the Indian strength that flowed through *La Reforma*. The Indian peasant was the populist foundation of Mexican reform, and Martí thought he saw important differences between a natural, growing America and the aging, posturing Europe from which he had just come. Fundamental to Cuban independence, Martí would argue, was freedom for slaves, and during this time in Mexico he broadened as a thinker and as a moralist.

In this respect he broke from Latin American thinkers of his time who had given up on European scholasticism — medieval attempts to "prove" the existence of God — only to mire themselves in the fashionable European "logical positivism" — a modern conceit that science will get you where God can't. Martí, the chain-gang veteran and the Cicero scholar, would have none of this intellectualism. "Abstractions are proved by abstractions," he wrote contemptuously. "I have an immortal spirit because I feel it, because I believe in it, because I want it."

In 1876, Lerdo was toppled by Porfirio Díaz, *La Reforma* ended, and night again descended on Mexico. Martí, although allowed to continue writing, became, in the chill of the new conservatism, a foreigner. His writing had to be confined to Mexican affairs and could not stray toward criticism of the Spanish and their Cuban slave colony.

Martí's position was tenuous. He had become a favorite of Mexico City's *tertulias*, the literary clubs, but he had neither sought citizenship nor saved any money. With the change of government in Mexico, he was transformed, almost overnight, from a welcome friend to a suspicious alien. In early 1877, under the pretense that he was going to Guatemala, he sailed for Havana. He used the assumed name "Julian Pérez," his mother's maiden name.

In Havana he saw only the futility of a revolution now nine years old. It was suggested that he would be welcome in Guatemala as other Cuban revolutionaries had been. After arranging for his family to return to Havana, Martí returned to Mexico City, determined to go on to Guatemala. Before leaving the city, however, he asked Carmen Zayas Bazan, the daughter of another Cuban exile living in Mexico City, to marry him when he returned. Then, alone, without a job and without a country, he set out.

By now, Martí's reputation, in several respects, preceded him. For one thing, work was easier to find, and Martí began teaching straightaway. For another, as biographer Felix Lizaso puts it, "Everywhere, from Southampton to the Atlantic Coast of Guatemala, there had been a woman's soul to comfort him." It is said that a young Guatemalan woman pined away and eventually died of longing when she found out Martí was engaged. After nine months in Guatemala, he returned to Mexico City to marry Carmen and bring her back with him.

But the most significant aspect of Martí's reputation was his inability to resist a fight. The diminuitive Martí — a "frail little man of genius" as Lizaso calls him — who had paid for his views with imprisonment, hard labor, and exile, would not accede to authority. His opposition to slavery and his insistence on democracy made him important enemies, and this image lay at the root of his appeal. He had neither won fights nor gathered armies, but the popularity of his writing as champion of common people was such that Guatemala's elitist regime eventually forced him to leave.

Rather than go to New York City, his first inclination, Martí followed his wife's suggestion to return to Cuba in the autumn of 1878. Her parents had just gone back, and it appeared that the insurrection, after ten years, was ending. The government guaranteed increased freedom. The hope was short-lived. The royal mentality reverted to its ancient ways. The authorities would grant Martí only temporary certification as a teacher, citing the old fact that he had never acquired his degrees. He found work in a law office and taught part-time.

He also found some work as a journalist, but, as might be imagined, his writing was inhibited. He found a forum, however, as a speaker, and in the spring of 1879, he was asked to speak at a gathering of prominent people in Havana.

His speech contrasted two kinds of political philosophies. One, he said, makes demands of its contemporary adherents without violating the spirit of its founders, its first heroes. To this kind of philosophy, Martí tipped back his head and quaffed a toast.

The other kind, he continued, turns its back on its followers, refuses to hear their needs, and fails to give voice to the truth. Rather than drink to this kind of political philosophy, Martí whirled and smashed his glass.

The captain-general was told of Martí's remarks. A week later, he showed up himself to hear Martí deliver the principal address honoring a noted violinist as part of a contest for promising young musicians. Martí, true to form, called the truce between the Cuban authorities and the rebels "a lying transaction." The captain-general is reported to have said: "I do not want to remember what I have heard, what I did not think anyone would ever say in front of me, a representative of the Spanish government. I am going to conclude that Martí is a madman...but a dangerous madman."

A Havana discussion group — a *liceo* — that had taken Martí in was censured by the establishment press. As a result of the news, he became more popular than ever. The attraction Martí's ideas had for Latin Americans outside Cuba was beginning to take hold among Cubans, who had never been allowed to read him. Then Martí's temporary teaching certificate expired, and his financial straits—Carmen had given birth to a son—grew worse.

His family's poverty, however, did not stand in the way of Martí's plotting. At the law office, as his employer nervously shifted clients to another room, Martí conducted strategy sessions. The authorities, meanwhile, had one eye on Martí and the other on fellow rebels Antonio Maceo, who was black, waiting in Jamaica, and José María Moneada, gathering an army in Oriente province at the eastern tip of the island, far from Havana and a traditional focus of insurrection. Calixto Garcia, only recently released from prison in Spain as a result of the truce, also plotted.

Finally, the authorities' nerves could stand it no longer. Martí was having coffee with a friend and fellow conspirator in September 1879, when a messenger called him away. He returned after a moment to tell his friend to stay and finish his coffee. He would not be returning.

Again exiled to Spain, he immediately traveled to France. By now his reputation was assured, so along his wandering route there were likely to be famous admirers, like Sarah Bernhardt in Paris. He went on to New York, where his writing in the *Hour* and the *New York Sun* would enhance his reputation as an observer of the cultures of both Americas.

In New York he enlarged his reputation in another way. Needing a place to stay, Martí was taken in by a Cuban émigré, Manuel Mantilla, and his Venezuelan wife, whose name, like that of Martí's wife, was Carmen. Carmen de Mantilla was a woman of great charm, and in the Mantillas' East 29th Street apartment she presided over the salons that Martí convened continually. Indeed, they cemented a relationship that left her, when Martí departed for Venezuela a year later, pregnant.

He began teaching in Caracas and founded a magazine that lasted two issues before running afoul of the authorities. In this case, Martí published a eulogy for Cecilio Acosta, whose record as a democrat had placed him in opposition to the despotic Venezuelan president, Antonio Guzmán Blanco. Guzmán made things hot enough for Martí that he was forced to leave hurriedly in mid-1881, after he had been in Venezuela less than nine months. His letter of farewell, which was published, increased his popularity among Guzmán's opponents, and Martí continued to write for a Caracas newspaper, but from New York.

In the judgment of Manuel Pedro González, a Martí biographer, "a less uncompromising attitude would have brought him wealth and social prominence." As it was, his attitude kept him out of work. Martí was the soul of a revolution that could not find its body. He returned to New York, where, in a testament to human compassion, Manuel Mantilla took him in again. Martí's wife and child were brought up from Havana and moved into the Mantilla apartment. Martí might have been satisfied with this arrangement, but his wife was not. After arriving in March, she took their son and returned to Havana and her family in November. That month, Carmen de Mantilla gave birth to a daughter.

Martí stayed in New York — save for brief trips to Mexico, Central America, and the Caribbean — planning, raising money, and recruiting fighters for a revolution that would not happen. He worked as a translator for D. Appleton and Company, the publisher, and he wrote about the arts, culture, and politics for newspapers from New York to Montevideo. During this period he recognized that a dangerous consequence of breaking the bonds of Spain would be avoiding the economic and cultural domination of the United States, with its "disproportionate craving for material wealth." The United States had hungrily eyed Cuba since buying the Louisiana Purchase from France in 1803 and the annexation of Florida in 1821. In 1823, John Quincy Adams had suggested that "laws of political as well as of physical gravitation" ruled the hemisphere and would bring Cuba into the U.S. sphere whenever it broke with, or was broken away from, Spain.

Living in the United States did nothing to ameliorate Martí's fears of such a fate. He saw the United States as exhibiting an unhealthy interest right across its southern neighbors. He wrote to a friend that he thought "my duty — inasmuch as I realize it and have the spirit to fulfill it — is to prevent the United States from extending itself through the Antilles and with that added momentum taking over our American lands. What I have done up to now, and what I shall do, is toward this end. It has had to be done in silence and indirection because there are things which, to be achieved, must be hidden; and should they be known for what they are they would raise difficulties too powerful to overcome.... I have lived inside the monster and know its insides."

When New York coachmen, mostly immigrants flooding into the country and working for less than a dollar a day, went on strike, Martí championed their cause against the private and government forces that sought to break their strike. He wrote that their goal was fundamental: "The employees, in mass, abandon the stables, demanding not higher salaries, nor seeking fewer hours, but because they are to be deprived of the right of association." Martí's defense of such causes has inclined modern adherents of several political stripes, from communists to reactionaries, to claim him. Thus today Cubans shout back and forth between Havana and Miami, each insisting that now, a century later, Martí would be on their side.

On which side one stood, Martí wrote, ultimately had to be made clear beyond words. He stated a personal principle when he eulogized abolitionist Wendell Phillips, whom he greatly admired. "An orator shines for his speeches," Martí wrote, "but he remains only for what he does. If he does not sustain his words with acts, his fame will evaporate even before he dies because he has been standing on a column of smoke." Martí would ultimately demonstrate how strongly he felt.

In Cuba, the rebellion had been dragged like a great, empty cannon with broken wheels. There was never enough support among the Creoles to throw out the Spanish, yet the royal occupation was so clearly immoral that the insurrection struggled on. By 1894, relations among the rebels themselves were frayed from long wear; there were half a dozen strategies, that many uses for every dollar raised, more frustration than could be measured. There was an apparent attempt to poison Martí while he was in Tampa trying to raise arms, ammunition, money, and men.

He went on to Key West, Mexico, and New Orleans. But although newspapers carried accounts of his efforts, for so long had Martí preached revolution and so many times had uprisings been put down that U.S. editors had increasing difficulty taking the movement seriously. In January 1895, however, the world, especially Spain, was shocked by a revelation. Perhaps the little man had not been standing on a column of smoke.

Because of confusion and dissension among the rebels, U.S. customs authorities discovered a shipload labeled "machinery" bound from Florida to Costa Rica that was weapons headed for clandestine unloading on the coast of Cuba. The authorities seized that ship and ordered that another, then two more, be searched. The proportions of the plot and the immediacy of action could not be determined, hence the seriousness of the situation could only be enlarged in Spanish imagination. Whatever was about to happen, it was bigger than people had realized.

Martí was chagrined. Like other rebel leaders, he was reduced to hiding from newspaper reporters.

But the news of aborted invasion had the effect of galvanizing rebel forces on the island and of increasing demands for support. In New York, Martí drafted a call to arms, a document owing more to romance than any understanding of military reality. The Spanish had been alerted, too. Nevertheless, Martí rhetorically charged. Émigrés were asked to mortgage their homes, if necessary, to raise new funds. Martí resolved to return to Cuba despite the setback, and he and an associate departed for Santo Domingo. There and in Haiti, at times on horseback visiting émigré enclaves, they searched for fighting men.

They got news of new outbreaks in Cuba and hastened their efforts. After so many years and so much death, it seemed that the time was finally coming to make it all count for something. "I called forth war," Martí wrote to a supporter. "With it my responsibility begins instead of coming to an end. . . . I shall raise the world. But my only wish would be to affix myself there, to the last treetrunk, to the last fighter, to die in silence. For me it is now time." As Martí and other leaders approached the point of landing, orders were for several small sorties to land at various points along the Cuban coast.

There was haste, and there was waiting. As Martí finally sailed slowly toward the coast of Cuba, he wrote to his daughter, María, in New York. The revolutionary was ever the pedant. He counseled her not to shy away, despite her tender years, from an effort to write a translation of a particular book from the French. He gave advice on style, and used his own experience as translator as an example. Above all, he said, write. "A page a day, my little daughter. Learn from me. I have life on one hand and death on the other, and a nation on my shoulders, and see how many pages I write to you?" The letter held out the request, "Wait for me as long as you know I am living."

In Haiti, Martí and five other rebel leaders found out that a schooner captain hired to take them to Cuba had reneged. Nevertheless, with the complicity of Haitian authorities, they found passage on April 5 on a run-down German freighter that would put them off on a small boat near the coast. They went over the side the night of April 9 into a rough sea.

Reaching shore, the small band found the village of Cajobal, where residents, reluctantly at first, took them in. They made their way toward a rendezvous with other rebels, and Martí, spending his first days and nights as a soldier, seemed ecstatic. The others, seeing his enthusiasm, told him that not only had he been recognized as the official delegate of the Cuban Revolutionary party, but he had also been named a major general of the Army of Liberation.

The five first found a small rebel group, then caught up with a column led by Maceo. There was Martí's first combat, in which he served as a medic. He sent a dispatch, as had been requested, to the *New York Herald.*

Martí was afraid, however, that for all his personal enthusiasm the revolution would again stall. He spurred Maceo to join forces with another column to mount a decisive assault. Maceo agreed, and the linkage was accomplished before the end of April. On May 19, the rebels approached the plain of Boca de Dos Rios, where they hoped to coordinate the efforts of both their cavalry and their foot soldiers. Spanish troops got there first.

When the battle was joined, Martí presented himself for orders in a battle that was quickly being dominated by the Spanish. Martí was ordered to the rear. Martí replied that he had encouraged the fight and was obligated to join it. When it was clear to the seasoned fighters around him that such an act was foolish, Martí spurred his horse toward Spanish emplacements. A friend named de la Guardia saw what he was doing and caught up to ride beside him. In the volley that ripped de la Guardia's horse from beneath him, Martí was knocked from his saddle.

His dead body fell too close to the Spanish lines to be recovered by the retreating rebels, and the Spanish refused to give it up until it had been demonstrated by the Spanish commander to his superiors.

When Martí's comrades got back to the rebel camp, they found an unfinished letter in which Martí, as always, was imploring, asserting his opinion, instructing, guiding.

Benito Juárez
1806–1876
(Mexico)

Builder of Democracy

For Latin America's former colonies, the last battle of independence was often followed by the first battle of civil war, and nowhere were centrifugal forces stronger than in Mexico, which is more than three times the size of Spain and Portugal combined. In addition, Mexico faced invasion by France, a determined effort not only to deprive Mexico of its independence, but to turn it into a bizarre, New World monarchy. No one did more to try to build the nation than Benito Juárez, warring with foreign invaders with one hand and building a nation with the other, maintaining his dignity all the while.

Benito Pablo Juárez was born on March 21, 1806, in a village of twenty Zapotec families in the mountains of Oaxaca, 250 miles southeast of Mexico City. In those mountains the vice-royalty, then dying, had never had much in-fluence, although the Church reached everywhere. Juárez' father, godmother, and grandparents carried him to a nearby village, Santo Tomás Ixtlan, in order to find a church where he could be baptized.

Both parents were dead by the time Juárez was three, so he and his two older sisters went to live with their grandparents, who also died within a few years, starting Juárez on a round of uncles and friends who saw to the children's lessons. Juárez, who left a considerable body of writing, would recall that he bought his uncle the whip to be used when he had not studied hard enough. By his own evaulation, however, Juárez remained an indif-ferent student. It became clear that "only by going to the city could I learn."

To the city he went, although legend has it that the trip had extracurricular motivation. Juárez allowed himself to be talked out of his uncle's sheep, which he had been tending, by passing brigands. Rather than face punishment, he trudged twenty-five miles to the state capital.

There, he found lodging at the home where one of his older sisters, who had left her drunken husband, was working as a domestic. The owner, Antonio Maza, a produce wholesaler and perhaps a European, helped to polish the manners of the rough-cut boy and put him into school at the only place available, the seminary. His "patrimony" as a full-blooded Zapotec allowed him to study free.

At age fifteen, Juárez completed his studies in Latin grammar and had to refuse ordination. The idea of becoming a priest, he later wrote, was something "for which I felt an instinctive repugnance," an early indication of his view on one of the most bitterly divisive issues of Mexican society, the relationship between Church and state. Juárez knew, however, that Indian priests were trained just well enough to lead the faithful in prayer, but were not allowed to give instruction or to rise in the Church's hierarchy.

Still wishing to study, Juárez talked Maza into allowing him to stay at the seminary, but with a broader curriculum. When a secular school — Oaxaca's first, an example of the nation building going on — opened, Juárez transferred. He eventually earned a degree in law, learning along the way Oaxaca's many lessons in politics. Away from the European affectations of Mexico City, the city provided a body of belief that convinced the young Juárez and others of the possibility of fulfillment of the nation's Indian heritage. Mexico remains a nation whose population is three-tenths racially and culturally Indian, six-tenths mixed, or mestizo, blood, and only one-tenth European. Oaxaca was one of the places where Mexico's Indian consciousness has been defined.

Notions of independence were strong there. While Juárez was growing up, both of the priests of independence, Hidalgo and Morelos, fought important battles in Oaxaca. An Oaxaca contemporary of Juárez was Porfirio Díaz, who both helped shape Juárez' role in politics and built his own dictatorship. In the wild and wooly politics of Oaxaca — a disgruntled politician once took a shot at Juárez as he sat on his front porch — one of the lessons Juárez learned was to distrust "the enthusiasm of the crowd, which rarely examines events to their depths and causes, and always admires and approves anything that seems to it new and extraordinary."

During Juárez' early teenage years, the defeated vice-royalty was replaced by the abortive "monarchy" of Agustín de Iturbide and the inept dictatorship of Antonio López de Santa Anna. One of the many legends depicting Juárez' humility is the story of how Santa Anna — very European and a staunch guardian of church prerogatives — was once, during a visit to Oaxaca, served in a restaurant by a young Indian waiter — Juárez.

For Juárez personally, independence settled an important conflict between him and his benefactor, Maza. Although Juárez wanted a secular education, there was still pressure from Maza to follow the priesthood. Independence settled the issue: Juárez was spared the necessity of defying his benefactor when anticlerical rebels sent all bishops back to Spain. Juárez' military career, such as it was, was also resolved during this period. In 1829, when he was still studying law and teaching physics to help support himself, Juárez was drafted. Quickly, however, the Spanish, who had invaded Tampico from Cuba, were driven out. Four years later Juárez was briefly commissioned a captain during one of the periodic wars between clerical and anticlerical forces, a war that quickly passed over an issue that is still unresolved in Mexico.

Juárez' personality clearly inclined him toward teaching, but his lack of money led him to practice law. It was not a career without obstacles, for both the Church and politics were thoroughly mixed in with the courts. The influence of the Church, Juárez wrote, "was almost omnipresent. . . so they could indulge with impunity in every excess and every injustice."

In 1834, the young lawyer represented complainants before an ecclesiastical court. His clients claimed they were being overcharged for religious services. Juárez' argument prevailed, although he knew it was because the local authorities were liberals and he himself was a liberal deputy to the state legislature. The same authorities allowed him to get the offending priest banned from the parish. Alas, with elections there was a change in administrations, whereupon the priest not only returned to the village but had his accusers, and any who dared take up their case, jailed. Juárez returned to the village and was jailed. Released after nine days, he returned to Oaxaca a wiser man.

Despite this volatile environment, Juárez' political career advanced. He was thought of as a puritan, standing just over five feet tall in his customary black suit, and he did nothing to dispel the image of a bureaucrat picking his way along the difficult, always changing paths of Mexican politics. He had a reputation for thoroughness, and he nurtured it. He was called – not always admiringly – "the little Indian," and he was willing to take on any administrative task, often turning the result to the benefit of his beliefs. He was appointed a judge and, eventually, president of the provincial court.

Mexico's internal struggles often ran parallel to the territorial ambitions of the United States. Where Americans saw their destiny manifest, Mexicans saw their territory being stolen. The United States was headed for San Francisco – founded by the Spanish in 1776 – and would absorb Texas and fully half of the land claimed by the Republic of Mexico along the way. In the Peace of Guadelupe Hidalgo, signed in March 1848, the United States paid $15 million, canceled all American claims against the defeated republic, and called home its troops. With a Prussian eye for detail, the United States filled in the Gadsden Purchase in 1853.

Throughout this turbulent period, Juárez' career was propelled by his administrative ability. While Mexican presidencies and personal ambitions rose and fell, somebody, quite simply, had to run the country, and one of those people was Juárez. In 1844, he was elected governor for the first of two terms. In late 1846 and early 1847, Juárez was one of nine men from Oaxaca to gather with other delegates in Mexico City — his first trip to the national capital — to revise the national constitution.

At that convention, the signal decision was made — to help pay the debt from the war with the United States — that part of the Church's property would be mortgaged. Secular-clerical conflict was again enflamed, and, Juárez recalled later, "I decided to go home and dedicate myself to the practice of my profession."

There was no escape, however. As the nation defined its democratic life, even Juárez' private life became an example, a model for people who had few models of modernity. In 1850, while he was governor, his two-year-old daughter, Guadalupe, died. In his grief, Juárez set an example by accompanying her body to a civic cemetery outside the city's walls to emphasize a liberal campaign encouraging hygienic burial. Conservatives considered such behavior blasphemous, although hygiene was not always possible in the traditional cemeteries administered by the Church, and Juárez wished to make his point.

"He is very homely," said his wife, Margarita, later, "but very good." Margarita, the daughter of Maza, Juárez' benefactor, was born just eight days after Juárez' twentieth birthday and married him when she was seventeen. Earlier, Juárez had sired two illegitimate children: a son with whom he maintained contact, and a daughter who became a drug addict and whose care Juárez entrusted to a long-time friend and his wife in Oaxaca. Tragedy also followed the large family — twelve children — born to Juárez by Margarita, and Juárez would bear countless domestic heartaches even as he wrestled with the republic's problems.

After leaving the governorship in 1852, Juárez became director of the Institute of Arts and Sciences, but within a year he was removed from the position by political opponents. Just weeks later, with Santa Anna back in power in Mexico City, Juárez was accused of inciting class warfare. As he prepared for a court proceeding in Ixtlan, he was arrested and ordered to Puebla, between Mexico City and the Gulf Coast. At Puebla, he was arrested by Santa Anna's son and taken to a wretched island prison off Vera Cruz.

In October 1853, along with his brother-in-law, Juárez was exiled, ending up in New Orleans. There he joined an émigré community, many of whom, like Juárez, had skin dark enough to make life difficult. The

Mexicans were appalled at the slave markets they found among people fond of casting themselves as hemispheric leaders. There were conspiracies to return, but for the time being Santa Anna was propped in place by receipts from what Americans know as the Gadsden Purchase.

Finally, in June 1855, making his way across the country to meet with a rebel leader, Gen. Juan Alvarez, Juárez was sidetracked in a typical display of his humility. On the trip, a rainstorm ruined Juárez' one good suitcoat, so he showed up at the general's camp wearing the traditional white cotton shirt and pants of a Mexican peon. When an officer spotted him and found out that he could read and write, Juárez was made, apparently without his objecting, a corresponding secretary. Only later was Alvarez told that a letter had arrived at the camp addressed to "Sr. Licenciado Don Benito Juárez." Chagrined, Alvarez promoted Juárez to his staff.

After Alvarez' troops forced Santa Anna, once again, into exile, those who took power separated themselves over a kind of litmus test of liberality. Juárez was among the *puros;* others, more willing to compromise, were the *moderados.* Juárez fretted lest "the clerical-military" forces that Santa Anna had represented retain too much power. Juárez warned about politicians and generals who had "joined the revolution only to adulterate it." Juárez was most committed to what he saw as the necessity of controlling the Church. He supported the initiative to deny clerics seats in the national and state legislatures because, as he wrote later, they "believed themselves to be representatives in the congresses only of their class." Most of all, this was Juárez' chance to enact real reform.

When Alvarez moved into the presidency, and before Juárez returned to Oaxaca to resume the governorship, Juárez was a major influence on laws that ended the three decades of "the era of Santa Anna," laws that presaged *La Reforma,* the intellectual, social, and legal basis of modern Mexico. Although Alvarez allowed himself to be replaced by Ignacio Comonfort, a moderate, causing other *puros* to leave the administration, Juárez, who had been named by Alvarez minister of justice and public instruction, stayed. Seeing his chance to sculpt lasting reform, he acted fast.

"What most led me to decide to go on in the Ministry was the hope that I had the power to seize an opportunity," Juárez wrote, "to initiate one of the many reforms that society needed to better its condition, thus making use of the sacrifices that the people had made to destroy the tyranny that was oppressing them."

Special privileges for the military and the Church were among the most serious abuses Juárez wanted to stamp out. "I was occupied with working on the law for the administration of justice," he explained. "The revolution was triumphant, it was necessary to make effective the promises of reforming the laws that hallowed the abuses of the despotic power that had just disappeared. The previous laws on the administration of justice suffered from this defect: they established special tribunals for the privileged classes, making permanent in society the inequality that violated justice and that kept up a constant agitation of the social body."

Because of opposition by both Alvarez and Comonfort Juárez was not able to effect as sweeping a change as he sought: absolute elimination of all special courts for clerics and military personnel. "It was, then, very difficult to get anything useful done under such circumstances, and that is the reason that the reforms I effected in the law of justice were incomplete, limited as I was to the removal of the ecclesiastical exemption in the civil branch and being forced to allow it to remain in the criminal. . . . To the military was left only their exemption in crimes and misdemeanors that were purely military."

The law was published in November 1855, and the following spring another law established a process for breaking up the Church's great landholdings, allowing sale to tenants. Over the next two years, Juárez would help write the Constitution of 1857, which sought finally to separate Church and state and establish public schools. Then Juárez returned to Oaxaca, where he was elected governor with nine of every ten votes cast.

At home, he set in place other liberal reforms, but even as laws were enacted, traditions chafed. Comonfort was centralizing power, and defenders of the old prerogatives were reasserting their strength. The 1857 Constitution required civil officials to take an oath of allegiance to the state, but clerics threatened all who did with excommunication.

Late in 1857, although he had asked them not to, friends put Juárez' name forward for national office, and he was elected to the nation's second highest position, president of the supreme court, next in line for the presidency. In addition, at Comonfort's request, Juárez doubled as minister of the interior. That meant that in December, when Comonfort tried to seize supreme power, Juárez was caught in the middle again. Juárez stated his opposition, and Comonfort had him thrown in jail.

Then, although Comonfort was forced into exile, Juárez was not allowed to ascend to the presidency. Juárez and his supporters contended that it was his constitutional right, and Mexico fell again into civil war. His side by far the weaker, Juárez took a cadre of about seventy *puros* and fled the capital. For the next ten years, driven just ahead of would-be captors, Juárez represented constitutional government, but on the fly. "But where is he?" wrote a contemporary. "I do not know the bit of earth where he is right now, but. . .in that corner will certainly be found the President."

Juárez was an exile in his own land. Defenders of the Church were determined that the *puros* meet their end. Liberal officials of the last regime also had to escape from Mexico City, sometimes in disguise. Juárez went first to Guanajuato, then Guadelajara, where he and his party were captured and threatened with being shot. They were freed only because confused, illiterate soldiers, unsure what they were fighting for, let them go.

On March 21, 1858, pushed toward the Pacific Coast, they saw in the distance an approaching band of Indians. The Indians had found out that the strange caravan was that of Don Benito Juárez, and they had brought wreaths of flowers in celebration of his fifty-second birthday. He was still their president.

On they went to Colima, where they were told the main constitutional army had been defeated. They labored on to New Orleans, where they caught a boat to Vera Cruz, a liberal stronghold. The government was finally off the road, and Juárez sailed into the port of Vera Cruz to a twenty-one gun salute. Margarita, then with eight children — ranging in age from infancy to fourteen years old — had arrived overland from Oaxaca, over difficult mountains.

Juárez was protected by governors defending their relative independence under federalism. In 1859 and again in 1861, Juárez issued decrees that institutionalized federalism and liberality, going for broke although he had no power. He had decided, he explained later, that this was an opportunity to speak his piece on the constitution and, at the same time, disestablish the Church once and for all. If he waited until he had real power, he reasoned, such views would cause civil war all over again. "Better one war than two," was his terse evaluation.

He decreed that all church property not used for worship was to be confiscated. This measure sought to correct an earlier, misguided reform that put church property up for sale, thus assuring that it would be bought up by the wealthy. The new decree was designed to put common land, *ejidos,* in the hands of peasants. He also decreed that the Church and state were separate, and while religious freedom was to be protected religion was not to spread its tentacles across state prerogatives.

In foreign affairs, more than decrees were needed. Mexico was in debt to almost every European capital that had a bank. Nations as powerful as Britain, France, and emerging Germany wanted their money and threatened to get it by taking customs receipts.

The United States, meanwhile, was sending mixed signals. Both the Union and the Confederacy wanted to buy Mexican commodities, but the Union also wanted to talk about a route to the West around the South. In the slave states, some leaders saw potential for added strength by acquiring northern Mexican states. Juárez found the former proposal troublesome, the latter odious.

To make matters worse, Juárez' representative in Washington, José María Mata, found himself dealing with mountebanks. Businessmen eyeing property in Mexico or just looking for opportunities there claimed expertise they did not have. Even President Buchanan had his eye on a piece of real estate in northern Mexico for a railroad right-of-way, and, more important, on the Isthmus of Tehuantepec, a narrow stretch across which an interoceanic railroad line might be built. When Buchanan had no luck with his representations to the government holding Mexico City, he turned to Juárez.

"I told him," Mata wrote to Juárez of Buchanan, "that I believed you would be willing to sanction any treaty that was based on principles of justice and was to the advantage of both countries." Mata had had enough of dealing with Washingtonians and wanted to return, but he counseled Juárez, "For my part, I consider it to the interest of Mexico to make those treaties, if in them the government of the United States binds itself to recognize and maintain in those routes the sovereignty of Mexico, and only in those treaties do I see a means of suppressing the rapacious spirit so prevalent in the southern states, precisely the ones closest to us."

Mata then made an eloquent statement regarding the future of relations between his country and the United States. "Perhaps I am deceiving myself," he wrote, "but I am convinced that Mexico is necessarily allied with this country, and that in order to preserve our independence and nationality it is necessary to adopt a policy that is based on fully liberal principles, that will serve the reciprocal interests of both countries, and that will permit the two peoples to come in contact with each other, so that they may know and appreciate each other better, and so that one country will lose its spirit of aggression and the other its mean distrust and absurd suspicion."

Without guarantees of Mexican sovereignty and dignity, Mata concluded, "in no case and for no reason should we consider the alienation of a palm's width of our territory."

Negotiations dragged on. U.S. military outposts spread across Mexico? The idea was out of the question for many Mexicans. Strengthen the forces of slavery? The notion was unacceptable to abolitionists. The figure of $4 million was discussed, with half going to settle American claims and half free and clear for Juárez' government. Was this a defensive alliance between the two countries, or a sale for hard cash? The "Treaty of Tehuantepec," which was never to be, did much to besmirch political reputations in both countries. Both the U.S. Senate and Juárez' cabinet — despite his support — rejected it. It was 1860, and the United States entered its own civil war. Half a century later the crossing would be built in Panama.

In March 1860 the siege of Vera Cruz was lifted as constitutionalist armies began to turn the tide. Toward the end of the year the civil war drew to a close. The successors of Comonfort fled into exile. It was the end of what Mexicans call "the War of the Reform." Juárez entered Mexico City, but his government was characterized by uncertainty. He expelled the ministers of Spain, Ecuador, and Guatemala, and the papal legate for their encouragement of reactionaries. Generals of the victorious forces arrested generals who had led the other side, and a kind of code emerged, born of necessity with almost constant civil war: if a commander had spared lives when possible, his life was spared.

The economy was in ruins. The design of a rational agronomy — a mixture of cash crops and sustenance — had to be ignored in the rush to satisfy creditors. Land redistribution would have to wait. The treasury was obligated to repay money stolen by commanders on both sides. The states took their cut of customs receipts before sending the diminished balance to the capital. Every month, the nation fell another $400,000 in debt.

Enter Maximilian. For four years, European arrogance would cause 40,000 Mexicans on both sides to be killed; 10,000 were wounded. Napoleon III, in an effort to prove himself his uncle's equal, provisioned and dispatched this "silly princeling," and Juárez was driven once again into internal exile.

In the autumn of 1861, Britain, Spain, and France signed an accord to collect their debts. The British insisted they held no territorial goals; the French and Spanish kept their own counsel. The divided United States was invited to join, but declined, coming up with absurd offers on its own. Confederates offered to return, in exchange for certain favors, California and New Mexico. The Union had in mind a $65 million purchase of mineral rights in several northern Mexican states.

In December 1861 and January 1862, matters were joined. Seven hundred British marines briefly landed at Vera Cruz. The Spanish invested the port city with 6,000 troops, and the French landed 2,500 soldiers and began to build troop strength by recruiting Mexicans. Juárez, in a gentlemanly if misguided gesture, gave permission to the invading commanders to move their troops inland away from the scourge of yellow fever along the swampy coast.

On May 5, a date that remains a proud symbol of Mexican history, the Battle of Puebla was fought. Puebla lies on the road from the coast to Mexico City. With heavy losses on each side, the French were defeated. For Mexico, however, satisfaction was short-lived.

During the rest of 1862, while Napoleon III sent more and more reinforcements, Juárez' government fought with itself. *Puros* worried about clerical power, demanding such measures as a reduction in the number of convents and a ban on sermons against the regime. With adversity at home and abroad, Juárez — trying to prepare a second defense of Puebla — also had to deal with the death of a daughter and his father-in-law.

The French surrounded Puebla with 26,300 troops, including 2,000 reactionary Mexicans, in March 1863. Twenty-two thousand Mexicans loyal to Juárez fought back, holding out for so long they were reduced to eating dogs and cats. The French commander offered the Mexican commander the presidency if he would surrender. He refused, finally falling back to defend Mexico City against an onslaught of reactionaries commanded by Comonfort. When a supply train headed for the city was taken by Comonfort's troops, the capital was lost.

In May 1863, Juárez presided over the last session of the legislature. "Great has been the reverse we have suffered, but...we shall fight on with greater ardor...because the nation still has life, and strong sons to defend her." Once again Juárez fled the capital toward the wilderness of northern Mexico.

Maximilian and his queen Charlotte—he a Hapsburg without a throne, she a daughter of Leopold I of Belgium—arrived in Mexico in the spring of 1864. For them was established a system by which reactionary notables "elected" them, and they created the monarchy of Mexico, an idea previously considered by Agustín de Iturbide and Aaron Burr.

Driven north were constitutionalist armies, importuning all the while to the United States for arms. The times could not have been darker. In January 1864, a delegation claiming wide support asked Juárez to resign. Juárez refused, writing later that under those conditions, "in which power had no attraction, neither my honor nor my duty permitted me to abandon the power with which the nation had entrusted me."

When Juárez' party decided to travel to Monterrey, the delegation preceding him tried to welcome him to the city with a four-gun salute only to have opponents steal the four cannons and turn them on Juárez as he prepared to enter. Informed of this reversal, Juárez simply spent the night at a nearby ranch and resolved to try again the next day. "Pick up for me the clothesbrushes that I left on the table where I was shaving," he calmly wrote to Margarita that night. "Remember me to our friends, and many embraces for our children.... I am your husband, who loves you."

The next day, the governor of Monterrey, who was doing a thriving business in contraband with the Confederacy, made clear he was in no mood to receive Juárez. When an aide suggested that the presidential carriage proceed with haste, however, Juárez countermanded him: "At a trot," he said. "The President of the Republic cannot run." Before the day was out, however, Juárez, who had been prudent enough to keep the carriage waiting, had to beat a hasty retreat.

In late spring Juárez' last child was born, and in early summer his first grandchild. At the same time, although Juárez could claim no control over his own country, he began to garner sympathy outside his country. In the United States there was considerable contempt for this imposition of foreign power, which was precisely what the Monroe Doctrine was supposed to prevent. The American press identified Juárez' roving presidency with the true expression of the Mexican people. Victor Hugo, William Cullen Bryant, and Hamilton Fish, among others, added their rhetoric to his support. Nevertheless, by autumn 1864 he had been driven north to Monterrey — the irascible governor had earlier fled to the United States — and was forced to send his family first to Matamoros and finally to refuge in New Rochelle, New York. Juárez was so close to capture at one point that his coach was riddled with bullets, before he, too, fled to the United States.

American reporters eventually hounded Doña Margarita as a curiosity. She spoke no English and was defenseless, although a son-in-law did what he could to protect her. When she traveled to Washington and attended, as the wife of the Mexican president, some function, the American press made much of her wearing "jewelry" while her husband lived in poverty, narrowly avoiding capture. Then, two of their three sons died. Margarita made clear in her letters to Juárez that she felt responsible. Juárez feared for her sanity.

"Poor Margarita," Juárez wrote to his son-in-law. "How she will have suffered." He confessed to subordinates that he himself had trouble focusing: "You will appreciate all that I suffer," he wrote after the death of his son José, "from this irreparable loss of a son who was my delight, my pride, and my hope."

On March 21, 1865, while Juárez and his party found brief refuge in Chihuahua, local leaders insisted on celebrating his birthday. When glasses were lifted in a toast to his wife and children, Juárez wept.

Meanwhile, his forces in the field, because of inferior numbers and incompetent leaders, suffered defeat after defeat. What saved the day was Mexico's size. Maximilian's troops, although 35,000 strong, could not be everywhere. In addition, Porfirio Díaz, that other son of Oaxaca, proved a competent commander. When captured, he made a daring escape and set about raising another army.

Maximilian also had another problem: governing a population that included liberals. He issued proclamations that weakened the Church's position, stirring Mexico's oldest resentments. In December 1864, Maximilian confirmed the laws of *La Reforma*, losing the support of the clergy without gaining the adherence of liberals.

In the spring of 1865 the end of the American Civil War encouraged both sides in Mexico. Napoleon III had earlier suggested that American slaveholders colonize the Mexican state of Sonora, and now Maximilian suggested that Southerners bring their slaves into Mexico. Such schemes contributed to stories that Maximilian was losing his grip, and Mexican royalists began deserting his cause. On October 3, 1865, Maximilian decreed that "rebels" be shot, and within a few days a governor, a general, two colonels, and a priest died before firing squads.

Juárez also hoped to get help from the renewed republic to the north, a nation he now felt more comfortable dealing with. The response, however, was more of the same — the U.S. predilection for trying to buy what it needed. When his emissary in Washington informed him of the latest cash-for-acreage proposition in early 1865, Juárez replied: "The idea that some people have, as you tell me, that we should offer part of the national territory in order to obtain help is not only anti-national, but prejudicial to our cause.... The enemy may come and rob us, if that is our destiny, but we do not have to legalize that crime.... If France, the United States or any other nation should take possession of any part of our territory, and if because of our weakness we should be unable to drive it away, we should nevertheless leave alive the right of succeeding generations to recover it." Those remarks would be engraved on the memorial Mexicans built to Juárez.

By the end of 1865, Juárez had been driven out of the country, to El Paso, Texas, and was threatened by a rival for the presidency. The French controlled Chihuahua, just below Juárez' refuge. It was up to Maximilian to destroy himself. U.S. Secretary of State Seward, with the Civil War past, applied pressure to rid the continent of foreign intervention. Maximilian's wife, Charlotte, off in Europe trying in vain to rally support, was going mad. Maximilian faced desertions and the crumbling of an empire that had existed only in his mind. In the countryside, as French and reactionary forces retreated, harsh reprisals began.

It appeared that Juárez had won the war of waiting. "Impatient people," went a Juárez axiom, "are limbs of Satan." Díaz retook Oaxaca, and the constitutionalist Army of the North, augmented by volunteers from Canada and the United States, began to drive south. Juárez hurried along, too, so fast that he almost got himself captured while parading about in front of his troops, exhorting them. "I have received the sermon on what seems to have been my tomfoolery on January 27 at Zacatecas," he wrote to Díaz. "[But] there are circumstances in life in which it is necessary to risk everything, if one wishes to go on living physically and morally, and it is thus that I see the circumstances of that day. I got away with it, and I am happy and satisfied with what I did."

Republican victories continued in 1866, and the French forces that had propped up Maximilian's regime were recalled to take part in European wars in early 1867. It became clear even to Maximilian that the end had come, and he sent a messenger to Díaz, camped at Acatlan, requesting terms. Díaz refused to negotiate, and as the messenger waited out the night to return, Díaz paraded his troops beneath the man's window — in a circle in order to multiply their apparent number. Reactionary forces, without French leadership and arms, fell away before the republicans.

The last major battle was Querétaro, where reactionary forces converged on a plain north of Mexico City. They numbered 9,000. Arriving, battalion by battalion, were republican forces three times that number, including the volunteers from North America and Europe. They had been attracted, in the evaluation of an opponent, by the fact that Juárez was "not a man, but duty incarnate."

The republicans surrounded the reactionaries, and Maximilian was captured trying to escape at night. Imprisoned, he sent a message to Juárez asking for a meeting. Juárez replied that he could have his say at the trial. Pleas for Maximilian's life included those from Victor Hugo and Giuseppe Garibaldi.

The trial took place in a theater. Maximilian refused to attend. A seven-number panel voted: three to banish, four to execute. On June 19, 1867, on the hill where he'd been captured, Maximilian and his two top officers were stood against a wall and surrounded on three sides by four thousand Mexican men at arms. As his final gesture, Maximilian stepped to the side and gave one of his generals the honor of standing in the center.

Knowing that Juárez had spoken of the day he might raise the Mexican flag over the National Palace, Díaz ordered a large flag sewn for the occasion be saved for Juárez' arrival. Juárez arrived late, delayed by rain, unable to pay his escort.

Margarita arrived with her five unmarried daughters and young Benito, her only surviving son. She brought the bodies of their two other sons. The family moved not into the national palace but into a hotel.

The task of rebuilding the country was too much for Juárez, as it was for everyone else. It was 1867, and he had stood for election in 1861. He called for elections, won easily, then had to satisfy himself with minor administrative victories while the army grumbled and priests won back the right to vote.

He suffered a stroke in October 1870, and his beloved Margarita died in their small house the following January. She was only forty-two years old. Juárez invited no one to her secular funeral, but respectful crowds lined the streets anyway.

Late in 1871, with Díaz, whom Juárez was probably holding at bay, and Sebastian Lerdo, Juárez' protégé, both impatient to succeed him, Juárez insisted on winning one more election. In July 1872 he went home from the presidential office complaining of chest pains. With forces loyal to both Díaz and Lerdo already forming in the hills, Juárez died in his bed, attended by one servant. Mexico's "Age of the Indian" was ended.

Pancho Villa
1878–1923
(Mexico)

Political Warrior

With Juárez gone, Porfirio Díaz did not delay long before overthrowing Juárez' successor and assuming dictatorial powers. He established a centralist government, imposed by an army that he dressed in uniforms copied from the French and Prussians. He turned back the clock.

The Spanish Crown had deeded virtually all of Mexico's land to fewer than five thousand colonists, and by the time Juárez became president half of the good land was owned by the Church. *La Reforma* certified some forty thousand transfers in an effort to redistribute the land to its original Indian owners, but when Juárez died the best land remained under control of the haciendas. The Age of the Indian was not an age at all, but a beginning; it had to be sustained. Díaz, however, used the land to enhance his power by distributing more of it to the haciendas. Large landowners were allowed to help themselves to both individual holdings and the Indian *ejidos*, farmed communally. To do this, Díaz chartered seventeen companies to survey traditional lands, allowing the companies to keep one-third of what they "found" uncharted and what they could "prove" unprotected by deeds. The legality of deeds was decided in Díaz courts; decisions were enforced by his ruthless rural police.

By 1910, after more than three decades of Díaz, more than 18 million acres, nearly one-third of the entire national territory, had been surveyed by Díaz' hand-picked companies and the land sold to new and old haciendas. Approximately five thousand Indian villages had lost their farms. Díaz, with his handsomely attired army, was seen abroad by leaders like

150

U.S. President Taft and German Chancellor Bismarck as a great leader. The foreign press described him as a hero.

Doroteo Arango, who would take the name Francisco Villa, was born on June 5, 1878, at the beginning of Díaz' regime. He is said to have weighed twelve pounds at birth. Although Villa was born in Central Mexico, he would claim as his domain the northwestern states near the Rio Grande, especially Chihuahua. It is a dry, barren region just below the land taken from Mexicans to form Texas, New Mexico, and Arizona. Roving country just below the belly of the United States, Villa embodied the dream of many Mexicans; he was an avenging cowboy, a pure, if rough, assertion of Mexican *machismo*, leaving in his dust the Colossus of the North.

At about the age of 17, while breaking horses on a hacienda, Villa killed the owner's son, who, according to legend, had molested Villa's sister. Villa fled to the hills and changed his name on joining the robber band of Ignacio Parra. When Parra was shot down robbing a stagecoach, Villa, who had become known as both intelligent and merciless, took over.

In 1908, when Villa was thirty-one, he retired from banditry, married Luz Corral, and opened a butcher shop in the city of Chihuahua. His markup was substantial: his men rustled the beef he sold. This picture of Villa as a bourgeois merchant in downtown Chihuahua might seem farfetched, but aspects of this image will recur. He was a simple, if exceedingly ruthless, man. Villa did not drink or smoke, and while he chased as many skirts as his shooting eye spotted, there was a bit of the burgher about him. He was stout, with spindly, bowed legs and pigeon toes. Even with his mustachio, when Villa wore a three-piece suit — which he sometimes did, even on horseback — he gave the impression of a German sausage salesman.

But friend and critic alike saw Villa as transformed on horseback. In the saddle, because of the disproportionate size of his torso, his five feet, ten inches seemed taller. The paunch disappeared, and so natural was his equestrian ability that at the head of his cavalry, *los dorados*, "the golden ones," Villa cut such a figure that he was dubbed "The Centaur."

In 1910, as Mexico's definitive revolution toppled Díaz, Villa was recruited by landowners, the very men who would later want him destroyed. During the Revolution, however, landowners needed their own armies even as Italian princes had needed *condotierri*, hired warriors. Villa was hired by supporters of Francisco I. Madero.

Madero, of Jewish ancestry, was a man in the most tenuous of positions. With a coal black beard and an intense glare, Madero was known to his liberal admirers as "immaculate," "incorruptible," even a "redeemer." Although he suffered from the liberal intellectual's tendency to ambivalence, supporters saw him as offering the perfect alternative to the long, oppressive night imposed by Díaz.

Madero was no more a warrior than Juárez. The masses believed in him because he did not appear to be seeking every opportunity to exploit them and because he had, insofar as possible, stood up to Díaz. In the reorganization that followed Díaz' flight, Madero was rising to the top. But the reorganization itself was rough. Even after Madero won his electoral mandate, it had to be defended against those who were unwilling to change. Villa was recruited to defend Madero's ascension to the presidency. He would continue to fight Madero's assassins, carrying on the struggle not as a bandit, but as an instrument of politics, a general, a cavalry tactician.

Because the decade was filled with civil war, it was also filled with opportunity for warriors. At the point Villa was hired, he was commissioned as a captain who commanded but fifteen men. Before long he was a colonel, commanding several thousand.

While only a devoted student of Mexican history should be expected to follow the power shifts that occurred in the capital during the war, the essence of the struggle can be seen in the hinterland. Outside Mexico City, where there were fewer politicians, peasants wanted to prevent centralists from exercising control over the whole nation. Peripheral, peasant-led movements had their own ideas about independence and reform. They insisted on the former and felt themselves capable of shaping, without help from the capital, the latter.

Generally, elitists — however they characterized themselves — opposed the peasant movements. What made the Mexican revolution so drawn out, painful, and seemingly impossible to resolve was that it was struggle in the most fundamental sense — the taking of power from elites who abused it and turning it over to masses who had difficulty administering it.

Villa's place was in the countryside; Madero would articulate liberal ideas, and Villa would fight. Madero's betrayal and murder would bring despair to the faithful, but Villa would go on fighting. In the process, Villa would teach himself to be a tactician.

Although Villa's forte was as a cavalry leader, Mexico's expanse meant there was a need to move troops — and horses — in large numbers over great distances. So a friend of Villa, Rodolfo Fierro, as unschooled as Villa, became a master of rail logistics, seeing to the coal that kept the trains running, moving thousands of troops, giving Villa's Army of the North a mobility beyond that enjoyed by many smaller European armies of the day.

Villa also was able to cope with another tactical problem of modern warfare. Because he could not count on sanctuary in mountain jungles, that traditional stronghold of guerrillas, Villa found himself pursued not only by horsemen but by airplanes. With airplanes, Villa was simply lucky enough to have been born before technology had caught up to him. Fleeing air pursuit, Villa's cavalry had only to cross mountains — over which the sputtering U.S. air force could not fly.

Villa's signal victory for Madero, and a victory for nontechnological warfare, came at the border of the United States in the spring of 1911. Villa, along with Giuseppe Garibaldi — a grandson of the Italian hero who was attracted to the republican cause Madero represented — and Pascual Orrozco, commanded forces that captured stoutly defended Ciudad Juárez. The republican army attacked with little more than rifles, tin-can grenades, and courage. While North Americans watched from their side of the Rio Grande, the peasant troops rooted defenders out of the city and established Madero's claim to the presidency.

If Madero was grateful, however, his commander-in-chief, Victoriano Huerta, was less impressed. The aging Huerta was all spit-and-polish in the sunlight, if a drunkard by night, and he did not appreciate Villa's loose style of command. Villa, for example, followed a managerial philosophy of allowing his troops to raise considerable hell after successful battles. Huerta, a man whose courage and whose orders were not to be questioned, insisted that Villa follow directions sent from headquarters. Villa, dismissing them as administrative foolishness, did not always follow orders. Finally, Huerta ordered that his unlettered subordinate be arrested.

Villa considered the whole affair a bad joke, even when he was clapped in the guardhouse at Huerta's order. He awoke from this interpretation when guards stood him in front of a firing squad. Villa, finally realizing that Huerta had not been kidding, was talking very fast when Madero's brother, a personal emissary, rode up to mediate. Huerta was not mollified, however, and had Villa confined to prison in Mexico City, accusing him of insubordination, subversion, and looting. The first charge was undeniably true and the second ludicrous. As to the third, Villa reasoned, how else was he to pay his troops?

Under guard, Villa was taken to Mexico City on June 7, 1912. There, federal prisons had become gathering places for men who had lost their grip on power. Villa met a principal lieutenant of Zapata, Gildardo Magaña, a polished urbanite who had joined Zapata's agrarian revolution. Magaña, who had studied to be a priest, began teaching Villa how to read and write. It is uncertain how much Villa learned, for after six months, on the day after Christmas when the compound was filled with visitors, Villa put on a pair of sun glasses, tried as best he could to look like a lawyer, and walked out. He next turned up in El Paso, where a newspaperman stumbled across him and wrote the predictable profile of a pistol-toting badman. Villa declined to dignify the story and refused to be interviewed.

The war raged on. In February 1913, reactionary cadets from the national military school seized the national palace and the federal prison, freeing two of Madero's principal adversaries. Fighting raged street by street. Because the fighting was confined to such a concentrated urban area, the damage within that core was the worst of any of Mexico's civil conflicts.

At the presidential palace, Madero's personal guard, the members of which had turned against him, burst into his office and began firing. A friend jumped in front of Madero, saving Madero's life but sacrificing his own. At that point the guardsmen hesitated, shamed by their own villainy, and were talked back into the hall by another Madero associate in the room as Madero wept over the loss of his friend.

Huerta played the unrest to his own advantage. Rather than defend Madero, Huerta grabbed the opportunity, reached agreement with the reactionaries, and, when Madero resigned a week later, ordered his arrest. Henry Lane Wilson, the U.S. ambassador to Mexico, called together the diplomatic corps to announce proudly that he had known Madero would be imprisoned and had encouraged it. Madero's downfall, Wilson predicted, would mean "peace, progress and prosperity."

Madero and his vice president, informed that they would be allowed to go into exile, left jail. They were in a carriage being escorted out of the city when they were stopped by a mob. Their guard stood aside, and both were killed. Huerta promoted the lieutenant and corporal who were in charge of the "guard," and both eventually became generals in Huerta's army.

Madero's faithful followers were both saddened and enraged. Villa, still in Texas, learned of events in the capital and reentered Mexico to begin gathering troops. Huerta, his alcoholism a severe hindrance, would not last much longer, but he clung to power while another coveted his place. This was Venustiano Carranza, a governor who dubbed his followers "constitutionalists" and who was able to recruit to his cause none other than Woodrow Wilson.

Wilson, a former university president, had vowed to "teach the Latin Americans to elect good men." Carranza, presumably, was his idea of a beginning toward that end. Wilson was also well aware that the Germans— who needed oil as much as Americans—had their talons in several Mexico City politicians. Part of Wilson's purpose was to minimize German influence in Mexico. For Villa, this unholy alliance between Wilson and Carranza meant a two-front war.

It took Villa no more than thirty days after his return to Mexico to gather 3,000 troops. They would follow him as long as they were well led and could count on plunder. Political idealism was at a minimum. They faced federal troops who followed their officers only because of regional prejudices, or because soldiering was the best available job, or because of naked fear. Federal officers shot troopers who did not fight to their satisfaction. There would be instances when Villa, about to execute captured federal officers, would have volunteers for the firing squad step forward from among the ranks of the captured federal troops. They wanted retribution, and Villa would give it to them. Then he would recruit the troops, for if Villa did not represent political ideals, he did represent a raw freedom, a kind of equality that common men understood. His pronouncements were simple promises that rang as true and were as easily fulfilled as any politician's promises.

Villa's army soon controlled all of the northeast except the cities of Torreón, Chihuahua, and Juárez, all three positioned along the long, north-south highway between El Paso and Mexico City. He took Torreón, closest to Mexico City, on October 1, 1913. Then he turned north toward Chihuahua, intending to take it and isolate Juárez, two hundred miles farther north, hard by the U.S. border. But he failed to take Chihuahua, so, rather than exhaust his resources, he circled the city and headed north for Juárez. On the way, he happened across a federal troop train on its way south.

As the train crossed the barren prairie, Villa's men stopped it and captured its passengers. Villa ordered the train backed up to a small station, where he sent a telegram north along the line to the commander of the garrison at Juárez. Engine broke down, Villa wired. A new engine and five box cars were needed. Then he sent a second telegraph message: A large force of rebels is approaching. What should be done?

The garrison commander took the sensible course, ordering the troop train to return to the safety of the garrison at Juárez. The train rolled into Juárez late on the night of November 15.

Many federal troops were shot down as they ran from the barracks in their underwear. When the federal troops were able to gather themselves and counter-attack, Villa repelled them. Rather than prolong his attack, he pulled out of town and headed back south toward Chihuahua. There, the dispirited garrison, informed of events at Juárez, abandoned the city on November 29. Villa declared himself the governor of Chihuahua.

By early 1914, Villa and Carranza in the north and Zapata in the south had squeezed Huerta's federal forces into a narrow strip between Mexico City and the Gulf Coast at Vera Cruz. President Wilson, trying to help Carranza, had already embargoed arms shipments to Mexico and now took the final plunge to force out Huerta.

With a U.S. fleet already floating off shore to stop the Germans from delivering arms to the government, Huerta's agents made the mistake of arresting U.S. marines on shore leave in Tampico. Huerta's government in Mexico City, realizing immediately that it had picked up a rattlesnake, apologized. Wilson, however, had the excuse he wanted. He ordered the occupation of Vera Cruz. Huerta's government crumbled; Carranza entered Mexico City.

Neither Villa nor Zapata, however, accepted Carranza as president or, as he wanted himself known, "First Chief." They had fought, at the very least, to avenge Madero; certainly they wanted to establish the states' rights to govern their own affairs; and, ideally, they both wished to institute reforms. They had not fought to replace a drunken tyrant with a brazen opportunist.

Wilson liked Carranza—but then American presidents had liked Díaz—although both Villa and Zapata understood that the only reason Carranza was in the national palace was because of the efforts of his brilliant field commander, Alvaro Obregón. They kept their forces intact, and there was stalemate. A convention to settle affairs was called in November 1914. It broke down in acrimony.

Carranza announced to foreign governments that Villa's Army of the North—30,000 fighters at its strongest—constituted a grave threat to the republic. Villa replied: If my army is such a threat, why don't you and I jointly commit suicide to settle everything? Carranza did not reply.

No one was strong enough to hold Mexico City for long, and in December Villa and Zapata went there to meet each other for the first time. The two guerrilla leaders appeared ill at ease with each other. They agreed that Carranza was, in Zapata's words, a "bastard." They tossed off a celebratory drink of brandy together, Zapata downing his impassively, the exuberant Villa nearly choking because he was unaccustomed to liquor. Zapata left to lead his forces against Carranza troops occupying Puebla. Villa promised he would send Zapata arms, including artillery—a promise he was unable to keep.

When Villa returned northward, Obregón chased him. Their opposing forces would conclude the civil war in the north, writing the final chapter in terms of modern warfare. Villa was of the past. Obregón was schooled in the trench warfare that was defining warfare in Europe. Villa knew frontal assault by cavalry, the tactic of wars gone by. Furthermore, his troops knew only the frenetic pace of constant fighting; without the discipline of the saddle, they were at loose ends. As they moved northward, a trusted lieutenant simply detached the train car carrying millions of pesos of payroll for his own men, and rolled off.

In March and April of 1915, Villa met Obregón and his trenches and barbed wire and machine guns and artillery. On the plains outside Celaya, near where Juárez' troops had beaten Maximilian, Villa's cavalry charged Obregón's fortified positions. After two great battles, there was no clear victor. Villa was pursued northward, barely surviving. When part of his troops were encircled, their commander escaped only by leading his cavalry outside the ring, telegraphing federal officers conflicting messages, then attacking from behind in their confusion. Villa's troops were reunited at Chihuahua.

Villa was running out of places to retreat to. Wilson spread troops along the long border to keep Mexicans out and guns from going across. He guaranteed Carranza's troops safe passage over U.S. territory to flank Villa as he was driven northward. Cornered — and perhaps trying to embarrass Carranza — Villa attacked the Texas town of Columbus the night of March 9, 1916. In response, Wilson sent Gen. John "Black Jack" Pershing in pursuit — a caravan of 10,000 soldiers, 9,000 horses, and reconnaissance biplanes that could not fly high enough to get over Mexico's mountains.

Carranza complained that this was going too far; Mexican sovereignty was being violated. Wilson ignored him. The upshot — except for once again training U.S. officers, like Lt. George Patton, for other wars — was that Pershing had more trouble with Carranza's troops than Villa's. Indignant that their country had again been invaded, Carranza's officers were hostile. Pershing never even got a glimpse of Villa or his army.

"I do not believe these people can ever establish a government among themselves that will stand," Pershing wrote to a friend in frustration. "Carranza has no more control over local commanders or of states or municipalities than if he lived in London." For his part, Villa's manifestos, issued from traveling headquarters, characterized North Americans as "barbarians."

Pershing never got close. On March 27, 1916, not three weeks after the attack on Columbus, Villa was shot from behind, either by accident or by a guerrilla who, impressed into service, feigned an accident. The bullet hit Villa above the right knee, the first time Villa had ever been shot. He very nearly died. The whole time Pershing raged about the countryside looking for him, Villa was holed up, recuperating.

Villa retired and outlived Carranza, who was shot by his own bodyguard in 1920 and succeeded by Obregón. Villa found contentment as a member of the bourgeoisie, investing in real estate. But, in the end, the landed class got him.

It is unclear whether Villa's death was motivated by an old grudge, a recent aggravation, an old political hatred, or the threat that Villa, a natural leader, might reenter political combat. It is possible that Obregón was behind it. It is known that the ambush was planned and executed by a rancher who had never met Villa.

On July 23, 1923, Villa and six friends rode in a convertible to Hidalgo del Parral, Chihuahua, to pick up payroll for Villa's employees. Three men were in the back seat. Two bodyguards rode the running boards. Another man rode in the front seat, while Villa drove.

Eight men, who had carefully planned the assault, charged out of a house they had rented for three months, waiting. They poured pistol and rifle fire into the car.

As the car careened to the side of the street and stalled, Villa, like an enraged bull, was the only one able to get his pistol from its holster to get off a shot. As his friends died around him, Villa fired and killed an attacker with a bullet through the heart. Then he slumped across the front seat, twelve bullets in his torso, four in his head.

What is most overlooked about the man who called himself Pancho Villa is that he represented deep sentiments of large numbers of Mexicans. He was not a bandit, but a political figure who spoke for simple people, people whose politics should be regarded more, not less, seriously precisely because of the simple nature of their needs. They believed in him.

Mexican historian Pedro Vives obviously recounts with pleasure — and in dialect — the story of one peasant telling another of how Villa's body was dug up three years after being buried so the head could be displayed — "in order," says the peasant, "that the people not keep saying that he's still alive."

Emiliano Zapata
c. 1880–1919
(Mexico)

Indian Reformer

Estimates of Zapata's year of birth range from 1877 to 1883, making him the same age as Villa, although their stories are different in both style and substance.

Elders of tiny Anenecuilco elected Emiliano Zapata president of their council in 1909, when he was approximately thirty years old. His principal task was to represent the village in its claims to native lands, part of a widespread effort by Mexican Indians to re-claim land taken by Europeans and mestizos who drew up documents based on nothing but force of arms. The elders chose Zapata because he was from a family that had prospered through hard work, and because Zapata, except for a brief period in Mexico City, had stayed in Anenecuilco. Although much of his past is unknown—he was the ninth of ten children, four of whom survived to adulthood—it appears that Zapata, for some teenage transgression, faced conscription into the army but was given the chance instead to work as a groom in Mexico City. It is said he returned to Anenecuilco embittered by the realization that too frequently horses lived better than Mexicans. But Zapata was not the first to have reached such a conclusion, and he was not the creator of a following. He was himself pushed ahead of the most powerful political movement of his day: the Indians' claims to their land.

Zapata's leadership consisted of balancing the efforts of regional chieftains like himself and of holding them together lest they lose heart and succumb to the bribery and threats of the central government. Because at the turn of the century new political ideas were finding expression all over the world, these unschooled, country people attracted leftist intellectuals who saw in them the natural foundation for widespread reform.

Reactionaries distrusted the Indian movements not only for their own force, but because of the way in which they focused the ideas of others. Zapata, for example, was rumored to have been influenced, while in Mexico City, by an anarcho-syndicalist who later led an abortive invasion of Baja, California. But the movement that propelled Zapata remained rural and indigenous; it was articulated as the "Plan of Ayala," land reform based on ideas that harkened back to those of Juárez and the *puros*.

In general, economists stress the importance of agrarian movements because they draw exceptional strength by mixing tradition with modern design. Scholars have documented scores of cases in Mexico where villages, independently of each other, asserted claims that were organized logically and were unsullied by personal greed. Peasants insisted that they could work the land more efficiently — with greater benefit to consumers and to the national economy — than could the *hacendados* who had stolen it. Today, Article 27 of Mexico's revolutionary constitution of 1917 is the foundation — or, perhaps, the unfulfilled idea — for agrarian reform. Article 27 directly resulted from pressure created by peasant movements like the one organized by Emiliano Zapata Salazar.

Unlike Villa, who made up a name for himself, Zapata bore a patronym and matronym that were part of history in Morelos, a small state just southeast of Mexico City. The name "Zapata" appears in records of the revolution against the Crown in 1810. Of José Salazar, his mother's father, there is the story of how he, as a boy, smuggled tortillas, tequila, and gunpowder through Spanish lines during the siege of Cuautla, a Morelos town that commands passage to both the south and west from the capital. Morelos's strategic location, in fact, would continue to be important to Zapata's efforts.

Throughout Mexican history, the state of Morelos — named for a revolutionary priest who insisted on the need to return their land to the Indians — has been important both because it is close to the capital and because it is agriculturally rich. It was in Morelos in 1869, when the state was chartered, that Porfirio Díaz ran for governor, hoping to begin his succession to Juárez' legacy. Díaz' defeat helped make Morelos' reputation for dissent and earned Díaz' enmity. By Zapata's lifetime, Morelos, still known for independence, was responsible for one-third of all sugar products in Mexico.

When Zapata was elected by the village elders, the specific dispute he was expected to help resolve was typical. Small farmers around Villa de

Ayala claimed that their ancestral lands were infringed upon by a neighboring hacienda. The farmers were planting in this disputed margin, and the hacendado wanted to collect rent.

From this instance, one of many disputes, a movement took its name and grew. The Indians' ancient assertions conflicted with those of the landowners who supported Díaz' harsh dictatorship. Morelos, especially, smarted under the whip of Díaz' oppression, and when the dictatorship gave way to Mexico's revolution of 1910 — the world's first socialist revolution — great, fundamental forces elevated simple men.

Francisco Madero emerged as the national "redeemer," and Zapata was linked to his future and lifted to prominence. What allowed Zapata to sustain himself, his military skills, were, like Villa's, learned on the job. There was ample time, for the "revolution" dragged on and on in virulent civil war. First came the fight to overthrow Díaz and put Madero in office. In May 1911, two days before Villa and others took Ciudad Juárez to establish Madero's regime in the north, Zapata successfully led 4,000 guerrillas against 400 federal soldiers defending Cuautla, assuring control of the south. For Zapata, however, that was just the beginning because he represented a movement that required more than military success. It required reform, and Madero's tendency to ambivalence caught Zapata in a dilemma.

While newspapers characterized him as "Attilla the Hun," he faced the responsibility of leading reform even as he had led his peasant army. His troops were returning to their villages by June, leaving him at the head of no more than an idea. Furthermore, landowners, too, had supported Madero. Now they complained that claims were being made on their land. Indians were making the preposterous argument that their deeds were spurious, or at least antedated by native rights. Madero called Zapata to the capital to give voice to the landowners' fears.

When Zapata returned to Morelos, it was becoming clear that his fight was not with one side of Mexican politics — neither liberals nor reactionaries could make it without landowners' support — but with the entire Mexican system of land tenure. The Plan of Ayala, that is to say, represented a profound threat, and the government was not long in responding. That summer while Zapata — already the father of at least one child — was being married to Josepha Espejo in Villa de Ayala, he was informed at the reception that more than a thousand troops commanded by Victoriano Huerta, the most powerful general in Mexico, had entered Morelos.

The landowners wanted the state under control, and they found a willing champion in Huerta, the disciplinarian who had ordered Villa shot. Of the Morelos farmers his report asserted, "These people are all bandits." He had overridden Madero's efforts to mediate and was pursuing Zapata to execute him. Zapata had become, in the words of a landowner, "a constant menace to the interests of cultivated Society."

Zapata fled, once bursting from the back door of a hacienda and dashing into the fields on foot as troops entered the main gate. Three days after his escape he was encountered, riding a mule, in the mountains of Puebla, eighty miles away. But the ferocity of Huerta's pursuit, rather than intimidating the peasants of Morelos, enflamed them, creating an idol. People who had called themselvles *maderistas* became *zapatistas*. By October 1911, Zapata commanded an army of 1,500 guerrillas and had pushed within fifteen miles of Mexico City.

During that autumn Mexico's agrarian revolution was defined more clearly than during *La Reforma* fifty years earlier. Zapata and his contemporaries wrote their program with a singleness of purpose that was unprecedented. "I am resolved," Zapata wrote to a friend with existential ferocity, "to struggle against everything and everybody."

A series of pronouncements informed the central government that its troops must be withdrawn from Morelos; "General Zapata" would keep order. The Plan of Ayala asked for small farmers to get the "justice they deserve as to lands" and that that justice be codified in a national agrarian law. Justice, the Plan of Ayala made clear, demanded expropriation of land from "monopolists."

John Womack, Jr., in his definitive biography of Zapata, notes the Plan of Ayala's "sense of history." Similarly, a Mexican psychologist suggests that Indian culture, as expressed in Juárez' and Zapata's leadership, has provided for a large proportion of the Mexican population "the necessary continuity of the psychic life in successive generations," a cultural assertion that cannot be broken.

Nevertheless, in early 1912, Huerta tried to end resistance with a strategy of "resettlement." If a village was deemed hostile, it was destroyed. The government identified outspoken opponents and burned their homes. In February 1912, Zapata's sister, mother-in-law, and two of his wife's sisters were taken hostage, and, for a while, the dissent subsided in a state tired of war. In a conciliatory gesture, the national assembly discussed a bill to prohibit further exploitation of Indian common lands, but took no action.

Then Madero's government fell, and Huerta took sole power. The possibility of conciliation ended. Huerta conceived of a bizarre plan to transport from the north as many as 20,000 field workers. The result would not be particularly efficient, he conceded, but at least the northerners would be less susceptible to recruitment by Zapata.

Some relief came in early 1913 with the inauguration of Woodrow Wilson, who was unwilling to recognize Huerta's government. As the closest thing Mexico had to a pacifier, Venustiano Carranza, safe in the north, announced his idea for a period of reconciliation. Huerta would have none of it. In a speech to Mexico City's exclusive Jockey Club, Huerta said that he would control Morelos using some "procedures that are not sanctioned by law but are indispensable for the national welfare." He predicted victory in about a month.

The effect was to force Zapata to organize a real army. Volunteering help was Manuel Palafox, a slightly built, short man in his late twenties with a pock-marked face. Palafox was a hustler whose instinct for survival had given him certain important managerial skills. He became the revolution's office manager. As the line was drawn between Huerta and Zapata, others from outside Morelos insinuated themselves into the movement. Morelos took on the characteristics of a government in exile.

Huerta's troops were able to take and hold the cities, but did not have the strength to reach into the countryside. In rural areas they could only destroy property, controlling nothing. When, in a typical maneuver, the government took Cuernavaca, the capital of Morelos, Zapata struck at the five hundred–man garrison in Jonacatepec, on the periphery of the state. Taking stores and guns, Zapata offered a pardon to any man who promised not to fight the revolution. The garrison commander joined Zapata and was put in charge of training troops and buying arms.

While Zapata's rebel government attracted outsiders, it was the planners, the intellectuals, who made their way to Morelos from the city. The fighters were natural leaders whose troops had known them since childhood. Close to Zapata was his older brother, Eufemio, a taller man whose black handlebar mustache was even more formidable that Zapata's. Eufemio had taken his share of a modest inheritance when their father died and drifted off to try his hand at business; he returned to fight.

One effect of local leaders' commanding his units was that Zapata sometimes had trouble in their seeing the greater scheme of things. Zapata commanded by persuasion and, if that failed, by threat. At one point "persuasion" meant threatening to rustle fifty cattle from a chieftain's territory if he didn't immediately send the six rifles Zapata had been asking for. His officers and men were continually being enticed to switch sides.

Socially and economically, the result of the warfare in Morelos was chaos. Fugitives from government oppression, forced to flee their villages, set up camps. Zapata's rebels encouraged the camps because they kept workers out of the fields. Morelos landowners had to contract with the government to keep one-third of their workers from conscription, registering them and arming them for self-defense, in order to maintain production. Homeless children roamed the countryside, and at least one group of widows formed under the leadership of a virago known as "La China" and traveled from town to town, some dressed in feathered finery liberated from shops.

Women also fought. In 1911, a *New York Times* reporter noted their "spectacular part" in battle. Juana Belén Gutiérrez de Mendoza, a teacher, took up the cause of poor Indian children, founded a newspaper, and was imprisoned for criticism of the government. She eventually made her way to Morelos, joined Zapata's army, and rose to the rank of colonel.

As the war dragged on into 1913, atrocities committed by the Huerta government became so blatant that some members of the puppet national assembly threatened to walk out in protest. Huerta simply had the deputies arrested, all 110 of them, and assumed dictatorial powers. But Huerta was unable to bring the country to heel; it was too large, with too many armies rampaging in too many directions. When the government pulled troops out of the south to counter threats in the north, Zapata's forces would spill out into the neighboring states of Puebla and Guerrero.

Zapata was unable, however, to establish and protect a strategic axis between Acapulco, on the Pacific Coast, and Mexico City. The Plan of Ayala excited the imagination of leftist planners, but his peasant army could not secure enough territory to give his ideology a base. Supply lines for guns and ammunition — which ended as mule trails into the mountains — stretched for hundreds of miles. Any chance of winning lay in an alliance with Villa, Zapata decided by the autumn of 1913. Partly to demonstrate the strength of his southern army for such an alliance, Zapata focused on Chilpancinango, the capital of Guerrero, and took it. It was the first time he had been able to take a state capital.

In the spring of 1914, Wilson precipitated the fall of Huerta with the brief occupation of Vera Cruz. As Huerta's troops flowed toward that port on the Gulf Coast, Zapata's rebels flooded into the unguarded area left behind. For the first time, Zapata occupied the six district seats of Morelos; he laid siege to Cuernavaca. But when Huerta fled into exile the next summer, the government was left to Carranza, an old Díaz supporter widely recognized for the opportunist he was. Zapata's forces were still contained in Morelos and parts of adjoining states. Now the forces of Carranza, who was endorsed by President Wilson and who chose for himself the title of "First Chief," stood between Villa and Zapata.

In late 1914, Villa and Zapata agreed to meet in Mexico City. Womack cautions against equating the two forces. Villa, he notes, was "the very incarnation of irregularity." His supporters were "more a force of nature than of politics, the Villista Party was commotion rampant." Zapata's troops, on the other hand, demonstrated a discipline rare for any civil war. "If they plundered," Womack suggests, "it was not for fun, but on business."

Before the meeting Zapata was reluctant, apparently distrustful. Because neither man liked cities, they first met in Xochimilco, the site of the "floating gardens," and, more important for Zapata, closer to his territory. It was like a meeting of an ostrich and an ox. Their personal differences are evident from photographs and were remarked by observers. Zapata's sister traveled with him, and a North American observer speculated that "everything she had on her person could probably have been purchased for about $5.00 American money." Villa, contrarily, was the height of fashion, donning an English-style pith helmet. When they were induced to enter the capital and pose for photographers at the national palace, it was Villa who was coaxed into the ornate presidential chair, its carved eagle above his head. He wore an officer's uniform with braided cuffs and carried a billed military cap like the ones that Díaz made his officers wear so they would look European.

Zapata wore the clothes of Morelos—tight pants for riding, a waist-length jacket, a huge sombrero. Photographs show Villa laughing. Zapata broods.

They could agree on their hatred of Carranza; Villa called him arrogant, Zapata called him a son of a bitch. But there matters rested. Villa was no help to Zapata in getting ammunition; he had trouble, despite his claims, getting it himself. Villa rode north, back to his anarchic, politically meaningless war and within months was defeated by Obregón at Celaya. Zapata went back to Morelos, to the last months of his revolution.

Carranza had earlier suggested alliance with Zapata, but Zapata regarded him a Cassius. "I see in him much ambition." Zapata wrote to an aide, "and an inclination to fool the people." In his refusal to compromise, critics began to see in Zapata a fatal egotism, but he persisted. "Revolutions will come and revolutions will go," Zapata told an emissary from Carranza, "but I will continue with mine."

Continue it did, tilting to the left as it went, although it is estimated that one-fifth of Morelos' population had been killed in the fighting against Huerta's oppression. Zapata stayed in the field, where he seemed more at home than dealing with the intellectuals planning the revolution. This meant he left headquarters affairs to Palafox, whose response to the heightened power was to abuse it, alienating field commanders by trying to impose control. When an informal delegation from Carranza arrived, Palafox, acting on his own, insulted men who knew something of agrarian reform themselves.

But Zapata's aides insisted that Carranza accept the Plan of Ayala and its explicit call for the return of Indian lands. And there questions of style exacerbated the dispute. In conferences and convention halls, as Mexicans tried to define themselves and their reborn country, there was a great deal of individual posturing, fiery speeches of hollow words. Zapata withdrew even further.

The Plan of Ayala was given whatever legal force Zapata could confer upon it in Morelos, but in the capital another law, "Article 8," was promulgated. It said that anyone opposing the revolution could have his land

and property expropriated. But Article 8 went unenforced outside Morelos; the revolution bogged down in a three-way argument among Zapata, Villa, and Carranza over who was the most revolutionary.

In Morelos, Zapata's government, galvanized by the civil war and having attracted planners from all over, overcame old antagonisms among villages and implemented programs beyond land reform, suggesting a model for the whole country. Schools got redesigned curricula. Members of the graduating classes of 1913 and 1914 of the National School of Agriculture arrived (as they did in several states) to help with land reform. The political climate was such that in some places it was dangerous to appear nonrustic — without the white cotton outfits of campesinos.

But, meanwhile, Carranza's army occupied Mexico City. Although it withdrew, his dominance was made clear. His principal commander was Alvaro Obregón, who, no less than Huerta, intended to extend that dominance to the outlying states. To Morelos he assigned Pablo Gonzales, an orphan who had grown up in city streets, a sometime peddler who emigrated to the United States but returned to make a career in Carranza's army. He had never led troops in a significant battle, and one way of winning notice would be to break the back of Zapata's government. He rescinded all state laws and organized the systematic theft of sugar, timber, and other resources from the villages. He started to coopt Zapata's field commanders. Into 1915, Carranza grew stronger.

Zapata's field commanders were trouble enough in their own right. One, a mystic, was convinced that God would ride with him and dictate whether Carranza forces should be allowed to pass. Another commander, who followed more traditional theology and tactics, threatened to shoot him. Zapata intervened, but when a patrol of the latter commander's men happened upon the mystic, they did, indeed, settle the dispute. They shot him.

Carranza had gotten Wilson's — that is, Pershing's — help in more or less pacifying the north. He then sought to prove he could control the south. In May, government troops took Cuernavaca, introducing the airplane, which bombed Zapata's troops. Zapata, arriving late for the battle, was nearly captured. Carranza introduced harsher and harsher measures, taking on the ugly demeanor of his predecessors. In Cuautla, a priest was hanged as a Zapata spy; in Jiutepec 225 prisoners were given a hasty military "trial" and shot en masse; in Tlaltizapan, which had served as Zapata headquarters, 286 people — 132 men, 112 women, and 42 children — were executed. By the end of the spring more than 1,200 prisoners had been sent by train to forced-labor camps in tropical Yucatan. Wilson's emissaries watched.

Zapata could have compromised, but his advisors insisted that he hold out for ideological purity. Field commanders, however, were inclined to blame purists for prolonging the agony. It was suggested that Zapata go into hiding to let Mexico City's always volatile political antagonisms take their toll on Carranza's government. Yet another suggestion was terror.

While it appears that Zapata held out against the idea of conducting a campaign of terror, he was forced to use only small guerrilla units—he could not risk a broad confrontation—and such a strategy must sacrifice control. His guerrillas tried to disrupt mills and factories and destory rail heads. For every act of that kind, however, Carranza commanders ordered executions. Finally, in late 1916, Zapata's troops stopped a train and resorted to abject terror, killing four hundred soldiers and civilians.

Eventually Zapata was able to reorganize along traditional military lines, acquiring medical and engineering units. As late as 1917 it looked as if Zapata might prevail when Carranza forces were withdrawn from Morelos. The U.S. embargo on arms was lifted, and Zapata was able to re-enter Cuernavaca. The concept of agrarian reform had been legitimated, at least to the point that it was under discussion in a constitutional convention.

Nevertheless, defections and intrigue continued in an environment now polluted by the black market prices engendered by World War I. In early 1918, Zapata lost Palafox, who for all his wild-eyed unpredictability, had in many respects been the soul of the agrarian movement. He had alienated men with his insults, his intransigence, and his zeal, and, in the end, he lost his most important supporter by turning Zapata against him with a homosexual indiscretion. So infuriated was Zapata that he almost ordered Palafox shot.

At mid-year, Zapata, seeking some way out of his impasse, contacted Obregón to suggest that he revolt against Carranza. It did not work, and by the end of the year Carranza forces, again under the command of the former peddler, Pablo Gonzáles, drove back into Morelos. Gonzáles had learned to be cautious, and even a revolt against Carranza would now invite U.S. intervention. Zapata could do nothing but sit tight. North American journalists called it the end of Zapata.

But in the spring of 1919, he pulled one last trick. A Carranza colonel, something of a hot-shot cavalry officer named Jesús Guajardo, had sworn to meet Zapata face to face. Before that could happen, however, Guajardo was ignominiously clapped in the guardhouse for tarrying at the cantina after Gonzáles had ordered him into the field. Hearing of Guajardo's plight, Zapata saw his chance for a coup. He wrote to Guajardo: Why not switch sides?

There were spies everywhere, and the letter was delivered to Gen. Gonzáles.

At first, Gonzáles used the letter to imply that Guajardo was a traitor; he humiliated him, driving him to tears of frustration. Then the general gave Guajardo the chance to redeem himself. He was instructed to play along with Zapata. A meeting was arranged.

Each was to arrive with a complement of only about thirty troops. Guajardo showed up with six hundred, including a machine-gun squad. Zapata and Guajardo talked, but Guajardo declined an invitation to dinner, saying he wanted to go back to pick up ammunition that had just arrived at his camp. They agreed to meet again at Chinameca hacienda, just thirty-five miles from Villa de Ayala.

At about 8:30 Thursday morning, April 10, 1919, Zapata rode down from his campsite with 150 men. He and Guajardo conferred at a small shop outside the hacienda. Because there was a report of Carranza troops in the area, they broke up the meeting and sent out patrols, Zapata riding with his patrol. When Zapata returned about 1:30 in the afternoon, all of Guajardo's troopers were inside the hacienda wall. The only Zapata trooper inside was an aide negotiating for delivery of 12,000 rounds of ammunition. Invited inside, Zapata said no.

A bit later, invited inside again, Zapata said yes. As he rode through the gate into the courtyard on a horse Guajardo had brought him as a gift, Guajardo's guard presented arms. Then they turned their sights on Zapata and fired. The aide, inside, rose from his chair and was immediately killed. Others, outside, were shot from their saddles trying to flee.

On his way back to Cuautla with Zapata's body draped over a horse, Guajardo stopped at Villa de Ayala to telephone ahead with the news. By the time the body was brought to Gen. Gonzáles and dumped to the ground, it was after dark, but Gonzáles examined it with a flashlight. The general made sure the body was well photographed, although some of Zapata's people, even after seeing the photos, refused to believe Zapata was dead.

Dolores Jiménez y Muro
Juana Belén Gutiérrez de Mendoza
Hermila Galindo de Topete
1910–1920

Women of the Mexican Revolution

At the turn of the century in Mexico, two ideologies converged to give impetus to the Mexican Revolution. Those forces were socialism and feminism, and while the former would not endure, the latter would impel Mexican women to create for themselves a unique and lasting place in their country's history. Because it was a popular revolution, a movement patched together out of many groups of intellectuals and poor people, the Revolution needed all the help it could get. There was much work to be done, and women played an important role. From the beginning, women were propagandists against Porfirio Díaz, and several were imprisoned for their words. When the shooting began, women, sometimes as leaders, fought and died beside men. Mexican women accompanied whole armies on the move by rail, on foot, and on horseback, foraging for food, keeping the soldiers in the field, and earning the respectful name, *soldaderas*.

Although their concerns were relegated to an undercurrent in the flow of a male-dominated society, Mexican women have long had their own pantheon of heroines. These exemplars were women who asserted themselves despite conditions that hindered their self-expression at every step. *Sor Juana*, for example, provided literary inspiration, while *La Corregidora* stood as a model for more combative, political instincts.

Sister Juana Inés de la Cruz, christened Juana de Asbaje y Ramírez in 1648, was the illegitimate child of a Basque captain and a Creole woman, the youngest of three sisters. Proving herself a precocious student, she was made a lady in waiting to the viceroy's wife. She left the court in 1667, when she was not yet nineteen, to enter a convent. In time, she entered another convent said to have a library of 4,000 volumes, probably an exaggeration since that would have made it the largest private library in the New World. In 1689, she published in Madrid her first volume of poetry and, in 1692, her second. Through her poetry, Sister Juana openly criticized the Spanish-Mexican cult of *machismo.*

Josefa Ortíz de Domínguez was the wife of a royal official, *Corregidor* Miguel Domínguez, in 1810, at the time Spain's colonial yoke was being broken. She conspired with and protected revolutionaries, and is best known for saving Father Hidalgo from capture.

These women head a long list of those who demonstrated revolutionary zeal, including Leona Vicario, a wealthy woman who joined insurgents in the countryside in 1810, and the saintly Beatríz González Ortega, who turned her school into a hospital during the Revolution of 1910.

That kind of feminine leadership formed a foundation for emancipation that began well before the Revolution of 1910. For reasons not completely clear, Mexican feminists began to register advances even under the regime of Porfirio Díaz, the dictator who managed to keep the great bulk of his country at heel. Anna Macías has noted: "When one considers that up to 1856 Sor Juana's dream of higher education for women had never been realized, the advances made by Mexican women between 1869 and 1910 were really remarkable and parallel other achievements of the Porfirian era, such as the building of railroads and a telegraph system."

Furthermore, it was during the series of civil wars that threw off Díaz' domination and shaped modern Mexico that women burst forth with a force that became legendary. "Women have taken a spectacular part in the revolution," wrote an anonymous *New York Times* correspondent in the issue of May 10, 1911. "With the first outbreak in Puebla in November, a woman of the family of Serdan made appeals to the people from house tops amid flying bullets to join the small bands fighting within, and was wounded. . . . At Casas Grandes, Patricinia Vásquez took an active part in the battle. In Guerrero, Margarita Neri, a wealthy girl and landowner, furious over excessive taxes, placed herself at the head of 200 laborers two months ago. She is now said to command 1,000 men under Gen. Figueroa."

There was example after example, a flowering of feminism under the harshest condition, war. Society was profoundly changed. Of that change, Angeles Mendieta Alatorre writes, "For the first time, women sensed and understood an undeniable truth: they were able to marry for love and not out of necessity because their preparation offered them economic independence — the ability and the determination to make their own decisions."

This change had to be wrought in a society in which *hembrismo*, or "femaleness," had been coined as the term denoting the submissive obverse of *machismo*. The changing ground rules of sexual relationships were portrayed by John Reed, the U.S. correspondent, who wrote of the casual alliances — "six-peso weddings" — encouraged by the Revolution. But tradition persisted, as described by Reed in his account of the *soldadera* "Elizabetta," whom he encountered "trudging stolidly along in the dust behind Captain Félix Romero's horse — and had trudged so for thirty miles. He never spoke to her, never looked back, but rode on unconcernedly. Sometimes he would get tired of carrying his rifle and hand it back to her to carry. . . . [He] had ordered her to follow him. Which she did, unquestioningly, after the custom of her sex and country."

That custom was radically, savagely reversed by stories of female officers and heroines among rebel forces, like *La Chata*, "Flatnose," and *La Corredora*, "the Scout." In Zapata's army there were several *coronelas*, like María de la Luz Espinosa Barrera, a motherless child of Yautepec, Morelos, who killed her husband's lover, then went off to serve the Revolution well for five years. There was Margarita "Pepita" Neri (mentioned by the *Times* correspondent above), who was described as somber, brave, and cruel, and who in reality came off the streets to better her position. She rose to lead hundreds of men, demonstrating a bestiality that could shock the toughest among them. And there was Jovita Valdovinos, daughter of a rebel chieftain, who demanded such perversities of her subordinates, it is said, that they were carried out only out of fear of what would happen if Jovita were disobeyed.

As colorful as these colonels and characters were, however, more lasting models for Mexican women include three whose intelligence and courage helped form the foundation for the Revolution and provided it with enduring values. They were Dolores Jiménez y Muro, Juana Belén Gutiérrez de Mendoza, and Hermila Galindo.

María Dolores Jiménez y Muro, born in Aguascalientes on June 7, 1848, remembered from her youth the end of Maximilian's abortive monarchy and Benito Juárez' hopeful presidency. A teacher, she wrote anti–Díaz essays for *La Patria* and *Diario del Hogar*, emerging as a kind of grande dame of the Revolution, earning for herself the description "virile, combative writer." So ubiquitous were Jiménez y Muro's writings — often under pseudonyms, sometimes male pseudonyms — and so shadowy was her life because of her revolutionary activities that historians concede the impossibility of gauging with certainty her full effect on the Revolution.

From 1900, Jiménez y Muro was active in the Precursor movement, made up of the earliest advocates of bringing to an end the long dictatorship of Porfirio Díaz. She worked on the staff of *La Mujer Mexicana* in 1905 and in 1907 joined the Mexico City group *Socialistas Mexicanos*, which included Juana Belén Gutiérrez, Elisa Acuña y Rossetti, and other female leaders. These women personified the intertwined forces of socialism, liberalism, and feminism. Those forces drew on ideas from around the world in a time of tremendous intellectual ferment, and the Mexican Revolution, as chaotic as it was, represented the combined eruption of those ideas.

In 1910, Jiménez y Muro helped organize the protest against Díaz' eighth term, and, for her effort, was jailed at Belén prison despite the fact that she was sixty-two years old. She was, in fact, placed in solitary confinement because in prison she continued to recruit. Upon her release, undaunted, she took part in 1911 in *el complot de Tacubaya*, an unsuccessful scheme hatched to put Francisco Madero into the presidency.

Important to the plot was its manifesto, a justification of the plot itself. The manifesto was an early articulation of revolutionary ideas. It restated and expanded upon a liberal program published five years earlier — and Jiménez y Muro was assigned the task of drafting it for publication on March 18, 1911.

The earlier statement had been a call for nationalist values and agrarian reform. Jiménez y Muro's proposals were more complex, forming a basis for later statements, including the drafting of a constitution at Querétaro in 1917.

Proposed was decentralization of school administration. Carranza later tried to effect this idea. Liberals were convinced of the need to free schooling from the clerical influences that mired education in Middle Age thought. Decentralization, as it turned out, did not work, the poorest states showing neither the capacity nor will to support their own school systems. The idea was another expression of Mexico's strong centrifugal tendency that pulls at national unity even today.

With a mentality that would be considered progressive in any city of the world today, the manifesto proposed lowering of tax values on urban rental properties in order to allow landlords to lower rents. Also envisioned was long-term financing for working-class housing. Included was that timeless proposal: higher pay for teachers. Other points called for an eight-hour work day, the return of farmland to its original owners, a requirement that Mexican workers be hired by foreign-owned companies, and the abolition of monopolies.

In the spring of 1911, Jiménez traveled north to Ciudad Juárez to observe the assault on the city by forces led by Pascual Orozco and Pancho Villa, the attack that broke the tough back of the Díaz regime.

Returning to Mexico City, her dissidence was re-ignited after Victoriano Huerta—the man who ordered the murder of Madero—took the presidency in February 1913. Her views landed her back in jail for three months.

When Emiliano Zapata was told of the manifesto Jiménez y Muro had written, he remarked on the point calling for restitution of villagers' land—a principal goal of his own—and asked to meet this spinster teacher who wrote revolutionary tracts. Jiménez y Muro traveled to Morelos to join Zapata, who promptly named her a brigadier general. By 1916, owing to her allegiance with Zapata, there was a price on her gray head.

After Venustiano Carranza replaced Huerta in the presidency, however, Jiménez y Muro was able to exercise some influence over the drafting of the Constitution of 1917, when she was in her seventieth year. She continued to live in Morelos until Zapata was assassinated in 1919. She returned to Mexico City, where she died on October 15, 1925.

Juana Belén Gutiérrez de Mendoza was born in Durango in 1880. Her background and surroundings—the arid, rugged country northwest of the capital—were much like those of Villa, and she grew up hearing of the exploits of those who opposed the government. Her grandfather, she was told, was a poor laborer who died in front of a firing squad for his political dissent, a particular point of pride for the family. Her mother and father are variously described as Indian or mestizo. Her father, Santiago Gutiérrez, earned a meager living as a blacksmith, a horse-tamer, or a farm laborer. She was schooled as a typographer and in 1901 joined the Precursors movement, early critics of the Díaz regime and the foreign-dominated elitism it represented.

Her first publication was a small volume of poetry. Such a modest work was still the typical effort for a female writer in Mexico, although that condition was changing. While words of war, revolution, and patriotism were still largely the domain of men, women were being heard at a time when Mexico, in turmoil, needed new ideas. A feminist movement took form even before the oppressive, traditional regime of Porfirio Díaz had been driven from the scene.

In the spring of 1901, Gutiérrez, along with fellow teacher Elisa Acuña y Rossetti, founded *Vésper*, a weekly newspaper. It is said that Gutiérrez sold goats she owned to buy the press. Based in Guanajuato, the newspaper defended the serflike miners of the region and attacked the Church for its "religious obscurantism," the common charge that Roman Catholic priests, by claiming that only they held the keys to heaven, kept illiterate peasants in a kind of servitude. Unlike other dissidents, Gutiérrez did not just attack Díaz and his retainers, but upbraided the Mexican people for cowering before the dictator. So strong was Gutiérrez' commentary that a male anti-Díaz editor paid her the same compliment as had been paid Jiménez y Muro, calling her writing "virile."

Indicative of the times and of Gutiérrez' style was her publication of hundreds of copies of Kropotkin's *La Conquista del Pan*. Prince Peter Alexeivich Kropotkin (1842–1921) was a progenitor of communistic anarchism, a "pure" communism that did not allow individual moderation; his ideas were part of the swirl of socialist thought being discussed across Mexico. Gutiérrez also contributed to *Excélsior*, the publication of a Mexico City antireelectionist group.

The newspaper *Regeneración*, an important organ of anti-Díaz propaganda, described in 1903 the place of *Vésper* in the fight: "Now," wrote *Regeneración* in 1903, "when many men have lost heart and, out of cowardice, retired from the fight...now that many men, without vigor, retreat...there appears a spirited and brave woman, ready to fight for our principles, when the weakness of many men has permitted them to be trampled and spit upon."

Eventually, an infuriated Díaz struck back, and Gutiérrez was arrested along with male writers of several opposition newspapers. Three and a half years after the founding of *Vésper*, in 1904, Gutiérrez and Acuña y Rossetti were thrown into Belén women's prison. Gutiérrez remained behind bars for three years and was then exiled.

During the years of Gutiérrez' imprisonment and exile, the movement that initially had as its goal the departure of Porfirio Díaz broke apart into the factions that would eventually tear Mexico to shreds through years of civil war. A major personalistic fight was between the Flores Magón brothers and Camilo Arriaga, the oldest remaining leader of the Precursors. Gutiérrez and Acuña y Rossetti (as well as Francisco Madero, the future president) sided with Arriaga. In the spring of 1910, Gutiérrez traveled to San Antonio to be with Arriaga in exile. There they reestablished *Vésper*.

Mexico was now close to armed revolt, and Gutiérrez returned to publication, warning that simply driving Díaz out would not end despotism. It was a warning that would prove prophetic.

The scheme to bring Madero to power, *el complot de Tacubaya*, was conceived in 1911 by Arriaga. When the plot was betrayed and arrests made, Arriaga was jailed and not released until Madero took the presidency in May.

Gutiérrez, however, turned away from Madero as his regime proved unable, or unwilling, to shed itself of the *porfiristas* whom, she thought, were a drag on Madero's resolve to solve Mexico's problems. Similarly, Carranza's promises were, in her view, hollow. Gutiérrez then joined Zapata, the leader who was for many the only true beacon of social revolution. She founded *Desmontada*, trying to cut through all of the conflicting claims to leadership arising from all the personalist factions. With "the countryside bristling with old logs," she wrote, explaining the publication's name, "one must dismount." After all of the war, Gutiérrez charged, after all of the death, "for all of the so-called principles inscribed on the flags of combat" — with the sole exception of Zapata's agrarian reform — "there is nothing else that merits the name of 'principle.'" Finally, with the murder of Zapata, Gutiérrez' last hope for national reform was lost. Her spirit, however, was not extinguished.

She returned to Mexico City in 1920 after Alvaro Obregón had taken power. At the age of sixty, Juana Belén Gutiérrez de Mendoza had diminished in neither eloquence nor conscience. She published a biweekly newspaper called *Alma Mexicana*, and told an interviewer that, alas, her advanced age had not enabled her to blind herself to the needs she saw everywhere around her. She could not "retire," find a peaceful corner and ignore her struggling country.

"I have that right," she said, "but I don't have a corner. In all the world's corners lives a pain; in all the world's corners is coiled a treachery with open jaws, ready to swallow; and I don't have the indifference necessary to ignore it, nor the cowardice to flee it, nor the gentility to accommodate it."

Juana Belén Gutiérrez de Mendoza died in Mexico City in 1942.

Hermila Galindo was also born in Durango, in Lerdo, on May 29, 1896. In 1909, when only thirteen years old, she put the shorthand and typing courses she was taking in addition to her regular schoolwork to a revolutionary use. A dissident lawyer gave a speech in nearby Torreón, denouncing the Díaz regime. The discourse was so harsh in tone that the president of the municipal council took the original draft in order that it not be published. Little Hermila, however, had made a verbatim copy, which was passed along to Díaz opponents for their use as yet another broadside at the embattled dictator.

Five years later, still a teenager, it was her fate to once again cross paths with the Revolution. This time the episode was the beginning of a career. Her family had moved to Mexico City, and Hermila had continued to be a precocious student. She was chosen to deliver a welcoming speech for Venustiano Carranza, who was to make a triumphal entry into the city after the fall of the short-lived dictatorship of Victoriano Huerta. Galindo's intelligence impressed Carranza. He needed the moderating image of women around him to assuage the feelings of many Mexican women who feared that the revolution would come down hardest on the Church. Carranza could not know, however, that Galindo's revolutionary zeal would soon shock everyone.

Carranza, a landowner and former governor, stepped into the presidency only to begin betraying principles and people. Once in power he was perceived as too conservative by the people who had fought to put him in the presidential palace. But while others turned against Carranza, Galindo did not. "She steadfastly supported Carranza," writes Anna Macías, "after he was elected president in 1917, and remained loyal to him despite mounting criticism of his venality, duplicity, and bad faith as the supposed leader of Mexico's peasantry and urban working classes."

Support, however, worked both ways. If Galindo remained loyal to a despot, she also used her position in the administration to espouse feminist positions — positions more radical than anyone had imagined. "Emboldened by Carranza's support," Macías continues, "between 1915 and 1919 Hermila Galindo adopted advanced positions on divorce, sexuality, religion, prostitution and politics which shocked even secular-oriented, middle-class women with some education." While it cannot be said that Galindo's efforts bore immediate fruit, her force was a necessary and large part of the groundwork for women's advances that came later. Carranza, in fact, made liberalized divorce law a part of his program, and liberalization occurred in most Mexican states.

In January 1916, at the First Feminist Congress in Yucatán, a paper by Galindo called "Women in the Future" was so radical as to retain the support only of those delegates labeled "extremists." Its central argument was that a woman's sex drive was as strong as a man's, a shocking idea barely fifteen years after the death of Queen Victoria. Galindo's notion led her to the conclusion that girls and young women needed sex-education classes in school. Even among most feminist militants, the conclusion was explosive, and its effect on Roman Catholic educators can only be imagined. Her ideas, however, found expression twenty years later during the presidency of Lázaro Cárdenas (1934–1940), when sex education was introduced to public schools.

Macías rendered this judgment in 1982: "Unlike her contemporaries, Juana Belén Gutiérrez de Mendoza and Dolores Jiménez y Muro, Hermila Galindo did not suffer imprisonment for expressing her ideas. However, she did have to face a great deal of hostility, scorn, and ridicule from both men and women for expressing unpopular views and for speaking up on a subject that still remains taboo in Mexico."

Similarly, at the constitutional convention at Querétaro in 1917, Galindo proposed giving women the vote. The proposal was rejected (liberals feared that enfranchising women would open a Pandora's box of support for the Church), but it was the beginning of a period of incubation. Mexican women finally won the vote in 1953, casting their first presidential ballots in 1958.

As Galindo's feminist efforts diminished, her writing turned to politics, always a slippery slope in postrevolutionary Mexico. Support for one candidate or another was sure to attract at least as many enemies as friends. In 1920, when Gen. Alvaro Obregón succeeded to the presidency, Galindo was unwelcome in councils of power. In 1923, she married Manuel Topete and retired to a quiet life. Galindo lived to the age of seventy-nine, having sown ideas that would flower only in more enlightened times.

Augusto Sandino
1895–1934
(Nicaragua)

The Visionary versus the Marines

The life of Augusto Sandino bridges the gap to modernity. His name, of course, was made known during the long struggle between Nicaraguan *Sandinistas* and the United States. During his lifetime, however, his rebellion brought him into direct conflict with U.S. forces, including dive bombers, as they staged their long occupation of Nicaragua in a vain attempt to shape that tiny nation's political future. U.S. marines chased Sandino over mountain trails, attracting to his cause worldwide attention. Rebels, from communists in neighboring El Salvador to the Kuomintang in China, found Sandino representative of all struggles during that volatile period, 1925 to 1935. They transformed him into a symbol.

Augusto Sandino was born on May 18, 1895, in Niquinihomo, a village of about a thousand inhabitants. His father was Gregorio Sandino, owner of a modest farm. His mother was Margarita Calderón, a servant. His birth to a servant and a landowner imbued him with a sense of both cultures that would run through his political thought. Although both parents were *ladinos*, of mixed blood, his father exercised some power in the community, while his mother was "Indian" twice over, both by virtue of her family and her low status. Sandino's private letters and public pronouncements would suggest that such distinctions be destroyed.

For several years the young Sandino lived with his mother and was known as Augusto Calderón. When he went to live in his father's house he took advantage of the ample library, reading its classics and eventually deciding his name should be Augusto "César" Sandino. He went to secondary school in nearby Granada and then went to work as administrator of his father's farm.

Although the elder Sandino was a supporter of Nicaragua's Liberal party, Augusto showed no particular interest in politics. For years, the country's Liberals and Conservatives had tugged at each other without upsetting a system dominated by the wealthy and their foreign financiers. Had Sandino stayed at home, it is likely he would have been submerged in this traditional system.

But in 1920, when he was twenty-five, Sandino got into a fight in Niquinihomo and shot a man in the leg. He fled the country.

There was plenty of work in Central America for a man with Sandino's education, both formal and practical, and Sandino worked for fruit companies in Honduras and Guatemala as he made his way north. He settled in the Mexican oil port of Tampico, took a common-law wife who bore him a daughter, and settled into Tampico's turgid political environment.

Tampico was a magnet for foreign capital and foreign workers, the former representing a single conservative force, the latter bringing in radical ideas from all over the world. The ideas found a hospitable environment in Mexico, still in the throes of its peasant revolution, the Indian aspects of which attracted Sandino. In addition, nowhere in the hemisphere could Sandino have been more thoroughly schooled in the effects of U.S. domination.

Sandino was something of an intellectual explorer in this environment. Like Juárez, Sandino found cause to admire the Masons. Sandino also studied yoga and the beliefs of the Seventh-Day Adventists. Added to this eclecticism was a hint of mysticism, suggesting a range of thought that has caused some to admire Sandino's hunger for new ideas. Others simply dismiss him as weird.

On May 14, 1926, just before his thirtieth birthday, Sandino quit his job as head of gasoline sales for Huasteca Oil Company in Tampico. He took $500 in savings and his revolver back to Nicaragua. Crossing the border, he immediately found work at the San Albino gold mine in the Segovia Mountains, the area that would become the province of his army.

Sandino began lecturing fellow workers on the need for political change. His eloquence on the subject divided listeners into those who saw him as self-centered and voluble and those who were impressed by his willingness to explain his views to the least educated *peon,* just as long as he would listen. Sandino was able to recruit twenty-nine workers into his "army," using his own money to buy rifles and ammunition from a Honduran gun-runner.

At that time, Liberals in Managua were trying to take power from a Conservative regime that was propped in place by the U.S. marines. From 1912, Conservatives had been able to count for support on the marines' arrival whenever needed to protect their interests and the interests of U.S. investors. Historian Hubert Herring has described Nicaragua at the time as "the virtual ward of New York bankers." In 1916 the United States' authority to intervene in Nicaraguan sovereignty was guaranteed in perpetuity by treaty. Sandino considered the treaty an outrage. In one of his first pronouncements from his mountain headquarters he calculated that the $3 million that paid for the treaty, "spread among Nicaraguan citizens, would not have bought each one a sardine on a cracker."

Without identifying his band with the Liberal party — although no one mistook him for a Conservative — Sandino led it in a raid on the government garrison of two hundred troops at Jicaro on November 2. It was the beginning of Sandino's personal war.

The Sandinistas were repelled, and, although no one had been killed, there was a general loss of heart among his men after the raid. Sandino decided that what was needed was an alliance with Liberal forces, so he led his disheartened guerrillas down the Coco River to the Atlantic Coast. At Puerto Cabezas he declared his allegiance to "constitutionalist" forces gathered there.

But Sandino's arrival was not welcomed, either by Juan Sacasa, the Liberal pretender to the presidency, or by José María Moncada, his field commander, despite Moncada's having been a friend of Sandino's father. Also, as Sandino learned more of his would-be allies, he, too, cooled to the arrangement. They were, in Sandino's view, much too willing to collaborate with foreigners in general and the United States in particular.

The United States was in touch with both sides of Nicaragua's civil unrest, manipulating the Conservatives while covering all bets with Liberals. Sandino was aghast at the role the United States was able to play between the two sides. After arriving in Puerto Cabezas, Sandino watched in dismay as Liberals complied with a declaration of the commander of a small contingent of U.S. marines that the city would henceforth be a neutral zone. The marines were to gather up all arms, take them out to sea, and dump them overboard. What kind of revolution, Sandino wondered, throws away its guns? Reacting as fast as he could, Sandino and some friends recruited passing prostitutes to help them hurriedly grab up some thirty rifles and six thousand rounds of ammunition that had been stacked for disposal. Then they quickly left town.

Although the Liberals admired Sandino's resourcefulness — he was made a Liberal general — he had to insist to Moncada that he be allowed to keep the rifles. Clearly, Sandino's allies were planning a less aggressive strategy than he was. In February 1927, Sandino's force won an important victory by defending its position against government troops, his men proving themselves under fire and then falling on their attackers as they fled, recovering weapons and ammunition left behind. Then Sandino turned his men, now numbering two hundred, to an attack on the government garrison at Jinotega. They succeeded in driving off the defenders and occupying the town, if only briefly. Finally, joining forces with another rebel column, Sandino went to the relief of Moncada himself, whose troops had been stalled in a drive toward Managua.

At this point, however, Liberal heads were turned. Moncada was persuaded to sign a truce urged upon him by Henry Stimson, whom President Coolidge sent. As a part of the truce, Moncada offered Sandino the governorship of a northern state and $10 a day for each day he'd spent in the field if he and his men would lay down their arms. Sandino declined, saying he would fight on alone. He declared, in one of the existential telegrams from his headquarters that would become a trademark, "I will protest for my own satisfaction if there is no one to support me."

This was more than posturing. Despite the small size of his force and the fact that he was no threat to the capital, Sandino could not be ignored. He had demonstrated a capacity for leadership and the ability to learn military tactics. In addition, his voice, although solitary, carried out over the rubble of opportunism that characterized Nicaraguan politics. If he could not be silenced, there was always the chance that, eventually, he would be followed.

Moncada enlisted the help of Sandino's father to go to Sandino's camp to convince him to give up. After the two talked, however, the father wrote to his other son, Socrates, encouraging him to join Augusto. Socrates became his brother's liaison with supportive groups in the United States.

In 1927, the year the Liberals laid down their arms, the United States made a fateful decision — to commit its marines to building an independent armed force for Nicaragua, one that answered to neither Liberals nor Conservatives. It would be called the National Guard. At the same time, New York banks assumed the bulk of the debt Nicaragua owed British banks. Finally, there was a $3 million payment against the possibility that Nicaragua might be the site of a transoceanic canal. To make sure Nicaraguan finances were handled in a manner Washington considered prudent, the money would be disbursed — how much to retire debt, how much for international development — at Washington's order. Against this kind of domination, Sandino protested.

He established as his base San Rafael del Norte, taking as his headquarters the house where the telegraph office was located and as his intended bride the daughter of the telegrapher. Sandino met Blanca Araúz, nineteen years old, as she tapped the key for his many messages and pronouncements. Blanca's sister, swept up in the revolutionary spirit, arranged for a mass to be celebrated in honor of the safe return of Sandino's troops from battle. The men comported themselves properly, according to Sandino, except for "some salvos from rifles and machine guns." Sandino smoothed things over by paying for the mass.

From his headquarters Sandino kept up a running correspondence with his adversaries. He conducted a kind of continuing debate, salted with insults, with the marine officers in pursuit. He warned one marine captain that if he and his men contemplated venturing into the Segovia Mountains, which Sandino considered his domain, "make your will beforehand." The marine officers generally had no trouble in replying in kind. Wrote this one, "Bravo! General. If words were bullets and phrases were soldiers, you would be a field marshal instead of a mule thief."

As the marines slogged through the mountains in search of Sandino, they were at the same time training the National Guard. Marine sergeants served as National Guard commanders. The idea — as durable as it was unsuccessful — was to train and equip a force that would be left behind after the marines had gone home.

Sandino either eluded these patrols or, at his choosing, ambushed them. Counterattacks chased Sandino to his mountain hideout, called *El Chipote*. Marine commanders would occasionally report to their superiors that Sandino's army, last seen disappearing into the undergrowth, had been "wiped out," but as long as Sandino and his men stayed deep enough in the mountains, they were safe. They were kept well informed by villagers.

In May 1927, Sandino married Blanca and prepared for his biggest attack, on the river port of Ocotal, in the heart of the Segovia Mountains. To taunt his enemies, he named a "governor" for the state of Nueva Segovia, allowed the nearby town of El Jicaro to be "renamed" Ciudad Sandino, and made it clear that just as soon as his troops took Ocotal he would appoint his own mayor.

Ocotal was defended by four hundred U.S. marines and two hundred Nicaraguan National Guard trainees. Sandino had eight hundred men. On his side, Sandino counted on surprise and stealth, infiltrating the town with spies and arming collaborators in the middle of the night. On their side, the marines had airplanes. Ocotal was a small beginning for modern warfare.

Sandino's awkward strategy might have prevailed against an enemy left to its own devices. But the planes and their bombs made the difference. When Sandino attacked Ocotal in darkness, the marines were able to hold out until morning, when two biplanes were called in from Managua. Dive bombing and strafing were introduced, and Sandino's revolution scattered for cover.

One marine was killed at Ocotal; at least fifty dead rebels were found in the streets, and it is assumed at least fifty more died in the houses or along the river or were carried away by Sandino's retreating troops.

The battle signaled the beginning of stalemate. Marine airplanes did not help them get into the mountains to drag Sandino out. But neither could Sandino come out when, within hours, he would be attacked from above.

President Coolidge called the Battle of Ocotal a "heroic action" by the marines. American critics, however, in phrases resembling those of the Vietnam era, called the use of bombs in a country with which we were not formally at war an "indecency" and "inhuman." The critics pointed out that marine body counts were likely to include civilians in a nonwar in which there were no "belligerents" but yet everybody *looked* like the enemy. The resulting charge and counter-charge turned Sandino, trapped with his troops in the Segovia Mountains, into an international celebrity.

In the eyes of U.S. policy makers, Sandino's notoriety made it imperative that he be stopped, so the giant's pursuit of the gnat began to take on epic proportions. Japan, involved on the other side of the world with sending its troops into Manchuria, was happy to have an example to throw in the face of the United States. International bullies shouldn't criticize each other, was the message. Sandino, meanwhile, was only too happy to be used as a global example.

Journalists who trekked into the mountains to interview Sandino found him wearing khakis or the type of clothes any bourgeois might wear for a day's hunting: checked jacket and high, lace-up boots. He did not wear a military uniform. North American journalists described him as short; Latin American writers saw him as of medium height. He was thin, with black hair combed straight back and delicate features, making him seem quite dapper. His day-in-the-country attire — topped by a ten-gallon cowboy hat that became his trademark — plus his natural gregariousness, made Sandino a kind of boulevardier of mountain trails. He and his troops wore kerchiefs of black and red, the colors of the international workers' movement — although while the troops' kerchiefs were cotton, Sandino's was silk.

In shaping his own image for the press, Sandino talked the way he dressed, with style. Replying to an associate who had asked for a photograph for a magazine article, Sandino cautioned that it be made "clear in any caption that I'm not a professional politician, just a plain artisan. My profession is that of mechanic, and up to my present age of thirty-three I have earned my bread, tools in hand."

Sandino argued that his goals were not earth-shaking. He wanted, he said, the chance to negotiate the withdrawal of U.S. marines and the redrawing of the canal treaty. He wanted a hemispheric conference to discuss the sovereignty of Latin American countries. "A man who doesn't even ask his country for a yard of ground to be buried in deserves to be heard," he wrote, "and not only heard, but believed. I am a Nicaraguan and proud that Indian-American blood, more than any other, flows in my veins, blood that contains the mystery of loyal and sincere patriotism."

The Battle of Ocotal had shown Sandino that he could not confront marines with their airplanes overhead, and had demonstrated to the marines that they could not easily subdue Sandino. The tiny war became one of running battles and ambushes: a marine or two would be killed in the jungle thickness, or several *sandinistas* would be bombed when a patrol plane spotted horses tied outside a mountain cabin. Sandino captured arms and ammunition, dragging his dead away from skirmishes so the government could not count to what extent he had been weakened. The longer the conflict dragged on, the more bitter the behavior. A marine pilot, his plane downed by small-arms fire, was executed and hanged from a tree; a photograph of his limp body was sent to Honduran and Mexican newspapers. The marines carried the image in their heads.

When the marines could never quite claim that Sandino was within their grasp, the State Department grew impatient. Marine commanders alternated between predictions that his capture was not far off and admissions that he was unlikely to give up and, furthermore, enjoyed the support of the peasants. Sandino added to their dismay in the autumn of 1927 when from *El Chipote,* his now well-fortified hideout, he issued his "Articles of the Defending Army of the National Sovereignty of Nicaragua." Sandino's notion of sovereignty meant that while his area chiefs were forbidden from stealing from peasants, they were allowed to "collect forced loans from native and foreign capitalists" as long as they kept records. He declared that he was neither politically committed nor beholden to anyone, but he informed his soldiers they would not be paid until after the cause was triumphant.

The marines' response was an all-out attack on *El Chipote.* The mountain redoubt had taken on a heroic aspect, bolstering Nicaraguans' faith that perhaps the United States would not always win. The slang term *chipote* was coined to suggest "impregnability," as if Sandino could laugh down the mountain at his impotent adversaries; the word could be translated to mean everything from "myth" to "back-handed slap" to the lump resulting from a blow to the head. Used by Nicaraguans, however, the word allowed them to laugh at the United States.

In January 1928, the marines closed in on *El Chipote* even as Coolidge, accompanied by Charles Evans Hughes and Secretary of State Frank B. Kellogg, traveled to a hemispheric peace conference. At the conference, held in Havana, Coolidge testified to the United States' determination to get along with neighbors. A cynic might suggest that Coolidge's peace talk risked misunderstanding as he simultaneously cheered on efforts to subdue Sandino, who was given one last chance to lay down his arms before a siege was ordered.

"The situation was getting tricky," Sandino would write afterward. "They were encircling us to prevent supplies' coming in, and the circle was constantly tightening." When the attack was sprung, it depended on air power. "During the sixteen days we were under siege," Sandino wrote, "the pirates' air squadrons paid us daily visits."

For sixteen days, four planes would appear in a wave, bomb, then be replaced by another wave. Two hundred horses were blown to bits. Cattle were killed by shrapnel. The stench of decaying carcasses became almost unbearable, Sandino wrote, and "the air was full of vultures for days. They did us a service by ruining visibility for the planes." When Sandino ordered a retreat, his men left behind straw figures topped by native sombreros. The planes continued to bomb the scarecrows.

The marines had shown they could destroy Sandino's refuge. Not so his image. American journalist Carleton Beals, visiting Sandino after he'd pulled out of *El Chipote,* described him in the *Nation* as "a man utterly without vices, with an unequivocal sense of justice, a keen eye for the welfare of the humblest soldier."

Despite such journalistic enthusiasm, however, the war dragged on with Sandino still unable to threaten Managua. U.S. planes continued to rain impersonal terror in the countryside, while small bands of Sandinistas inflicted what damage they could on isolated mines or defenseless towns. There the two sides stood.

Knowing he had to step up his capacity to make war, Sandino decided to go to Mexico for materiel and moral support. Before he left, Sandino tried to open talks with Moncada, who was elected president in the U.S.-sponsored election of 1928. Moncada rebuffed him. Sandino departed overland for Mexico, leaving behind a confused army, uncertain whether his departure represented defeat. Almost daily, guerrillas were surrendering to a government amnesty.

Sandino traveled overland through Central American countries in the spring of 1929, sometimes greeted as a savior, sometimes treated like a pariah. Reaching Mexico, he cooled his heels.

The government of Mexico gave Sandino and his companions a house in Mérida, but otherwise studiously ignored him. He was free to make speeches and entertain reporters, but the materiel and spiritual support he sought from Mexico were not forthcoming.

He wrote letters to the Radical president of Argentina, Hipolito Yrigoyen, and to the Republican president of the United States, Herbert Hoover. Sandino was informed that his ideas dovetailed perfectly with those of the mystical Victor Haya de la Torre of Peru, whose dream of a united, Indo-Hispanic continent was attracting intellectuals. Sandino got news that a division of the Kuomintang army in China was named for him. But he could not get what he needed from the Mexican government.

After six months and a frustrating trip to meet the president and other national leaders, who yielded nothing, Sandino gave up. All he got was words from men who faced him squarely, but had their backs to the Rio Grande.

When Sandino returned to Mérida he and his associates began contacting real estate brokers. They drove in a caravan into the countryside as if looking for a permanent residence in exile. When the press, the spies, and the curious, all of whom had followed, were lulled into accepting the pattern of trips from which Sandino always returned, one day the cars did not come back. Sandino slipped back across the border carrying the only Mexican acquisitions that would aid him in his fight: two submachine guns, disassembled and listed with customs as carpenter's tools.

The stalemate in Nicaragua in Sandino's absence had enabled the United States, by early 1930, to get closer to the day when the marines could live up to the promise of pulling out. Officers and noncoms had been busily training the Nicaraguan National Guard. The stated purpose was to create an apolitical peace-keeping force to replace army officers too inclined to take sides between Liberals and Conservatives.

Part of the State Department's strategy — antiguerrilla strategies are timeless — was to "relocate" any Nicaraguan and his family if there was some indication he identified with Sandino or one of his regional chiefs. The result — such results are similarly timeless — was to spread from the towns where people were uprooted to wherever they were relocated stories of an impersonal, hostile government flailing blindly at a man officials insisted was just a common bandit. More thoroughly than he could have done it for himself, Sandino's message was being carried.

At the same time, no strategy of relocation could eliminate the necessity of capturing or killing Sandino. Only now the National Guard would have to do what the Marines could not. When Sandino returned to Nicaragua the frequency of raids increased, and in June 1930 Sandino returned to the fray himself by taking command of four hundred troops at El Saraguazca Mountain, not far from Jinotega, where he had led his first successful attack three years before.

The Guard was no more effective than the marines had been, but no less inclined to call in air support. Sandino was wounded in the leg. The battle was inconclusive, but the world read in an Associated Press dispatch of marine planes that "got away with bullet-perforated wings." Ineffective on the ground, badgered from the air, Sandino clearly still dominated the newswires.

Sandino let it be known that he claimed "control" of the rural areas of the northern states from the Atlantic to the Pacific. In towns, he said, his supporters watched and waited. He celebrated the fourth anniversary of the Battle at Ocotal by issuing a proclamation that spoke grandly of a kind of pervasive presence among the populace and a humane relationship among his troops. "I am in no way different from any rank-and-file soldier in the armies of the world," he proclaimed. "My voice is not arrogant, nor does my presence evoke terror as many might imagine. We have, however, fulfilling our duty as citizens, had the pleasure of seeing under our feet in humiliation a number of exalted chiefs and officers of the arrogant army of the United States, the would-be annihilator annihilated."

The bombast extended to calling Hoover "a rabid but impotent beast," casting aspersions on members of the Hoover administration, and suggesting that the wife of the U.S. ambassador to Nicaragua "now runs the Yankee legation in Managua." The earthquake that shook Managua in 1931, he said, was divine retribution. A world war, he predicted, would destroy most of mankind.

Sandino adopted a style of life as exotic as his pronouncements. In the mountains, moving constantly, he took, in the absence of Blanca, a mistress, Salvadoran revolutionary Teresa Villatoro. But by the spring of 1931, like a guilty husband, he proclaimed that although love ought to be unfettered he recognized social convention. He summoned Blanca to join him at his headquarters. Teresa left. Before long, Blanca was pregnant.

"My little Blanca," he called her in a letter, fondly describing "her .38 pistol and her .44 Winchester rifle." She shot up too much ammunition practicing, he complained gently, but admitted that "all I can do is permit her to do anything she likes."

In 1932, the State Department sponsored a presidential election as the final building block of its strategy. Sandino called for voters to abstain, but the appeal was unsuccessful. After the election, the State Department insisted, Liberals and Conservatives were to share power no matter which party's candidate won the presidency. The marines were to be pulled out, and democratic institutions were to develop under the watchful protection of the National Guard. Elected president was Sacasa, the man to whom Sandino had declared allegiance in his first days as a revolutionary. Sacasa, consolidating his government, bequeathed unusual power on one man, making him foreign minister in addition to his post as chief director of the National Guard. That man, educated in prep school and college in the United States and trained by the marines, was Anastasio Somoza.

Sacasa extended to Sandino the chance to cooperate with the new government. Sandino chose as his emissary Blanca, four months pregnant, who, despite being manhandled a bit by National Guardsmen, began the process of reconciliation. With the marines gone, a proclamation declared, "an era of basic renovation in our public life is opened. . . . In order to deepen this most noble tendency, the undersigned agree to make respect for the Republic Constitutions and basic laws the foundation stone of their respective political programs."

Amnesty was granted, and Sandino was authorized by the national government to control land in the valley of either the Coco or Segovia River to establish and advance his agrarian policies. In exchange for disarming the main part of his army, he was allowed to retain a personal guard. Sandino returned to the mountains.

But he was concerned about the strength and independence of the National Guard. This concern crackled through contentious messages between Sandino and Somoza. Sandino's regional chiefs let him know they needed ammunition because of attacks by National Guard patrols. Somoza opposed all such accommodations. Sandino, powerless, tarried in the administration of agricultural reform. Strong in his mind was the example of Zapata's reforms in Morelos. Strong must have been as well the example of Zapata's betrayal.

Sandino thought to organize a political party to enter national politics. Sacasa asked that he wait. So he did, turning back to his farming. In June 1933, Blanca gave birth to a girl and died. Sandino named the infant Blanca Segovia, left the child with her grandmother, and rode back into the mountains.

Fighting continued between government patrols and former Sandino soldiers. Sandino complained in messages to Sacasa that the National Guard was constantly provoking trouble, overstepping its bounds, demonstrating that the independent role on which Somoza insisted was "unconstitutional." Sacasa was powerless to intervene. Nevertheless, Sandino decided to go to Managua to argue his case.

He arrived on February 16, 1934, to confer with Sacasa and other administration officials, including Somoza. Somoza privately assured the U.S. ambassador that he should not be alarmed by the apparent hostility and that the ambassador would be informed of any plans Somoza might have. Sandino, meanwhile, embarked on a round of discussions with government leaders, one of whom informed the ambassador that Sandino, as flowing with ideas as ever, at times failed to make sense.

There is evidence, however, that Sacasa had no trouble understanding Sandino's suggestion that the National Guard be reorganized. The idea could not help but be appealing to the president since he could not control it any other way. His predecessor, Moncada, had feared the independence of the Guard, but only because he sought to control it himself. Preventing political control of the Guard, however, was the keystone of U.S. policy, notwithstanding the fact that that policy had created a monster.

On the morning of February 21, Somoza was noticed by the U.S. ambassador to be especially exercised over something, although he did not know what. That evening, Sandino and his father and several friends were expected for dinner at the presidential palace.

After dinner, Sandino talked on about exploitation of gold deposits in the Coco River basin, one of his myriad ideas. When it came time, about ten o'clock, for the guests to leave, Sandino shared a car with his father and Sacasa's agriculture minister, the man responsible for bringing Sacasa and Sandino together in the negotiations that led to peace. Sandino also invited to ride with him two old, trusted generals from the days of campaigning in the Segovia Mountains. The two generals sat in front with the driver, the other three in the back seat. In a car following was Sacasa's daughter.

The presidential palace was on a hill, and when the cars reached the bottom of the hill, where the street passed through a National Guard post, there was a car in the middle of the road, apparently stalled. Sandino's car stopped, and a National Guard sergeant stepped up to the car window in the dark. The two generals in the front seat reached for their pistols, but Sandino stopped them, saying his companions in the back seat were not fighters. Sandino and the two generals were arrested. Sacasa's daughter came forward to protest, but when it did no good she drove away back toward the presidential palace.

Sandino and his two companions were driven to the Managua airfield. National Guard officers would later say that their instructions came from Somoza, and that he had assured them the U.S. ambassador knew full well what was happening. They signed a conspiratorial document entitled "The Death of Caesar."

Sandino and his companions were told to stand together on the dark airfield, watching while soldiers took from the back of a truck a tripod-mounted machine gun. The officer in charge of the squad, a Mason like Sandino, did not have the courage to stay to face what he was about to order. He gave instructions to his men to commence firing when they heard the sound of his pistol, then walked over the crest of a nearby hill, out of sight.

One of the generals with Sandino searched in his pockets for souvenirs to be taken to his family. Sandino, hoping to buy time while Sacasa's daughter alerted the president, asked for a drink of water. He was refused. He asked to be allowed to urinate. He was refused again. Then he, too, searched through his pockets for souvenirs until one of his companions stopped him, telling him to preserve his dignity and get it over with.

In any event, Sandino is said to have found nothing in his pockets, leading him, in the moments before the machine gun blasted all else into silence, to utter the frustration of rebellion. "Screwed," he said. "The politicians cleaned me out."

Juan Perón
1895–1974
(Argentina)

Monarch of the Working Class

Some parts of the life of Juan Perón read like a radio script, in which, of course, the radio actress Eva Duarte plays herself. There is about both of them a staged quality, contrived, so that in the end there is no sense of tragedy, no inclination toward pity for them, just a feeling that their audience—"the shirtless ones" was the melodramatic phrase—was used for corrupt purposes. Yet peronismo lives on, representing a strong force among Argentines, a political movement that has outlived the follies of its progenitor. It does so because Juan Perón touched a nerve among working people, one that had been ignored, if not oppressed, by Argentine elites. For that reason, Juan Perón deserves to be remembered.

Juan Domingo Perón was born on October 8, 1895, about sixty miles south of Buenos Aires, near the village of Lobos, where his father worked for a judge. Although some biographers portray Perón as having been born in an impoverished setting, a more sober judgment is that his parents, of predominately Spanish and Italian origins, were members of Argentina's growing middle class. Perón himself, as have other politicians, contributed to the image of poverty-stricken early days. Indeed, there is something in Perón's mythical background for everyone.

On the one hand, Perónist publicists claimed that his grandparents were friends of a colorful bandit, Juan Moreira, who operated in the southern part of the province. On the other hand, Perón himself claimed to an electorate dominated by Italian immigrants that his great-grandfather had been a Sardinian senator. To this claim there was attached speculation that the family name had been Peroni.

When Perón was five years old, his father, suffering hard times, moved the family to Patagonia, a barren province where Argentina and Chile squeeze together at the bottom of the continent. There the father found work as a hired hand. Later, he was able to move the family back to the province of Buenos Aires and to buy a sheep ranch near the Atlantic Coast.

When Perón was ten, he was sent to Buenos Aires to military school, where he proved a natural athlete and was trained as a horseman, a crack shot, a boxer, and a fencer, later winning the foils championship of the army. He grew tall, with a broad chest and shoulders. Striking was his smile and his dark hair, combed straight back, which accentuated his aquiline profile. These manly attributes would not discourage political opponents from whispering in later years of his "effeminacy."

One reason for the slur was, obviously, the jealousy of men not so endowed. In Perón's shadow, men found solace by mocking him. There was also the fact that there would emerge weaknesses in Perón's character. And in a country influenced by Spanish and Italian notions of male dignity, even a man who so carefully crafted his own image would not long be able to disguise such flaws. It is particularly embarrassing, of course, for the *macho* to need a woman to provide the drive for his leadership, and even Perón's supporters would have to concede that he would not have risen half so far without the intellectual and psychological toughness of his second wife, whom the crowds called "Evita."

Nevertheless, Perón's military career was relatively distinguished, considering that he served in an army at war only with its own civilian population. At the age of eighteen he graduated from military school as a second lieutenant and, soon afterward, completed officer training with the rank of captain. He went on to more military schooling and in 1929 was appointed to a post in the war ministry. While at the ministry, Perón also taught, developing sufficient background in military tactics to write four books.

Yet by 1930, when he was thirty-five years old, Perón was still a captain. In ensuing years, however, his résumé was enhanced with service at the Argentine war college and as an aide to the army chief of staff and to the minister of war. In developed countries, rapid broadening of an officer's experience is possible only in time of war; in Argentina, Perón was able to rise by virtue of participation in the coup that deposed Hipolito Yrigoyen, the grand old man of Argentine liberalism.

By 1930, the liberalism that once promised to organize Argentina's formidable cultural and economic strengths into political dynamism had withered. It had always been held suspect by the landed classes, and after independence in 1829 the tension between the cosmopolitan Buenos Aires and the agricultural provinces evolved into a corresponding split between industrialization and the interests of landowners. For a while, it appeared that liberalism would triumph, a necessity for Argentina's many graces to be accepted in the world community. Liberal ideas were written into the Constitution of 1853, and waves of European immigrant workers flocked to Argentina in the mid–1800s, filling, by 1880, the ranks of the Radical party.

But liberalism barely managed to struggle into the twentieth century. When Irigoyen was elected president in 1916, he proved to be the last hope. In 1930, Yrigoyen was eighty years old and senile, unable to keep his own aides from raiding the Argentine treasury. The military placed in power civilian puppets, but the end had been written for any hope of a two-party system in which a liberal opposition would compete for power. Capt. Perón had learned the way government worked.

In 1936, now a lieutenant-colonel, Perón was assigned as military attaché in Santiago de Chile, the capital of Argentina's traditional Andean enemy. Perón, at once charming and devious, became a friend of the Chilean president, Arturo Alessandri — until Perón was discovered trying to buy Chilean defense secrets. Alessandri later told scholar Joseph R. Barager that when he found out about his Argentine friend's duplicity he called him into the presidential office and pointed out the window at Chile's most effective line of defense: the snow-capped peaks of the Andes. Perón was declared persona non grata in Chile.

Perón was ready for further training, so in 1939, with Europe dominated by warlike fascist states, Perón was sent to observe Italy's Tyrolean troops. He spent nearly two years studying military organization in several countries, including Germany and Spain. Argentina's upper classes were strongly drawn to European customs; commercial ties with Great Britain were important, and cultural ties with Italy, Germany, and Spain exerted strong influences. Argentine elites — like many of their counterparts in Brazil, Paraguay, and several other Latin American countries — saw totalitarian government, with its parallel excitement and control of the masses, as the answer for Argentina's future. Perón's own writings disclose his admiration for Alexander the Great, Hannibal, and Napoleon and his fascination with the views of the German officers he had interviewed.

In the late 1930s and early 1940s, banking on widespread sympathy, German agents operated openly in Argentina. At a hemispheric conference of foreign ministers in Rio de Janeiro in January 1942 — a month after the attack on Pearl Harbor — Argentina, with Chile, held out against the overwhelming sentiment of other Latin American nations and the machinations of the United States. Argentina and Chile insisted on retaining diplomatic ties with Spain, Germany, and Italy.

Argentina might have sustained this diplomatic position had the country's puppet civilian leaders shown any subtlety, any finesse. The regime would have become, effectively, a puppet of the Axis. But in 1943, after leaders' arrogance and corruption caused a popular outcry, an embarrassed military threw out the civilian government and took over itself. Perón was named administrative head of the war ministry.

The post was important for its control of personnel assignments. More important, Perón's mentor was Edelmiro Farrell, minister of war and vice-president of the new regime. Perón would move up, a notch at a time, an understudy studying the lead role. Indeed, the man in charge of the new military regime, Pedro Ramírez, did not last long, mostly because he was yet another example of that enduring Argentine type, the clumsy general. While in power, however, he helped set the stage for Perón's approaching time in the spotlight. Ramírez reaffirmed the embrace between reactionaries and the Catholic Church, rescinding nineteenth-century prohibitions against Church teaching in public schools. Also during the Ramírez months, political parties were outlawed; leaders who signed a petition calling for the return of constitutional government lost their jobs. The internment of labor union leaders was continued. Finally, however, when U.S. and British agents presented evidence of Ramírez' continuing collaboration with Axis agents, the general had to go. Into his spot moved Perón's benefactor, Farrell. Into the vice presidency moved Perón.

Like the student who gets smarter than his teachers, Perón was augmenting his power by forging links beyond the officer corps. The most important base of his strength was his leadership of the vaguely secret, reactionary "Group of United Officers," but he reached out to workers as well. This was his signal contribution to the art of Latin American demagoguery. It would one day make him president when the officer corps turned on him.

Perón perceived that more was needed to take — and hold — leadership in the rough realities of Argentine politics than force of arms. He asked for and got directorship of the Argentine Department of Labor and Social Welfare (a subcabinet position newly created and thought to be powerless), then led the department into independence from the Department of Interior. That meant Perón was able to create his own bureaucracy, by virtue of which he got cabinet rank. He also got the undivided attention of workers.

The organized labor unions had seen their support among politicians wither. Disaffected, they saw in Perón an unprecedented chance for alliance, popular numbers added to military strength, held together by

Argentina's fierce nationalism. The combination proved a heady one. Using Perón's rhetorical power for recruitment, the metal workers' union, as one example, grew from a nascent 1,500 members split off from other unions to 300,000 strong. The overarching General Confederation of Labor—to the directorship of which Perón appointed the elevator operator from the apartment building where he and Eva lived—would grow from a membership of 300,000 in 1943 to 5 million during Perón's presidency.

This ligature between labor and the military is significant in that elites of other Latin American countries have traditionally seen organized labor as something to be controlled, kept weak. This has ensured one kind of elite domination, but it fails to realize the potential of developing another. None, however, dare climb atop mass movements save those confident of their ability to stay there. Perón mounted the back of a workforce ready to regain strength achieved, then lost, under the Radicals.

Perón's rhetoric, style, and shrewdness led labor to a position without precedent in Latin America, in the process assuring his own position. Collective bargaining was carried out under Perón's auspices. Wage demands were satisfied, and workers were kept on the job. Should a union choose to take matters into its own hands, picket lines were dispersed and workers replaced. For this sacrifice of independence, unions won wage and salary increases in virtually all segments of the economy, including white-collar, agricultural, and maritime. Perón's most dramatic device was the "thirteenth month" of wages, a Christmas bonus. It was the vigor of the Argentine economy that enabled Perón to make good on his high-flown promises, but he would be the man on the balcony, raising his hands in victory and delivering the bounty. He would later write that he never learned how to be president, but his military training had taught him how to "lead."

The strategy even tended to neutralize those unions influenced by communists, and the case of the tough meatpackers union demonstrates Perón's flamboyant style. The union, run by Cipriano Reyes, was moving toward a strike when Perón's statements made it clear that he supported the workers. But Perón perceived that simple statements were insufficient to the style he was beginning to establish, so Perón left his office and was driven to the heart of the packing district, down at the docks along the La Plata River. There he met Reyes, threw his arm around the union leader's shoulders, and walked up the main street with him. When the strike was settled, Perón had won a valuable friend, one who would become a frequent visitor to Perón's apartment.

By late 1943, Perón was consolidating power. He lost no opportunity to enhance his image with the masses by grandly announcing social programs. In December, with the combination of flourish and cash that endeared him to common folk, he appropriated 500 million pesos for low-income housing. It was about this time that he met Eva María Duarte.

It is harder to separate fact from fantasy with regard to Eva Perón than it is with Perón himself. Snobs on one side, zealots on the other, and Eva Perón's own flair for the melodramatic confuse the picture. Like Perón, she was from a small town south of Buenos Aires; she was illegitimate, poorly educated, and ostracized by people in her hometown even before she worked her way up to ostracism by Buenos Aires society. By virtue of pluck, wit, and beauty, Eva Duarte made herself an actress and commentator at a Buenos Aires radio station. By ingratiating herself with the right officers, she had gained entry to circles surrounding the power of the military dictatorship.

Then, when her contacts began losing interest and wandering away, she dramatized, on the radio, reforms instituted by Perón's department of labor and social security. Stories told of great improvements in common people's lives wrought by government programs. With either foresight or careful planning, this was done before she met Perón. It was as much a clever gimmick to make broadcasts popular with working-class people as a ploy to catch a rising star. Either way, it worked. Eva Duarte, even at twenty-three, had been taking care of herself long enough to recognize that good copy for her radio broadcasts might last longer, in Argentina's volatile politics, than a coup leader.

One version of how Perón and Eva met is that after he had given a speech at the dedication of a project, she approached with her microphone, narrating. She was next to him when an elderly woman approached and kissed Perón's hand, a show of emotion that drove Eva to even greater heights of praise. Perón overheard, was flattered, and turned to ask her name.

For some time, the two openly shared an apartment on Buenos Aires' Calle Posadas while their separate careers flourished. Perón continued to build support among workers; Eva built an audience.

Both his supporters and her audience saved Perón's career when opponents made their move in 1945. On October 10, amid increasing demands for a return to civilian government — and even calls for Perón to be executed — Perón was forced to step down from all three of the posts he had acquired or created. He was minister of war, secretary of labor and social welfare, and vice president. Perón's power, it was clear to many, far outstripped that of the president, his benefactor, who was indecisive and politically weak next to this master puppeteer of the masses. On the night of October 11, with his enemies calling for his head either figuratively or literally, Perón resigned. He did so, however, on a national radio hookup orchestrated by Eva. It is widely suggested that Perón, visibly shaken, wanted simply to save his own hide. Eva Duarte provided the grit to stage-manage his departure so that Argentine workers would be sure to know they were losing their savior.

After the resignation, Perón met Eva back at the apartment. They drove to the river and rode in a launch through the small islands of the La Plata River delta to a resort used by Buenos Aires businessmen as a weekend hideaway. The spot offered quick access to safety across the border in Uruguay. But alert river patrols spotted the couple and they were arrested. That night, after first being returned to their apartment, Perón was placed aboard a gunboat and taken to the prison island of Martín García. All during his arrest, Perón, said to be shivering with the dampness, complained of his pleurisy. The same night, he wrote to the president, complaining of rain coming in at his cell window; he was moved to a more comfortable room. He also asked to be allowed to go into exile, and this night, as much as any time in Perón's career, fixed his reputation for weakness. He seemed unable to conduct himself with the dignity expected of a deposed leader. And on this night, wrote Argentine journalist María Flores, Eva, "in that moment of weakness, gained her hold."

Despite melodramatic claims that obscure just what Eva's effect was, it is certain that while Perón was held she went to the streets, working the doorbells of friends and potential enemies, cajoling the former and threatening the latter. If Perón was to be saved, he needed help. Those with influence were asked to exercise it. Those without it were invited to join her in the streets. Those who did not properly reply to her entreaties were never forgiven. Biographer John Barnes describes her as "a woman of incredible humourlessness, startling energy, and corroding rancor, who had an absolute inability to forget and forgive."

Instrumental in turning out the crowds that freed Perón was Cipriano Reyes, the leader of the meatpackers' union. Crowds, including a significant portion of roughnecks, began filling Buenos Aires' broad boulevards, shouting "Viva Perón." When the crowds were disparaged in a newspaper headline as *descamisados*, the shirtless ones – a reference not to their literal shirtlessness but their being without jackets in Buenos Aires' relative formality – Perón jumped on the term. He made a point to assure his followers that he welcomed the support of the shirtless. In fact, they would become putty in the hands of Eva.

In response to Perón's resurgent popularity, Argentine elites, including Perón's enemies in the military, simply missed their opportunity. They were indecisive, and when support for Perón mounted, they caved in. On October 17, a day that would live in the memory of *peronismo*, the General Confederation of Labor declared itself at the side of the crowds chanting "We want Perón." Perón was brought to a balcony of the presidential Casa Rosada and introduced by Gen. Edelmiro Farrell, who had nurtured Perón's career and now saw it overwhelm his weak presidency. Here, Farrell told the huge throng gathered in the plaza below, was "the man we all love...the man who has conquered the hearts of all Argentines."

Not quite "all," but Perón was where he wanted to be. Still complaining about his imprisonment's effect on his health, he told the crowd how he loved his *descamisados,* and how his poor little mother had also been worried about his whereabouts. From now on, he said, he wanted to be just one of the people. Dramatically, he took off his sword belt and handed it to the president. With teary eyes, he sent the crowd home.

A paradox was created. Both elections, to satisfy the middle class, Perón, and the masses, were needed. Political parties, prohibited by the military, were again allowed, and elections were scheduled for February 1946. Perón, whose first wife had died of cancer, married Eva Duarte.

As the elections approached, Perón's opposition again slept at the switch. Elites were convinced they would roll to a presidential victory, but Perón continued to play on themes most appealing to the masses, something the elites were unwilling to do. Then, on the eve of the election, the United States lent its support to Perón's opposition by issuing a 131-page pamphlet entitled "Consultation among the American Republics with Respect to the Argentine Government." Because of its cover, it was called "the blue book." For misbegotten tactics, the episode deserves a prize.

The blue book is credited to Spruille Braden, a former ambassador to Argentina who had been promoted to assistant secretary of state. Braden joined that long line of U.S. envoys, official and amateur, who overestimated their expertise in Latin American affairs. The book thoroughly documented connections between the Argentine hierarchy — especially Perón — and Nazi government officials. Perón condemned the pamphlet as an unacceptable intrusion into Argentine affairs. The majority of Argentines, already convinced that the United States was uncultured to the point of barbarity, roared its disapproval of the book. Perón turned the presidential race from one between him and his principal opponent to one between him and Spruille Braden. Of more than 2.7 million votes cast, Perón won 56 percent; in the electoral college, his margin was 304 to 72; his supporters won overwhelming majorities in both houses of the national assembly.

Anyone sympathetic to Juan Perón and the role he played in Argentine history might prefer to end his story here, in 1946. He had served as catalyst for the workers' consolidation of power. His own power was formidable. He had organized the beginning of a corporate state. However, every system in which powerful classes, at the top, attempt to "balance" competing interests, tends, ultimately, to turn inward, ignoring international realities, resisting internal pressures.

Perón took people in, in every sense of that expression. The man who wrote that "the Nazis had the right idea" and called Mussolini "the greatest man of this century" offered his nation a grab-bag of duplicity and reforms, spurring the working classes to euphoria, rewriting the 1853 constitution, liberalizing divorce laws, and creating havoc with the economy.

During the presidential campaign, the Church sought to conserve its power with a pastoral letter that warned Catholics to beware of candidates who would separate secular from sacred education. Perón cast himself as the logical extension of the conservative, God-fearing, military government that preceded him. Although some Catholic leaders rejected Perón's vision of a "new Argentina," others fell in line. Perón placed the latter on policy-making councils.

After he was elected, schools adopted curricula that extolled the virtues of militarism, the fatherland, and Perón and Eva. Higher education was governed by its own set of rules, but the rectors of the six campuses of the national university were appointed by Perón.

The labor movement was controlled by Eva, who proved even more effective than Perón in communicating with the masses. In charge of the General Confederation of Labor was placed the man who had operated the elevator in the apartment building where the Peróns lived before their marriage.

Eva was also given control of news media in a country with a respected newspaper tradition. The once-proud *La Prensa* was hounded out of existence and *La Nación* was reduced to subservience. Other newspapers, with wealthy Argentines buying stock to assure control, were turned into *peronista* propaganda sheets.

Peronists in control of Congress impeached four of the five supreme court justices, and the chief justice resigned. Throughout the country, lawyers willing to assure the safety of Peronist programs took over the courts.

There were legitimate reforms. During Perón's presidency, a five-year plan called for improved electrification and, in fact, some forty-five power plants, large and small, were constructed.

Eva was head of a ministry of health that initiated relatively effective campaigns against tuberculosis and malaria, both of which were lethal diseases in Argentina because health care outside Buenos Aires was still rudimentary. Finally, the same plan that promoted electrification also called for female suffrage, and women helped reelect Perón to his second term.

There was an international acclaim that reassured Argentine masses that all they had been led to believe about Argentina's cultural leadership might be true. In 1947, Eva was sent on a well-publicized tour of Europe to meet Franco, to be received by the premier of France, to pay the obligatory visit to Italy, and, of course, to be received by Pope Pius XII. At home her charitable foundation — extolled by the poor, maligned by the grand dames of Argentine society who had lost their major public function — brought donations from hundreds of thousands of people.

While hardly "dismantling capitalism" as he claimed to have done,

Perón straddled the cold war in foreign relations and returned substantial control of industry to domestic investors. Sixty percent of industry had been foreign-owned and 30 percent of profits had been flowing out of the country, mostly to British pockets. Gas and electric companies, telephone companies, and other enterprises, under threat of expropriation, were placed in Argentine hands.

More complex needs of the society were not so easily mastered. Perón's "system" of government, which he called *justicialismo,* was unsuccessful in harnessing the country's disparate forces. The term *justicialismo* suggested a middle path between capitalism and communism at the height of the cold war, but a wandering path it was. His five-year plan ran out of money, and, like so many revolutionary leaders in Latin America, Perón was unable to restructure the reality of long years of elite domination. His task was to distribute wealth and opportunity without destroying the economic structure that had produced wealth, without scaring off the elites whose domination was so resented.

Change, though, there was. Argentina's quasi-independent central bank was completely nationalized. The telephone system was expropriated from its American owners. The railway system was taken from the British. Steps like these cannot be overlooked in evaluating Perón's place in helping a proud, if confused, nation claim its rights. Perón was created by forces that surged from Argentine frustrations, and it is foolish to suggest that he was nothing more than a political Narcissus, manipulated by his wife and associates. The accomplishments, like the blunders, were his. But, in short, Perón's unsophisticated leadership, applied to a nation divided, managed to snatch defeat from the jaws of success. Change was not progress, but confusion.

Perón's path had been cleared by prosperity. His presidency began at the end of World War II, when Argentina sat atop grain and beef surpluses needed by a hungry Europe. Mounds of sterling reserves resulted from wartime trading. Resources were in place to boost Argentina into something like the position of Latin American leadership that its people thought was its destiny.

To handle Argentina's postwar trade cornucopia, Perón created, grandly, the Argentine Institute for the Promotion of Exchange. Typically, however, accounts were not precise. Income had a way of disappearing. Poor management led, eventually, to such paradoxes as the need in 1952, during Perón's second term, to "meatless days" in a nation accustomed to one of the highest per capita meat consumption rates in the world. Eventually it was discovered that ranchers, realizing that Perón's middlemen were taking a cut from producers' profits, scaled back production. The same happened to grain production. A national agriculture with so much promise was threatened with ruin.

In addition, the economy was not being infused with productive investment. Speeches portraying Perón as standing up for Argentine rights — a place on the United Nations Security Council, for example — satisfied national sensitivities, but did not build factories. Stress was on image. Peronist agents among labor unions in other Latin American countries were disruptive, meddling in politics, supporting conservatives, glorifying Argentina's leadership in the hemisphere. Meanwhile, unrest grew at home.

In September 1951, there was a coup attempt, during which some say Eva had to pull Perón from premature refuge in the Brazilian embassy so he could lead loyal army troops. In October, an abortive attempt by the General Confederation of Labor to put Eva on the ticket as vice presidential candidate had to be withdrawn. Eva, embarrassed, said she was really too young, anyway, to satisfy the constitutional requirement.

Capable of enflaming dislike in all directions, Perón was especially irritating to Great Britain. Close relations between the two countries are as old as Argentine independence, which the British were instrumental in winning. British interests in Argentina ran deepest in cattle and grain operations, and Britain financed and built Argentina's railroads. But as the British struggled to rebuild after World War II, a war in which many Argentines had flaunted their support for the Axis, Argentines engaged in what was seen as price gouging. British coal, machinery, and petroleum were shipped in return for Argentine leather, meat, and grain at exchange rates favorable to Argentina. When Argentina expropriated the railway system, a bitter dispute led first to Argentina's sterling reserves in England being frozen, finally to a price of 150 million pounds for the railroads.

In July 1952, an era ended when Eva Perón died. Great crowds of Argentine humanity had loved, if not Perón, this woman who seemed to understand them. Hundreds of thousands of Argentine working-class people thronged to see her lying in state; hundreds were trampled, eight of them to death. Her autobiography, *My Mission in Life*, was made compulsory reading for schoolchildren. Streets and schools were named for her. And with Eva gone, Perón's administration, already in trouble, increased its speed downhill. The former elevator operator was fired from his position over the labor movement. Eva's brother, Juan, was fired from his job as secretary to the president — and found in his apartment with a bullet in his head. The bullet, of the caliber used by military and police officers, was fired from too far away to have been suicide.

The Church, either because it questioned the morality of its choice or because it realized it had bet on the wrong horse, turned on Perón. Perón's response was typically clumsy. When two clerical emissaries were sent to the Casa Rosada, they found themselves hustled onto a flight for Rome. When Perón's thugs vandalized cathedrals, the crudeness of the acts sapped the last patience Argentines had with their precocious son.

Perón decorated the presidential residence at Olivos, outside Buenos Aires, and apartments in the city with mirrored bedrooms and installed garish bars. The world learned of his predilection for teenage girls. His favorite was a thirteen-year-old. Asked how he could besmirch the memory of Eva with a thirteen-year-old, his smug, insensitive reply was that he was not superstitious.

In April 1953, with his support disintegrating, with the economy shriveling, Perón did what he did best; he held a mass rally. Perón was a political leader who did as much as any in the hemisphere to demonstrate the effectiveness of rhetoric, to take Hitlerian speaking style and add television. The glossy magazines carried pictures of Perón as a virile, dynamic leader because that was what the people wanted to see. To his rally, held in Buenos Aires, hundreds of thousands gladly came. After his speech, they churned through the downtown streets, burning the Jockey Club, a symbol of patrician complacence, and destroying the headquarters of opposition parties. For another two years, before their enthusiasm waned to a level the military and the Church could jointly overpower, the masses insisted on Perón.

In June 1955, disaffected Catholics rallied where the workers' crowds had been, showing leaders of Perón's opposition that they, too, could count on numbers. By September, Perón was forced to flee aboard a gunboat along the same path that had seemed so close at hand a decade earlier. This time, the crowds would not save him. He wandered to Paraguay, Panama, Venezuela, the Dominican Republic, and finally to Spain, where he was taken in by his old idol, Francisco Franco.

The massive working-class discontent that propped up Perón did not subside, but floundered on in search of a leader. In late 1963, a visitor to southern South America could not help but be struck by the electric atmosphere that the absent Perón could still create by the mere possibility of his presence, even after eight years in exile. He was rumored to be on his way from Spain, and there was in conversations in the streets and cafés a sense of hope, or dread, an expectation that transcended ideas and programs. He was said to be flying first to the coast of Brazil, then down to Montevideo, then crossing the La Plata River in a decisive sweep back to power, without armies, certainly without programs, transported by expectations alone.

The governments of Argentina and Brazil, however, demonstrating international cooperation, turned Perón back the same day he landed in Brazil. He was bundled back to Spain.

In 1972, however, such was the state of Argentine politics that Perón was asked to return. He proved unable to achieve the gargantuan task of bringing order to a society split between the working classes and a military mentality, and died eighteen months after his return. Some considerable part of the disorder, of course, he had helped create.

He was succeeded by his third wife, Isabel Martínez de Perón, whom he had married in exile. Although she affected the style and dress of her fabled predecessor, Eva Duarte de Perón, she was no more able to solve Argentina's Gordian political problems.

Peronismo, with its shifting allegiances, its inclination toward mobs, its tendency toward complaints rather than consensus, remains deeply entrenched in Argentine politics. There are the old crowds and the sons and daughters of the old crowds, the old roughnecks, the old images. *Peronismo* might still represent as much as one-third of the Argentine electorate, a third with which the military and the oligarchs and the Church would rather not have to contend, a third that remembers that for all the corruption and confusion, working-class wages and self-esteem increased dramatically. It was a third that prevailed in 1989 to elect Peronist Carlos Menem president of the republic after too many dark years under the boot of the military.

Peronismo, its critics say, is political vulgarity, and Perón himself was an inept, cowardly demagogue. *Peronistas* still are able to argue, however, how well they both compare with so much that has befallen Argentina since.

María Eva Duarte de Perón
1919–1952
(Argentina)

Angel of the "Shirtless Ones"

Few women have ever been so vehemently damned and so passionately adored. Biographer J. M. Taylor, discussing "the myth" of Eva Perón, writes of the division of feeling, with one side convinced she was "an ideal of pure and passive womanhood incarnate," and the other side seeing her as "manipulated by specialists dedicated solely to the task." Eva Perón was unique. In a sense, she created herself, rising above abject poverty, driving herself relentlessly, boldly turning events to her advantage, molding an image of glamor, profoundly affecting Argentine reality. She encouraged her *descamisados*, her shirtless ones, toward a hope they could not otherwise have known. She was, remarks historian Hubert Herring, "perhaps the shrewdest woman yet to appear in public life in South America."

Several authors have remarked upon the dusty, barren hopelessness of a small Argentine town like Los Toldos, where Eva María Ibarguren was born on May 7, 1919, with the help of an Indian midwife. It is thought that the Ibargurens were in Los Toldos because Eva's grandmother had followed the army there during the campaign to clear Buenos Aires province of Indians. For Eva and her family, one of the most depressing aspects of Los Toldos was that everybody knew everybody else's business. Eva was the fifth of five children born to Juana Ibarguren by Juan Duarte, a landowner and plantation manager who refused to let the children of his mistress take his name.

Duarte, after all, had three children by his wife, the sister of the mayor of nearby Chivilcoy. When he died in 1926, his family tried to prevent Juana Ibarguren and her brood from attending the burial. But Juana Ibarguren insisted. She had spent fifteen years as a cook on one of his plantations, and felt that, under the circumstances, he had really not been such a bad father. With a will that would later be shown by her youngest child — in fact, all her children did relatively well for themselves — Juana Ibarguren, plump, pretty, and determined, stood her ground at the cemetery gate. After a standoff, cooler heads prevailed. Duarte's wife was prevailed upon to allow Juana Ibarguren and her children to pay their last respects.

In 1930, Juana Ibarguren — she would eventually refer to herself as "the widow Duarte," conferring a kind of legitimacy on her children — hired a truck and driver and removed her family to a larger small town, Junín. There, she would be under the protection of her new provider, Oscar Nicolini, who is variously described as a postal worker and a minor politician. Like Duarte, he was married, older than Juana Ibarguren, and a reasonably good provider.

Although Junín was a step up from Los Toldos, Eva had bigger things in mind. She wanted to be an actress, so, at the age of fifteen, she made up her mind to get to Buenos Aires, as bright a metropolis as there was to be found in the Americas in 1935. Argentina prospered as the rest of the world hurtled toward World War II. The center of Argentina, if not the world, was Buenos Aires. One night when Augustín Magaldi, a dashing tango singer whose troupe was appearing in Junín, returned to his dressing room, there was Eva, thin, dark-haired, and determined.

Magaldi was but the first of a string of men who helped Eva Duarte in her career, but what allowed her to succeed, without notable talent, was shrewdness, a flair for the dramatic, and an unembarrassed willingness to grasp the moment. By March 1935, after months of search as the Argentine winter approached, she had gotten a small part in a stage comedy with one of Argentina's leading actresses and, more important, one of the country's leading actors. He helped her find both a place to stay and further acting jobs, and Eva Duarte's career improved to minor dramatic parts that were as short-lived as her love affairs. In time, however, she maneuvered her way up from bit parts on the stage to the company of the military. Her success with Argentine army officers, some of whom were running the country, put her near, at least socially, the salons of power. She once astounded girlfriends by picking up the phone in her dressing room to place a direct call to the president of Argentina, a general. He accepted the call.

Eva Duarte's social connections were not lost on her first major employer, who gave her better and better parts in radio dramas, knowing full well that radio was controlled by the government. Eva Duarte was careful to include among her favored friends those officers who controlled radio communications, and as her contacts broadened, her salary grew, to a level unheard of for other radio actors. Fleur Cowles, a hostile biographer, pays perhaps unintentional tribute to Eva Duarte's capacity for survival by describing her as "doing a turn in a mediocre slot on a mediocre show with a mediocre audience at Argentina's leading radio station." That was precisely Eva Duarte's greatest strength, employing her limited resources in ways, and with results, others could only imagine. She did not waste time with anyone or anything that was not a leader.

By 1940, at the age of twenty, Eva Duarte was simply among the first of her generation to learn how to manipulate radio, a medium that was reaching the masses and that she would later employ to full political advantage. This was the day of primitive technology, and one of Eva Duarte's principal benefactors was the man who made a fortune by cornering the market on radio headsets. Another was a soap manufacturer who simply bought her a show of her own. Working-class Argentines, nonetheless, were transported beyond their own environment through all manner of programs. By 1944, at age twenty-four, she was playing the great empresses of Europe in historical radio dramas written specifically for her by Francisco Muñoz Aspiri. Movie parts followed.

None of her parts was the stuff of great literature; radio was a medium for the masses; her movies were decidedly Grade B. One detractor recalled that as an actress Eva Duarte was "cold as an iceberg." Nevertheless, Eva Duarte had shaped herself, on posters and in show-biz magazines, into someone who was a far cry from the impoverished little girl of the provinces. Her accent and grammar would always be ridiculed by the highborn, but her words were being heard and read by hundreds of thousands.

In 1944, she met Col. Juan Perón. He was forty-eight, she was twenty-four. Suggesting the mythology that has been built around their relationship, biographer Fleur Cowles writes that she had heard at least seven different accounts of the historic meeting. It was most likely either at a gala party to raise money for earthquake victims, or at a neighborhood appearance of Perón, where Eva Duarte showed up with a microphone and crew to record his utterances. In the former instance, the rest of the story is that they stole away from the glittering affair to a riverfront tryst. In the latter instance the story goes that an elderly woman approached Perón, increasingly considered a hero to the masses, and kissed his hand, whereupon Duarte launched into dramatic description for her radio audience that Perón overheard and found flattering.

In any event, it seems likely that Eva Duarte would have engineered a meeting eventually, for there is general agreement that once the two met, she moved swiftly and surely to cement, as it were, the relationship. Within a very short time, they had adjoining apartments on Calle Posadas. Neighbors reported seeing Perón, a widower, in his robe, bringing in the morning delivery of milk, which attentive soldiers delivered to her door.

Perón at that point held three posts: vice president, minister of war, and secretary of labor, although his real strength derived from the loyalty he claimed among the officers who had, in 1943, overthrown the civilian government. Here, then, was the strongest protector of all for Eva Duarte. She immediately introduced him to Muñoz Aspiri, her script writer and image maker. Muñoz was named director of propaganda in the subsecretariat of information. Her mother's paramour, the erstwhile postal clerk, was named director of mail and telegraph.

For her part, Duarte, through her continuing radio broadcasts and her astute political maneuvering, became a conduit for information about all the good things the military government could deliver. Recognizing that the first information about benefits would associate her name with those benefits, she announced to her listeners the military government's initiatives. She interviewed common people who were beneficiaries of government policy. She put a human face on government institutions.

In doing this, she began speaking for herself, changing her role from that of observer, or reporter, to spokeswoman and, finally, to benefactress — not just for the regime but for all of the country. On a program called "Toward a Better Future," she spoke as "the voice of a woman of the people."

As Perón's power grew, so did Eva Duarte's. The Office of Labor and Welfare, a Peronist power base created only a year before, ratified her ascension to head of the Radio Association of Argentina. This gave the association official recognition to represent radio workers at a time when the government was negotiating with competing unions for precisely that right. As an important token of her new post, Duarte was moved into a government office. She had climbed, thereby, from a radio actress to "the voice of Argentina" to an official mediator between the government and radio workers. Perón and the military, imitating the Spanish and Italian systems, were developing corporate fascism, in which labor groups, agricultural associations, industrial combinations, and so on have direct lines to policy makers. Eva Duarte was consolidating power within that system, implementing powerful moves that perfectly complemented those of Perón.

She was transporting herself from the demimonde of second-rate theater to the highest councils of power. Only five feet, five inches tall, she could be assertive in private with men who often bristled at this unexpected display of feminine will power. At the same time, she played a role of public passivity: "In an almost childlike way I live and dream each of the characters whom I portray," she told her audience of listener-citizens. "With this fresh and sincere voice I would like to proclaim how loyal I am to all of you. . . . It hurts me to think that I do not reach your ears."

By October 1945, however, opposition had mounted. Either because they were contemptuous of Eva Duarte's role in their government, or because they resented Perón's assumption of so much power, or for both reasons, the military officers who had brought Perón to a position of power now wanted him out. Perón was forced to quit all three of his posts; Eva Duarte was immediately fired from her job on the air and, without Perón's protection, lost her semiofficial position as head of the radio association.

Adversity was to be Eva Duarte's metier. At this point, in fact, both critics and supporters alike say that Eva Duarte thrived on what seemed to be sure defeat. Her provincial toughness withstood the challenge when, by all accounts, Perón, the symbol of *machismo*, was ready to crumble. Argentine journalist María Flores writes that Eva, "in that moment of weakness, gained her hold." At the end of the day, they met at the apartment they shared.

"Perón was ready to give up," writes John Barnes, a biographer. "But Eva was not prepared to let him. First, she screamed at him, telling him to pull himself together and act like a man. Then she got to work on the teleophone." Her calls went out to junior officers who owed their advancement to Perón. They came in small groups, according to Barnes, "leaving half an hour later pumped full of Eva Duarte's adrenalin." She spoke to labor leaders, reminding them that Argentine elites were no more accustomed to dealing with workers as equals than they were with assertive women. If Perón fell, their conduit to power would be gone.

Eva told Perón to go to his office to clean it out. Meanwhile, she induced labor leaders to raise a crowd and lead it to the government building where his office was located. She called her mother's old and close friend, Oscar Nicolini, who, as head of the mails and telegraph, controlled national radio. He was to set up a national hookup emanating from the steps of the building, she instructed.

Perón, hatless and in civilian clothes, emerged from the building to hold a carefully staged "impromptu" news conference. His statement included an edict that industrialists share profits with their workers, but only if "the workers are decided to defend your interests."

Later that night, the couple was found at their riverfront hideaway. Perón, convinced he might be shot for his role in the 1943 coup when naval cadets were killed defending the government, quaked with fear. Eva Duarte, apparently afraid of nothing, screamed obscenities. Perón was exiled to Martín García Island. Eva Duarte was set free. Historians have noted that the military committed a fatal and irreversible error by not having it the other way around.

Staying at a friend's house, she sallied forth to knock on doors, by turns threatening and cajoling former friends. At one point she was pulled from a taxi and set upon by thugs. "That was the worst aspect of my Calvary in the great city!" wrote Eva later, unabashed by the biblical comparison. "The cowardice of men who were able to do something and did not do it, washing their hands like Pilates, pained me more than the barbarous blows given me when a group of cowards denounced, shouting: 'That's Evita.'" Those who did not reply favorably to her entreaties were never forgiven.

Labor leaders responded. A general strike was called for October 18, but the workers' zeal was not to be contained, and on October 17 a demonstration erupted. It was Perón who appeared on a balcony to the roar of the masses gathered in the main plaza, but it was Eva Duarte who put him there.

Five days later they were married. Perón was elected in February 1946, and as First Lady, Eva Duarte de Perón was uninhibited by tradition. "No woman had ever assumed the title in so official a manner, writes J. M. Taylor. "Attacks rained down on the presumption of a mere starlet of radio drama and cinema."

Eva Ibarguren, the illegitimate bumpkin, who had made herself Eva Duarte, the radio star, now had helped win for herself a role as Eva Perón, the First Lady. Still, she aspired to an image the masses, quite literally, would sanctify as their "Lady of Hope," but that she would want to be called "Evita." She traveled throughout the country, refining that image, to the dismay of critics and to the delight of the masses. Her constant companion and confidante was Isabel Ernst, whose title was "Labor Secretary to the Presidency of the Nation." Muñoz Aspiri, the scriptwriter, turned his pen to this larger drama. Eva Perón, of course, was her own best director.

"A few days of the year I act the part of Eva Perón," she would explain later, with the help of a ghostwriter, "and I think I do better each time in that part, for it seems to me to be neither difficult nor disagreeable. The immense majority of days I am, on the other hand, 'Evita,' a link stretched between the hopes of the people and the fulfilling hands of Perón, Argentina's first woman *peronista* — and this, indeed, is a difficult role for me, one in which I am never quite satisfied with myself."

Just as she had presumed to be "the voice of the Argentine people," she shifted her speeches from explanations of government policy to her own expression of the people's needs. Her power grew with her independence; her agenda was long.

She wanted housing for working-class families; she initiated a childcare plan that included summer camps for middle-class children; she militated for safe drinking water; she wanted help for female immigrants from the interior; she promoted junior soccer, which included a medical exam that was for some children their first; she helped organize college-student housing.

When her efforts overshadowed government agencies, there was resentment. Either they were not doing their jobs, which caused resentment of her effectiveness; or they were doing their jobs, which caused resentment of her grandstanding.

Undaunted, at least in public, she would remark later, "I have discovered a fundamental feeling in my heart which completely governs my spirit and my life. That feeling is my indignation when confronted with injustice. . . . I think now that many people become accustomed to social injustice in the first years of their lives. Even the poor think the misery they endure is natural and logical. They learn to tolerate what they see or suffer, just as it is possible to acquire a tolerance for a powerful poison."

Withal, she was a controversial figure. She traveled — typically, without Perón, although with Isabel Ernst — on an exhausting round of personal appearances, her popularity growing as the Argentine working class convinced itself that here, for all her faults, was a champion. During 1946, she progressed from shouts of derision when she appeared at a February rally, to the title of "First Worker of Argentina" in July and, in December, to "Queen of Labor." During the December ceremony, in Tucumán, either seven or nine people (reports vary) were crushed to death in the enthusiastic crowd.

When the high-born matrons of the *Sociedad de Beneficiencia*, a snobbish charitable organization associated with the Church, said she was "too young" to be their president, she sarcastically suggested that maybe they would prefer her mother. Historian June E. Hahner notes that Eva Perón's "illegitimate birth was never forgotten or forgiven by the country's social elite once she achieved power." Power, however, allowed Eva Perón in September 1946 to take over the office of the *Sociedad* and make it the base for what became Fundación Eva Perón, the beginning of her empire. Importantly, she was sharing her power by empowering others. Before her first year as First Lady was over, she was making weekly feminist speeches.

Her views, especially in a traditional, male-dominated, snobbish society, were radical: "Although it is not fundamental in the feminist movement," she said, "the vote is its most powerful instrument. . . . 'Politics' is not an end, but a means."

"I think that men, in their great majority, above all in the old political parties, never understood this properly. That is why they always failed. Our destiny as women depends on our not falling into the same error."

She proposed a special tax on all workers — a device that would later be used to fund her foundation — for "fixing a small monthly allowance for every woman who gets married, from the day of her marriage."

As wily as she was determined, Eva Perón let no others scrape off any of the residual power that accrued to her efforts. She formed the *Asociación Pro-Sufragio Feminino* to win the vote for women, but when other wives of political leaders tried to form "sister" clubs, she rejected them, making public statements that their efforts were not to be confused with hers and that their funds were not to be mixed with hers.

Her appeal — and it was uniquely hers — was spiritual at its base, political in its expression, and intimately feminist: "Everything, absolutely everything, in this contemporary world, has been made according to man's measure."

> We are absent from governments.
> We are absent from parliaments.
> From international organizations.
> We are in neither the Vatican nor the Kremlin.
> Nor in the commissions of atomic energy.
> Nor in the great business combines.
> Nor in Freemasonry, nor in other secret societies.
> We are absent from all the great centers constituting a power in the world.
> And yet we have always been present in the time of suffering, and in all humanity's bitter hours.

She reclaimed her prominence in labor affairs. In early 1947 she met twenty-six labor delegations in one day. Her friendships included a number of Argentine image makers — publishers, theater people, and industrialists who understood the value of advertising to the leadership of a mass democracy. Reporters who went to her suite of offices described a consummate politician, listening to simple folk from the countryside who came to ask for housing or work, speaking with cabinet members who needed her help or could help her, moving among groups, being reminded of other appointments, distributing government largesse, demanding political quid pro quo. She sometimes dispensed houses to needy families; she often dispensed peso notes from a supply she kept ready on her desk.

Her power was manifest in two ways: directly, on her own; and indirectly, by influencing her husband. She served as president of an international conference on social security; she took a seat at the table for labor negotiations, dealing with striking bank employees, newsvendors, and railway workers. She held weekly meetings with labor leaders who were the mainstay of Peronist power. At the same time, she influenced Perón's selection of cabinet members. It is said that she would meet with "her" selections before they went into formal cabinet meetings, sometimes delaying their arrival so long that disgruntled military officers had already left.

"Thrilled or alarmed," writes historian Taylor, "Argentina watched Eva's growing contacts with organized labour, her activities in social welfare, her feminist initiatives, and her influence in the press."

In January 1947, she bought the newspaper, *Democracia*, and was widely credited with, or accused of, influencing the news coverage and editorial policy of two others. Newspapers in general had to respond to a blizzard of press releases about her nonstop, if contrived, activities. Critics, meanwhile, portrayed her as a threatening influence on affairs from the congressional to the social. When a compliant congress passed a Perónist law that prohibited insulting the presidency, newspapers could be, and were, closed for criticizing her. Radical Party opponent Ernesto Sammartino used his congressional seat to compare Argentina to a cart mired in the mud, stuck because it was being pulled by a mare. To escape arrest he fled across the river to Montevideo, joining other critics of the Peróns.

In 1947 Eva Perón raised her controversial image to the international level. She accepted an invitation from Francisco Franco, who had also been a "neutral" tool of the Axis during World War II. Such a trip, observes one biographer, was "thought by those who dreaded her growing consequence and magnetism to confirm all their fears."

The navy denied her a ship, so she flew. Five hundred thousand Argentines saw her off; 300,000 Spanish greeted her. It was a private trip, but she was accorded authority to sign certain agreements with European governments. She granted a shipload of wheat to Spain and approved a loan for the purchase of wheat and meat to France. She met, and was, of course, photographed with, Franco and French President Vincent Auriol. She was received by Pope Pius XII. In Switzerland, however, she was the target of tomatoes, which the anti–Perón press back at home chronicled with glee. As a result, two newspapers were closed.

When British royalty, presumably on the advice of Parliament, declined to invite her for a stay, she turned toward home and not only lunched with the president of Brazil, but attended a special session of the Chamber of Deputies convened in her honor. Friendly newspapers coined the term *presidenta* for her.

On the trip, she had collapsed from exhaustion, continuing over the advice of her physician. Detractors were suspicious, thinking the fainting *Madona de los Humildes*, as some called her, was just another public-relations trick. Indeed, after the trip, she gave up the flashy clothes and hats that had been her trademark, and a new image emerged. She appeared in tailored suits; she went hatless, her hair pulled severely back into a bun; she wore simple dresses or a blouse and sweater. The collapse had been real. Eva's health was delicate all her life, as time would demonstrate.

She returned to Argentina on August 23, 1947, and Congress approved female suffrage shortly after that. It should be noted that this was six years before a similar empowerment was achieved in "revolutionary" Mexico. Congress also approved the nation's first law allowing divorce. Eva Perón was reaching the zenith of her power.

As president of the Perónist Women's party, she led legions whose electoral power was great and untested. The party was a springboard for women to run, successfully, for Congress. With government appropriations, private donations, and deductions from workers' wages, she created the Eva María Duarte de Perón Foundation of Social Aid. Incorporated in June 1948 and with a fund of 23,000 pesos after five months, its treasury held 2 billion pesos by 1952. She was able to fill warehouses of staples for low-income people at officially controlled prices.

Her family moved into positions of control as well. Brother Juan Duarte, an erstwhile soap salesman and ne'er-do-well, was first made inspector of government operations, then installed as Perón's private secretary. Her sisters and their husbands were handed sinecures in the courts and the ports, the schools and the mails.

How could this child of dusty, provincial streets find acceptance in the tight, arrogant society of Buenos Aires? "The oligarchy has never been hostile to anyone who could be useful to it," she wrote, with tough wisdom. "Power and money were never bad antecedents to a genuine oligarch."

Nevertheless, the military was resentful of her role and contemptuous of the evidence of mounting corruption in the regime. In 1949, the army refused to allow her into Campo de Mayo, a camp outside Buenos Aires, and it appeared there would be a confrontation between the Peróns and the military. The Peróns prevailed, for the time.

On January 9, 1950, Eva Perón collapsed at a public ceremony in the middle of a hot summer day. She was experiencing pelvic pain, fever, and vaginal hemorrhaging. Her ankles were badly swollen. It became known that for about a year sexual activity had been impossible. On January 12, 1950, a hysterectomy was reported to the press as an appendectomy.

Although the end of her life was near, she drove herself obsessively, as if determined to make herself the martyr her enemies had mocked. Her personal physician quit in May 1950, after she flared up at him one day and slapped him after he admonished her not to work so hard. He later added that a reason for his resignation was concern over the increasing corruption in the administration.

Preparations for the coming election — Congress had repealed the prohibition against a president's succeeding himself — were under way. Despite increasing criticism of the administration and acrimonious distrust of her role by the military, labor leaders wanted Eva Perón to stand for vice president. On August 22, 1950, a *cabildo abierto*, a huge town meeting, was to be held. Labor saw it as the chance to announce that both Peróns would be on the ticket. Perón was ambivalent. Eva, who may have known she was dying of cancer, certainly understood the seriousness of the opposition to her candidacy.

Perón appeared on the dais without her, but the crowd would not accept that. The first speaker could not be heard over calls for Eva, and she was brought to the stage. Presumably very weak, always emotional, and witnessing the greatest outpouring of sentiment she had ever seen, she broke into tears. Knowing that she could not be a candidate, she said only, "I will always do what the people may say." Then her words wandered. "I prefer to be 'Evita' rather than the president's wife," she said, "if 'Evita' is said in order to alleviate pain in my country."

Disjointedly, she "proclaimed" Perón president. When Perón stepped to the microphone, however, someone shouted, "Let Compañera Eva speak," and when Perón ended his remarks that request was taken up by others. The moderator, a labor leader, insisted that she accept the vice presidency, telling her that she was "the only one who can and must occupy" the post. She took the microphone to beg for time. The crowd would not have it. They became unruly, perhaps suspecting that their Lady of Hope was in the control of the same old political forces that had for so long oppressed them. They began to clamor while shouted debates took place on stage. Perón, upstaged and irritated, wanted an end to the proceeding. Eva, pitifully, asked the crowd for a two-hour delay. She wanted to be allowed to make her announcement on the radio.

Immediately, newspapers reported that she had taken the nomination, and her candidacy was announced by the *Confederación General de Trabajadores*, the blanket labor organization that Perón created. Army commanders and units loyal to them grew restless. On August 31, nine days after the assembly, Eva Perón read an announcement broadcast at eight o'clock that night.

In her renunciation, she tried to describe a place at the head of her *descamisados* that ought to be distinct from an official position in the government. "This decision comes from the most intimate part of my conscience," she said, protesting too much that the decision was hers, "and for that reason is totally free and has all the force of my definitive will." She wanted it remembered "that there was at the side of Perón a woman who dedicated herself to carrying the hopes of the people to the president, and that the people affectionately called this woman 'Evita.' That is what I want to be."

Her illness worsened. When, on October 17, Loyalty Day, she made a public appearance, it was the first time in three weeks she had been out of bed. Then she underwent another operation, which was kept secret, and, in November, yet another. She still was able to record a speech from bed to be broadcast November 9. On November 11, a ballot box was brought to her hospital room for her vote in the first Argentine election allowing female participation.

In early December there was enough of a remission that she was able to take short drives around Buenos Aires with her husband. She made a

Christmas speech and on Christmas Day met with reporters. Her agrarian plan was inaugurated, providing equipment to farmers and increasing the acreage available for crops. These last vital signs encouraged her followers to believe she would fully recover, but only a superhuman effort made that possible.

On May Day, 1952, she not only appeared at an assembly, she managed a short speech. Her last remarks, perhaps as she contemplated her own death, tended toward harshness, an insistence on judging others. Biographer Taylor describes "a definite element of violence in her rhetoric." Eva Perón herself had admitted that "all my life I have been prone to be driven and guided by my feelings," and the end was no different.

A week passed, and on her birthday she appeared on a terrace of the presidential residence, waving to the crowd. She was so weak, however, that she had to be held up. The Chamber of Deputies designated her "spiritual chief of the nation," and on May 23 she addressed governors and legislators at the residence. Again, there was violence in her message. It would later be publicly revealed that in spite of her condition, Eva Perón, hearing mounting criticism and fearing an anti–Perón coup, used Social Aid Foundation money and the good offices of Dutch royalty to buy 5,000 pistols and 1,500 machine guns to arm the workers.

Her last public appearance was at the inauguration ceremony for Perón's second term, June 5, 1952. A specially built support made of wire and plaster held up her thin, cancer-ravaged body in the open car as the couple was driven on the triumphal procession. "Like every woman of the people," she had written, "I have more strength than I appear to have." She managed to stand through the ceremony.

In bed, she began *Mi Mensage*, but never finished it. When U.S. publishers refused to publish *La Razón de Mi Vida*, Argentine workers called a protest strike for July 4.

On July 26, 1952, her death was announced at 8:25, two hours after it occurred, but Eva Perón's journey was not over.

There was a plan to convert the Buenos Aires monument to *descamisados* to a huge crypt, the largest in the world, and construction was begun. Her body, immaculately coiffed, a rosary in her hands, lay in state while two lines of mourners filed slowly past. "I never knew they loved her so much," Perón remarked to a friend after watching Argentines weep over the glass-covered coffin. "I never knew they loved her so."

Although Perón said she would lie in state "until the last citizen of the Republic has been able to see Compañera Evita," it proved impossible because of a rather bizarre scheme to embalm her for all time. The embalming process required a series of steps at certain times. On August 9, her body was carried at the head of a procession to the Congress. Two days later, she was pulled to the labor ministry on a gun carriage drawn by forty-five men and women dressed alike in white shirts and black trousers. Nurses and cadets swelled the ranks of mourners. Some 2 million people, kept in relative order by 17,000 soldiers, thronged the route.

There, at the labor ministry, her body was to remain, safe amid rumors that her enemies might "kidnap" her before the huge crypt was complete. Her book, *La Razón de Mi Vida*, was assigned to countless schoolchildren. Postal boxes were assigned and kept open for people to write to her. The pope was asked to make her a saint. On the radio, commentators continually recalled her birth date, her renunciation of the vice presidency, the day and time of her death.

In 1955, however, after Perón was deposed and hustled into exile in September, there was no rest for the body of Eva Perón. The value of the goods and assets of her various foundations, agencies, and funds were estimated at $700 million, a staggering sum. The tales of her opulence seemed to have been borne out. The site of the crypt, still under construction, was dynamited — deep had run the hatred and jealousy. Jorge Luís Borges, the literary giant, dismissed Eva Perón. "No one ever seemed capable of speaking of Eva Perón in dispassionate terms," notes historian Hahner. "Those who benefited from her large charity foundation glorified her. Others vilified her. But certainly no one ignored Evita." So high was the emotional tenor that the military was afraid Eva Perón's body would be used by Perónists as a mystical rallying point. One night, a squad of soldiers showed up at the labor ministry, and the body was taken away. No one knew where.

In June 1956, Eva Perón's body was found, hidden in a sealed wooden crate marked "radio equipment" and stacked in the basement of a government building. Its journey to that point had been a troubled one. An army officer in whose apartment it was briefly hidden had been murdered, leaving a pregnant widow. Hardly had this story come to light, when Eva Perón's body disappeared again.

There was, for some time, only a paper trail. All there was left of Eva Perón, the woman who had so moved the masses, was the signature of a priest who had claimed the body in January 1957. It was not publicly known where he had taken it.

In 1971, as Argentines continued to demonstrate their inability to form a stable, democratic government (the divorce law was repealed; the number of women holding office diminished), Perónists called for the return of their hero. Perón was living comfortably in exile in Madrid, married for the third time. Because of political pressure in Buenos Aires, it was disclosed, after a decade and a half, that in a cemetery in Milan, Italy, was the coffin of "Maria Maggi," whom documents claimed to be an Italian citizen who died in Argentina and had been shipped "home." The body of Eva Perón was disinterred and shipped to Perón's house in Madrid.

The coffin was opened under the watchful eyes of Isabel Martínez de Perón, Eva's successor, Perón, and Dr. Pedro Ara, the embalmer. Her hair was dirty, and the end of a finger was broken off. Repairs were made.

Perón was returned to power in 1972 and after eighteen months died in office. He was replaced by Isabel Perón, who copied Eva's dress, hairstyle, and gestures — to little avail. Isabel had been careful to leave Eva's body behind in Madrid, but Perónists clamored for her return. Rumors flew that there had been mutilations. In 1974, Isabel Perón had Eva Perón's body shipped home to a televised reception, although the gesture was of no help in saving her stumbling regime.

In 1976, the body of Eva Perón was secretly taken to an exclusive Buenos Aires cemetery and enclosed in the Duarte family crypt. Eva María Duarte de Perón had finally found, in a way, acceptance.

José Figueres
1906–1990
(Costa Rica)

At the Center of Latin America

José Figueres, the five-foot, three-inch Costa Rican known as "Pepe," helped construct one of Latin America's most admired democracies. To supporters he is a Cincinnatus of the hemisphere, a patrician who tilled the soil, entering politics only to save the republic, an archetype of democratic moderation. Detractors, however, had a different image. He was labeled both Nazi-sympathizer and socialist and, finally, seen as a tragic Faustus, who

sold his soul to the Central Intelligence Agency and to a hoodlum of international finance. The truth takes something from both portraits. Figueres was a man of wide interests who was always impatient for action. One of Latin America's most determined leaders, Pepe Figueres placed himself at the center of many storms.

It is a humorous irony that so desperate were critics to find fault with José María Figueres Ferrer, that they pointed out that he was conceived by his parents before they left Barcelona. So, although he was born on September 25, 1906, in the tiny village of San Ramón, Costa Rica, a few months after they immigrated, he would be called by some *el catalán*, as if he did not belong in their tiny country. San Ramón is in the coffee-growing hills northwest of San José. There his father, Mariano Figueres Forges, practiced medicine, specializing in electrotherapy, the use of electrical current to ease neurological and muscular discomforts.

José Figueres was the first of four children born to Paquita Ferrer Minguella de Figueres, and from the beginning he did things his way. The schools in San Ramón were not good, a fact that put Figueres early on the road to self-education. As with Sarmiento, self-study would leave Figueres widely read, but without a degree. Because of his father's specialty, Figueres was interested in electricity even as a boy. He set up a small laboratory in his bedroom and enrolled in the International Correspondence Schools of Scranton, Pennsylvania, improving his knowledge of both electricity and English. By the time he was ready for high school, his father had taken the family to San José to establish a clinic.

The elder Figueres insisted, against his son's objections, that the youngster attend Colegio Seminario, where, according to a biographer, "the German priests were stern disciplinarians, and the curriculum ignored the sciences and discouraged free inquiry." The father wished his son to follow in his footsteps, but the son was showing signs not of the calm deliberation one associates with physicians, but the erratic temperament typical of some leaders. Young Figueres suffered from depression, tried to run away, and, it is said, attempted suicide. His father responded by switching him from boarding to day student. Still, after four years of the five-year secondary curriculum, Figueres peevishly dropped out.

In 1924, at age seventeen, Figueres went alone to Boston to study electrical engineering at Massachusetts Institute of Technology. When MIT conditioned its acceptance on his taking preparatory courses, Figueres had no patience for the idea. He left the school after six months and would later disparage "canned education." He turned, instead, to the Boston Public Library and charted his own course. When money from home was offered to help him return, he turned it down and stayed, working as an electrician for Salada Tea Company.

Moving to New York, he worked as a translator during the day and took classes in electrical engineering at night. In New York he was joined by Francisco "Chico" Orlich, a boyhood friend and scion of a wealthy family in San Ramón, and Alberto Martén, another boyhood friend. At the Liceo de Costa Rica, the three had been influenced by teachers who awoke them to political ideas. Those ideas now got full discussion as the three grew to maturity in New York City.

Figueres returned to Costa Rica at his father's insistence in 1928. With a stake provided by his father and the Orlich family, he established in San Cristóbal, south of San José, *Sociedad Agricola Industrial San Cristóbal*, a holding company that managed coffee plantations in four towns and used the capital to develop a down-at-the-heels farm. He named the farm *La Lucha Sin Fin*, Struggle Without End. Although only thirty-five miles south of San José, La Lucha took seven hours to reach on horseback. His brother Antonio worked the farm with him.

They developed the farm's former crop, maguey, the thick, broad leaves of which yield tough fiber for making rope suitable for heavy marine use. *Cabuya* fiber was processed to make gunny sacks for coffee beans. They brought in water through bamboo conduits with sufficient force for hydroelectric power. In building the business, Figueres also developed the area, introducing schools and libraries, recreation areas, better roads, telephones, and clinics. He became known as "Don Pepe," a respectful compromise between the informality of his education and the fact that he was the boss.

In 1934, Figueres married Henrieta Boggs Long, a teacher from Birmingham, Alabama, whom he met in San José. Although the Depression meant that sometimes they had to issue scrip in place of pay, Figueres' enterprises prospered. By 1942, as the war raged in Europe and Asia, San Cristóbal operated Costa Rica's largest rope-and-twine factory. Critics called Figueres paternalistic, although the leader of the Costa Rican Communist party, Manuel Mora, conceded that Figueres was not cheap with wages. Figueres called his workers "comrades," and argued that conflict between the classes was a useless concept in a developing country. Daniel Oduber, a protegé, wrote that Figueres was "a 'socialist' before it was fashionable to be one."

Figueres was drawn ineluctably into Costa Rican politics. The country had long been dominated by the "Generation of '89," men of the previous century who had encouraged democratic participation, but then, as they grew older, could not let go of the reins of control. Personal followings, the bane of Latin American politics, allowed Costa Rican presidents to alternate with hand-picked successors. Rafael Calderón Guardia epitomized this history.

In 1940, Calderón won the presidency with the full support of his predecessor, León Cortéz Castro. Upon taking office, Calderón cast himself as a populist, absorbing "New Deal" goals and the ideas of the recent papal encyclical, *Rerum novarum.* He instituted a social security system and proposed a minimum wage, an eight-hour working day, and adequate housing for working-class families. He reopened the University of Costa Rica, which had been closed since 1888.

There was a darker side, however. Liberals eventually began to grumble over his readmitting the Jesuits — expelled for poking their sharp minds into political affairs — and reintroducing religious instruction in the public schools. More seriously, The Calderón regime was accused of corruption.

Calderón also divided opinion by interning German and Italian residents. Costa Rica had declared itself on the side of the Allies in World War II, but Calderón took this declaration to the limit of his powers, and beyond. He confiscated the property of foreign owners despite their contribution to the Costa Rican economy. Figueres was among those coming to the defense of the emigrés.

In 1940, the year of Calderón's election, Figueres had helped found the Center for the Study of National Problems. He and colleagues like Orlich and Martén dubbed themselves the "Generation of '40." They were *centristas*, critical of Calderón, of the corruption that infused his regime, and, especially, of his alliance with the communist leader Manuel Mora, whose party enjoyed widespread support among banana workers.

In February 1942, by-elections brought matters to a head. Calderón forces were accused of ballot-box stuffing. As the nation seemed ready to topple Calderón's regime, however, his communist supporters saved him. Figueres, once called a socialist, was now labeled a "fascist" because of the center's opposition to the communists.

In this heated atmosphere there occurred, on the night of July 2, a crucial event. At a dock of the Atlantic port of Limón — which was not blacked out, as it should have been — a United Fruit Company freighter was being loaded when two torpedoes from a German submarine slammed into its hull. The ship sank in shallow water, and twenty-four workmen, most of them trapped below deck, died.

Without a visible enemy to confront, embarrassed by carelessness that had cost so many lives, and whipped up by Mora's communists, some people reacted with a protest march, demanding internment of "traitors." Twenty thousand angry Costa Ricans gathered at San José's main plaza, and in their march to the presidential residence they deteriorated into a rock-throwing, looting mob. Their targets were presumed Nazi sympathizers, but they ransacked Italians' and Germans' businesses indiscriminately, included in their binge a warehouse belonging to Figueres, and even stoned the church and school of Spanish monks. One hundred and twenty-three buildings were damaged and seventy-six people hurt. Calderón never tried to calm the mob.

The church and the center pointed their fingers at the communists. Figueres blamed Calderón, whom he felt let the situation get out of hand. Figueres, outraged, bought time on the radio to speak his mind. He linked the government's inability to quell the riot with its weakness in protecting shipping. "The worst form of sabotage," he said acidly, "is an inept ally." Swept along by his own rhetoric, he widened his criticism to the government's social security program, charging Calderón: "You assure us of a decent burial and let us die of hunger."

As Figueres' harangue continued, police threw open the studio doors. The police chief grabbed his coat, but Figueres kept on talking. "The police order me to stop," he blurted. "I'll not be able to say what I think ought to be done, but I can summarize it in a few words: the government ought to get out!"

Figueres was held incommunicado. One defender insisted Figueres had only said "what the honest and conscientious citizens of the Republic are feeling and thinking." Calderón, unassuaged, wanted Figueres exiled, but he stayed, stubbornly, in jail. Friends finally convinced him that to prevent confiscation of his lands he should accept exile.

He went to Mexico, where Martí had gone in exile. Also like Martí, Figueres sent his wife home to Costa Rica to give birth to their first child, whom they named Carmen after Martí's daughter. From Mexico Figueres sent home for publication his essay, *Palabras Gastadas*, sketching his ideas for Costa Rica's future.

Those ideas were expanded to Central America in general — then dominated by dictators — by his friendship with Rosendo Argüello, Jr., who had fled to Mexico from Nicaragua in 1936, when Antonio Somoza took power. Figueres and Argüello were among the authors of what came to be called the "Caribbean Legion," a plan to rid Central America of dictators.

Meanwhile, as Figueres looked abroad for enemies, the political situation in Costa Rica worsened. Calderón's heir was Teodoro Picado, who tried to make their politics more palatable by downplaying the alliance with the communists, fearing it risked losing the Church's support. Mora, in turn, put the best face on the communists by changing their name to *Vanguardia Popular*. The corruption did not cease, however, and criticism became more vocal.

In September 1943, the Center for the Study of National Problems invited people to submit ideas for postwar society, publishing them as *Ideario Costaricense*. Figueres' essay suggested eliminating personalism in politics by introducing a professional civil service. Never one to miss an opportunity for insult, Figueres referred in his essay to Calderón officials as "cutthroats."

The presidential election of 1944 put such feelings to a test. The Popular Vanguard, or communists, using tough banana workers and encouraged by Calderón, formed *brigadas de choque*, bands of thugs. They disrupted gatherings of their opponents and broke into radio stations and newspapers. Their opponents bombed Mora's home. With emotions at a fever pitch, Teodoro Picado was elected.

Figueres' friends refused to accept the outcome. They sent Orlich to Mexico to induce Figueres to buy arms and to organize a revolution. Figueres shared their impatience, but was concerned about the safety of his employees, who were being harassed, and decided to return to Costa Rica.

His return sparked a demonstration, as thousands accompanied him from the airport to the downtown offices of *Diaro de Costa Rica*, a newspaper. Figueres grandly predicted a "Second Republic." More crowds welcomed him back to La Lucha, but he shunned further public displays, convinced that electoral politics were not the answer. He wanted fighters now, not voters, and began writing his views for the new weekly newspaper *Acción Demócrata.*

Figueres rejected the notion of agricultural diversification, saying rather that Costa Rica should capitalize on its tradition of coffee growing. Diversification meant overlaying the economy with a new network of services, he contended, from roads to electrical lines. Why not, Figueres asked, heighten coffee production, bringing the cash necessary to import other goods? As for land reform, he declared that the important goal was to divide the profits earned from the land among all workers, not to subdivide the land into inefficient parcels.

His ideas attracted the intellectuals of the Center in a general blending of views among opponents of the regime. As a result of this blending, a convention was held on March 11, 1945, and *Partido Social Demócrata*, the PSD, was formed. It was the first time a Costa Rican party had grown around ideas, not around a personality. The platform demanded the vote for women and, to preclude fraud, creation of a separate "branch" of government to oversee elections.

The PSD made Figueres treasurer, but ignored his counsel. He believed armed revolt was the only lasting answer to Costa Rica's problems. At one meeting, Figueres, frustrated by his colleagues' talk, berated them for their timidity and ended his lecture by slamming his pistol on the desk. That, he told them, was the only way. After personally publishing a denouncement of the Picado regime without consulting other PSD leaders, Figueres quit the party. Martén and Orlich followed their impatient friend.

Spoiling for a fight, Figueres dispatched Arguello back to Mexico to buy guns with the more than $400,000 Figueres had raised. Arguello promised to match that sum. In a tragicomedy of errors, however, Arguello bought the guns, hid them, but then could not, despite bribes, get them out of the country. Meanwhile, Costa Rican by-elections simply strengthened the hand of Picado and Calderón.

Figueres rejoined the PSD, but still fought with its members. One PSD leader, taking a page from Figueres' book, staged his own coup attempt, but failed. Now, thwarted at the ballot box and in the field, the PSD sought accommodation with Picado, much to Figueres' disgust. Again, he quit.

To end this confused turning against themselves, the opposition called a mass convention for February 1947 at the National Stadium in San José. There, 2,000 delegates were to settle on an acknowledged leader. Figueres was nominated, and the choice was clear: Should the opposition follow the fiery ways of Figueres, or espouse moderation? Just before the convention was called to order, headlines told of the discovery by Mexican police of the clandestine guns; Arguello was arrested and the weapons seized. An embarrassed Figueres ran third in the balloting.

The convention settled on support for Otilio Ulate, a tall, engaging man whose lack of strong commitment to any one idea enhanced his value as a standard bearer for disparate groups. His opponent would be Calderón.

The election campaign, as always, was violent. Discussion often degenerated into street fights. Then, on July 20, 1945, a riot in Cartago galvanized the opposition. Although there were no deaths, many people were injured, and it was clear that Picado's government was not going to uphold public safety. Opponents of the regime protested by calling a strike, first in Cartago, then nationwide. Figueres welcomed the action, appearing one afternoon on a balcony of *Diario de la Costa* before an enthusiastic crowd in the streets below. With chalk on a huge blackboard, he printed "*HUELGA,*" "STRIKE." Eight people were killed the first day. Ulate was forced into hiding.

Figueres was convinced there was no chance for electoral reform. By November 1947, he had disclosed to Ulate that he planned to equip and train an army in the countryside. Guns for the enterprise suddenly became available when an ill-begotten invasion of the Dominican Republic, launched from Cuba, failed. Two million dollars' worth of small arms were being held by the revolutionary government in Guatemala. The Dominican invasion had been backed by Cuba, Guatemala, and Venezuela, so a committee from those countries would determine how the weapons were to be allocated. Figueres argued that Costa Rica was next in line for revolt. To get the arms, Figueres signed a pact in Guatemala City on December 16, 1947. Parties to that agreement — the backbone of the "Caribbean Legion" — agreed to overthrow the governments of Costa Rica, the Dominican Republic (Rafael Trujillo), and Nicaragua (Anastasio Somoza). Now Figueres had his arms, if he could muster an army to use them.

On February 4, 1948, Figueres called together at La Lucha the seven who would form the cadre of his army. None had a military background, and they could hardly be described as centrists. Three were in hiding, suspected of having bombed the car of communist leader Mora. Two others had been part of the short-lived rebellion of the year before. One, Frank Marshall, had been a high school student in Germany in 1936 and was reputedly a Nazi sympathizer.

The election was held on February 8, and Ulate won, 54,931 to 44,438. However, Calderón thugs simply took matters into their own hands. A day after the election, many of the ballots, stored at a girls' school in San José, were burned in a mysterious fire. Two days after the election, there was a petition to cancel the result because of irregularities. Four days after the election, crowds were in the streets, claiming they had not been allowed to vote.

Each side blamed the other. Analysis seemed to make it clear, however, that Ulate, no matter how much cheating occurred, had won by at least 9,000 votes. Nevertheless, Calderón forces were understandably incensed when the director of the elections office dropped out of sight only to reappear at Figueres' side, a trusted officer of his army in the countryside. Costa Rica moved to the brink of civil war.

On February 28, one day before the deadline that would have reopened the voting in Congress, a special committee appointed by Picado decided, two-to-one, to declare Ulate provisional president. Calderón refused to accept the committee's judgment.

He insisted that Congress reopen the voting. As the congressional debate restirred the controversy, police were dispatched to the home of an Ulate supporter, where there was a small meeting. After a heated exchange in front of the house, police shot and killed one of the men at the meeting. Although another national council of reconciliation was hastily convened, the die was cast. Figueres waited in the countryside, his small army ready. "Don Pepe did not have to make a revolution," notes biographer Ameringer. "One was delivered to him."

Figueres' plan was to descend from the mountains, block the Inter-American Highway, and create an occupied zone in the southern part of the country, near the border with Panama. After airlifting in arms and equipment, he would take San Isidro, then fall on Cartago, southeast of San José. Figueres thought that the taking of Cartago would break the government's will.

The Costa Rican army numbered about three hundred men, not well trained and owing little allegiance to either Calderón or Picado. When Calderón tried to take command of the army, Picado refused, then failed to take charge himself, while Figueres grew stronger.

On March 11, thirty of Figueres' men took San Isidro de El General, a small town with a dirt airfield. They captured three DC-3s, a type of aircraft none of the rebel pilots had ever flown. Despite that fact, two planes were immediately flown to Guatemala for arms and ammunition. Figueres, commanding what was barely an army, had an air force. Back came the planes with six hundred rifles, a few machine guns, ammunition, and seven Dominicans and Hondurans ready to fight. The "Caribbean Legion" had landed.

Three days later, Figueres took Frailes. With the government turning his right flank and growing in strength, he had to immediately retreat into the mountains. Another rebel force was at La Lucha, meanwhile, headed by Alberto Martén, who was second in command. Martén, knowing he could not withstand the predicted government assault and afraid to bury the weapons entrusted to him, placed the weapons in trucks and lumbered away over dirt roads. That clumsy retreat turned out to be just the right thing to do. Fearful that he would be run down by faster-moving government troops, Martén established a perimeter at El Empalme, on the Inter-

American Highway. The chance tactic turned out to be perfect; the rebel forces had their "northern front." Government troops destroyed La Lucha, which was left undefended, but they went no further. Businessmen were making a revolution.

Figueres began daily broadcasts to the tiny nation, opening each one with Beethoven's Fifth Symphony, a sort of theme for the rebels. His army, as volunteers reached it, grew to seven hundred, including a priest, Benjamin Núñez, the rebels' rifle-toting chaplain. In San José, saboteurs knocked out three-fourths of the electricity for the city and guerrilla activities in other places suggested that support for the rebels was widespread. By all appearances, San José was surrounded.

On March 20, however, a week after Figueres made his move, Picado responded with what force he had. Three hundred banana-plantation laborers, rallied by the communists, drove the rebels halfway out of San Isidro before a counter-offensive regained the town for Figueres' army. At Empalme, a government attack on the rebels was thrown back after only forty-five minutes.

Picado panicked, and hastily flew to neighboring Nicaragua to ask Somoza for help. Somoza, fearful of both the international rebels commanded by Figueres, the Caribbean Legion, and of Picado's communists, offered support only if Picado would betray the communists. It is unclear whether Picado refused the aid under those conditions, or, treacherously, accepted: Nicaraguan troops were later reported seen in Costa Rica, but were of no effect.

Figueres kept up his propaganda war. He issued a First Proclamation of the Army of National Liberation, spurring Costa Ricans to join in sabotage to hasten the government's fall. "We are on the way," he boasted. As if to corroborate his claim, a more determined government attack on Empalme was again thrown back. Figueres then ordered, of all things, an air raid. One of his DC-3s zoomed in over the palms of San José, and from it a bomb was dropped into the courtyard of the presidential residence.

In search of a truce, the archbishop of San José traveled to the rebel encampment, but Figueres would have none of it. Instead, he issued a Second Proclamation. Those who accused him of being "reactionary, bourgeois or retrogressive," he said, did not know him. His victory in the civil war would signal the beginning of a "war against poverty . . . the greatest good for the greatest number."

In San José, confusion reigned. Figueres' lofty pronouncements made it unclear who the rebel leader was. After all, it was Ulate — in hiding in San José — from whom the election had been stolen. It was Figueres, though, who was at the center of the maelstrom. Confusion was exacerbated by the fact that Figueres was surrounded by Caribbean Legion friends who spoke of a utopian Caribbean, cleansed of dictators. On the other side, Picado's army was strongly supported by those other utopians, communists. Picado was also counting on help from the communists' arch-enemy, Somoza. The United States encouraged Somoza to help only if Picado would disavow the communists' support.

In early April, Figueres prepared for a final blow. He moved on Cartago, just south of San José, while at the same time sending a parallel force to take Puerto Limón on the Atlantic.

The rebels entrusted with occupying Limón — whom Figueres called "the Caribbean Legion," a name that had not actually been used theretofore — did so easily. To take Cartago, however, Figueres needed the help of nature. For maximum mobility, Figueres had each man carry his own supplies. The army set out walking, moving at night along narrow trails. As they neared San Cristóbal Norte, dawn threatened to expose them as they crept past government emplacements of artillery and machine guns. Recognizing the danger, Figueres hid his men in the forest until, in the early morning light, a fog bank descended on the mountains. Hidden by the fog, the men moved silently past the danger in what became known as "the phantom march."

At Llano de los Angeles, they hid until nightfall. Padre Núñez baptized a local baby while they rested, and when darkness came they moved in three columns to easily take Cartago. Securing nearby towns, the rebel army was joined by the Caribbean Legion approaching from Limón.

On April 13 was the showdown. A government force advanced on Cartago from the south along the Inter-American Highway. The two forces met at Tejar, and the rebels prevailed in one of the most fiercely fought battles of the civil war. In forty days, the war had taken two thousand lives.

Figueres delivered his terms at the Mexican Embassy to a small group that included foreign mediators. He called for unconditional surrender and demanded that Congress appoint him, Martén, and Fernando Valverde Vega, another of "the original seven," as first, second, and third designates to oversee the restructuring of the government. Ulate was left out in the cold. A conflict that cost two thousand lives, Figueres calculated, had been for more than just a change of presidents.

Padre Núñez took over negotiations, which boiled down to a standoff between Figueres and the communist Mora. They met on a cold, overcast night after ten o'clock on April 15 on the rise at Ochomogo. Figueres assured Mora that the rebellion was a revolution for social and economic reform.

Mora offered to join forces to stave off a rumored invasion from Nicaragua. Mora finally gave up, at least partly because he feared continued division would invite a Nicaraguan invasion. Indeed, on April 17 Somoza ordered Nicaraguan National Guardsmen to be flown to Villa

Quesada, thirty-five miles inside Costa Rica, but when Picado read a statement that the Nicaraguan incursion was unwelcome, the troops were withdrawn.

The rebel army entered San José on April 24, and there was a victory parade four days later. Figueres wore a khaki uniform without military adornment; the guns and jeeps of the conquering army were decorated with flowers. "Arms bring victory," Figueres proclaimed. "Only laws can bring freedom."

Ulate claimed the presidency, and on May 1 Figueres agreed. Importantly, however, a governing junta, with Figueres as its head, would hold power for at least eighteen months, two years if necessary. Then there would be elections for an assembly to write a new constitution, and Ulate would take over for a four-year turn. "Don Pepe was now free to make his revolution," writes Ameringer, "but he had only eighteen months, possibly two years, in which to do it."

The junta that Figueres headed included old friends Orlich and Martén. The junta's resident radical was Núñez, who served as minister of labor and social welfare. Figueres' protégé, Daniel Oduber, was secretary-general. "We are a government of the middle class," Figueres said. Ethical standards were to be the foundation of the new, and succeeding, governments. A merit system was written for civil personnel. Social progress was to be made possible without communism.

Such goals, while noble, rang hollow until Figueres underlined his intent. Over the loud complaints of elites, Figueres took the startling step of nationalizing Costa Rica's banks. He called it "the democratization of credit." He also shocked elites by declaring a 10 percent tax on wealth. Although definitions of taxable wealth were poorly drawn and administration of the tax was weak, it served notice as to how deep the Figueres revolution was intended to reach. Elites resisted, lied about their holdings, boycotted, and turned to the junta's enemies for relief.

Almost immediately, as an economy measure, the junta fired three thousand government workers, including some teachers. There were accusations of a "Caribbean reign of terror," with Figueres cast as Robespierre, replete with charges of torture, unjust impoundment of wealth, and dismissals of junta opponents from government jobs. Figueres, it was claimed, recovered damages for destruction of his plantations — which in several cases was severe — amounting to ten times their true value. Figueres did, in fact, emerge from the revolution with a sizable bank account.

Before the end of the year, however, in another marked departure from Latin American practice, Figueres and the junta disbanded the army. Only civil police were retained to keep order.

Disagreements still ran deep. Opponents said Figueres was disavowing promises. Ulate, anxious about his long-promised presidency, organized an electoral sweep in the December 8 election of delegates for the constitutional assembly. Thus, the junta, which kept its most important promise to allow elections, was summarily swept aside in them.

In addition, Figueres' old Caribbean Legion pals detected cold feet because he did not immediately mount an offensive against neighboring dictators. Nicaragua was supposed to be next, but Somoza was strong, and Figueres had his hands full with Costa Rica. Costa Ricans complained about Legionnaires who were encamped, with Figueres' protection, in Costa Rican bases.

Caught in this verbal crossfire, Figueres suddenly found himself under armed attack. On December 8, when the junta was but seven months old, Somoza launched an attack on La Cruz, Costa Rica, in an attempt to return Calderón to power. Figueres, of course, had no army, but a volunteer militia pushed Somoza's soldiers back. Sixteen Costa Ricans were killed.

Trying to calm continuing criticism from domestic opponents, Figueres addressed the constitutional assembly in January 1949, describing himself and Ulate as on parallel paths for Costa Rica's ultimate benefit. Convention delegates were unreceptive. It was bluntly suggested that he retire, like Cincinnatus, to his farm. Another delegate suggested that his rebel army turn in its arms. He responded to the former suggestion by saying he would not be dismissed like a bandit, like a Costa Rican Pancho Villa. To the latter suggestion, Figueres invited anyone who had the nerve to come and take the weapons.

His popularity was not enhanced. He was not pupular enough to win an election and not strong enough to rule by fiat. In March, with the junta ten months old, Figueres persuaded Ulate to agree to extend its life. In the interim, he reasoned, elections would be held in October and the new constitution would take effect in November. Thus Figueres would have several months to work his way with newly elected officials.

The strategy had its problems. Figueres was a man who could alienate friends, so working with adversaries was not easy. In addition, events were moving much too quickly. Figueres was infuriated when a split among his oldest friends on the junta pitted conservatives against radicals. It led to a half-hearted coup attempt — Figueres dramatically offered to settle differences with his fists — that collapsed of its own lack of support in half a day. Despite the brevity of the revolt, six lives were lost.

Democratic debate proved no more effective. Figueres submitted to the convention a draft constitution that envisioned state control of the economy and social systems. Conservative delegates spurned the proposals. Piqued, Figueres told Ulate to go ahead and take over the government; he had had enough. Ulate, though, recognizing chaos when he saw it, declined. Nevertheless, conditions convinced Figueres to withdraw his request for extension of the junta's life. He had exhausted his already limited patience. The two leaders agreed to submit a single slate of candidates for national elections in the fall of 1949. Like it or not, Figueres said, "destiny" had cast them together.

One final insult to Figueres' pride, however, remained. The compromise slate of candidates submitted by a caucus of Ulate and Figueres representatives failed to include Figueres as candidate for first vice president. Figueres, beside himself with anger, threatened to divide the country by running against Ulate for president. Ulate supporters responded with a proposal to prohibit junta members from ever running for office. This would have blocked Figueres from the presidency later, so, to prevent that, he agreed to a compromise slate and gave up on being first vice president. Figueres' ambition had been profoundly frustrated, but the compromise was not in vain; the October elections were fair and unmarred by violence.

The Constitution of 1949 retained old guarantees and included new programs, like social security and a code protecting workers' rights. The convention delivered the constitution on November 7, 1949, and the next day Figueres turned over the government to Ulate.

Figueres "retired" to four years of being appointed to international conferences. He came to symbolize, in those days of the cold war, "the democratic left." Figueres was widely identified with Victor Raúl Haya de la Torre of Perú's *Alianza Popular Revolucionaria Americana*, or APRA, and with Rómulo Betancourt of Venezuela's *Acción Democrática*, or AD. Luís Muñoz Marín of Puerto Rico, the author of "Operation Bootstrap," was another friend. In the United States, Arthur M. Schlesinger, Jr., Chester Bowles, and Norman Thomas asked Figueres' opinion. He may have been the eye of a storm in his own tiny country, but Figueres was avidly courted in the hemisphere.

In March 1952, he announced his candidacy to succeed Ulate, but a question remained as to whether he could unite a following. On a dais, after so many years of lecturing abroad, he was a bit pedantic. He tended to lecture, to talk down to his audience. In the end, however, the informal style that had served him so well in building his business had not left him. Away from the lecturn, his personality shone through; he related to crowds when he was among them. Banana workers, remembering the civil war, never took to him, but *campesinos* did.

A sad aspect of the campaign was that he and his wife, Henrietta, were divorced just before the election. Less than two years later, while he was president and on a speaking tour to the United States, he would meet Karen Olson, a Dane who was a naturalized U.S. citizen. He was forty-seven years old; she was twenty-three and studying for her doctorate in sociology at Columbia University. They married quietly in Costa Rica in February 1954.

The election was delayed from May 31 to July 26 to register women, who were newly enfranchised, but on July 26, 1953 — the same day Fidel Castro stormed the Moncada barracks — Figueres won with a 65 percent majority, 123,444 to 67,324 for his opponent, Mario Echandi. Figueres' party, the PSD, won 30 congressional seats, the other three parties a total of 15.

He was now president of the only democracy in Central America, and evidence of that fact was everywhere about him. He was host to Rómulo Betancourt of Venezuela, who, already in exile in Havana, had fled to Costa Rica because he was unwelcome after Fulgencio Batista's coup in Cuba. Figueres was also host to twenty-two assassins on their way to Nicaragua to kill Somoza. These circumstances, portrayed in headlines, did not endear Figueres to nearby dictators.

There was, as well, pressure from the left: Jacobo Arbenz of Guatemala had begun expropriating the property of United Fruit Company, which had extensive holdings in Costa Rica. To follow suit, Figueres said it was time for a gradual departure of United Fruit Company. "The gradual and judicious withdrawal of the economic occupation would be the rectification of one of the gravest errors, or anachronisms, prevailing in the American hemisphere," he said. He went after a 50-50 split on profits like the arrangement Betancourt had achieved with foreign oil companies in Venezuela. He also wanted to eliminate the company's tax avoidance on imports of equipment and supplies.

In June 1954, he signed a contract enabling the government to take over the health services the company had provided. The company also agreed to higher taxes, although the rate was 30 percent, not the 50 percent Figueres sought. He settled for a daily minimum wage of $2.40, although the workers wanted more and struck to get it.

Figueres' government designed other programs, but progress was slowed after 1954 when coffee prices declined. Still, his international reputation grew. After repelling yet another Somoza-sponsored invasion in January 1955, Figueres was portrayed by Adolf Berle, an old Roosevelt hand, as a hero in Washington. Figueres suspected, however, that while he was being praised in some Washington circles he was being targeted in others. He blamed the Central Intelligence Agency for backing Somoza.

Figueres remained a target for critics, both domestic and lethal. Throughout 1956 he was criticized by Costa Ricans for spending so much time abroad. Then, in the spring of 1957, assassins contracted by Rafael Trujillo of the Dominican Republic were arrested in San Juan as they calculated the best time and place to strike.

When his term came to a close, Figueres hoped to hand the presidency to his old friend "Chico" Orlich. That, of course, was the way Costa Rican politics had always worked, the very system Figueres had helped to dissolve. So there was justice of a sort when, in February 1958, Mario Echandi, beaten by Figueres four years earlier, made a comeback with the support of old Figueres antagonist Otilio Ulate. Echandi also beat the indomitable Rafael Calderón, trying his own comeback.

So the country underwent peaceful change, but Figueres was once again a prophet with less honor in his own country than in international assemblies. In the spring of 1958, after riots dogged the path of U.S. Vice President Richard Nixon's South American tour, Figueres was called upon to testify before a subcommittee of the U.S. Congress. Nixon's delegation had been jeered and spat upon in Montevideo, and Nixon was briefly trapped in his car cavalcade by a stone-throwing crowd in the streets of Caracas. "People cannot spit on a foreign policy," Figueres told the subcommittee, explaining that Nixon merely represented his country, which Latin Americans felt had turned its back on the hemisphere. "If you talk human dignity to Russia," Figueres asked, comparing two dictatorships, "why do you hesitate so much to talk human dignity to [the people of the] Dominican Republic?" Figueres' words were published throughout Latin America.

He remained one of the best-known Latin American spokesmen for the Latin American idea of progressive democracy. He watched with satisfaction when Rómulo Betancourt was elected president of Venezuela in late 1958, and he excited hostility in Cuba in 1959 when he dared to support the United States in the global cold war.

International pride, however, leads to international sins. To propagate his ideas, Figueres used the Institute of Political Education in San José, an arm of his party, now called *Partido de Liberación Nacional.* The institute was a font for progressive democratic ideas, inviting lecturers, publishing essays, and generating discussion. Like all such institutions, however, it needed funding. So, in April 1959, when Figueres was introduced to Romanian refugee Sacha Volman, an answer appeared to be at hand. An avid anticommunist, Volman opened doors for Figueres, flattering his already sizable ego. Volman seemed to know everyone, and suddenly, Figueres was more popular than ever before for lectures. His name was linked with that of Richard Nixon, of Nelson Rockefeller. Funding flowed.

Because it was a time of heightened conflict in the Caribbean and Central America — Cuba sent insurgents to Panama; Costa Rica invaded Nicaragua — never was the dissemination of democratic ideas more necessary, in Figueres' view. Unfortunately, that was also the view of the CIA, which turned out to be the source of the funds Volman provided. Figueres knew this, and when the facts were made public in 1960 the institute was branded an ignominious tool of U.S. policy, the policy Venezuelan mobs tried to spit on.

Figueres' ego was salved a bit the next year when President John F.

Kennedy, in announcing the Alliance for Progress, remarked, "In the words of José Figueres, 'Once dormant peoples are struggling upward toward the sun, toward a better life.'" It soon was reiterated, however, that Figueres' words, while convenient for quotation in speeches, went unheeded in the formation of policy.

For example, Figueres insisted that Rafael Trujillo ought to be "the first target" of overthrow in the Caribbean. The advice was ignored. Kennedy focused on that double-whammy of U.S. fears: a Latin American, communist dictator — Fidel Castro. In April 1961, Figueres tried to warn Kennedy away from what became the fateful Bay of Pigs invasion, but was unable to do so. Then, when Trujillo was assassinated by Dominican officers on May 30, 1961, Figueres' involvement with tainted U.S. policy became more pronounced. The assassination was carried out with the complicity of the CIA and, perhaps, Figueres, whose Institute of Political Education was then harboring a rival Dominican, Juan Bosch. There seemed no end to the entanglements.

Figueres' was a lonely voice crying out for moderation in the midst of excess. "Latin America is now in a grave economic situation," he told a U.S. college audience in 1962, "which is being converted into a serious political situation."

Although he was able to help Orlich win the presidency in 1962 — perpetuating the important, ordered succession of Costa Rican presidents that continues to this day — and in October 1963 he began a lectureship at Harvard University, Figueres' fortunes were in decline. In November 1963, Kennedy was shot. Figueres traveled from Kennedy's college to Kennedy's funeral, walking sadly along Pennsylvania Avenue behind the caisson, dwarfed by the throng and the tall, gaunt figure of Gen. Charles de Gaulle next to him.

Figueres, however, like Sarmiento, could not step out of the arena. Unable to help his one-time protégé, Daniel Oduber, win the presidency in 1966, Figueres slid deeper into his role as handmaiden to U.S. policy. In 1967 *Ramparts* magazine revealed that "the J. M. Kaplan Fund Inc.," was yet another funnel for CIA money — a funnel pointed, once again, toward Figueres' Institute of Political Education.

In 1970, after regaining the presidency for himself with 55 percent of the vote, Figueres found that the world had become a complex thing indeed. A Central American border dispute required his service as comediator alongside the oldest of his antagonists, Nicaraguan dictator Anastasio Somoza, the man he had once vowed to depose. To make matters worse, in the middle of Figueres' term the notorious international financier Robert Vesco showed up in Costa Rica. Vesco was eager to escape extradition to the United States for prosecution of his alleged crimes, and he was willing to pay for his stay. Vesco's investments in Figueres' interests would once again stain Don Pepe's reputation, fueling his critics' antipathy and embarrassing his supporters.

Figueres' career was like that, never avoiding controversy, never shirking involvement, never shunning risk. He insisted, as if compulsively, on returning to the center of the storm, and for that, Figueres is still admired. He died at his San José apartment on June 8, 1990, of a heart attack at the age of eighty-three. He was eulogized by the *New York Times* as "Costa Rica's Fierce Pacifist."

Fidel Castro
1926–
(Cuba)

Socialist Revolutionary

Fidel Castro took up arms to shape the first socialist revolution in Latin America that was made to last, a revolution the United States failed to prevent and could not erase. As a result, Castro has remained a hemispheric pariah as far as the United States is concerned, although Latin American democracies have long since learned to live with Cuba. In recent years, Cuba has become even more unusual, a socialist island ever more lonely as it is deserted by its European retainers.

Fidel Castro's father was Angel Castro y Argiz, a Galician and soldier in the army sent to suppress the Cuban insurrection of 1898. Without formal education, he built a small farm in Oriente province into a prosperous cattle ranch of more than 23,000 acres. The plantation—two and a half years after the father's death—would be broken up by the revolution. Angel Castro's first wife, who died, bore him two children. He married Lina Ruz González, the mother of seven more of his children, after Fidel was born on August 13, 1926. Because the parents of Lina Ruz de Castro were also natives of Galicia—a coastal province at the northwest corner of Spain that once was an independent kingdom—Castro is said by some to be *puro gallego*, a Spaniard on an island of Creoles.

Because neither of his parents had gone to school, there was no thought of sending Fidel until, the story goes, he threatened to burn the house down. He was sent to live, not altogether happily, with godparents

234

and enrolled in a Jesuit school. Later, he was moved to the prestigious Colegio Belén in Santiago, the provincial capital. Oriente is a province noted for its independent turn of mind, prosperous and isolated at the eastern tip of the island—far from Havana, the corrupt urban "leech" of Cuba's agrarian riches. Santiago would serve as political classroom for the young Castro, just as its Moncada barracks would provide him with the first laboratory to test his theories.

Castro was athletic and unusually tall. He graduated from high school with a citation in the yearbook for "defending with bravery and pride the flag of the school." He went to Havana to study law in 1945.

At the university, campus politics were practiced with a zeal that bordered on thuggery. While Latin American campuses have traditionally sheltered critics of their governments, and while student activism typically includes rock throwing, Havana University was in a league of its own. Campus leaders, for example, oversaw the organized sale of black market textbooks. During the time Castro was at the university, several students were murdered, and although no convincing evidence has ever been adduced that he played a role in the deaths, Castro earned a reputation for toughness in a tough environment. If, as it is said, he carried a pistol while a student, he was not alone in the practice.

More substantial evidence describes Castro's role in the events of the spring of 1948. Castro and two fellow students were sent by campus organizations to Bogotá to an international convention of university students. Thus, they were in the Colombian capital on April 1 when Jorge Eliécer Gaitán, a popular leftist, was murdered on a downtown street. Enraged followers of Gaitán tore his assailant to pieces and the ensuing riot became known as the *bogotazo*, an explosion of mob violence. Castro and at least one of his fellow Cubans appear in reports resulting from a special investigation; they distinguished themselves in a chaotic situation for having done their best to fan the flames of chaos. That Castro played any direct role in the beginning of the riot or contributed to its aftermath—decades of virulent clashes between Colombian Liberals and Conservatives—has never been demonstrated and seems naive. Yet it is clear that Castro, even as a student, encountered no revolutionary conditions he wouldn't try to improve upon.

Indeed, while he was still at the university, Castro took part in an abortive attempt to overthrow, by seaborne invasion, Dominican dictator Rafael Trujillo. The idea of overthrowing Trujillo was supported by Venezuelan authorities and, at first, Cuban President Ramón Grau San Martín. But pressure from the U.S. ambassador to Cuba subtracted Grau from the equation. Nevertheless, a tiny expeditionary force set out from the coast of Cuba, and when a coastal patrol boat closed in, Castro dove over the side to escape. Another legend was born in that Castro is said to have swum to shore without letting go of his submachine gun.

With revolutionary politics as his principal extracurricular activity, Castro also found time to marry. He and Mirta Díaz-Balart, a philosophy major, were married in the autumn of 1948 and honeymooned in Miami. A son, Fidelito, was born on September 1, 1949.

Castro graduated the next year. With two partners, he began practicing in Havana, a city with political and juridical systems known for their corruption and an economy tightly controlled by sugar interests.

The sugar economy prescribed all other conditions in Cuba after the Spanish were driven out. The royalty was ended, but reality lingered on. And into the twentieth century Cuba's sugar economy was increasingly dominated by North Americans. Absentee landlords thus made themselves heirs to the feudal system that had evolved from the hemisphere's last slavocracy. Thousands cut cane to put sugar onto a world market that paid richly in foreign exchange for the owners to buy imports. Plantations were already becoming vertically integrated — controlling not only growing, but grinding, transportation, and distribution as well. American capital and organizational skills accelerated the consolidation, linking the system with railroads, and building a one-crop economy without rival anywhere in the colonial world. This system flourished in the 1920s, but when it began to slow it dragged all else with it. By the 1950s, it had slowed considerably.

By that time about one-third of Cuba's population was destitute despite the fact that the island's per capita income was third highest in Latin America. The lights of Havana's casinos created a glow over the city that could be seen clearly from hovels without hope of electricity.

Political solutions to the imbalance, however, were not apparent. Many, if not most, politicians were for sale. Cuban government had staggered since the U.S. army and the Platt Amendment had left Cubans to their own devices early in the century. The most egregious example of Cuban self-governance was President Gerardo Machado, of whom Castro heard as a child. Machado's skills at leadership earned him the sobriquet "the butcher" before he was overthrown by the coup that eventually elevated to the presidency Fulgencio Batista.

By contrast with Machado, Batista's first term was enlightened. When he retired to opulence in Miami in 1944, Batista was followed by two civilian presidents, and it appeared that Cuba might have righted itself in the sea of democratic practices. When national elections were again scheduled for June 1952, Castro intended, as a member of the Orthodox party, to run for congress.

His law practice was successful, although the cases he accepted tended toward those with social implications, not high fees. He had joined the *ortodoxos*, which began as a splinter group but was built to a substantial populist force by the charismatic Eduardo "Eddy" Chibas. The enigmatic

Chibas brought his own career to a bizarre end by shooting himself in the head at a radio studio at the end of an emotional speech, but the party continued. Castro had found a political niche and was confident of election.

In late 1951, however, Batista returned. He led a second successful coup, terminating any chance of continued reform by democratic processes. Deprived of his seat in Congress, Castro took the Batista government to court. He petitioned a special court, charging that Batista had violated the Cuban constitution written in the 1940s. Had the court accepted the petition and found Batista guilty on all counts, he would have faced jail terms adding up to something over a century. Castro also brought suit in the Court of Constitutional Guarantees, claiming, understandably, that the coup was illegal. The Court of Constitutional Guarantees, in an opinion that both recognized Latin American realities and prophesied the island's future, dismissed Castro's complaint, acknowledging instead that revolution "is the font of law."

Castro took the court at its word. The following year, on July 26, 1953, he led nearly two hundred men and several women in an attack on the Moncada barracks in Santiago. Simultaneously, seven others staged a coordinated attack on the small garrison at Bayamo, on the highway about sixty miles west of the city. From the outset, the plan was shot through with mistakes.

The Santiago attack was to have two waves. The first wave, led by Castro, intended to emerge from the cover of a carnival crowd to take the main sentry post and occupy the nearby civic hospital and the palace of justice. But as they rolled up to the gate in a caravan of cars and trucks, they saw a government patrol, by chance, emerging from the guardhouse. The ensuing firefight alerted the garrison, and the few rebels who succeeded in taking the hospital were quickly isolated and surrounded.

The second rebel wave, more heavily armed, got lost in the streets of Santiago. Its caravan drove around helplessly until it was too late.

When Castro signaled retreat from the attack on the main fort, his brother Raúl was able to extract his squad from the palace of justice, but no one could cover the escape of nineteen men and two women trapped at the hospital. The assault at Bayamo was no more successful. Fidel Castro's first attempt as a guerrilla was a dismal failure.

In the assault on Moncada, three rebels were killed and approximately one hundred captured. Sixty-eight prisoners were summarily executed. Fifty rebels, including Fidel and Raúl Castro, escaped. The inchoate revolution had won nothing but its name, the 26th of July. For days after the attack, as government troops hunted down the rebels, residents of Santiago — including parents of captured rebels — were subjected to grisly reports, smuggled out of prison and into the streets, of torture and slow death. The stories were not all true, but they were strong enough to embarrass even a populace accustomed to political savagery. The archbishop of Santiago was pressed to intervene, and his efforts tempered the government's fury, although it is less certain, as some stories suggest, that he was personally responsible for saving Castro's life.

Some of those who escaped were hiding in the woods, and they came out, cautiously, hoping to face prison rather than execution. Castro and two others were spotted and captured at the home of a sympathizer — fortunately, for them, by a junior officer who disapproved of the slaughter that had already taken place. Castro was first brought to trial with several others, and he insisted on speaking in his own defense.

One morning as the trial began, however, he was not in the courtroom. The judge was told Castro was too ill to continue. In his cell, Castro, fearing that he would be killed, managed to smuggle out a note, which one of the defense attorneys plucked from her coiled hair in the courtroom. He was not sick, Castro wrote, but being forcibly detained. His trial was postponed.

The incident illustrates the porous nature of the Batista regime. When a jailor was ordered to poison Castro, he refused. So weak was the Batista government, so shot through with corruption and ambiguity, that it was incapable even of carrying out its own nefarious tactics. It was in Batista's prison, in fact, that Castro began his climb toward prominence. Only one of many opponents of the Batista regime, Castro used his rhetoric to climb to a position of preeminence. Had Castro, as the twenty-six-year-old leader of the Moncada assault, been one of the five dozen rebels executed, the hemisphere would doubtless have changed less over the past thirty years. But had a less determined person been captured, one less capable of turning imprisonment into a forum, so, too, would history have been different.

Castro's trial was held at the civic hospital; it drew a standing-room-only crowd of nurses, another example of the regime's lack of control. Although the trial was closed to the public and press accounts censored, full news, including Castro's remarks, carried across the island. His own lengthy closing statement, polished by editing, was published and distributed widely as the first formal suggestion of what Castro had in mind for Cuba. He spoke of a "return" to the Constitution of 1940, free elections, and made his assertion, "History will absolve me."

He was sentenced to fifteen years on the Isle of Pines, where Martí had been sent. Reaching the island in October 1953, Castro organized in the barracks what came to be known as the "Abel Santamaría Academy," named for a fellow rebel who was captured in the Moncada attack and tortured to death. Castro was sole lecturer, other prisoners his pupils. The authorities clapped him in isolation.

Yet his ideas — written in lemon-juice "invisible ink" between the lines of letters, or smuggled out in match boxes — were communicated, largely through the efforts of Haydée Santamaría, Abel's sister, and Melba Hernández. "No weapon, no force," he wrote, "can overcome a people who decide to fight for their rights." As many as 20,000 copies of his prison pronouncements were printed and circulated.

Early in Castro's imprisonment Mirta served as a link between her husband and the rebel movement. When she had trouble supporting herself and young Fidelito, however, her brother, in the time-honored tradition of Latin American politics, used his position to help. He simply had her name added to the payroll of Batista's interior department. Checks were issued regularly. When this was discovered and publicized, Castro took it as a reproach to his ability to support a family and as an accusation of hypocrisy. His family, after all, was sustained by the very government he sought to overthrow. His relationship with Mirta deteriorated, and before he left prison she had filed for divorce; she took their son to the United States.

Batista, without significant opposition, perpetuated his regime with an "election," but by the spring of 1955 he was under pressure—manifest by a vote in the Cuban House of Representatives—to grant amnesty. Families, including Lydia Castro, a sister, had begun to demonstrate at the main gate of the Isle of Pines prison camp. Batista relented and pardoned the July 26 rebels, who, as they rode the train back toward Havana, were greeted by occasional crowds of sympathizers.

Several veterans of the Moncada assault, almost immediately after they were released, left for Mexico City to await Castro. At first, Castro stayed, using his popularity to give his opinions to Havana reporters, but the attention was a mixed blessing. Eventually access to the news media was choked off by Batista supporters, and Castro found himself under the scrutiny of government agents. Following Raúl, he went to Mexico City.

In the Mexican capital the small group of Cubans was joined by a short, ill-kempt Argentine, as intense about politics as he was loose about his personal habits. He was knocking about the continent in search of a cause, and the Cubans had one. With their gutteral Caribbean pronunciation, they were amused by the slow, Italian-influenced accent of this newcomer. They were taken with his use of the affectionate "ché," a common term at the bottom of the continent, and so dubbed Ernesto Guevara with the name, and it stuck.

The Cubans, given new life by the Latin American tolerance for rebellion, rented a farmhouse and underwent combat training by a veteran of the Spanish civil war. Long marches through the volcanic mountains toughened them for a war the dimensions of which they could only try to imagine. Castro went to the United States where, like Martí, he spoke to émigré groups seeking support. After each discourse, a wood-and-papier-mâché machine gun would be passed around for donations.

Help was welcome from anywhere. Although Castro was then denouncing the *ortodoxos,* accusing them of collaboration with the Batista regime, Castro supporters were accepting donations from the Authentic party — whose funds bought the yacht used for Castro's miniscule invasion — another anti–Batista group. There was, in fact, relatively broad opposition to Batista, which would later lead to the accusation that Castro "stole" the revolution.

The Cubans in Mexico were closely watched by both Cuban agents and Mexican authorities. Once when Castro's car was stopped in Mexico City and the stock of weapons it carried confiscated, he replaced them only to be stopped again, losing the replacement arms. When, finally, arms and ammunition were gathered and stored aboard the *Granma,* eighty-two men, along with their provisions, crammed themselves on. The plan was to arrive on the south shore of Cuba on November 30, 1956.

Castro planned to coordinate the arrival of his small army with an uprising in Santiago. Then, gathering provisions hidden near their landing point, they would link up with another hundred men at arms and establish a base in the Sierra Maestra. However, tactics at first seemed as ill-fated as they had been at the Moncada barracks. Against all advice, Castro insisted on telegraphing his punch by repeatedly boasting that his force would invade before the end of the year. So Batista's army was prepared. In addition, he ignored warnings that the planned uprising in Santiago was unlikely to occur. Indeed, the uprising was immediately suppressed, the waiting troops were too far back in the mountains to make the rendezvous, and the yacht arrived late, past the designated point and too overloaded to be beached. The boat was finally anchored off a swamp, and its hapless expeditionary force waded ashore carrying what it could. Batista's army and air force attacked.

Although the rebels made it from the coast into the mountains, they were immediately surrounded. Castro reacted by splitting his force to avoid the capture of everyone. But one group of fourteen was trapped and promised treatment as prisoners of war if they surrendered. When they surrendered, they were shot. Radio stations in Havana reported that the entire invasion force had been wiped out and Castro killed.

In fact, the rebel forces were splintered, and for the second time in his short military career, Castro was forced to flee for his life. With two companions, he wandered, trying to regroup what was left of his forces. Others also wandered, living on sugar cane. At one point Castro and his two companions hid from a group of men they could see, but could not identify. It turned out to be Raúl and two others — who had seen them and were trying to hide. Eventually, as stragglers from the *Granma* gathered themselves again, Castro's army numbered twelve men.

Theodore Draper has suggested that at this precise point Castro distinguished himself by having the iron will, not to say madness, of a revolutionary hero. Rather than escape from the island in order to start again, Castro clung to the Sierra Maestra like a tick to a dog. The men with him, mostly city-bred and unaccustomed to living off the land, were reduced to hunger, wandering, confusion. They were largely without arms. Men who were with Castro during those months recalled that when they rested, complaining of their plight, they would look over at Castro, who was not paying attention but gazing at the sierra, planning.

Within six months, he had learned the mountains that would be his refuge for two hard years. Castro's strategy, like Sandino's, was shaped by the terrain and his weakness. He claims to have won the war with five hundred guerrillas, and even more objective estimates confirm that his forces never exceeded about eight hundred fighters at their strongest. He was able to win by virtue of his own tenacity and because of the corruption of the Batista regime, unable to rally either people or army to its own defense. Guerrillas picked off army outposts, disappearing back into the mountains to await the next opportunity, to sustain themselves, and to train the recruits that filtered in from the farms and out of the city.

Castro, meanwhile, kept himself accessible. Foreign correspondents, in a stream led by Herbert Matthews of the *New York Times*, legitimated Castro's rebellion by according him a forum with their interviews. When Batista functionaries claimed Castro had been killed, there he was, with Matthews, in a photograph in the *Times*. One CBS correspondent became so enthralled with Castro's homilies that he became a spokesman for Castro's ideas, and the network had to pull him off the assignment.

As he had from prison on the Isle of Pines, Castro built a constituency, national and international, by issuing pronouncements from the sierra. From prison he had promised a return to the Constitution of 1940. Now he predicted a future of promise without bounds. Because Castro dealt in generalities, the U.S. State Department, sensitive to American business interests on the island, saw Castro as no threat. The 26th of July movement seemed nothing more than one of many pairs of hands pushing at the side of Batista's toppling structure.

Opposition was varied. In March 1957, four months after the *Granma* landing but independent of Castro's direction, Havana students attacked the presidential palace to assassinate Batista. The attempt was unsuccessful, but students who escaped fled to the mountains of Central Cuba, creating another "front" there, or made their way to Castro's forces in the western sierra.

In May, a trial was held for the twenty-two men captured from the *Granma* and one hundred more people accused of participating in the failed Santiago uprising. The three-judge panel — reflecting Cuba's deep ambivalence — split. Two judges insisted on freeing the defendants. Manuel

Urrutia,* speaking for the court, held that the defendants had the right to
rebel against an unjust regime.

In the autumn, naval personnel at Cienfuegos revolted. Batista ruth-
lessly bombed the base into submission, ending the uprising and creating
even more opposition.

Meanwhile, Castro's small army eluded air strikes and attacked only
when victory was assured. The same month as the Cienfuegos revolt, it
mounted its first successful raid against a small garrison on the south coast.
Vital to Castro's force was that it preserve its unity. The rebels had time,
and time had to reveal that they were the only opposition force able to hold
itself together without being killed, captured, or coopted. Even Cuba's
traditional, Soviet-oriented communists — later to be so closely examined
for their influence on Castro — was at that point condemning Castro as a
"putschist," a selfish bourgeois who sought power for himself. So toothless
were the communists that Batista felt safe appointing them to his cabinet.

Not all threats to the rebels were external. Fighting alongside Castro
was Eutemio Guerra, who was a spy, disclosing the band's position whenever possible. Then Guerra's superiors assigned him a bigger job: assassinate Castro. He planned to shoot Castro at close range with a pistol, dis-
couraging pursuit as he escaped down the mountainside with two hand
grenades.

As Guevara later told the story, one frigid night in the mountains
Guerra asked Castro to lend him a blanket. Castro replied that because he
only had one blanket they would both be better off sleeping side by side,
sharing their two coats, the blanket, and their bodily warmth. They did so,
Guevara wrote, while either lack of nerve or absence of opportunity prevented Guerra from carrying out his assignment. After later betrayals,
Guerra's purpose was discovered, and he fell to his knees, asking quick execution. The request was superfluous, but Guevara notes that the revolution saw to it that Guerra's two sons were provided an education.

In the spring of 1958, the rebel army had accumulated sufficient numbers to launch a column of fifty-three fighters. Led by Raúl Castro, they
moved into the Sierra del Cristal, broadening the attack, although the
rebels were still confined to the southeastern end of the island. It was a
significant expansion, and Batista's generals, trying to crush the rebels
before they strengthened themselves further, tried to surround them. During the summer, soldiers were sent around the island, landing on the south
coast to push upward, into the Sierra Maestra toward the main body
of about three hundred rebels. The strategy nearly worked, but Castro

---

*Castro would later reward Urrutia for his courage by making him the first president of
postrevolutionary Cuba. Then he would dump him as one of the first thrown overboard when
the revolution began its swerve to the left.

withdrew into a perimeter less than twenty miles across and fought off the attack. Counterattacking, Castro took government prisoners. He turned them over to the International Red Cross. His small army had achieved a military respectability that meant Batista's defeat eighteen months later.

With bolstered confidence, Castro sent Guevara and Camilo Cienfuegos at the head of 150 rebels aimed toward the island's waist, tightening the pressure on Havana on the north coast. They captured two towns and more government troops in sometimes bloody fighting; both sides knew that the end was near for one or the other. In the south, the Castro brothers increased pressure on the garrison at Santiago.

Then came the end. Batista staged an election, but it was window dressing for a deserted building. On New Year's Eve 1959, Batista flew into exile, and Guevara and Cienfuegos led their troops into Havana three days later. Ironically, Castro, at his camp, heard the news on the radio. He had just successfully negotiated the surrender of the Moncada and Bayamo garrisons at Santiago, against which the 26th of July movement was forged five and a half years earlier. He and Raúl led their troops across the island toward Havana, entering the city on January 8. Castro rode into the city atop a tank with his son, who had been in school on Long Island, riding beside him.

Some insight into Castro's attitudes upon his entering Havana is gained from a letter hung on the office wall of Celia Sánchez, who was rewarded for her revolutionary work with a position in the new government. Enlarged and framed, the letter was sent to her by Castro during the Sierra Maestra campaign. He described watching government troops firing rockets made in the United States at the home of a friend. "I swore to myself," he wrote, "that the Americans were going to pay dearly. . . . When this war is over, a much wider and bigger war will begin for me."

At first, Castro insisted that his role would be only as head of the armed forces. His choice for administrative positions included both communists and men who had proven themselves as administrators under Batista. It was clear, however, that regardless of their titles or backgrounds they were not the ones sought by the crowds. Those people, spilling over with requests so long suppressed, went to Castro and his rebel soldiers, whose beards identified them with the future. The result was total confusion.

Castro, with enemies not only from the deposed regime but also from among other Batista opponents, kept closest to himself the men and women who had been with him in the mountains. Beyond them, he counted on those who had supported him from the cities. Neither represented a strong cadre of administrators. By mid–February 1959 he had decided to name himself prime minister. He began replacing cabinet members. The principal qualification for service became loyalty to the prime minister.

In the immediate aftermath of the revolution there were approximately six hundred executions, a modest number by some standards in Latin America and elsewhere. Trials were often hastily arranged, sometimes held in public arenas and televised.

But revenge did not substitute for solutions, and the island's economy was in shambles. Some Cubans, opposed to Castro's takeover, tried to keep it that way; saboteurs and snipers cropped up, trying to frustrate reorganization of the island's resources. In addition, an exodus of middle- and upper-class Cubans had already begun. While it relieved antagonistic pressure on Castro, it also threatened to strip the economy of both capital and managers. It is at this juncture that Castro is accused of failing to return Cuba to the democracy that was struggling to find itself in 1952. Doing that, Castro knew, risked perpetuating U.S. domination, something he was determined to change. He persisted, and what followed was change of enormous proportions, creating equally enormous problems.

U.S. President Eisenhower, more concerned about the communists in Castro's administration than he had been about those in Batista's, recognizing the vulnerability of American-owned sugar plantations and following the precedent of every president since James K. Polk, was belligerent. Early in 1959, Eisenhower threatened, unless Castro disavowed his increasingly leftist orientation, to reduce American imports of Cuban sugar. Castro, anxiously trying to consolidate power and stifle opposition, accepted Eisenhower's challenge — and the aid eagerly offered by communist governments. The resulting strain in U.S.-Cuban relations quickly became a severe break.

For a few weeks, there was ambivalence as neither side could get used to setting policy in a situation unique in the four and a half centuries since the hemisphere had been colonized. Castro came to the United States in April and addressed newspaper editors. In May, at a meeting of Latin American ministers in Buenos Aires, he proposed a $30 billion "Marshall Plan" funded by the United States. Then he returned to Cuba and nationalized agriculture.

Oil refineries met the same fate. Before the revolution, U.S. and British refineries had processed petroleum from Venezuela, but after Castro took power the supply began to dwindle, threatening the already precarious state of the economy. Cuban requests for oil from Venezuela and Argentina were to no avail. The alternative was to bring in crude oil from the Soviet Union, but when the first tanker arrived, the refineries refused to accept it. Castro nationalized the refineries, and by the middle of 1960, Nikita Krushchev was blustering that the Soviet Union would protect its new Cuban ties with "rocket firepower."

More immediately necessary, however, was to prop up the Cuban economy with Soviet-bloc transfusions of money, goods, and management. The resulting advice was not always helpful. Advisors from land-locked East European countries sometimes misunderstood island conditions, planning warehouses inland while imported food rotted at the dock. Guevara joked about Coca-Cola that was like syrup, toothpaste so hard it could not be squeezed from the tube. Exacerbating Cuba's domestic disarray—pockets of armed resistance persisted in the interior—was the United States, which busily organized international disapproval.

Castro had difficulty coping, and was inclined to paper over the problems with political poses. Wearing army fatigues and probably longing for the simpler problems of the sierra, Castro often reacted to problems by driving off to the countryside, the scene of his military successes, to make pronouncements. Agrarian reform, he declared, was crucial to answering Cuban economic problems, but rewriting ancient laws of land tenure was no easier in Cuba than it had been anywhere else in Latin America. In May 1959, when the Castro family's holdings were nationalized, brother Ramón and sister Lina were outraged. Ramón later joined the government to administer agricultural reform in the eastern end of the island, but other landowners were not so easily mollified.

The long-term idea was that sugar had to be replaced by a variety of crops. Cane-cutters had to be released from the feudal characteristics of the sugar economy, which locked Cuba into dependence on erratic, occasionally glutted, world markets. For the time being, however, sugar brought in dearly needed cash, so the symbol of the revolution became pictures of government, business, and professional people, machetes in hand, toiling in the fields. "Fellow *macheteros*," Castro was fond of saying at the beginning of hortatory speeches that went on for hours. Those who failed to demonstrate revolutionary fervor he called "scum." Self-exiles were "worms."

Then, on January 3, 1961, the United States and Cuba broke diplomatic relations, and the United States instituted an almost total embargo on goods shipped to the island. In the spring, impatient with this hemispheric upstart, the Kennedy administration trained, transported, and gave logistic support to an army of refugee invaders. The Bay of Pigs invasion failed. "We regarded him as an hysteric," remarked Arthur Schlesinger, Jr., the historian and advisor to Kennedy, explaining the United States' hysterical policy.

The next year, Khrushchev moved to make good on his bluster, dispatching ships loaded with missiles for emplacement on the island. Kennedy called the bluff with a naval quarantine, which succeeded in turning around the Soviet ships. To Castro's humiliation, the drama played out well above his head; it was clear that in the largest sense Cuba's place in international politics would be determined by the superpowers.

Judgment of Castro's place in the contemporary affairs of the hemisphere has never lent itself to objectivity. Differing opinions will be heard in the exile community in Miami, in a Havana schoolroom, in a poor *barrio* of another Latin American country, languishing under another Batista.

The most lasting criticism is that Castro and his army of the Sierra Maestra "stole" the Cuban revolution from other anti–Batista groups and, since, have driven away or imprisoned opponents. Cuban poet Armando Valladares, released from prison in 1986 after twenty-two years, writes of having met inmates who were the very Cubans "who helped the Revolution come to power, students, professionals, *campesinos*." Valladares, who was imprisoned for criticizing the government, tells of brutal torture for those who refuse "political rehabilitation."

Have Castro's policies improved the lot of Cuba, which had the highest per capita income in Latin America in 1959, in comparison with other Latin Americans, which, in the aggregate, owed U.S. banks roughly $350 billion in 1986? Judgment has always amounted to a balance. Some shake their heads at the rationing caused by shortages; others point to the new classrooms and the virtual elimination of illiteracy. Some call Castro an adventurer in the serious world of international relations; others see him as an expression of realities too long denied.

Domestically, as early as 1970 Castro pointed out that while Cuba's population had grown from 6.55 million people in 1958 to 8.25 million, the nonworking population had been reduced, by his measurement, from 686,000 to 75,000. During that time, he claimed, spending on education had tripled, the number of public school teachers increased fivefold. The number of scholarships, not counting for children in kindergartens or the revolutionary *circulos infantiles*, had been increased from 15,698 to more than a quarter of a million. But at the same time, he conceded, 300,000 to 500,000 Cubans had already fled the island. Individual departures, although severely restricted, continued, and when in 1980 the port of Mariel was opened 120,000 Cubans left their homeland.

Internationally, despite having to yield to Soviet direction on the large questions, Castro has managed to play a revolutionary role other Latin American rebels could only imagine. He has made himself pariah or hero, depending on one's point of view, providing soldiers and civilian workers to revolutionary governments from Angola to Nicaragua. He has given ideas teeth. In exile, Martí warned of U.S. domination; Castro has embodied anti–United States sentiment. In the mountains, Sandino sent down proclamations; Castro has shipped arms and soldiers. "We will never get on our knees at the feet of imperialism to beg for peace," he said in a typical speech in 1980. The speech, marking the twenty-seventh anniversary of the Moncada attack, was aimed at encouraging the Sandinista government of Nicaragua.

Such public pronouncements, over a period approaching three decades, have shaped our image of Fidel Castro. But a private moment recorded by the Colombian novelist Gabriel García Márquez affords another view. Márquez describes Castro standing at the dock, seeing off a Cuban expeditionary force bound for Angola. The troops were sailing on a rusting freighter, one so old and ill-equipped that fifty-five gallon drums holding water and fuel were lashed to the deck. Hatches were locked open so air could circulate and the fumes from fuel, crudely stored below decks, would not collect and blow up the ship. Castro looked at the woebegone example of international revolution and offered a historical observation: "Anyway," Castro told the troops, "you'll be more comfortable than the expeditionaries on the *Granma.*"

Ernesto "Ché" Guevara
1928–1967
(Argentina/Cuba)

Existential Rebel

Ernesto Guevara, two years younger than Fidel Castro, also grew up in a middle-class family, although one with decidedly more liberal politics. Guevara's mother, Celia de la Serna de Guevara, was an active dissident in Argentina. Although she protected her frail, asthmatic son, it may be presumed that she transmitted her revolutionary idea that events can be controlled, that things can be made better. Guevara acted on that idea not in the schizophrenic political environment of his native country, but in Cuba. It seems clear, however, that had Guevara not met Castro in Mexico City he would surely have made some other revolution in some other place, as, in fact, he would die trying to do in Bolivia.

The family of Ernesto Guevara de la Serna moved from Rosario, where he was born on June 14, 1928, to Buenos Aires when he was two years old. They hoped the new environment would relieve his asthma, but the condition persisted, and his sister Celia would recall their father sleeping with his tiny son's head on his chest because his breathing improved with his head elevated. When the tortured breathing that would plague Guevara all his life continued, the family moved again, this time when he was four, settling in Alta Gracia, in Córdoba province. Finally, his health improved.

Because of the asthma, he at first did not attend school, learning at home from his mother. Later, Celia de Guevara would drive him to school on the days he was able to attend, directing his brothers and sisters to get his assignments when he was forced to stay home.

There were four other children, two brothers and two sisters, in a closely knit family. Both Ernesto Guevara Lynch, a civil engineer, and his wife were of old colonial families, his partly Irish in origin, hers Spanish. What was left of inherited lands, however, had been sold, and the family's economic status was firmly middle class. That combination — patrician heritage and middle-class reality — had produced political views that were strongly expressed. Although weakened by asthma herself, Celia de Guevara was an ardent socialist, vociferous enough to get herself jailed briefly in 1964 in Argentina's always volatile politics.

The family's political tutelage didn't end with Celia de Guevara. An uncle, the family poet, contributed to the children's political education by traveling to Spain during its civil war, a war that divided world opinion as no other war had. He returned to write a book, *Spain in the Hands of the People*, which Ricardo Rojo, a long-time friend of Guevara, credits with helping to begin Guevara's leftward trek. Such was the political involvement of Guevara's family that in the 1950s, even as Guevara fought in Cuba's Sierra Maestra mountains to overthrow the Batista government, his second cousin was serving as Argentina's ambassador to that government.

Early in life, Guevara began a practice — on foot, bicycle, and motorbike — of observing Latin America, like a Darwin examining the subjects for whom he would later adopt a universal theory. Refusing to let his asthma interfere, he toughened himself playing rugby in school and first, while still a schoolboy, walked about Argentina, later embarking on longer motorbike and motorcycle trips. In 1950, his letter to the manufacturer of the "Micrón" motorbike served as a testimonial used by the company in its advertising. Under a picture of the twenty-two-year-old Guevara was his endorsement for a machine that could carry him "4,000 kilometers through the Argentine provinces." The next year he and a friend set out northward into Chile on motorcycles, working at odd jobs as the need arose.

On these trips he cultivated, if that is the proper term, his ability to eat when food was available, to do without when necessary. His rugby teammates nicknamed him "Pig" because of his careless disregard for manners, but he began to take on something more like the digestive system of a snake. He would eat prodigious amounts of food when invited to table — and when he knew there was a period of abstinence coming. When times were lean, he bore them, apparently happily, by eating almost nothing. It was as if he were schooling himself in survival.

Although good in mathematics, Guevara confounded family predictions that he would follow his father's career as an engineer. He chose medical school, taking a particular interest in tropical diseases and focusing on leprosy. He was also interested in archeology, the study of Latin America's ancient Indians.

In his travels he indulged these interests, visiting in Peru, for example, both Macchu Picchu, an ancient settlement, and a leper colony. The trips, however, always seemed to find their principal justification in adventure, in survival. Leaving Peru, Guevara and a friend went on to Colombia, were deported, and ended up in Venezuela. Then, while his friend stayed behind in Caracas, Guevara hitched a ride on a transport plane carrying thoroughbreds to Miami. He later told friends he survived in the city on Cuban *café con leche.*

He returned to Buenos Aires to complete medical school, crowding into one year, as had Martí, a heavy load of classes, as though there were many pursuits more important than school. He graduated in the spring of 1953 when he was twenty-five years old. As soon as he was able — he was declared unfit for military duty because of his asthma — he set out, by train, to rejoin his friend in Venezuela.

As Guevara continued his travels, he was intent upon observing the Indians in the highlands, silent, sullen, and often stoned on *coca.* He rode with them, standing in the backs of trucks to better scrutinize them, declining the privileged seat in the cab that was offered because of his European appearance. Among his observations was that the Indians were suspicious of him; although politically unorganized themselves, they seemed unreceptive to outside ideas. It was a lesson later driven home. Nevertheless, at the time Guevara was traveling, it was popular to believe that Bolivia provided fertile ground for revolution because the political consciousness of its miners, it was thought, could be mixed with the peasant strength of its Indians. He would return to test precisely that theory.

In Bolivia, Guevara met Rojo, an Argentine political refugee. As a tattered band of students traveled about Latin America without apparent aim, Rojo convinced his new friend to go to Guatemala, where it appeared a new day was being built. Guatemala, Rojo convinced Guevara, was where the model revolution was in progress. There, struggling since World War II to overcome the dominance of U.S. interests, the archetype of which was the United Fruit Company, a series of revolutionary governments had labored to survive. Guevara abandoned the idea of putting his medicine to work for lepers and decided he would work, instead, for revolutionaries.

Guevara and a companion struck out up the isthmus by ship, foot, and thumb. They stopped in Costa Rica, where José Figueres' liberal government provided sanctuary for political exiles, some of whom belonged to the romantic "Caribbean Legion," democratic activists in a hemisphere dominated by military dictators. At sidewalk cafes, Guevara met Rómulo Betancourt of Venezuela and Juan Bosch of the Dominican Republic.

He also met escaped Cuban survivors of the 26th of July raid on the

Moncada barracks. Rojo recalled: "To both Guevara and myself, it seemed that these excited young men were living a fantasy. They talked of summary executions, dynamite attacks, military demonstrations in the universities, kidnappings, and machine-gun fire; and they talked in a way so natural that it made our heads spin. . . . It was from them that Guevara first heard about Fidel Castro."

Guevara reached Guatemala just months before the CIA-directed coup that ended the ten-year experiment. Because he refused to join the Communist party, he was denied a license to practice medicine, but stayed to work in the bureaucracy. He did not leave the country until the government of Jacobo Arbenz was at the point of collapse. Guevara watched the Arbenz government let itself get thrown out in the summer of 1954 by a small, rag-tag army conscripted by the Central Intelligence Agency and organized in Honduras — then as now a jumping-off point for U.S. policy. The government fell, in Guevara's view, because internal dissent and confusion prevented a concerted counterattack.

During the final days, Guevara was informed by an Argentine diplomat that his name was on a list of people to be executed by the new regime. His participation in the revolutionary government, although short-lived, had made at least enough of an impression to mark him for death. This was the first instance of Guevara's unfortunate capacity for sticking up, as short as he was, like a lightning rod. He tended to give full rein to his contempt for anyone less committed than he, and it was not a characteristic easily overlooked. He took refuge in the Argentine embassy, but declined the chance to return to Buenos Aires. He chose safe-conduct to Mexico City.

There he made a paltry living selling books door-to-door or as a street photographer, working in the latter enterprise with a Guatemalan with whom he shared his apartment. In Mexico, Guevara married Hilda Gadea, a Peruvian woman of Indian-Chinese extraction he'd met in Guatemala. Rojo called her "an unselfish companion of the exiles." When their daughter was born in February 1955, she was named for her mother.

Hilda was a friend of several Cuban expatriates waiting in Mexico City for Castro to be released from prison. Among them, Guevara found a spiritual home. When Guevara was again given the chance to return to Argentina, as Perón finally was driven out, for the second time he declined. He stayed in Mexico City and was introduced to Castro one summer night in 1955. Talking into the morning, Guevara threw in his lot with the planned invasion. In November 1956, although Castro excluded other foreigners, Guevara took his place with eighty-one Cubans on the *Granma*. His asthma exacerbated the seasickness that afflicted everyone, and Guevara was ill throughout the voyage.

Immediately upon landing, Guevara later wrote, he was put to a test. Batista forces were instantly upon them; would he remain the force's physician or take arms? Under fire from the air and ground troops, the small force was confused and split up. Guevara and several others saw as their only escape a field of sugarcane. He had to decide whether to concern himself only with the wounded, or to fight. "At my feet were a pack full of medicine and a cartridge box," he wrote. "Together, they were too heavy to carry. I chose the cartridge box, leaving behind the medicine pack."

He was wounded in the neck and chest before staggering to relative safety with his comrades, several of whom were even more severely hurt. Batista's troops set the cane field afire, but Guevara was among the survivors who made it until nightfall and escaped.

He continued in a dual role, acting as doctor to the rebels, occasionally caring for wounded Batista troops, and, out of necessity, even becoming a dentist. But Guevara's bravery — a seeming lack of concern for safety despite having been wounded twice — attracted notice. The Cubans were impressed that exceptional courage was being shown by a man who was fighting not for his own country, but theirs. During the battle at Uvero, an early, successful clash that did much to build rebel confidence, Guevara volunteered to recover some rifles lost by nervous rebels under fire. Castro began to trust Guevara in a guerrilla war in which commanders were also teachers, confessors, kind uncles, and harsh judges all rolled into one. No one was a professional soldier, so as raw recruits straggled in from the city, they had to be motivated and reassured as well as trained. Eventually, Guevara was given command of a column.

Guevara's importance to the Cuban revolution, however, was not as a fighter. Guevara himself kept his record as a warrior in context. He wrote of returning to one battle site from which he had been forced to take to his heels: "There I found a piece of my blanket tangled in the brambles as a reminder of my speedy 'strategic retreat.'" Like Archilocus of Pylos, Guevara's contribution to the lore of battle was more lyrical than tactical. His diaries reveal the everyday drudgery of living off the land, learning all that could be learned from the peasants, fighting an enemy that had more of everything except will.

If Guevara was compelled to rebel, so was he obsessed with the idea of recording everything, from inventories to emotions, in his diaries. That writing is relatively free of the leaden dogma that characterizes much communist "literature." In the case of twenty-five months in the Sierra Maestra, his diaries, edited after victory, provide one of the most complete chronicles of guerrilla warfare. His descriptions of battles, his observations of both enemy and ally, his expression of his own and others' feelings, all distinguish Guevara as neither a great leader nor a great warrior, but as a simple human being experiencing the kind of warfare only imagined by the many who would rebel, but do not.

"That night the weapons arrived. For us it was the most marvelous spectacle in the world: the instruments of death were on exhibition before the covetous eyes of all the men. . . . A few days later, on May 23 [1957], Fidel ordered new discharges, among them an entire squad, and our force was reduced to 127 men, the majority of them armed and about 80 of them well armed. . . . There remained one man named Crucito who later became one of our best-loved fighters. Crucito was a natural poet and he had long rhyming matches with the city-poet, Calixto Morales. Morales had arrived on the *Granma* and had nicknamed himself 'nightingale of the plains,' to which Crucito . . . directed in mock derision at Calixto, 'I'm an old Sierra buzzard.'"

From the moment the rebels landed—"disoriented and walking in circles, an army of shadows, of phantoms, walking as if moved by some obscure psychic mechanism"—until they entered Havana, it was Guevara who gave voice to the revolution. From rebel headquarters, Castro issued pronouncements, declarations, manifestos. But as supreme commander he was kept safe during battles. It was Guevara who recorded the terror. "His name was Armando Rodriguez and he carried a Thompson submachine gun," Guevara tells us from precise notes and shared experience. "Toward the end, he had such a terrified and anguished face whenever he heard shots in the distance that we called that expression *cara de cerco*, 'the face of the surrounded.'"

Movement, distrust, constant vigilance: these, Guevara lectures, were the cardinal requirements of successful guerrilla tactics. In the early days the rebel army risked extinction, eating raw crabs, making reed straws to suck water from tiny pools among the rocks, drawing weak sustenance from sugarcane. If hunger did not incapacitate them, disease was the next risk. Guevara contracted malaria. If the army outside the sierra could not penetrate the rugged terrain, spies were always possible. Guevara recounts the story of Eutemio Guerra, the peasant who worked his way into the rebel force, betraying the rebels' position three times while awaiting his chance to assassinate Castro, a chance only narrowly missed.

When fifty new men, many recruited in Santiago, were marched in, it took weeks to determine whether they had the mettle, mental and physical, to remain. "A few other boys left us," Guevara writes, "a fact that was to the advantage of the troops. I remember one of them had an attack of nerves, there in the solitude of mountains and guerrillas. He began to shout that he had been promised a camp with abundant food and anti-aircraft defenses, and that now the planes harassed him and he had neither permanent quarters, nor food, nor even water to drink. Afterward, those who stayed and passed the first tests grew accustomed to dirt, to lack of water, food, shelter and security, and to continually rely only on a rifle and the cohesion and resistance of the small guerrilla nucleus."

Guevara's notes also record his sense of personal development. At first he felt conspicuous, as if his nickname, *el argentino*, were the Cubans' way of isolating him. Although he was willing to risk his own neck, he tended to be tentative in command. He was reprimanded by Castro for not being assertive. Then, a delivery of weapons, distributed on a strict merit system, assured him of his worth when he was placed in command of an automatic-rifle squad. "In this way," he recounted, "I made my debut as a fighting guerrilla, for until then I had been the troop's doctor, knowing only occasional combat. I had entered a new stage."

In late 1958, Batista's generals made a last attempt to destroy the rebels before the staged elections planned for November. The army moved into the sierra and encircled Castro's army, but fell far short of the victory needed. "After two and a half months of steady skirmishing," Guevara wrote in a kind of gleeful accounting, "the enemy had a thousand casualties—dead, wounded, captured and deserters. They had abandoned to us six hundred weapons, including one tank, twelve mortars, twelve tripod machine guns, and an impressive quantity of automatic weapons, not counting an incredible amount of equipment and ammunition of all sorts, plus four hundred and fifty prisoners, whom we turned over to the Red Cross at the end of the campaign."

When the time came for what would be the rebels' final offensive, Guevara marched his column toward Santa Clara, the railroad center for the central plain, under difficult conditions. Without trucks, through a cyclone, under fire, twice surrounded, the column staggered into Las Villas province, new territory for the guerrillas. Guevara conceded that closer to Havana the peasants were not as sympathetic as they had been in Oriente. In mid-October, he reached the relative safety of the Trinidad–Sancti Spiritus mountain range. His mission was to upset the elections.

With Camilo Cienfuegos, another column commander, Guevara directed the decisive battles up to and into Santa Clara, a city of 150,000. The battle for the city Guevara sketched, including the story of a soldier he encountered in a rebel field hospital during the battle.

It was a man, now mortally wounded, whom Guevara had earlier found disarmed and asleep "at the height of a battle" and whom Guevara had ordered "with my customary dryness, 'Go to the front lines barehanded and come back with another gun, if you are man enough.'" In the field hospital, from his makeshift bed, the man reached up, "touched my hand and said, 'Remember, major? You sent me to find a gun at Remedios. . . . I brought it here.'" The soldier died "a few minutes later. It seemed to me that he was pleased to have proved his courage. Such was our Rebel Army."

Victory was more complicated. The administration of a thoroughly dependent, undeveloped, historically exploited island economy and the design and construction of a new society were problems considerably more intractable than beating Batista's army. The infighting; the counter-revolutionary sabotage; the difficulty of understanding, then improving, the economy; the embargo by the United States — these were not battles the men of the Sierra Maestra could win with automatic weapons. Guevara, ultimately, retreated from those wars and sought once again the kind of war he understood.

Guevara brought to Havana an easy grace that captured imaginations in a way the looming figure of Castro did not. As director of the National Bank, Guevara signed new money, simply, "Ché." For admirers, the signature signaled revolutionary flair, but for Guevara, it completed a journey. He had been dubbed "Ché" in Mexico City by the same Cubans who would isolate him in the sierra as *el argentino*. Now the name fluttered like a banner.

To Castro's dead-pan, long-winded *jefe máximo* of the new society, Guevara played a kind of intelligent jester — committed, but with a sense of humor. He made light of the new leadership's inability to manipulate the economy the Yankees had left behind. Coke tasted like bitter syrup and toothpaste turned so hard it could not be squeezed from the tube, Guevara admitted. But, patience, socialist morality would prevail. What was needed at the moment was style, and he was the embodiment of that style.

In mid-1959, six months after he and Cienfuegos had led their troops into Havana — and about the time five new cabinet ministers were being forced to resign — Guevara was sent abroad as a kind of traveling spokesman for rebellion. He cut a rhetorical swath for three months from Yugoslavia and Egypt to Ceylon and Japan. As far as international sympathizers were concerned, Guevara was a fetching symbol, with his beret, his scant beard, his good looks, and his ability to turn a phrase.

In December 1959, heading a trade mission to East Germany, Guevara met Haydee Tamara Bunke Bider, the attractive daughter of a college professor. Two years later she would visit Cuba on his invitation. To whomever was watching, it would have appeared the natural consequence of the meeting of two attractive people committed to the same ideas. It would eventually be revealed, however, that this was an early piece of an international jigsaw puzzle, a puzzle that would only be understood after Guevara and "Tanya the Guerrilla" were both dead.

In Havana, after the hardships of the mountains, Guevara slipped easily into the role of international celebrity, compensating at the banquet table for the years of deprivation in the sierra. His friend Rojo, who had not seen him since before the *Granma* expedition, found him well fattened. The breast pockets of his khaki shirt, however, still bulged with asthma medicine, and his face was bloated from cortisone. Also, his old friend was now cautious enough about assassination attempts that he carried in his

Jeep a cigar box filled not with his favorite Cuban cigars but with U.S.-made fragmentation hand grenades. Rojo found all Havana in preparation for the invasion that would come in February 1961 at the Bay of Pigs. During the invasion, Guevara, already bearing scars in the neck, chest, and foot from the sierra campaign, managed to get wounded again — by dropping his automatic pistol and shooting himself in the cheek.

In addition to being a major in the army and directing the National Bank — and serving as chairman of the committee directing the new Bank of Foreign Commerce — Guevara was chosen to direct industrial development. Schooled as a physician and having shown aptitude as a guerrilla, he was a prime example of how the Cuban revolution's enormous possibilities had to be realized by people outside their fields of competence.

Castro created an all-powerful Instituto Nacional de la Reforma Agraria, or INRA, and it was from that fount that all policy was to flow. Guevara's industrial development office was a part of that structure. Edward Boorstein, an American economist who went to Cuba, wrote: "You could see and feel in the halls and offices of the INRA headquarters in Havana that it was a revolutionary organization. Here were not the prim, old-line functionaries of the National Bank or Treasury, but bearded rebels in uniform, carrying arms. The working hours were not the 9-to-5 of the ordinary government worker. They were the irregular hours — the nocturnal hours — of the guerrilla fighter. Meetings could start at midnight and last till daybreak."

Guevara had remarried, a Cuban woman, Aleida, and happily adopted the practice of working on administrative matters until midnight, then sitting, talking with friends and drinking *mate*, the traditional tea that Guevara made from herbs brought to him from Argentina. Guevara warned his colleagues that they were being observed by their fellow Cubans, who would be quick to notice signs that old, corrupt ways might be allowed to return. If style was important, it had to convey frugality and honesty.

There was also a hidden side. It is important to recognize that virtually from the day he walked into Havana from the sierra, as he assumed his role of public spokesman, worked as a member of the cabinet, went home to visit his family, received awards from other nations, and spoke at lecterns from New York to Punta del Este, Guevara's hand was in subversion. As he did tricks for his many admirers with one hand, the other was out of sight, making rebellion.

He hung an oilcloth map of Argentina in his bathroom, the better to contemplate revolutionary options in his native land, and in 1961-62, he helped establish a "revolutionary focus" in the northern mountains. Using Cuban fighters, it was led by an Argentine friend, Jorge Masetti, who was known as *El Segundo* to recognize Guevara as the principal leader. By the spring of 1964, it was wiped out, casting Guevara into grief over the loss of friends, but not convincing him that the Cuban model could not be transferred. While the world was transfixed by the missile crisis in 1962, Guevara was supporting another rebellion in the mountains of Peru, a movement eradicated by 1965. In both instances, a reasonably efficient, trained, motivated military found and destroyed the rebel forces, but Guevara was still convinced his design would work. He envisioned an axis of rebellion from Peru through Bolivia into northern Argentina. "Violence is the midwife of new societies," he assured Rojo.

In public, Guevara became a spokesman for hope. If the United States would not buy Cuban exports, the socialist nations would have to. Guevara went to Europe, to Asia. With his eagerly reported statements in the press, he became the embodiment of the notion that the Cuban revolution could be exported.

Eventually, however, after the trade agreements were signed and the loans extended, words began to have a hollow sound. His capacity for talking rather than for listening made enemies at home among confused, pressured cabinet members. He was a bit too quick with opinions that rolled over delicate relationships.

In 1964, while Guevara's public image was maintained, changes were occurring. His inability to accept others' ideas, his arrogance, isolated him in the cabinet. If at lecturns from Geneva to Algiers he was the toast of international rebellion, in Cuba he was an annoyance. There was the impression that a breach had been opened between Guevara and Castro — although the reality was that the two were clandestinely planning subversion on two continents.

In April, after arranging to send Cuban troops to help Congolese rebels, Guevara wrote in a private letter to Castro that "the time has come for us to part." Guevara went briefly to Africa with the troops, but reality directed him back toward his old interest, revolution in Latin America.

Divesting himself of his rank and Cuban citizenship, he wrote, not altogether accurately, "Nothing legal binds me to Cuba.... The only ties are of another nature; those that cannot be broken as appointments can." From then on, Guevara wrote, he would "carry to new battlefronts the faith that you taught me, the revolutionary spirit of my people, the feeling of fulfilling the most sacred of duties: to fight against imperialism where it may be. This comforts and heals the deepest wounds."

What bound him to Cuba was both illegal and secret: logistical support and volunteers for his revolutionary adventures. Guevara dropped from public sight, but he and Castro remained inextricably joined. With his wife expecting their fourth child, Guevara said publicly that he wanted to work in a factory, to absorb himself with the simpler tasks of building a new economy. It was widely interpreted not that he was going underground, but that he was being banished to some minor post.

His mother, in a letter he would never see, written only weeks before she died of cancer, asked why Cuba's revolutionary leaders spent so much time winning the sympathies of the people rather than improving government. "It seems to me true madness," she wrote, "that with so few heads in Cuba with ability to organize you should all go cut cane for a month as your main job when there are so many and such good cane cutters among the people." His plans, she suggested, meant "that the madness has turned to absurdity." With the tenderness of a mother and tenacity of an old socialist, she insisted that if he was unappreciated in Cuba he should go back to Ghana or Algeria to do revolutionary work. "Yes, you will always be a foreigner. That seems to be your permanent fate."

At the time Guevara was assembling 125 Cuban fighters to join Congolese rebels, but the six-month expedition was a failure. The Congolese annoyed Guevara with their corruption and lack of willingness to fight. He urged Castro to drop Cuba's support, and, undercover, returned to Cuba.

In October 1965, six months after Guevara had last been seen in public, Castro made public his letter renouncing his responsibilities in Cuba. He was still not seen in public, however, and the effect, for his many admirers, was mysterious, romantic.

In fact, plans were well advanced toward a Bolivian "focus." A network of supply and information was established by operatives from Cuba, including the East German woman, the one known as "Tanya." Posing as an Argentine national, she adopted several covers and was able to broadcast advice-to-the-lovelorn over a radio station — sentimental messages that carried codes for Guevara's guerrillas, whom she would later join. Castro, Guevara, and their intermediaries made contact with Bolivian communists, although the effort was half-hearted and never risked allowing the divided, Moscow-oriented party to interfere. Bolivia was the keystone in a potential series of revolutionary enclaves in Argentina, Paraguay, and Peru, and neither Castro nor Guevara was prepared to let European party dogma get in the way of Latin American design.

"Once again I feel between my heels the ribs of Rosinante," he wrote to his mother and father in the spring of 1965. "Once more I hit the road with my shield upon my arm. Almost ten years ago today, I wrote you another letter of farewell. As I remember, I lamented not being a better soldier and a better doctor. The latter no longer interests me; I'm not such a bad soldier."

Into Bolivia traveled a man carrying the passport of Ramón Borges Fernández. The passport, one of two the man carried, showed he had flown from Havana to Prague to Frankfurt to Brazil to La Paz. The man was portly, clean-shaven, wearing heavy horn-rim glasses, and bald. His occupation was identified as "businessman." Guevara had transformed himself, as his mother said, into yet another foreigner.

Using the code name "Ramón," Guevara was headed for a remote farm in Nancahuazú. Eight stalwarts of the sierra who had accompanied him to the Congo were with him. Out of Nancahuazú operated seventeen Cubans, all officers of the Cuban army, and three Peruvian veterans of the unsuccessful revolution there. To them they would gather twenty-nine Bolivians—as in the Cuban experience some city people, some peasants—and depend on a small, fragile network of operatives in the city. It is unlikely that Guevara knew Haydee Tamara Bunke Bider was a double agent. While working for him, she was also employed by East German security forces—and, in turn, the Soviet KGB. Apparently, her role was to keep an eye on Guevara and Castro, who had a marked tendency to make revolution on their own, independent of Moscow, as they were doing now.

"A new stage begins today," Guevara wrote on November 7, 1966, upon arriving at the safe house in Nancahuazú. He had last been seen in public in March 1965, and it amused him greatly that when his driver found out who his passenger was the shock almost killed them both. "While heading toward the farm on his second trip, 'Bigotes,' who had just discovered my identity, almost drove off a cliff, leaving the jeep stuck on the edge of the precipice. We walked about 20 kilometers to the farm." Five days later he reported, "My beard is growing and in a couple of months I shall start looking like myself again."

But nothing would ever be the same. Nancahuazú was in the middle of a vast, rugged wilderness that would have swallowed the entire island of Cuba. The land was uninhabited for great stretches, and the guerrillas wandered aimlessly. They had to hide even from hunters for fear of discovery. What natives they did encounter spoke an Indian dialect the guerrillas had not planned on. The peasants, unlike those of the Sierra Maestra, were often hostile and informed on them. Government broadcasts capitalized on the fact that so many of the guerrillas were foreigners. Government troops, on the other hand, were largely natives of the area, recruited nearby, defending their homeland, able to communicate with their countrymen. And whereas Batista had cowered in Havana, Rene Barrientos, the Bolivian leader whose own background was a humble one, would fly out to inspect his troops with a machine gun slung jauntily from his shoulder. He once landed within 250 yards of where Guevara lay hidden.

Less than four months after Guevara arrived in Bolivia, the first of his fighters was lost, not to hostile fire, but to the hostile environment. Exhausted from marching over the mountain terrain, he slipped and fell from a rock into a treacherous stream and was carried away. Once again Guevara's diary was the chronicle of the effort, but this time it was written mostly in despair. "Nothing new from La Paz. Nothing new here."

Simply holding the group together was a burden. There were continual arguments with the Bolivian Communist party over who was in charge. To join Guevara was to defy the party line. "I spoke to the entire group, giving them 'the facts of life' on the realities of war," he wrote on December 12. "I emphasized the one-man command system of discipline and warned the Bolivians of the responsibility they took in violating the discipline of their party in adopting another line." After listening on the radio to a Castro speech broadcast from Cuba that referred to their tiny, isolated fight, Guevara wrote: "He referred to us in terms that obligate us even more, if that is possible."

Yet very little was possible. In February 1967 a second rebel drowned. By March, with the group almost as large as it would get, about forty fighters, he despaired. "The men are getting increasingly discouraged at seeing the approaching end of the provisions, but not of the distance to be covered."

On March 23, there was a seductive success. An ambush killed seven government soldiers and a civilian guide and captured mortars, radios, boots, and eighteen prisoners. "A major and a captain, prisoners, talked like parrots," Guevara wrote in a tone that conveyed elation.

Guevara heard on the radio that the government still denied guerrillas were operating in the country. Then he heard that their base camp had been discovered. Two deserters were captured. Military attachés from Argentina, Brazil, and Paraguay had flown into La Paz to observe. Was this the continental revolt Castro had promised?

Barrientos ordered bombing raids and declared, yes, Guevara, the feared Guevara, was there with the guerrillas, but now he was dead. Another Bolivian leader said, yes, and not only was Guevara dead, they were all dead, all of them. Guevara listened to the radio and hung on.

Guevara treated his prisoners humanely and released them after trying to give the impression he headed a well-organized, efficient, and large force. On April 10 another ambush caused nineteen government casualties; the government, in retaliation, suspended activities of the Bolivian Communist party. Then Guevara heard that sixteen U.S. Special Forces "advisors" would train a Bolivian battalion, something rebels never had to deal with in Cuba. He wrote: "We may be witnessing the first episode of a new Vietnam."

What he was witnessing was the beginning of the end. On April 17, the group, forty-five rebels, was inadvertently split, a mistake, caused by the rugged terrain, that would prove fatal. Five days later a clash killed four guerrillas and wounded several others in Guevara's reduced group. Two more clashes followed. "It will take time to transform this into a fighting force," he wrote, adding hopefully, "although morale is rather high."

The government, perhaps getting reports on both halves of the guerrilla army, estimated it at twice its size, but kept up the pressure. Guevara, who figured by early May the rebels had killed twenty-three soldiers, placed his hopes on a miners' revolt and accelerated help from the Communist party. Neither occurred.

His analysis for May: "Total lack of contact" with the other half of the group. "Complete lack of peasant recruitment." Guevara called for a "National Liberation Army," asking Bolivians "to close ranks, to weld the tightest unity without distinction of political colors." It had all the effect of a manifesto issued by Sandino.

Guevara was trapped, cut off. He was satisfied with the government's acknowledgment it was he, in fact, who led the guerrillas. The thought of retreat, leaving Bolivia, never occurred to him. "I am now 39," Guevara wrote on June 14, "and am relentlessly approaching the age when I must think about my future as a guerrilla; in the meantime, I am 'complete.'"

In early July, Guevara's group decided to stop a truck on the road near tiny Samaipata — but another stopped behind it. Then a third driver stopped to see what was happening, and a fourth because the road was blocked. The episode would represent the final, exuberant cry of the guerrillas. They finally got around to going into town, capturing two shocked local policemen and the chief of the post. "Then they took over the barracks and ten soldiers in lightning actions," Guevara cheered. "The action took place before the whole village and many travelers in such a way that the news will spread like fire."

The news spread across the world, but the guerrillas left town without taking medicine Guevara needed for his asthma. Denied a safe zone and forced to constantly move, Guevara fell too sick to march. He had to hold himself on horseback and be floated across streams on rafts. Nights in the mountains were cold. When their tape recorder was lost so was their ability to capture radio messages for decoding. Their comptroller in La Paz absconded with a quarter of a million rebel dollars. Caches of arms were discovered. Deserters led the army closer.

"July 27: My asthma hit me hard." On August 26, "Everything went wrong." Guevara's mistakes were exacerbated by the army's increasing efficiency. "August 30: The situation is becoming desperate." The jungle was so thick that the macheteros in front could not keep going at the altitude they were forced to travel.

On August 31 the other, separated, column was caught fording a stream and wiped out, the East German woman along with them. Even before learning of their demise, Guevara wrote in his monthly analysis, "It was, without doubt, the worst month we have had so far in this war."

In late September, a village official apparently warned the army the guerrillas could be found near Alto Seco, a dot on the map at 1,900 meters, and on September 26, after climbing to 2,280 meters, Guevara's group was cut to pieces by a pursuing army patrol.

September analysis: "It would have been a month of recuperation and it was just about to be, but the ambush in which they got Miguel, Coco and Julio ruined everything and we have been left in a dangerous position. . . . The army appears to be more effective in its actions, and the peasants do not give us any help and are turning into informers."

Nevertheless, on October 7, Guevara wrote, "We completed the 11th month of our guerrilla operations in a bucolic mood." After resting, "the 17 of us set out with a very small moon. The march was very tiring and we left a lot of traces along the canyon. . . . Altitude 2000 meters."

On October 8, Guevara fought his last fight. He and his remaining sixteen men were trapped in a shallow canyon. Guevara was second in the guerrilla column when it made contact with a Bolivian ranger patrol. In the lead, a Bolivian miner returned the patrol's fire and the guerrillas tried to retreat. They were unable to scramble their way back up the slope or to make their fire effective. Guevara was hit in the legs, and the miner, Simón Cuba, carried him. Guevara was hit again.

Cuba propped Guevara against a tree and tried to defend him until he was cut down. Guevara tried to fire his machine gun with one hand, but was hit yet again, in the leg. Then a bullet hit his trigger, splitting the gun's stock and knocking it from his hand before ricocheting into his right forearm. He was defenseless and captured.

Although bleeding, Guevara was not mortally wounded. He spoke to the two officers in charge, a captain and a colonel. They had him placed on a makeshift stretcher and carried to the village of La Higuera, where he was set down in an empty room of the schoolhouse. They left. Decisions had to be made.

Was Guevara, the international figure, to be taken to Vallegrande for medical help? If so, should he be given preference over wounded soldiers? The colonel was on the phone. The decisions would be reached in La Paz.

The next day, Guevara was sitting on the floor of the schoolroom, propped with his shoulder against the wall, when the captain and the colonel returned. The captain walked behind him. With a machine gun, he fired a burst, hitting Guevara four times in the neck and upper back. The colonel fired his pistol once into Guevara's heart.

His body was taken to Vallegrande and displayed on a table in a public laundry.

Bishop Romero
1917–1980
(El Salvador)

Modern Martyr

In Latin America, oppressive governments have always sought the complicity, or at least the docility, of the Roman Catholic Church. During colonization, the Spanish king, commissioned by the pope, was secular head of the Church; he counted on priests to do his bidding. From the beginning, however, some priests answered to a higher law, standing at the side of the oppressed. Father Bartolomé de Las Casas won the title "Protector of the Indians" in the early sixteenth century; the Mexican priests Hidalgo and Morelos led the Mexican rebellion; Jesuits have periodically been at odds with kings and *caudillos*, and, in modern times, some priests, compelled by their understanding of Christianity, have gone into the hills to join guerrillas. Archbishop Romero, by inclination a conservative man who opposed public demonstrations of dissent, was cast into the middle of the continuing civil war in Latin America's smallest country. That war is being fought over ancient and fundamental questions of land tenure and the exploitation of workers, but Romero could have remained safe in his priestly vestments. He chose, as a matter of conscience, to step into the line of fire.

Oscar Arnulfo Romero y Galdámez was born on August 15, 1917, in Ciudad Barrios, in El Salvador's highlands near Honduras. It was a small town without electricity, reached only by foot or on horseback, in an area where Indian blood was dominant. His father, Santos, from a nearby village, was sent to Ciudad Barrios by the government in 1903 to serve as postmaster and telegrapher. He operated both services out of a modest stucco home on the plaza and married Guadelupe de Jesús, who bore him eight children, one of whom died in infancy. Santos, who also sired several children outside the family, augmented his income by growing cacao and coffee on twenty acres outside of town.

Oscar was the second oldest child. He was of medium height and rather wiry, and had his mother's prominent chin. Throughout his life, his nature seemed to balance between frailty and tenacity, fatigue and a fearsome temper. As a boy, he delivered telegraph messages in the town and learned how to operate a telegraph and read Morse Code. He attended the small school overseen by a single teacher, learned to play the flute and harmonium, and, at the age of twelve or thirteen, was apprenticed to a carpenter.

According to Romero's principal biographer, Father James R. Brockman, S.J., the youthful Romero himself broached the subject of studying for the priesthood, to the dismay of his father. His brothers and sisters were not surprised, having noticed their brother visiting the church on his own. He went off to the seminary at San Miguel, but left during the Depression to work in a gold mine near Ciudad Barrios, perhaps to help pay the medical expenses of his ailing mother. Two brothers also worked at the mine.

The Depression weighed hard on El Salvador, a country barely twice the size of New Jersey and dependent on coffee exports. It is a country that never has rested easily, although at times it has been kept quiet by agreement among the dominant families. At other times it has been split by civil war. From 1913 to 1930, fueled by high coffee prices and administered by a relatively stable government, El Salvador progressed. But coffee prices crashed in 1930, and the next decade witnessed a harsh civil war that installed a dictatorship; the 1940s gave birth to another war to unseat that dictatorship. So its history continued, the army and national guard by turns taking power and mediating between conflicting elites.

In 1937, after three years' absence, Romero returned to his studies and was sent to the national seminary run by Jesuits. Seven months later, having proved himself a scholar, he was sent on to study in Rome. Romero was in Rome at the outset of World War II. While there, he learned of the deaths of his father — and the subsequent loss of the family farm to creditors — and of a brother. He was ordained in the spring of 1942 and intended to stay in Italy to earn a doctorate, specializing in "ascetical theology." But the war made it impossible, and he returned to say his first mass for friends and relatives in January 1944.

His first parish was in a small mountain village, but he was soon called to the city of San Miguel to serve as diocesan secretary. Because others in the family were unable to take care of her, his mother lived with Romero until her death in 1961. His diocesan duties included editing a weekly, and Romero developed into something of a stylist; his homilies, when saying mass at a small colonial church in San Miguel, were broadcast over a local radio station. However fluid his style, Romero's view of the Church was staunchly conservative. Protestants complained when he refused to let them use the cathedral to honor the nineteenth century patriot Gerardo Barrios because Barrios had been a Mason. Brockman dryly notes of Romero's position in the community: "By refusing Christian burial to Masons, he alienated various families."

In the mid–1950s, Romero participated in a month of devotions conducted by Jesuits, whose role in the Salvadoran civil war would be pivotal. "Romero had had at least indirect exposure to Ignatian spirituality through his Jesuit teachers in San Salvador and Rome," Father Brockman writes. "There is nothing quite like making the exercises themselves, however. Some clue to their effect on him is the phrase from the exercises that he later took as his episcopal motto: 'Sentir con la iglesia,' To be of one mind with the church."

Father Brockman, himself a Jesuit, recognizes that the "effect" of jesuitical training must be, by turns, extolled or explained. This is especially true in the context of Latin America. Founded by Spanish soldier-turned-priest Ignatius Loyola in 1534, the order has trained some of the sharpest minds of the Church. Yet it has also earned for itself a reputation that inspires the second definition of Jesuit: "one given to intrigue or equivocation."

The Jesuits' predilection for "intrigue" has continually put the order's members at loggerheads with governments. In 1767 — after French Jesuits refused absolution to the king's Enlightened mistress — the strain became so severe that Charles III of Spain expelled all Jesuits from Latin America. Other priests declined to defend or protect them, and Jesuits were literally packed up and shipped back to Spain.

Also of significant effect on Latin America and on Romero was a series of liberalizing influences on the church. These began with the conferences of bishops in Rome from 1962 to 1965 that are known collectively as Vatican II. Latin was joined in the liturgy by parishioners' own languages; lay members were given more of a place ceremonially and administratively in the life of the Church; the hierarchical mentality of the traditional Roman Catholic Church was modified, softened. The Church opened up, and the new atmosphere was perceived by many as a threat. The liberality was seen by conservatives as blasphemous. Reformers looked to a new spirit of cooperation.

To apply the principles of Vatican II, Latin American bishops convened in Medellín, Colombia, in 1968. New principles for the Church, in Latin America, would apply side-by-side with very old, very oppressive economic and social conditions. Decisions made at Medellín were especially radical because they signaled change in an environment of oppression. The conference at Medellín allowed communication among those priests whose most leftward inclinations have come to be associated with the term "liberation theology." That term encapsulates the notion that the Church belongs firmly at the side of the poor and must accept, as a legitimate worldview, the Marxist interpretation that maldistribution of wealth creates class conflict.

In 1967, as these ideas were beginning to spin about in discussions, Romero was transferred — despite parishioners' petitions to let him stay — from San Miguel to the capital, San Salvador. He was given the title of monsignor and named secretary-general of the national bishops conference. In the spring of the next year he was named executive secretary of the Central American Bishops Secretariat.

Romero was known as thorough, contemplative, and conservative. When he was named auxiliary bishop in May 1970, the elaborate ceremony marking his elevation was seen by some as an example of the Church's historic "triumphalism" — which so often placed clerics at the shoulder of oppressors, softly assuring the oppressed that their kingdom was in heaven. Romero's conservative reputation had much to do with his continuing progress within the hierarchy.

By coincidence, the day after Romero's elevation to bishop 123 priests convened in San Salvador to discuss the implications of Vatican II and the Medellín conference. Because liberalization was so painfully controversial, about half of the clerics in the country indicated their opposition to change by staying away. "To a person schooled in a vision of life in which one must accept suffering and seek peace and harmony at any price," writes Father Brockman, "such ideas involve a considerable readjustment of attitudes and preconceptions."

By autumn of 1970, reflecting the pressure of his new position, the tensions within the clergy and the country, and the fact that a priest's life under such circumstances is filled with demands, Romero was ill. There would be rumors that his sickness was more than physical, that he was mentally ill. He went to the home of a lay friend, whose family cared for him. He remained virtually isolated at their home for weeks.

When he returned, his responsibilities were multiplied. He was named, in May 1971, editor of the archdiocesan publication. He moved it, editorially, toward being more conservative, avoiding the ferment of Medellín altogether. Two years later, Romero's conservatism put him at the head of an assault on new ideas as they were written into the curriculum of a Jesuit high school. Parents were complaining; here were liberal ideas, awakening ideas, foisted on the sons and daughters of the upper class. Romero warned against "false" ideas and "demagogy and Marxism." The liberality of Medellín should not be taken too far, Romero wrote.

Again, in late 1971 and 1972, Romero was forced by poor health to take time off. It was as if there was a battle within as to whether he could withstand the rigors of a public life, especially in a forum so torn by dissent. At the end of 1972, to place his steady, conservative hand on an institution drifting leftward, he was named rector of a Jesuit seminary. Among the transgressions noted was that seminarians were taking philosophy courses at a nearby secular college and playing volleyball in gym shorts. Romero's attempts at reform — there were severe problems of finance and management — were less than successful, testing his resilience to criticism.

The Church's internal wrangling affected him personally in 1974, when Salvadoran bishops elected him their delegate to a synod in Rome. He first accepted, then resigned and was replaced by Arturo Rivera Damas, a bishop identified with the liberal wing of the Salvadoran clergy. Seeing his mistake, Romero then changed his mind again and decided he wanted to be the delegate after all. The matter was left to the Vatican hierarchy, which picked Rivera.

In December, Romero was named bishop of Santiago de María. This made him, rather than an "auxiliary" in the archdiocese of the capital, a bishop in his own right, with his own diocese, his own flock. He was a contemplative man, but now he was being drawn toward daily contact with parishioners and the priests who felt responsible for them. He was nearing the conflict that divided Salvadoran society, and the proximity would change him. Instrumental to the well-being of many people, especially in his diocese, was a land reform bill being discussed by Congress. Although weak and eventually watered down even further, the law signaled the possibility of change. Opposed to the law were the well-organized associations of Salvadoran businessmen and landowners. Supporting reform were peasant organizations, many of them put together with the direct participation of priests.

Confrontations were usually one-sided and always brutal. Soldiers would enter a town where a peasant organization was being formed. The officer in command would search for "weapons and subversive literature." The search would lead to the town's church, where sacred places, the sacristy or catafalque, would be opened (sometimes shot open). Articles, not excluding communion wafers, would be scattered. Priests who helped the peasant organizations were condemned as communists, making the soldiers, like Inquisitors, the "true" representatives of the Church. There was that twisted hatred peculiar to the mentality that heaps anticommunism on top of religious zeal. It bore bitter fruit. Soldiers, conscripted from the villages and barrios, were expected to carry out all manner of atrocities.

On November 29, 1974, six people were killed and two of their widows beaten. Men were stripped naked and humiliated by national guardsmen and police. On May 7, 1975, a priest and three of his friends were arrested, blindfolded, taken into San Salvador, and beaten. A "subversive" pamphlet was found, or planted, in the priest's mass kit. On June 21, 1975, five campesinos were shot and hacked to death, their homes ransacked. The last of these atrocities occurred in Tres Calles, a town in the diocese of Bishop Romero.

The bishop went to the national guard commander and wrote a letter to the president of El Salvador, Col. Armando Arturo Molina. Still deferential to authority, Romero, referring to the mass he said for the slain men in Tres Calles, said he regretted that protest songs had been sung. He did not believe, he said, in public expressions of dissent.

At about this time, in May, Romero had been named a "consultor" to the Pontifical Commission for Latin America, an important vehicle for information and opinion about the region to the Vatican. Made up mostly of Vatican officials, the commission includes one member and three consultants who are Latin American bishops; Romero, Brockman notes, had received "singular recognition." The experience forced him to contemplate and express his understanding of the forces acting on his country and the region. Later that year, after traveling to Rome, he set down his views. Although he conceded that the Salvadoran government was oppressive, Romero was still convinced that the place of priests was alongside authority. He criticized dissenting priests as "politicized." Brockman notes Romero was "blind to his own political stance in support of the government. . . . That only a year and a half later his closest helpers would be those whom he pronounced suspect in this document is proof of a radical shift by then in Romero's viewpoint."

Indeed, the beginning of the transformation was imminent. In the summer of 1976, Romero, in order to learn more of plans to strengthen the land reform law, instigated a study. The priests who conducted the study were critical of the government's proposal, calling it weak in the face of centuries of injustice. No social progress was possible as long as a relatively few families owned the vast majority of arable land, forcing the bulk of the population to work as day laborers. Romero took the results of the study to the president. Nothing happened. The proposal, in fact, as weak as it was, eventually was emasculated by Congress in response to the complaints of landowners, who saw even slight change as a threat. Romero was learning realities. The lessons would get harsher.

At the outset of 1977, a new archbishop was needed for the archdiocese of San Salvador. Luis Chávez y González, at seventy-five, had served as the tiny nation's only archbishop for thirty-eight years. On a scale of such considerations in the tense, antagonistic environment of El Salvador,

Chávez was a liberal. He had looked to the well-being of believers, not just the wealthy. So his departure was welcomed by elites. A possibility to replace him, however, was Bishop Rivera, who was even more liberal. Rivera was popular with the masses and the clergy of the capital and just as unpopular with their adversaries. The choice of the Vatican, where Salvadoran divisions were well known, was Bishop Romero. His conservatism, presumably, would provide stability. Romero knew his elevation was not universally popular and wrote to priests of the diocese that he hoped to serve in a "spirit of cooperation."

At the same time as Romero's elevation, the political atmosphere of El Salvador was growing hotter. In the weeks before Romero was to take over as archbishop, the government had thrown out of the country two seminarians and four priests — a Colombian, an American, a Belgian, and a Salvadoran — accusing them of organizing peasants. Their treatment in captivity ranged from relatively gentle to cattle prods. The two seminarians and the Salvadoran (actually a former priest) were Jesuits, and traditionalists' hostility was directed at foreign priests and Jesuits.

Contributing to the atmosphere of crisis were preparations for a presidential election in February. The establishment of El Salvador had decided to exchange, as president, a colonel for a general. Elected was Gen. Carlos Humberto Romero, former minister of defense and public security. The fraud was massive.

The election was held on a Sunday, and two days later Romero took over as archbishop. When Salvadoran bishops visited Molina, the outgoing president, to present their new archbishop — whose elevation Molina had not even noticed — they got a lecture on how the Church had been misguided by new and dangerous ideas. While Romero returned to Santiago de María to bring his belongings to the capital, crowds protesting the election fraud gathered in San Salvador's Plaza Libertad. On Sunday night, one week after the election, the crowd was ordered to disperse, and when more than a thousand refused to leave troops opened fire. Many people took refuge in the church on one side of the square, where they were trapped until Rivera and Chávez helped negotiate their release. Romero hurried back to the capital.

The shootings and beatings, sometimes of priests, continued. Priests were thrown out of the country or, once out, prohibited from returning. On March 4, troops surrounded the home of the parish priest of San Martín, just east of the capital. Townspeople protected him, so the troops ransacked a house where four seminarians lived and left. On March 12, as another priest drove to say Sunday mass in the small town of Aguilares he was shot and killed. With him in the car were a fifteen-year-old boy and a seventy-five-year-old man. They were also killed. The priest killed that morning was Rutilio Grande, a Jesuit and an old friend of the new archbishop.

Father Brockman suggests that the assassination of Grande radicalized Romero, and it certainly drew the archbishop fully into an unholy war that would over the next three years kill hundreds of people, mostly farmers but also ten priests. Romero's thinking, his growing anger, can be seen in retrospect in his public statements, his homilies and pastoral letters. Although his first pastoral letter dips into an unreal placidity — "We are passing through a very beautiful Eastertide" — it begins to focus on what he will see as the Church's mission. Delivered on April 10, 1977, less than a month after Father Grande and his two companions were killed and as the country was convulsed by civil unrest, he draws on the ideas of the Medellín conference. He concurred that the Church must be "truly poor, missionary and paschal, separate from all temporal power and courageously committed to the liberation of each and every man. . . .

"The church cannot be defined simply in political or socio-economic terms. But neither can it be defined from a point of view that would make it indifferent to the temporal problems of the world. As Vatican II puts it: 'The mission of the Church will show its religious, and by that very fact, its supremely human, character.'" Romero linked the church's evangelical function to "human advancement." He would tread nowhere, he made clear, that the words of the popes and of Jesus Christ and the apostles did not lead. But, following them, he would bring Salvadorans "to have a clearer idea of the liberation that the church promotes."

Romero was offering a dialogue, he said, but with the offer came a moral warning. "From the perspective of our identity as a church, we also realize that our service to the people, precisely because it does not, as such, have a political or a socio-economic character, must seek sincere dialogue and cooperation with whomever holds political and socio-economic responsibility. The church does not do this because it has some technical competence or because it wants temporal privileges, but because the political community and other elements of society need to be reminded that they are at the service of the personal and social vocations of men and women."

Four months later, on August 6, he delivered his second pastoral on the holiday celebrating the Savior as the national patron saint. While the message of the Church is a message of hope, he said, "it is not an innocent hope that the church proclaims. It is accompanied by the blood of its priests and campesinos; blood and grief that denounce the obstacles and the evil intentions that stand in the way of the fulfillment of that hope. Their blood is also an expression of a readiness for martyrdom."

At the time, the streets were filled with accusations, in government-controlled newspapers and crudely printed flyers, that priests were part of a conspiracy. Increasingly, Romero himself was the target of vituperation. He responded that the mission of the Church "comes alive in an archdiocese that, out of fidelity to the gospel, rejects as a calumny the charge that it is subversive, a fomentor of violence and hatred, Marxist, and political. It comes alive in an archdiocese that, out of the persecution it is undergoing, offers itself to God and to the people as a united church, one ready for sincere dialogue and cooperation, a bearer of the message of hope and love."

Romero pointed out that the accusations leveled at activist priests had some historical precedent. "From the beginning of Jesus' public life, these denunciations brought in their train frequent attacks upon him. They brought personal risk and even persecution. The persecution was to go on through the whole of his life until, at the end, he was accused of blasphemy and of being an agitator among the masses. For these reasons he was condemned and executed."

Because of his place at the center of a storm, observers outside the country began to recognize his courage. Early in 1978, Romero received an honorary doctorate at Georgetown University; later that year British ministers of Parliament and others nominated him for the Nobel prize for peace.

In August 1978, again on the national holiday, Romero went straight to the heart of matters. His third pastoral was coauthored by Bishop Rivera and opposed by Salvador's four other bishops, who thought the message too radical. "The Church," they wrote, "which is the extension of the teaching and salvation of Christ, would be wrong to remain silent when faced with concrete problems.

"The testimony of the Second Vatican Council, always the point of reference for the teaching of Pope Paul VI; its application to Latin America through the documents of Medellín; the recent popes; many Latin American episcopates; and our own tradition in the church of El Salvador; show us that the church has always made its presence felt when society clearly seemed in a 'sinful situation,' in need of the light of the word of God and the word of the church in history. This prophetic mission of the church in the defense of the poor, who have always had a special place in the heart of the Lord, numbers among its apostles in Latin America such men as Fray Antonio de Montesinos, Fray Bartolomé de Las Casas, Bishop Juan del Valle, and Bishop Antonio Valdivieso, who was assassinated in Nicaragua because of this opposition to the landowner and governor, Contreras.

"To these eloquent testimonies of the church, both universal and local, we join today our own humble voice. . . .

"We realize we risk being misunderstood or condemned, through malice or naivete, as inopportune or ignorant. It is, however, our honest intention to dispel the inertia of the many Salvadorans who are indifferent to the suffering in our land, especially in rural areas."

The principal goal of this pastoral letter was to defend priests' work with community organizations, seen by landowners as threatening. Romero and Rivera saw them as not only necessary to the dignity of the common people, but instrumental for social progress. For the church, they were an extension of its ministry. And, yes, that meant that priests and Catholics must work side-by-side with communists. So complex was the issue that the two bishops issued with the pastoral letter three appendices for Salvadorans to study.

Salvadorans must analyze for themselves, the letter continued, the national situation. "The first conclusion of any impartial analysis of the right of association," they offered, "must be that groups in agreement with the government or protected by it have complete freedom. Organizations, on the other hand, that voice dissent from the government — political parties, trade unions, rural organizations — find themselves hindered or even prevented from exercising their right to organize legally and work for their aims, just though these may be. . . .

"The church is aware of the complexity of political activity. However, and we repeat, the church is not, nor ought it to be, an expert in this sort of activity. Nevertheless, it can and must pass judgment on the general intention and the particular methods of political parties and organizations, precisely because of its interest in a more just society."

Of violence, the bishops spoke a truth that is still, for the most part, only whispered in Latin America. "The most acute form in which violence appears on our continent," they wrote, "and in our own country, is what the bishops of Medellín called 'institutionalized violence.' It is the result of the unjust situation in which the majority of men, women and children in our country find themselves deprived of the necessities of life. . . .

"To those who hold economic power, the Lord of the world says that they should not close their eyes selfishly to this situation. They should understand that only by sharing in justice and with those who do not have such power can they cooperate for the good of the country, and will they enjoy the peace and happiness that come from wealth accumulated at the expense of others."

A year later, on August 6, 1979, the killing continued. Nothing had changed. "In El Salvador," Romero wrote in what would be his last pastoral letter, "new kinds of sufferings and outrages have driven our national life along the road of violence, revenge and resentment." Latin American bishops had recently met in Puebla, Mexico, ten years after the Medellín conference to renew their commitment to the social and economic change envisioned there. But Romero returned to a nation tortured. His unflinching view of the torturers was what made him so dangerous.

"Analysts of our economy point out that, if it is to function well, it needs a large and cheap labor force. Producers of coffee, sugar cane and cotton, which go to make up the agricultural export trade, need unemployed, unorganized campesinos. They depend on them for an abundant and cheap labor force to harvest and export their crops. On the other hand, the agricultural and cattle-raising sector of the economy is the one that pays the most taxes to the public treasury — which is one of the reasons it has the greatest influence upon the government.

"And still today many industrial and transnational corporations base their ability to compete in international markets on what they call 'low labor costs,' which, in reality, means starvation wages."

Romero also attacked the shibboleth of "national security." Citing the statement issued at Puebla, Romero denounced "this new form of idolatry, which has already been installed in many Latin American countries. In this country it has its own particular way of working, but substantially it is identical with that described at Puebla: 'In many instances the ideologies of National Security have helped to intensify the totalitarian or authoritarian character of governments based on the use of force, leading to the abuse of power and the violation of human rights. In some instances, they presume to justify their positions with a subjective profession of Christian faith.'"

This frail, introspective man, against all predictions, had turned into the conscience of Latin America. Vilified in slanderous publications, he had even received death threats, he told his parishioners. Yet he kept up his attacks, knowing they were against men whose predilection for the most obscene forms of violence was well documented. "The omnipotence of these national security regimes, the total disrespect they display toward individuals and their rights, the total lack of ethical consideration shown in the means that are used to achieve their ends, turn national security into an idol, which, like the god Moloch, demands the daily sacrifice of many victims in its name."

Leaving no doubt as to the profundity of the change he felt was needed, Romero continued. "The church sincerely believes that without such changes the structural bases of our whole malaise will remain. The full liberation of the Salvadoran people, not to mention personal conversions, demands a thorough change in the social, political and economic system. . . . I realize that some terrorist activities induce a state of mind in the powerful that hardly favors serenity and reflection. But they ought to overcome that preoccupation and generously lay down the basis for a democratic evolution, so that the majority of the population may participate equitably in the national resources that belong to all."

During the summer of 1979, the archbishop brought together representatives of the democratic opposition to the government, seeking "a dialogue." In October, the government was overthrown. The coup was led by younger officers. In place of the fraudulently elected Gen. Romero was established a five-man junta of three civilians, including José Napoleon Duarte, and two colonels.

Speaking to the governing board of the National Council of Churches in New York City in November, Romero said, "Violence is the outstanding characteristic of my poor country at the present time. Full of anguish, I must agree with the final document of Puebla: the 'muted cry' of people pleading for a liberation that never came is now 'loud and clear, increasing in volume and intensity.' It comes from blood-stained and tragic experience. At the base of all violence is social injustice, accurately called 'structural violence,' which is our greatest social evil now." He told the governors that in the first half of the year there had been "406 assassinations and 307 political arrests, all due to this violence."

Returning to El Salvador, he found leftists withdrawing their support from the junta and he supported them, agreeing that the junta was unresponsive to the country's greatest needs. In January 1980, Romero accused the defense minister of being an obstacle to reform and asked that he resign.

He was critical, as well, of U.S. assistance. To such criticism, a State Department spokesman blandly insisted that weapons were critical to land reform; they were used, he said, for "protection and security provided by the Salvadoran military for the new owners and the civilian technicians and managers helping them." The archbishop was not convinced. He wrote to President Carter in February 1980, asking that he rescind an effort to arm, equip, and train three Salvadoran batallions. "Instead of favoring greater justice and peace in El Salvador," he told Carter, "your government's contribution will undoubtedly sharpen the injustice and the repression inflicted on the organized people, whose struggle has often been for respect for their most basic human rights.

"The present government junta and, especially, the armed forces and security forces, have unfortunately not demonstrated their capacity to resolve in practice the nation's serious political and structural problems. For the most part they have resorted to repressive violence."

He got a reply from Cyrus R. Vance, the secretary of state, assuring him, "We share a repugnance for the violence provoked by both extremes." The letter came in March.

Virtually every public utterance of the archbishop had become an event. He had inflamed the judges of the country by suggesting that they had sold out to the oligarchy. In his sermon on March 23, 1980, his last sermon, he referred to the army's "genocide against the Salvadoran people." Speaking to the common men who filled the ranks of the army — and inciting them, some said, to mutiny — he pled, "You don't have to comply with the orders of your superiors if they oppose God's laws. I implore you to cease the repression."

The next evening, as he had promised, he was celebrating an evening mass in memory of the mother of Jorge Pinto, editor and publisher of *El Independiente* and a man who had been persecuted for opposing the government. All day, Romero, sixty-two years old, had been preoccupied with arrangements for Palm Sunday, the following Sunday. But he kept his promise to say the mass, going to the chapel at Divine Providence Hospital because his own Metropolitan Cathedral was filled with dissidents taking refuge there from the authorities. The same thing had been happening in churches all over the country. At the chapel, Romero led the congregation in the 23rd Psalm — "and I will dwell in the house of the Lord forever" — and chose as the Gospel reading the Book of John — "Whoever wants to serve me must follow me."

His homily, which had gone on for about ten minutes, concerned the return of Jesus. He was associating that with the concept of justice. "This is the hope that inspires us Christians," he said. "We know that every effort to better society, especially when injustice and sin are so ingrained, is an effort that God blesses, that God wants, that God demands of us."

A red car with as many as four men pulled up at the chapel's main entrance. As Archbishop Romero talked on, standing behind the altar and facing the congregation, a man walked into the back of the sanctuary, took aim, and fired a .22-caliber bullet that entered his heart and lodged in a lung. It seems, somehow, particularly obscene that the assassin apparently was not an enraged Salvadoran, but a hired killer, skilled in the use of his weapon, able to murder professionally, with a single, small-caliber bullet.

The archbishop pitched backward. There might have been other shots fired to intimidate the parishioners as the red car sped away. Several people fell on Pinto to protect him. As the archbishop lay dying, a nun knelt and softly kissed his forehead. He whispered, "May God have mercy on the assassins."

Select Bibliography

Doña Marina

Baudot, Georges. "Política y Discurso en la Conquista de México: Malintzín y el diálogo con Hernán Cortes." *Anuario de Estudios Americanos* 45 (1988).

Cantu, Caesar C. *Cortés and the Fall of the Aztec Empire.* Los Angeles: Modern World, 1966.

Díaz del Castillo, Bernal. *The Discovery and Conquest of Mexico, 1517–1521.* Trans. Alfred Percival Maudslay London: George Routledge and Sons, 1928. (From the copy by Génaro García.)

Long, Haniel. *Malinche (Doña Marina).* Santa Fe, N.M.: Writer's Editions, 1939.

Morris, J. Bayard, trans. *Hernando Cortés, Five Letters.* New York: Robert M. McBride, 1929.

Padden, R. C. *The Hummingbird and the Hawk.* Columbus: Ohio State University Press, 1967.

Prescott, William H. *History of the Conquest of Mexico.* 2 vols. London: Richard Bentley, 1849.

Rodríguez, Gustavo A. *Doña Marina.* Monograph, Imprenta de la Secretaria de Relaciones Exteriores, Mexico, D. F., 1935.

Solis, Antonio de. *Historia de la Conquista de México.* Buenos Aires: Espasa-Calpe Argentina, 1947.

White, Jon Manchip. *Cortés and the Downfall of the Aztec Empire.* New York: St. Martins, 1971.

Toussaint L'Ouverture

Alexis, Stephen. *Black Liberator.* Trans. William Stirling. New York, 1949.

Beard, John R. *The Life of Toussaint L'Ouverture, the Negro Patriot of Hayti.* Boston: Wendell Phillips, 1863.

Heinl, Robert Debs and Nancy Gordon. *Written in Blood.* Boston: Houghton-Mifflin, 1978.

Korngold, Ralph. *Citizen Toussaint.* New York: Hill and Wang, 1944.

Simón Bolívar

Bushnell, David, ed. *The Liberator, Simón Bolívar.* New York: Knopf, 1970.

Collier, Simon. "Nationality, Nationalism and Supranationalism in the Writings of Simón Bolívar." *Hispanic American Historical Review* 43/1 (Feb. 1983).

Lecuña, Vicente. *Crónica razonada de las querras de Bolívar.* New York: Colonial, 1950.

Madariaga, Salvador de. *Bolívar*. New York: Schocken, 1952.
Masur, Gerhard. *Simón Bolívar*. Albuquerque: University of New Mexico Press, 1948.
Sherwell, Guillermo A. *Simón Bolívar, Patriot, Warrior, Statesman, Father of Five Nations*. Clinton, Mass.: Colonial for the Bolivarian Society of Venezuela, 1951.
Trend, J. B. *Bolívar and the Independence of Spanish America*. Clinton, Mass.: Colonial for the Bolivarian Society of Venezuela, 1951.

Manuela Sáenz

Ballesteros de Gaibrois, Mercedes. *Manuela Sáenz, El Ultimo Amor de Bolívar*. Madrid: Fundación Universitaria Española, 1976.
Rambos, Humberto. *Bolívar Intimo: Cartas*. Caracas: Talleres de B. Costa-Amic, 1967.
Rumazo Gonzalez, Alfonso. *Manuela Sáenz, La Libertadora del Libertador*. Bogotá: Ediciones Mundial, 1944.
Von Hagen, Victor Wolfgang. *The Four Seasons of Manuela*. New York: Duell, Sloan and Pierce – Little, Brown, 1952.

José de San Martín

Metford, J. C. J. *San Martín the Liberator*. Oxford: Basil Blackwell, 1950.
Mitre, Bartolomé. *Historia de San Martín*. 3 vols. Buenos Aires: Editorial Universitaria, 1968.
Orfila, Alejandro. *The Liberator General San Martín*. Washington, D.C.: Organization of American States, 1978.

Bernardo O'Higgins

Amunátegui Reyes, Miguel Luis. *Don Bernardo O'Higgins: Juzgado por algunos de sus contemporáneos*. Santiago: Imprenta Universitaria, 1917.
Archivo de don Bernardo O'Higgins. Tomos 1–31. Santiago: Editorial Nascimento, 1946.
Balbontín Moreno, Manuel, and Opazo Maturana, Gustavo. *Cinco Mujeres en la Vida de O'Higgins*. Santiago: Arancibia, 1964.
Cabello Reyes, Carlos. *Genio y Figura de Bernard O'Higgins*. Santiago: Editorial Cultura, 1944.
Carrasco, Adela. *Pensamiento de O'Higgins*. Santiago: Editorial Nacional Gabriela Mistral, 1974.
Clissold, Stephen. *Bernardo O'Higgins and the Independence of Chile*. London: Rupert Hart-Davis, 1968.
Kinsbruner, Jay. *Bernardo O'Higgins*. New York: Twayne, 1968.
O'Higgins Pintado por Si Mismo. Santiago: Ediciones Ercilla, 1941.

Domingo Faustino Sarmiento

Alberdi, Juan Bautista. *Proceso a Sarmiento.* Buenos Aires: Imprenta la Industrial, 1910.

Anderson Imbert, Enrique. *Una Aventura Amorosa de Sarmiento: Cartas de Ida Wickersham.* Buenos Aires: Editorial Losada, 1969.

Bunkley, Allison Williams. *The Life of Sarmiento.* Princeton, N.J.: Princeton University Press, 1952.

Guerrero, César H. *Mujeres de Sarmiento.* Buenos Aires: Artes Gráficas Bartolomé U. Chiesino, 1960.

Rojas, Ricardo. *El Profeta de las Pampa.* Buenos Aires: Editorial Tosada, 1945.

Sarmiento, Domingo Faustino. *Facundo...Civilización y Barbarie.* Mexico, D.F.: SEP/UNAM, 1982. (*Facundo* was first published in 1845).

_____. *Obras Selectas.* Buenos Aires: Editorial la Facultad, 1944.

_____. *Recuerdos de Provincia.* Buenos Aires: La Cultura Argentina, 1916. (Originally published in 1850).

_____. *Viajes en Europa, Africa i America.* 3 vols. Buenos Aires: Libreria Hachette, 1958. (Originally published in 1851).

Pedros I and II

Bernstein, Harry. *Dom Pedro II.* New York: Twayne, 1973.

Burns, E. Bradford. *A History of Brasil.* 2d ed. New York: Columbia University Press, 1970.

Calogeras, João Pandiá. *A History of Brazil.* Trans. Percy Alvin Martin. New York: Russell and Russell, 1963. (Originally published in 1939.)

Corréa da Costa, Sérgio. *Every Inch a King.* Trans. Samuel Putnam. New York: Charles Frank, 1950.

Drescher, Seymour. "Brazilian Abolition in Historical Perspective." *Hispanic American Historical Review.* 48/3 (Aug. 1988).

Oliveira Lima, Manoel de. *The Evolution of Brazil.* New York: Russell and Russell, 1966. (Originally published in 1914.)

Reichmann, Felix. *Sugar, Gold and Coffee.* Ithaca: Cornell University Press, 1959.

Simmons, Charles Willis. *Marshal Deodoro and the Fall of Dom Pedro II.* Durham: Duke University Press, 1966.

Tarquinio de Sousa, Octavio. *José Bonifacio, emancipador del Brasil.* Mexico, D.F.: Fondo de Cultura Económica, 1945.

Williams, Mary Wilhelmine. *Dom Pedro the Magnanimous.* Chapel Hill: University of North Carolina Press, 1937.

Worcester, Donald E. *Brazil: From Colony to World Power.* New York: Charles Scribner's Sons, 1973.

José Martí

Foner, Philip S., ed. *José Martí, Major Poems.* Trans. Elinor Randall. New York: Holmes and Meier, 1982.

Gray, Richard Butler. *José Martí, Cuban Patriot.* Gainesville: University of Florida Press, 1962.

Kirk, John M. *José Martí, Mentor of the Cuban Nation.* Tampa: University Presses of Florida, 1983.

Lizaso, Félix. *Martí, Martyr of Cuban Independence.* Trans. Esther Elise Shuler. Albuquerque, N.M., 1953.
Mañach, Jorge. *Martí, Apostle of Freedom.* Trans. Coley Taylor. New York: Devin-Adair, 1950.

Benito Juárez

Cadenhead, Ivie E. *Benito Juárez.* New York: Twayne, 1973.
Roeder, Ralph. *Juárez and His Mexico.* New York: Viking, 1947.
Smart, Charles Allen. *Viva Juárez!* Philadelphia: Lippincott, 1963.
Solana y Gutiérrez, Mateo. *Psicología de Juárez.* Ed. B. Costa-Amie. Mexico City, 1968.

Pancho Villa

Herrera, Celia E. *Francisco Villa ante la Historia.* Mexico, D.F., 1939.
Lansford, William Douglas. *Pancho Villa.* Los Angeles: Sherbourne, 1965.
Mason, Herbert Molloy *The Great Pursuit.* New York: Random House, 1970.
Peterson, Jessie, and Thelma Cox, eds. *Pancho Villa: Intimate Recollections by People Who Knew Him.* New York: Hastings House, 1977.
Torres, Elias L. *Twenty Episodes in the Life of Pancho Villa.* Trans. Sheila M. Ohlendorf. Austin, Tex.: Encino, 1973.
Vives, Pedro A. *Pancho Villa.* Madrid: Ediciones Quorum, 1987.

Emiliano Zapata

Black, C. E. *The Dynamics of Modernization.* New York: Harper and Row, 1967.
Dromundo, Baltazar. *Vida de Emiliano Zapata.* Mexico, D.F.: Editorial Guarania, 1961.
Newell, Peter E. *Zapata of Mexico.* Sanday, Orkney, U.K.: Cienfuegos, 1979.
Parkinson, Roger. *Zapata: A Biography.* New York: Stein and Day, 1975.
Reyes, H. Alonso. *Emiliano Zapata, Su Vida y Su Obra con Documentos Inéditos* Mexico, D.F., 1963.
Womack, John. *Zapata and the Mexican Revolution.* New York: Knopf, 1969.

Dolores Jiménez y Muro, Juana Belén Gutiérrez de Mendoza, Hermila Galindo de Topete

Cockcroft, James D. *Intellectual Precursors of the Mexican Revolution.* Austin: University of Texas Press, 1968.
Hahner, June E. *Women in Latin American History.* Los Angeles: UCLA Latin American Publications, 1976.
Macías, Anna. *Against All Odds: The Feminist Movement in Mexico.* Westport, Conn.: Greenwood, 1982.
Mendieta Alatorre, Angeles. *La Mujer en la Revolución Mexicana.* Mexico, D.F.: Talleres Gráficos de la Nación, 1961.

Phelan, John Leddy. "México y lo Mexicano." *Hispanic American Historical Review.* 36 (1956): 309–18.

Reed, John. *Insurgent Mexico.* New York: Simon and Schuster, 1969. (Compiled from dispatches to *Metropolitan* magazine and the *New York World,* this volume was first published in 1914.)

Romero, Ricardo. *La Mujer en la Historia de México.* Mexico, D.F.: Costa-Amic Editores, 1982.

Turner, Frederick C. *The Dynamic of Mexican Nationalism.* Chapel Hill: University of North Carolina Press, 1968.

Augusto Sandino

Bermann, Karl, ed. *Sandino Without Frontiers.* Hampton, Va.: Compita, 1988.

Campos Ponce, Xavier. *Sandino.* 3d ed. Mexico, D.F.: Editores Asociados Mexicanos, 1979.

Macauley, Neill. *The Sandino Affair.* Chicago: Quadrangle, 1967.

Selser, Gregario. *Sandino.* Trans. Cedric Belfrage. New York: Monthly Review, 1981.

Vives, Pedro A. *Augusto César Sandino.* Madrid: Ediciones Quorum, 1987.

Walker, Thomas W. *Nicaragua, The Land of Sandino.* Boulder, Colo.: Westview, 1981.

Juan Perón

Alexander, Robert J. *The Perón Era.* New York: Columbia University Press, 1951.

Baraguer, Joseph R., ed. *Why Perón Came to Power.* New York: Knopf, 1968.

Cowles, Fleur. *Bloody Precedent.* New York: Randon House, 1952.

Scobie, James R. *Argentina.* New York: Oxford University Press, 1964.

Eva Perón

Barnes, John. *Evita: First Lady.* New York: Grove, 1978.

Boroni, Otelo, and Roberto Vacca. *La Vida de Eva Perón.* Buenos Aires: Editorial Galerna, 1970.

Flores, Maria. *The Woman with the Whip: Eva Perón.* New York: Doubleday, 1952.

Fraser, Nicholas, and Marysa Navarro. *Eva Perón.* New York: Norton, 1980.

Taylor, J. M. *Eva Perón: The Myths of a Woman.* Chicago: University of Chicago Press, 1979.

José Figueres

Acuña Valerio, Miguel. *El 48.* San José: Lehmann, 1974.

Ameringer, Charles D. *Don Pepe: A Political Biography of José Figueres of Costa Rica.* Albuquerque: University of New Mexico Press, 1978.

Baeza Flores, Alberto. *La Lucha Sin Fin.* Mexico, D.F.: Costa-Amic, 1969.

Bonilla, Harold H. *Figueres y Costa Rica.* San José: Editorial Sol, 1977.

Figueres Ferrer, José. *América Latina: Un Continente en Marcha*. San José: EIDED, 1966.
Gleijeses, Piero. "Juan José Arévalo and the Caribbean Legion." *Journal of Latin American Studies*. 45 (1988).

Fidel Castro

Boorstein, Edward. *The Economic Transformation of Cuba*. New York: Monthly Review, 1968.
Farber, Samuel. "The Cuban Communists in the Early Stages of the Cuban Revolution: Revolutionaries or Reformists?" *Latin American Research Review*. 18/1 (1983).
Franqui, Carlos. *Family Portrait with Fidel*. New York: Random House, 1981.
Matthews, Herbert. *Fidel Castro*. New York: Simon and Schuster, 1969.
Meneses, Enrique. *Fidel Castro*. Trans. J. Halcro Ferguson. New York: Taplinger, 1966.
Sutherland, Elizabeth. *The Youngest Revolution*. New York: Dial, 1969.
Szulc, Tad. *Fidel: A Critical Portrait*. New York: Morrow, 1986.
Yglesias, José. *In the Fist of the Revolution*. New York: Pantheon, 1968.

Ernesto Guevara

Guevara, Ernesto. *Reminiscences of the Cuban Revolutionary War*. Trans. Victoria Ortiz. New York: Monthly Review, 1968.
James, Daniel. *Ché Guevara, A Biography*. New York: Stein and Day, 1969.
_____, ed. *The Complete Bolivian Diaries of Ché Guevara*. New York: Stein and Day, 1968.
Rojo, Ricardo. *My Friend Ché*. New York: Dial, 1968.

Archbishop Romero

Brockman, James R. *The Word Remains, A Life of Oscar Romero*. Maryknoll, N.Y.: Orbis, 1982.
Delgado, Jesús. *Oscar A. Romero: biografía*. Madrid: Ediciones Paulinas, 1986.
Erdozain, Plácido. *Monseñor Romero, Mártir de la Iglesia Popular*. San José, C.R.: Editorial Universitaria Centroamericana, 1980.
Keogh, Dermot. *Romero, El Salvador's Martyr*. Dublin: Dominican, 1981.
Walsh, Michael J., trans., *Archbishop Oscar Romero, Voice of the Voiceless. The Four Pastoral Letters and Other Statements*. Maryknoll, N.Y.: Orbis, 1985.

General

Anna, Timothy E. "Spain and the Breakdown of the Imperial Ethos: The Problem of Equality." *Hispanic American Historical Review*. 42/2 (May 1982).
Blomberg, Pedro. *Mujeres de la Historia Americana*. Buenos Aires: Librarías Anaconda, 1933.
Connell-Smith, Gordon. *The Inter-American System*. London: Oxford University Press, 1966.

Herring, Hubert. *A History of Latin America.* 2d ed. New York: Knopf, 1961.

Lewis, Oscar. *Pedro Martínez: A Mexican Peasant and His Family.* New York: Random House, 1964.

Martin, Cheryl E. "Reform, Trade and Insurrection in the Spanish Empire." *Latin American Research Review.* 19/3 (1984).

Rock, David. *Argentina, 1516–1982.* Berkeley: University of California Press, 1985.

Wilkie, James W., and Albert L. Michaels, eds. *Revolution in Mexico: Years of Upheaval, 1910–1940.* Tucson: University of Arizona Press, 1969.

Williams, Eric. *From Columbus to Castro: The History of the Caribbean, 1492–1969.* New York: Harper and Row, 1970.

Index

Adams, Jerome R.

Liberators and patriots of Latin America

$25.95

28,942
Copy 2

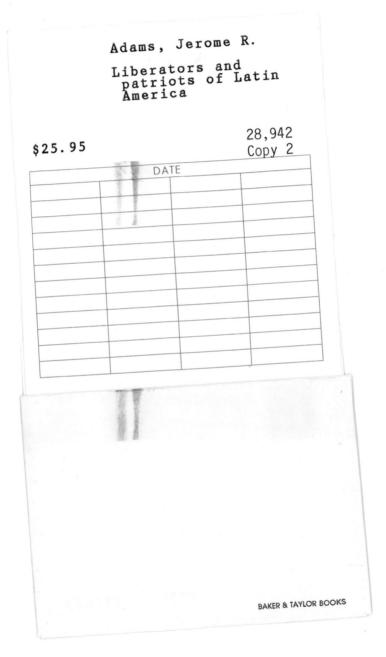

DATE			